- A Portrait of An Era -

Slavers, Traders and Privateers

Liverpool, the African Trade
and Revolution, 1773-1808

Frank Howley

"I have not come here to be insulted by a set of wretches, every brick in whose
infernal town is cemented with the blood of an African."

(Actor George Frederick Cooke, on being hissed and booed by an audience at
Liverpool's Theatre Royal for being drunk).

Acknowledgements

My thanks to Sheila for her support and encouragement, and to Mike and Pete for reading the first draft and offering their editorial comments. I would also like to thank staff at Liverpool Central Library and Merseyside Maritime Museum for their help in locating historical records.

Cover illustration: Liverpool from the Rock Perch, 1797, by J.T. Serres, Binns Collection C97, Liverpool Record Office.

First Published 2008 by Countyvise Limited,
14 Appin Road, Birkenhead, Wirral CH41 9HH.
Copyright © 2008 Frank Howley.
The right of Frank Howley to be identified as the author of this work has been asserted by him in accordance with the Copyright, Design and Patents Act 1988.
British Library Cataloguing in Publication Data.
A catalogue record for this book is available from the British Library.
ISBN 978 1 901231 98 4

Contents

Introduction

Picture a forest of masts and yards with sails well furled, beneath which a hundred wooden ships line the docksides. Weather-beaten seamen are hoisting bales and casks from the holds, while iron rims rattle over rough cobblestones as carters take their loads. Departing from this scene, a brig is hauled by ropes and capstans to join the multitude of craft on the open water, while a gathering of women and children follow its progress along the quayside to the river. From there they wave their last farewells, fearing that some of the men may not return but will go to a watery grave. As the crew unfurl the sails, the brig begins a yearlong voyage to Africa and the Caribbean, passing a battered, war-torn vessel limping home after a recent encounter with an enemy privateer. Meanwhile, pressgangs stalk the narrow streets and alleys of the town nearby, peering into smoke-filled alehouses, dingy cellars and filthy courtyards, abducting unwary victims to man the King's ships.

This was Liverpool in the age of George III, and this is the story of how it was mired in slavery and shaped by the events of two revolutions. At its heart lies an account of the pernicious trade in slaves, of which Liverpool had the major share. It shows how slaving ventures were planned and fitted out, and provides an insight into the working lives of crews and the dangers they faced at sea. It also shows how millions of Africans were made captive by their own countrymen, and were then bartered for goods before facing the horrors of the Middle Passage. In addition, the narrative traces the progress of the abolition movement and the obstacles it faced from both merchants and Parliament, until the eventual passing of the Slave Trade Act in 1807.

However, as the pages of its weekly papers show, far more of Liverpool's ships were trading with Ireland than with African merchants and princes. The town also had extensive trading links with America and Europe, but found its lifeblood threatened as its ships were attacked and its men pressed into service during the wars of the American and French revolutions. Threading through this narrative, therefore, is an account of these two great conflicts, and of their impact on Liverpool. The life of the town is further illustrated through a series of sketches that provide an intimate portrait of its social fabric over the course of a third of a century. These include a chronicle of its riots, political corruption, crimes and calamities, and of efforts to deal with the growing problems of slum poverty and sanitation.

Although written partly with the local interest in mind, the main purpose of this book is to provide a portrait of an age that will appeal to a wide readership. Liverpool's population more than doubled in just thirty years due to migration from all over the British Isles, so that it had yet to develop the unique character by which it later became known. It held much in common with many large Georgian towns, sharing the same mob culture, drunken revelries, ham theatrical performances and quack medical remedies. Besides being Britain's second largest port, its metal foundries, glassworks, sugar refineries, numerous breweries and potteries made Liverpool widely representative, even boasting four cotton mills by the end of the 18th century. Liverpool was also bow-windowed shops and busy street markets, coaching inns and taverns, yet all of this was within a few minutes walk from surrounding fields of local produce and open countryside.

Three themes are therefore interwoven to make this narrative of Liverpool, and of momentous events well beyond, culminating in a bloody battle off Cape Trafalgar, and concluding with the end of the British slave trade. While drawing on previous research, much of this book is based on original sources, including newspapers, letters, ships' logs, parliamentary papers, and many other contemporary writings. By reproducing selected extracts from these fragile and often faded pages, it is hoped that readers will find the story enhanced, as their authors' words are brought to life and given new resonance.

Explanatory Notes

Monetary values

To understand examples of prices and wages given in this book, it is useful to know that, prior to decimalisation in 1971, British currency was based on a system of pounds (£) shillings (s) and pence (d). In 'old' money:

12 pence = 1 shilling

20 shillings = £1

240 pence = £1

There was also a guinea coin in the Georgian era worth 21 shillings, which was discontinued in the 19th century. Ignoring the effects of inflation, one penny today is therefore roughly equivalent to 2½d in old money, while five pence has the same notional value as one old shilling.

There is no exact measure of the relative values of the pound in the late Georgian age compared with the present. From 1773 to 1790 one pound was roughly equivalent to £90 today. That value had fallen to £70 by 1795, and to around £47 by 1800, but recovered to around £57 by 1807. (The pound fell as a result of the war with France, but during the following century it remained fairly steady with an average value of about £67, until the marked drop that came with the two world wars).

However, earnings seem to have been much lower in relation to the prices of staple products compared with the situation today. In 1775, a skilled artisan or full merchant seaman could expect to earn about £2 10s (£2 50p) per month, or £30 a year, equivalent to £2700 in today's money, whereas wages today are perhaps ten times higher. Living standards for the majority were very low, with many families living in overcrowded slums, and barely subsisting on a basic diet of bread and vegetables. Food, rent and clothing accounted for most expenditure, but because there was not the range of consumer goods we now take for granted, expectations were very different from the present.

Quotations, References and Footnotes

All quotations retain the original spellings, but punctuation has been altered to reflect modern usage. People had a tendency to pepper their writing with numerous commas and semi-colons, creating long, complex sentences that are difficult for the modern reader to follow. Capital letters were also overused, but these have mostly been retained as they were originally written.

Numbers in the text indicate footnotes at the bottom of the page, which are used in preference to endnotes for ease of reference. Plain numbers indicate references to sources, which some readers may wish to ignore. Most of the original documents used are kept at Liverpool Record Office (LRO) and are shown either by name or catalogue reference. Sources from books are referred to by author's name and title when shown for the first time, but further references are given by surname only, followed by the abbreviation 'op. cit.,' (from the Latin opere citato) to indicate that the work has already been cited in full. 'Ibid' (from the Latin ididem) indicates that a reference is from the same source as shown in the footnote directly above. Bold numbers indicate additional information that is not included in the main body of the narrative to avoid disturbing the flow, yet which readers are likely to find useful.

Chapter One

Nancy was coming home. On a grey November day in 1773 she steered an easterly course, driven by the brisk autumnal southwesterly that filled her sails. As the 120-ton, American-built brig cleared the coast of Anglesey, the hills and mountains of North Wales shrouded in mist to starboard, her captain and crew were filled with anticipation and relief at the thought of their homecoming. It was nearly a year since they had last set foot on Liverpool's narrow streets, spent time with loved-ones, or lived outside the confines of their small wooden world. They returned to a safer place, free from storm-driven seas, tropical disease, and the ever-present threat of revolt by their wretched human cargo now languishing in Jamaica.[1]

As his vessel approached Liverpool Bay, Captain Cunningham gave orders to trim the sails. He knew all too well the dangers of being driven onto sandbanks that were hidden at high water, a fate suffered by many a crew. Once stranded, wreckers would plunder their cargo, keeping what they could quickly use or safely conceal and smuggling what may prove most profitable. Now under much reduced sail, *Nancy* neared the outermost buoy off Hoyle Bank, and Cunningham ordered a shift of course some forty-five degrees to southward. Ten miles ahead stood the lighthouse by the Cheshire shoreline at Mockbeggar, [2] and three miles beyond stood another on Bidston Hill. These were brought into line as the helmsman gradually turned the wheel from starboard to larboard and back, enabling *Nancy* to ease her way through the channel between the Hoyle and Burbo banks. As she did so, *Nancy* flew her owners' colours high upon her masts, which were relayed by the lighthouse keeper to Liverpool several miles beyond.

As they neared the coast, *Nancy's* crew shifted course eastwards into the Rock Channel, taking constant soundings in the shallow waters to avoid the treacherous Beggars Patch. They were well aware of those that eyed their ship from the Cheshire shore, hoping for a wreck to plunder. Cunningham consulted David Tuohy's written instructions and Burdett's navigation chart,

---

[1] *Lloyd's Register* for 1776 shows the *Nancy* was built in Virginia in 1771. *Nancy's* draught in the water when fully laden was 11 feet, so the depth of the vessel from the keel to the main deck would have been about 16 or 17 feet. Such a vessel would have two decks separated by a height of about 5 feet 6 six inches, and a hold below the lower deck. Its length would be about 70 feet from bow to stern, its breadth around 20 feet at its broadest across the beam. Brigs had two masts with sails set across the breadth of the vessel, except for a mainsail that was at right angles to the rest and in line with the keel.

[2] Now known as Leasowe lighthouse.

and gave orders to clear the first of three buoys to larboard.[3] Then he directed the vessel a little towards north, clearing the next buoy to starboard to follow the course of the deepest waters. *Nancy* now made for the third buoy, and, with little water beneath her keel, for the narrow gap between the treacherous Red Nose rocks and the sandbank off shore. Rumour had it that the Noses were riddled with a labyrinthine network of smuggler's caves, and all on board were anxious to remain afloat to secure their remaining wages. Cunningham spied the tower of Walton Church through his telescope, then found the Bootle marks and adjusted his course to bring them in line. As *Nancy* drew towards the Perch marker, which gave warning of rocks beneath, the crew watched nervously and breathed a sigh of relief as she slid by.

Navigation chart of Liverpool Bay and the Mersey by P.P. Burdett, 1771 (LRO)

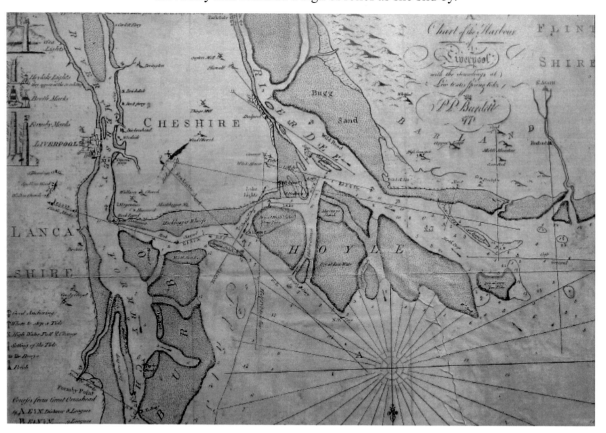

---

[3] Tuohy was a merchant with long experience as a captain, and provided written instructions to others in his service (Tuohy Papers, Liverpool Record Office, TUO 380/4/13). The most up-to-date chart was produced by P. P. Burdett in 1771. With the shifting of sandbanks over time, the Rock Channel is no longer navigable. All shipping now enters the Mersey through the Crosby Channel, which has been deepened with dredging, and is kept free of sediment by submarine revetments of limestone blocks constructed on either side to prevent inflow.

A detail from George Perry's Map of Liverpool, 1769 (LRO) showing the area around the Old Dock.

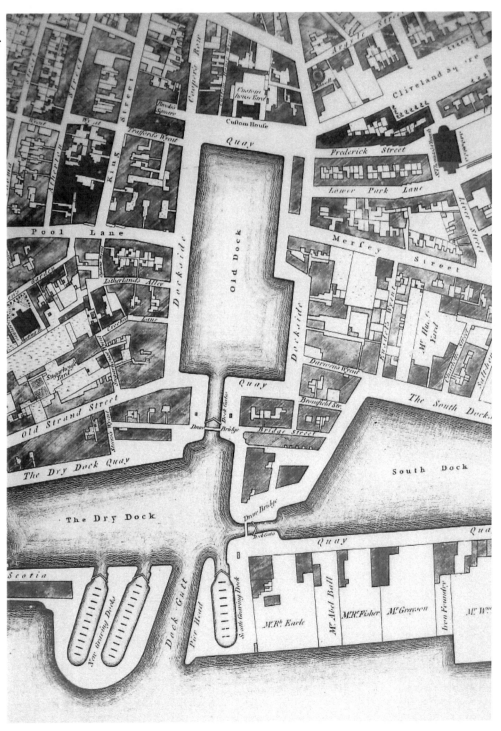

Once cleared, *Nancy* veered southwards into the deeper, safer waters of the River Mersey, passing the gunpowder magazines and *Mother Redcap's* notorious tavern on the Cheshire coast to starboard. Care was needed in guiding *Nancy* through the busy river traffic, as all manner of ships, brigs, snows, sloops, hoys and small boats thronged the waterway. Between their masts and sails, the windmills, domes and steeples of Liverpool were now clearly visible. Smoke billowed from Mr. Brooke's limekiln, river craft were taking shape in Mr. Dutton's boatyard, and the tower of Liverpool gaol stood a little beyond. On the North Pier of George's Dock, a small gathering awaited the arrival of a ferryboat to carry them across the Mersey. Nearby, piles of timber from North America and the Baltic lay ready to be transformed into masts and sail yards.[4]

As *Nancy* approached the Old Dock, she let slip her anchors to await the return of the next high tide to flood the entrance between the dry graving docks. Her crew now danced and sang to the sound of fiddle and drum, sharing the last of their rum and smoking clay pipes to pass the time. Their rhythms competed with the sawing and hammering of shipyards nearby, where ribs and planks of oak and elm were rising from keels on the slipways. On the return of the tide, and the dock master's instructions, the crew of the longboat towed *Nancy* through the narrow gut entrance and on towards its mooring beyond, aided by ropes and capstans along the quayside. But, when *Nancy* came to rest on 22nd November, there was much still to be done before the crew could collect the balance of their wages and return to their homes, as her cargo of sugar and rum had yet to be unloaded.[5] It was their job to hoist the casks and barrels from the hold and lower them to the quayside,[6] from where they would be taken by carters to David Tuohy's warehouse, and those of his business partners throughout the town. But not before the duty men had been aboard, checked the inventory, and delivered their report to the Customs House at the head of the Old Dock.[7] After agreeing the documentation, Cunningham could now supervise the unloading and complete his book-keeping by paying the men their remaining wages and signing them off.

Surrounding the Old Dock was a variety of businesses and private residences, but the east side was dominated by the Customs House. This was built of red brick and ornamental limestone, and was accessed by means of a short flight

---

[4] Description based on George Perry's map of Liverpool, 1769.

[5] *Williamson's Liverpool Advertiser* for 26th November 1773 lists the *Nancy* as having arrived from Jamaica on the 22nd laden with sugar and rum.

[6] Marcus Rediker, *Between the Devil and the Deep Blue Sea* (1987) p89-91.

[7] This was Liverpool's first dock, which was opened in 1715 but not completed until 1721, and was filled in just over a century later. It was situated roughly where Canning Place and Paradise Street now meet, and was the first fully enclosed commercial dock in Britain.

The Old Dock, 1773. The Customs House is on the left beneath the flag, and the spire of St. Thomas's Church is just right of centre (Local Illustrations Collection 264, LRO)

of steps leading through a double-arched entrance. Inside was a fine reception hall replete with decorative pillars and arches, through which a number of offices led.[8] To one side of this civic building lived Mayor Thomas Wilson, while merchant James Blair lived on the other, close to glass grinder William Heys and a cheese warehouse. On the north side of the dock were the merchant houses of Alix and Goodridge, and Birch and Brown; navigational instrument maker William Drury; sail makers Rose and White; gunsmith William Turton and victualler David Danson. Dock master William Hutchinson lived on the west side by the gates, where his presence was demanded at any time of day or night according to the tides. So, too, did boatman Thomas Mills, and slopman John Pulford, supplier of cheap, ready-made clothing to seafarers and the poor. Cooper William Gregson ran his business on the south side, close to Higginson and Yates' corn warehouse, Robert Crossland's tar oil warehouse, Seddon's anchor smithy, and the mug warehouse of Parker, Lickbarrow and Company[9] Each overlooked a forest of masts, yards, furled sails and rigging, beneath which men toiled endlessly, loading and unloading the hogsheads, barrels,

[8] Richard Brooke, *Liverpool As It Was, 1775 to 1800* (first published 1853) p74.
[9] *Gore's Liverpool Directory*, 1773.

bails and boxes stacked beside each vessel on the cobbled quayside. Using windlass, block and tackle, they heaved and pulled, their boisterous cursing and banter echoing around the dock. Those who witnessed this from within their premises were well placed indeed, for this was the heart of Liverpool, from which its life-blood flowed. In this town trade was all.

When all was done, *Nancy's* crew were paid off and drifted away into the surrounding streets and alleys. Although some were Liverpool born and bred, others were, like many seafarers, migrants drawn largely from farming communities impoverished by the enclosing of land for the benefit of wealthy landowners. Some looked for adventure and were willing to trade the hardship of the soil for that of the sea, while others sought new skills in the hope of greater prosperity. By 1773 Liverpool's population had reached thirty-four thousand and was growing fast due to the constant demand for labour. Although perhaps a quarter of the workforce were seamen, there were far more craftsmen and labourers, many of whom worked to keep Liverpool's trade afloat. These included shipwrights, rope and sail makers, sugar and salt refiners, brewers, carters and warehousemen, not to mention the hundreds of pottery and glass workers, or the foundry men working iron and copper.[10] Liverpool was a melting pot of humanity crammed into a mere square mile, its streets a jumble of Georgian town houses, warehouses and workshops, once respectable residences now in disrepair, backhouses, and sundry dilapidated cottages from a bygone age.[11] It was to the latter abodes that many of *Nancy's* crew now returned, while others repaired to their subterranean cellars beneath those more fortunate merchants and tradesmen who supplemented their earnings from rents. Cheek by jowl, wealth and poverty rubbed shoulders in pursuit of a common interest – to make a living from the sea.

Liverpool's trading interests were many, which was clearly apparent from the pages of its two weekly newspapers.[12] The port served Lancashire, Cheshire and the Midlands by exporting such products as cloth, pottery, salt and cheeses, but much of its trade was with Ireland, from which it imported linen and agricultural produce in exchange for manufactured goods. However,

---

[10] M. J. Power, *The Growth of Liverpool*, in *Popular Politics, Riot and Labour: Essays in Liverpool History 1790-1940*, Ed Belcham, J, Liverpool University Press, 1992, p27.

[11] Scenes of 18th century Liverpool can be seen in several collections of watercolours and sketches at Liverpool Record Office, a small selection of which are produced in this book.

[12] *Williamson's Liverpool Advertiser*, and *The General Advertiser*, printed by John Gore.

due to the poor state of the roads and the limitations of the horse and cart, Liverpool's ships carried goods all round the British Isles. They also traded extensively with Europe, importing Swedish iron, Baltic timber, flax and wheat, and wines from Italy, Spain and Portugal. Then there was the West Indian trade, involving chiefly the import of sugar, rum and some cotton, while all manner of fine manufactured goods were exported to the islands to supply the plantation owners and their families. Although many ships traded directly with the Caribbean Islands, others did so at the end of the 'middle passage' that brought human cargoes from West Africa. Indeed, Liverpool had gained notoriety, for it now conducted nearly two-thirds of Britain's share of the slave trade.

Liverpool also owed much of its prosperity to trade with North America, but this had been damaged in recent years by deteriorating relations between Britain and the thirteen colonies. While Parliament was content to leave them to run most of their own affairs, it was determined to maintain control over their economies. The Navigation Laws ensured that all trade was under the control of the British government, which expected the colonies to serve as a market for British-made goods, provide products not otherwise available in Britain, and accept restrictions on what they could manufacture. It was also felt that they should pay their way, particularly for defence, as Britain supplied most of the troop garrisons. After all, it was only ten years since Britain had won control of Canada and the 'Ohio Country' west of the Appalachians, in a struggle with France lasting nine years. Indeed, many Americans accepted the need for protection, especially in Canada with its French majority, and on the western frontiers where attacks by native 'Indian' tribes resisting European westward expansion led to constant insecurity. [13]

American society was deeply divided by the different interests of its various groups - merchants, farmers, plantation owners, puritans, Quakers, Scots, Irish, Germans, and so on - and there was, as yet, no real American identity. Each colony had its own assembly, but there was little cohesion and much squabbling between them. Most Americans even resented their own governments and remained loyal to George III, but any attempt at control from Parliament was regarded as intrusive. However, America was costing Britain dearly, and revenues lost through smuggling outweighed what was raised. In 1765 the government had tried to impose a tax on paper for legal documents and newspapers, proof of payment being shown by a stamp. Although the British had long taken the stamp tax for granted, many Americans had been incensed, and its introduction gave birth to a propaganda campaign under the

---

[13] The Anglo-French war in America, 1754-1763, became part of a wider conflict that included the Caribbean, in which Britain seized several French islands. However, these were returned to France at the Treaty of Paris in recognition of British control of Canada and all territory east of the Mississippi.

slogan 'No Taxation Without Representation'. Thus began a heated debate that would lead to the birth of the United States.

Opposition to the government was led by a small group of wealthy, influential Americans such as George Washington in Virginia and Samuel Adams in Massachusetts, who regarded the stamp duty as the thin end of the wedge. For the first time, representatives of the separate colonies met to discuss an issue of common concern. At the Stamp Act Congress held in New York, they acknowledged the king as their supreme head, but declared that Parliament had no right to tax Americans without the consent of their assemblies. Although the government decided to repeal the stamp duty, it reaffirmed its right to impose taxation, and presented each colony with a separate quota in the form of a requisition under royal prerogative. Boston's reaction was to refuse to supply royal troops with supplies. New York followed a similar line until its assembly was suspended, and many Americans now asked why they should support troops who might be used against them. In 1767 the government tried a new measure by imposing duties on American imports of paper, glass, lead and tea, in addition to existing duties on sugar, which led to further outrage and a movement within some colonies to stop imports from Britain. By 1769 British exports to America had fallen by fifty per cent. However, this action also hit American ports like Boston, where economic distress set in and angry mob violence became the norm. The duties were eventually withdrawn with the exception of that on tea.

Meanwhile, in Boston, where the largest British garrison was stationed, hatred towards the four regiments had intensified due to rumours about soldiers' drunken, disorderly behaviour and violations against women. On 5th March 1770 a mob attacked troops who were standing guard around the customs house with its receipts inside. The soldiers stood firm as children threw snowballs and adults hurled stones, until one was knocked down and the order was given to fire in defence. Five Bostonians were killed, but the troops withdrew to their barracks under further stoning. The event was soon dubbed the 'Boston Massacre' by more radical elements.

Days later, an estimated ten thousand crowded through Boston's narrow streets to mourn the dead, and the propagandists saw an opportunity. Over the following days, a local copper plate engraver, Paul Revere, crafted an image to appear with somewhat partial accounts of the Boston Massacre, which was printed in pamphlets and broadsheets far and wide. But some were not convinced. Readers of the New York Gazette, for example, read warnings that "property will soon be precarious," and that "it's high time a stop was put to mobbing." [14] But the radicals kept busy with their 'Committees of

---

[14] Quoted in S. Watson, *The Reign of George III*, 1960, p193.

Correspondence', spreading rebellious ideas and organising revolt. However, few Americans welcomed rebellion, and the colonies relapsed into disunity. Trade with Britain gradually resumed and calm was restored.

And there the matter might have ended but for a popular beverage, a tax on which the British government had retained in order to avoid a complete climb down. Most colonists showed their disapproval by drinking smuggled tea, and customs duties fell by seventy per cent. To answer this, and to help the East India Company out of its financial difficulties, the government passed the Tea Act in 1773. This authorised the company to ship its enormous surplus of tea direct to the colonies, and to sell it through their own agents in America after paying minimal duties. The company would be able to sell tea at half the previous cost, effectively giving them a monopoly. Although welcome to ordinary tea drinkers, it would also put American shippers, merchants, and even smugglers out of business. It was not in their interests that cheap tea should find favour with local palettes. Radical propaganda began making the case that the East India Company's tea was bad for American business, and therefore bad for America.

The first consignment of nearly three hundred chests of Darjeeling tea arrived in Boston harbour aboard the *Dartmouth* on 28th November 1773. Further shipments followed soon after in the *Beaver* and the *Eleanor*. Over the next fortnight, stirred on by Adams and his protest meetings, Boston mobs roamed the harbour threatening violence if the cargoes were landed on the quayside. By 16th December, the captain of the *Dartmouth* agreed under pressure to return his cargo to England, but British officials denied him permission to clear the port and threatened to seize the vessel for non-payment of duties. When Adams learned of this he gave the signal for a well-planned operation that soon gained notoriety. Several dozen of his supporters, disguised as Mohawk tribesmen, converged on Griffin's Wharf where the three ships were moored. Cheered on by the mob, they boarded the ships, took nearly 350 chests from the holds, broke them open, and threw them into the sea. This was the 'Boston Tea Party.'

Soon after the tea had been left floating in Boston Harbour, the *Nancy* was towed into one of Liverpool's narrow graving docks for maintenance and repairs. As this was gradually drained of water, the *Nancy's* keel settled onto wooden blocks, and the vessel was shored up by timber supports. Although built just three years earlier, exposure to seawater had led to a coating of weeds, barnacles and other crustaceans that needed to be removed by scraping and burning. Once cleared, the hull could be caulked by hammering oakum – old unpicked rope mixed with tar – into any gaps that had opened in the planking. Finally, the hull could be coated with a mixture of tar and sulphur, the latter providing some measure of protection against *Teredo navalis*, or sea worm. This was the scourge of any ship venturing into tropical waters, causing great damage by boring through timbers below the water line. In addition, repairs were needed due to the stresses and strains of a long sea voyage and the damaging effects of storms, particularly to her masts and sails.[15]

Among those engaged were carpenters employed by Roger Fisher and Jones, who charged £78 10s 10½d for the work and materials, while Earl and Grayson charged £44 3s 5d for ironwork.[16] Replacement and repair of sails cost £56 19s 2¼d, which went to sail makers John Burton and John Robinson. Block makers William Neale and Company supplied new pulleys for the rigging and lifting gear, while Abbot and North provided the ship's tar. Walter Cahoon supplied medicines, John Nunn, the iron hoops, and additional goods and services were provided by chandler Robert Davison and plumber James Aspinall. Edmund Alcock charged £4 8s 7½d for painting, while aptly named John Leather provided leather for the repair of the ship's water pumps. Finally, James Gildhart, co-investor in the forthcoming voyage, provided the storage butts. Total charges for repairs and refitting came to £1056 10s 10½d. Included in the bill were various sundry payments. One labourer received nine shillings for six days work, and another received 2s 3d for one and a half days. Two carpenters shared £1 12s for six days labour, while two riggers earned just over ten shillings each for five and three-quarter days. John Huddleston was paid two shillings to lay a new cooking hearth, and two shillings for the bricks and mortar on which the stove would be re-sited.[17]

During the refit the *Nancy's* owners were preparing for her next voyage. Like many merchants, David Tuohy had been master on board many vessels, but had since branched out as a merchant. Much of his trading interest lay with Ireland, but he also invested heavily in the African trade. Early in 1774, Tuohy and business partner William Speers had formed a consortium with fellow merchants James Gildhart, Henry Trafford, and the Yates brothers, Thomas and John. From mid-February, goods that would be used by the *Nancy's* next master in his bargaining for slaves were accumulating in warehouses. Luke

---

[15] *Lloyd's Register*, 1776, shows that the *Nancy* had been repaired in 1774. Long voyages to Africa and the Caribbean always took their toll on wooden sailing vessels.

[16] See Monetary Values in the explanatory notes following the introduction.

[17] Tuohy Papers, LRO 380 TUO/4/7. The total bill would be equivalent to about £95,085 in today's money. The carpenters each earned the equivalent of around £72 for six day's work, while the labourer only received about £40.50p in today's money for his six days.

Mann received the final manifest on 5th April, headed "Invoice of Sundry Merchandise shipped by Messrs. Speers, Tuohy & Company on Board the Brigantine *Nancy*, Luke Mann, Commander for Angola, being on the proper accounts of said ship, owners of said ship, and consigned to said master to be bartered for slaves, ivory, gum &c."

Among the many fabrics listed were a hundred 'pieces' of blue baft, or course cotton cloth, in lengths of twelve yards valued at twenty seven shillings each. There were thirty-six yards of blue Angola cloth valued at six shillings per yard, and the same quantity of red Angola cloth priced at a shilling extra. Also included were eighty-six yards of linen in four foot widths at a shilling a yard, silk cloths with gold trim, and various pieces of chintz and other fabrics. Ready-made fabrics included twenty-four dozen worsted capes at 4s 9d each, while of finer quality were four red and four blue cloaks valued at thirty shillings each. Clothing included check shirts and shoes at 2s 6d, frocks and trousers at 2s 10d, jackets at six shillings, plus hats and stockings. The *Nancy's* liquor cargo included twenty gallons of wine at 5s 6d a gallon, a puncheon of rum containing 100 gallons, and nearly 900 gallons of brandy, but there was also a large quantity of bottled beer and tobacco. The munitions included thirty barrels of gunpowder and 320 powder kegs, 500 muskets valued at 7s 6d each, and fourteen gross of knives. There were also various types of pottery, including eighty-three dozen mugs valued at sixteen and eight pence each depending on whether they were large or small. In addition, The *Nancy* was to ship six beds and sets of bedding for the benefit of African merchants or princes. Finally, to feed the slaves and seamen, there were nine barrels of rice, ninety-two bushels of kiln-dried wheat, and large quantities of barley, beans and sugar, but the pork and beef was reserved for the crew. The total value of the cargo amounted to £2303 3s 4d, on which sum customs duties of £72 12s 1½d had to be added at a rate of three per cent.

Before the *Nancy* could be loaded and the ship got underway, several tons of ballast, consisting of stone aggregate and pig iron or lead ingots, had to be distributed evenly throughout the bottom of the hold to increase stability in the water. Only then could her cargo be stowed, with the heaviest casks, puncheons and hogsheads laid into the ballast, followed by the lighter barrels, firkins, boxes and bales. This was a crucial job for the *Nancy's* crew, as the stability of the ship depended on how well the vessel sat in the water. How securely the cargo rested, especially in rough seas, was a responsibility that ultimately lay with the ship's master. By early April 1774 the *Nancy* was ready to sail, and Mann received these instructions and terms of employment for himself and his officers:

"Captain Luke Mann   Liverpool April 5, 1774

Sir,

You being appointed to command our brig 'The Nancy', now ready for sea, are to observe these instructions through the course of your present intended voyage to Africa & America.

You are with the first opportunity of wind to proceed to sea through the South Channel, and when clear of the land direct your course for the innermost of the Cape de Verde Islands, taking care to allow for an Easterly current that always sets in upon the Coast of Barbara, while many ships have been lost and their crews made slaves.

From the Cape de Verdes shape your course to the southward so as to pass Anna Bona to the Westward, by which means you may fall in with the coast of Angola well to the Southward , say at Ambrosse in the latitude 7 deg. 47 min south, where we mean you to fix your trade and barter your cargo as per invoice hereunto assessed amounting to £2377 15s 5 ½d for good merchantable slaves, taking care always to purchase none that are old or sickly, but young slaves from 4 ft 4 inches high to 4 ft 6 inches …. And in case you cannot finish your purchase at Ambrosse in these months we would have you stay only until you get about one hundred and fifty slaves on board and then proceed to Cape Benda and finish your purchase on the best terms you can. We apprehend you may purchase slaves at Ambrosse for 7 or 8 pieces of India goods,[18] but must observe not to let any slaves pass you that are good, for the current prices at Cape Benda are from 12 to 14 pieces India goods on a prime slave, and likewise to keep your presents until you go to Cape Benda, though we have not the least doubt that you may get all the slaves you want in six weeks or two months ……

When your purchase is finished you are to go directly to Antigua and there apply to Wm. Livingston Esq., where you will find our letters lodged, but in case you get no letters you are to put your cargo into Mr. Livingstone's hands to sell for our a/c on the best terms he can, unless he advises you to the contrary and directs you to some other market. Should it be Jamaica you are to put your cargo into the hands of Messrs. Hibberts, who we have entire confidence in. And you are to have £5 per month wages, £4 on every £104 on the net sales of the slaves sold on a/c of the owners for your coast commission, and £2 per cent on ditto for your privilege. Your chief mate, Mr. Wm. Evans, is to have £4 per month wages and one slave on an average with the sales, he paying the owners the first cost on an average with the general purchase. Your Dr., Mr. Daniel Vaughan, is to have £4 per month wages and

---

[18] Indian cloths, particularly cotton.

one shilling per head on all the slaves sold on a/c of the owners for head money. Your 2nd mate, Mr. James Pennell, is to have £3 15s per month wages and liberty to purchase a boy slave about 4ft 4 inches with his own goods. Should he fall short of goods you are to supply him with what he may want, he paying the owners the first cost. All your other officers and people are to have the wages set opposite their respective names in the articles, and there is no other adventure gratuity or privilege allowed you or any of your people save what is here mentioned under the penalty of one hundred pounds, beside the forfeiture of your commission and privilege to the owners. In case of your death, which God forbid, your chief mate Mr. Wm. Evans is to succeed you in your command and follow these instructions with this difference only, that he is to have the coast commission, say £4 in every £104 on the sale of the slaves actually purchased after your death and the whole of the privilege to be remitted home to the owners to be disposed of as they may think proper.

You must observe not to go into the River of Congo on any account as that will cancel the Insurance, and must not go on shore a little to the Southward of Congo River at a place called Cape Paderoou that lies between Congo River & Ambrosse. The house that sells your cargo in the West Indies must draw the bills for the proceeds as follows:- One sixth in favour of Mr. James Gildart; one sixth in favour of Mr. Henry Trafford; one sixth in favour of Mr. John Yates; one sixth in favour of Mr. Thomas Yates; one sixth in favour of Mr. David Tuohy; & one sixth in favour of Mr. Wm Speers, all at equal dates.

You will be careful of your powder & brandy as many fatal accidents happen from both, and as dispatch is the life of the African Trade we desire you will make all the prudent dispatch in your power both in your purchase and in getting your wood and water on board. You must not give your slaves too much provisions [as] they are accustomed to low diet in their own country. Exercise, a clean ship with pure air, and as much indulgence as you can prudently show them is the best medium. Carry a uniform and steady command with your officers & people, no ill treatment to any of them. In case they deny their duty they are to be mulct of their wages and a memorandum made in the logbook & signed by two or more of your principal officers. And, as you have plenty of provisions on board, you will not stint the people, but give them plenty of such provisions as you may think proper, say barley, peas &c. You will get your provisions out of the rooms as often as convenient and air them upon deck in the outward bound passage, and safeguard them and keep an account how they are expended.

You must take care during your purchase not to unsort your cargo of any one article, as that will undoubtedly hurt your trade, but keep a regular a/c of what you pay, and then you can always know what you have upon hand. ….. If any customs are required where you slave at, agree for them as low as you can, say 10 or 20 trading pieces to be paid when you are half slaved, which perhaps you may prolong until your purchase is finished. Make all the dispatch you can from the West Indies, and we hope you have no reason to be at any great expense there as the vessel is new and well fitted out. Be also frugal in your disbursements and sleep on board your own ship. We remain wishing you health & good voyage and a safe return. Your assured friends and well wishers, Speers, Tuohy & Co."

After checking the invoice of goods and reading his instructions, Luke Mann wrote his acceptance letter next day, stating "I bind and oblige myself to be accountable." Three days later, *Nancy* was on her way down the Mersey in pursuit of that pernicious trade. [19]

Following the Boston Tea Party, and similar actions in other American ports, a new government under Lord North introduced a series of harsh new laws during May and June 1774. Under these Coercion Acts, Parliament suspended the Massachusetts assembly, declared the colony in crown hands, and closed the port of Boston. Officials were to be appointed by the crown, and would escape the local justice system if accused of capital crimes in the execution of their duties, such as quelling riots or collecting taxes. Furthermore, troops were to be quartered throughout all the colonies to preserve order and isolate resistance, and colonists could be required to provide accommodation in their own homes for Redcoat soldiers.

The colonial assemblies held a congress in Philadelphia in September 1774. An association was formed to stop all trade with Britain unless the Coercion Acts were repealed, and the Committees of Correspondence were to organise the boycott. A Declaration of Rights demanded the rescinding of thirteen commercial Acts passed by Parliament since 1763. It was rejected outright and events moved swiftly. The Massachusetts military governor, General Thomas Gage, tried to enforce martial law throughout the colony, but with just four thousand troops was only able to hold Boston. Meanwhile, the Patriots now had about ten thousand men in the militia. They set up the Committee of Safety in October, and most of the colonies started drilling and arming. Cannon and powder were seized from British military bases, agents were sent to Europe to buy munitions, and neither the French nor Spanish governments could be dissuaded from supplying the Americans. The Patriots

---

[19] *Williamson's Advertiser*, 15th April 1774, shows the *Nancy* left Liverpool on the 9th.

began stockpiling munitions at Concord, a village twenty miles from Boston, where the illegal Massachusetts Assembly was now meeting regularly. In January 1775, merchants from Liverpool and every major British port met at the *King's Tavern* in Cornhill, London, to persuade the government to restore good relations and repeal the Acts that had led to resentment in America. Resolutions were carried by a large majority in favour of conciliation, but fell on deaf ears. Within a month eight thousand tons of shipping was returned to Britain due to the blockade.

From the vantage point of his Boston foundry close to the Charles River, Paul Revere was observing the British military closely. His suspicions were aroused in mid-April by preparations being made to a number of landing craft.[20] He guessed that Governor General Gage would order a force to Concord to seize the munitions and arrest patriot leaders Sam Adams and John Hancock, sending them to the gallows and thus dealing a blow to their outlawed Provincial Assembly. Revere rode to Concord on 16th April to rouse its people, who were soon concealing guns, powder and shot throughout the neighbouring countryside. Adams and Hancock left for nearby Lexington, where a militia of 'minutemen' had been formed to resist a Redcoat incursion. Content with these preparations, Revere returned to Boston and arranged for lanterns to be placed in the belfry of the Old North Church to signal the movement of troops.

On the evening of the 18th April 1775, the Redcoats were preparing to set off across the Charles River under cover of darkness, hoping to avoid notice. From there they would make their way to Cambridge and on to Concord via Lexington. But Revere was already ahead of them as he awaited the signal from his vantage point in Charlestown across the river from Boston. Seeing two lanterns appear in the belfry, he set off immediately to warn his compatriots. As he reached Lexington, Revere made for the tavern, where Captain John Parker and some of his men were awaiting news. They were soon joined by William Dawes, who had taken an alternative route from Boston, and by Samuel Prescott from Concord, who was anxious for information. While Parker mustered his militiamen, Revere called on Jonas Clark and roused his sleeping guests, Adams and Hancock, to warn them. Then, with Dawes and Prescott, Revere made for Concord five miles further on.

On the village green in Lexington, Captain Parker was finding it difficult to maintain discipline. Despite their pledge of 'ready at a minute's notice,' the long night of vigilance led some of the militiamen back to their beds. As the sun began to rise on the 19th, the head of the British column appeared, and the remaining seventy or so minutemen were instructed by Parker, "Stand your ground, don't fire unless fired upon, but if they mean to have a war, let it begin

---

[20] I am indebted here to U-S-history.com, from which this account is largely based.

here." The leading officer brandished his sword and called on the militia to lay down their arms and disperse. Now realising the odds, Parker reluctantly gave orders to obey, but a rogue shot rang out in the heat of the moment. In the confusion, the Redcoats fired a volley. As the smoke cleared, the bodies of eight dead and ten wounded patriot rebels were found on the ground. One Redcoat was slightly injured in the engagement.

Meanwhile, soon after leaving Lexington, Prescott, Dawes and Revere had run up against a roadblock. A party of Redcoats had been diverted from the main body to prevent any rebels from Lexington making for Concord to give warning. Revere and Dawes were captured, but Prescott managed to avoid capture owing to his intimate knowledge of the area. When he reached his destination just after midnight, the church bells were sounded to summon the local militia. By the early hours, several hundred had gathered and started towards Lexington, where the first shots of the conflict were about to be fired. A while later, and some distance down the road, they spotted a column of Redcoats advancing towards them from their recent engagement, and retreated to a hilltop outside the town to await events.

When the British reached Concord they began searching for weapons, and found several caches hidden in and around the town. As they did so, the militia left their hilltop retreat, anxious about events below. They confronted a Redcoat contingent stationed at a bridge over the Concord River, but the British retreated to join their comrades after a brief exchange of fire. Having destroyed the weapons, their commander decided to withdraw his forces, fearful of being overwhelmed by a growing opposition. At first, the Concord militia simply watched the withdrawal, but its members were soon tracking the Redcoats, taking cover, and firing into the retreating column. The rout continued all the way to Boston, joined by militiamen along the route, as news of the Redcoats' predicament spread. Meanwhile, Revere and Dawes were released owing to their captors' fears for their own safety. By the time the British reached Boston they had suffered 273 casualties in return for about sixty of the rebels.

By the end of May, Generals William Howe, Henry Clinton, and John Burgoyne had arrived with British reinforcements to secure Boston. The rebels, meanwhile, had their own ideas. On 16th June they took up positions on the Charlestown Peninsula overlooking Boston, from where they hoped to drive the British out. Working under cover of night, they began constructing defensive earthworks on Breed's Hill, but struggled to complete them next morning under heavy bombardment from British ships in Boston harbour below. General Howe now ordered a direct assault on the American positions, and three thousand Redcoats were landed on the west of the peninsula, from where they marched in close formation up Breed's Hill towards the enemy's well-defended positions. As they came within range, a volley of musket fire cut through flesh and bone, and the Redcoats scattered in a hurried retreat. Yet discipline demanded courage, and the British regrouped for a second attack, but were once more decimated. After an hour's delay, during which reinforcements were brought up, a third attack was made. By this time the Americans were running low on powder and were unable to resist the enemy. Many were shot in the back as they fled from their defences, leaving over four hundred dead or wounded. By the end of the battle, however, there were over a thousand British casualties, the heaviest loss they were to suffer in one engagement over the coming years. The British now took control of the peninsula and erected defences on Bunker Hill close to the recent scenes of slaughter, while the rebels began training and reorganising in the surrounding hinterlands under their new commander-in-chief, George Washington. The die was now cast, and over the coming months a new Continental Army began to take shape.

Meanwhile, having returned to Liverpool from his long voyage to Angola and Antigua, Luke Mann had been expecting to command the *Nancy* on its next voyage. Instead, he found himself assigned to the *Derby,* and as the repercussions of the growing American conflict were being felt in Liverpool and other ports, its crew were soon at the centre of the biggest storm in Britain for many years.[21]

---

[21] Lloyd's Register for 1776 shows Mann was originally to command the *Nancy* for the next voyage during 1775-76, but his name is crossed out and is shown clearly against the *Derby.*

Liverpool from the South Shore, Pictorial Relics, Herdman, Plate 35

Chapter Two

By the evening of 25th August 1775 the crew of the *Derby* were filled with rage. While they were refitting the ship for a slaving voyage under Luke Mann's command, a rumour spread that seamen's wages would be slashed from thirty shillings a month to twenty throughout the port. After completing the rigging, several of the crew set off to confront the *Derby's* owner, John Yates, to demand the thirty-shilling rate.[1] When they reached Yates' fine house in nearby Cleveland Square his reply was blunt. There were now over two thousand unemployed seamen in the port, so why should merchants pay thirty shillings when hands would work for less. Trade was down, and all must share the burden. Sailors, carters, carpenters, ropers, sail makers and many more must tighten their belts and make ends meet in these depressed times. Indeed, just weeks earlier, a writer in *The General Advertiser* had lamented, "Our once extensive trade to Africa is at a stand; all commerce with America is at an end. Peace, harmony, and mutual confidence must constitute the balm that can again restore the health of the body politic. Survey our docks; count there the gallant ships laid up and useless. When will they be again refitted? What will become of the sailor, the tradesman, the poor labourer during the approaching winter?"[2]

While the crew's delegation listened to Yates they could not help but notice the opulence of the tree-lined square surrounded by handsome town houses. This contrasted sharply with the narrow streets and alleys with which they were familiar, with their back-houses and damp cellars, and their poverty-stricken inhabitants. True, profits had been hit hard, but surely it was they who were feeling the main brunt of the war against the American rebels. Trading with the colonies risked attack from enemy privateers, and now Lord North's government had forbidden the export of arms and gunpowder, which African merchants valued so highly. Liverpool's slave trade was on its knees, forty of its Guineamen now lying idle.[3] To make matters worse, the return to port of several Greenland ships, after a season of fishing and whaling, further swelled the ranks of the unemployed.

---

[1] Thirty shillings (£1 10s) was the average monthly wage for ordinary seamen. Experienced able seamen earned up to twenty shillings more, but all would have been threatened by a cut. Inventories from a few years later show wages about 50% higher than the 1775 rates, the rise reflecting the dangers to crewmen during wartime. *Lloyd's Register* for 1776 shows J. Yates & Co. as owners of the *Derby* and Luke Mann as captain. John and Thomas Yates had been shareholders in the *Nancy* voyage commanded by Mann during 1774-75 (see p.13 above). Although contemporary reports give Yates as captain for the forthcoming voyage of the *Derby* in 1775, clearly they hired Mann for the job (see footnote 21, p17 above). Both Yates's are listed in *Gore's Directory* for 1774 (there was none in 1775) as living in Cleveland Square.

[2] The *General Advertiser*, 29th July 1775.

[3] Guineamen were slaves ships destined for anywhere along the coast of West Africa, whether the coast of Guinea or not.

Talk of hardship by wealthy merchants, dressed in their finery and housed in style, cut no ice with men whose families knew of nothing else but poverty. What did Yates and his sort know about parish relief or the workhouse. For seafarers' families, the good times were those when enough was on the table to feed hungry mouths. To own a powdered wig meant parting with as much as Yates was now prepared to pay them for a month. Sorely angered, when the men returned to the *Derby* with his reply there was no stopping the crew. Climbing the ratlines with knives and cutlasses, they cut the rigging so recently fitted, dropping the ropes onto the deck to cheers of support from fellow tars throughout the dock. From the quayside, hundreds of on-lookers watched the wanton destruction in amazement. Amongst them were the customs men, but it may have been Hutchinson, the dock master, who was first to raise the alert. Within minutes a party of constables was advancing towards the *Derby*. Armed with muskets, pistols, cutlasses and batons, they seized nine of the crew, bound them with ropes, and led them through the gathering throng of seamen and their supporters to the town hall, known locally as the Exchange. Awaiting them were the hastily assembled magistrates, whose affiliations lay entirely with the merchants. Justice was swift, and the nine, along with a riotous woman, were soon on their way down Water Street to be incarcerated in the prison by the Old Tower. [4]

Meanwhile, realising the threat to their own livelihoods, dozens of angry seamen set off to disable any ship ready to sail. Among the first were the *Grace*, *Glory* and *Providence*, each bound for Jamaica. [5] As the destruction began, news spread like wildfire throughout the neighbourhood. Men, women and children soon began hurrying towards the docks to witness the seamen strike one ship after another, cutting and slashing their ropes. [6] But, when news of the nine circulated, the collective thoughts of several large and excited crowds now focused on securing their freedom. From Liverpool's three docks, the Old, the South, and George's, poured hundreds of seamen armed with handspikes and clubs, women and children in tow, all converging on the ancient sandstone edifice of the gaol. Ten steps below ground lay seven dim, filthy dungeons, each about six feet square. It was here that the men, along with other felons, were being held, three or more to a cell. Before long, a mob of two or three thousand people had begun to lay siege. First they smashed the windows

Liverpool Tower Gaol, 1804, Pictorial Relics, Herdman, Plate 2.

---

[4] This account is based on those in Brooke, op. cit., p.326-343; H.R. Hickins, *Origins of Working Class Politics, Liverpool 1756-1791*, in *Building the Union – Studies on the Growth of the Workers' Movement: Merseyside 1756-1967* (1973) p15-19; and R.B. Rose, *A Liverpool Sailors' Strike In The Eighteenth Century*, Lancashire and Cheshire Antiquarian Society, Vol. 18 (1958) p85-91.

[5] Listed as due to sail in *Williamson's Liverpool Advertiser*, 25th August 1775.

[6] Marcus Rediker, op. cit., p110 & 205, suggests such actions were quite common among seafarers and gave rise to the use of word 'strike' in the sense of stopping work. Such damage would have been more easily repaired than slashing the sails, for example, as seamen were quite used to splicing ropes and might therefore avoid having to pay the costs.

of the tower, where debtors where lodged in more congenial circumstances than those below ground. The rioters then threatened to destroy the prison if their shipmates were not released forthwith. In fear of the consequences, the authorities released the men, who were then carried aloft in triumph by the cheering crowd. In the confusion, however, it was noticed that only eight of the nine had been released. Turning back, the rioters demanded the ninth, adding the release of the woman for good measure. Now they made their way back to the docks, where they paraded jubilantly in the warm evening air, fuelled by rum and ale. Meanwhile, the destruction continued, and only by midnight did the celebrations die down, as the crowds melted away into the narrow streets and alleys close by.

Saturday 26th August began more peacefully, with many a reveller recovering from the previous night's excesses. During the morning they congregated at the 'Ladies Walk' at the north edge of the town, close to Mr. Brook's limekiln and brickyard. Here they could organise, away from unwanted attention under the cover of an avenue of trees, to debate their next course of action. While some urged caution, fearful of what might result from further rioting, most demanded to press the power of the merchants and those they saw as their agents - the magistrates and members of the so-called Common Council. One of the more vociferous seamen was elected leader, and with a touch of irony dubbed General Gage after the military governor of Massachusetts where the American rebellion was underway. 'Gage' suggested a show of force. Before long he was leading hundreds of sailors along Old Hall and High Streets, and into the corn market in front of the Exchange. Under the banner of a red flag, 'Gage' delivered a proclamation stating their right to refuse to work without "redress and support" from the merchants, before leading his cheering supporters through the town, parading to the sounds of pipe and drum.

Sunday was a quieter day, during which cautionary sermons echoed from pulpits in church and chapel. In St. George's and St. Peter's, St. Nicholas's and St. Thomas's, congregations were reminded to love thy neighbour and refrain from violent action. For the rest of the day the seamen kicked their heels and waited for the Sabbath to end.

At 9.00am on Monday 28th the sailors met at their rendezvous at the Ladies' Walk. However, about 150 were soon scouring the docks to persuade reluctant tars to join their strike.[7] Boarding and searching vessels, they showed no hesitation in taking off anyone still working, including three men on board the *Elizabeth*. When the second mate and boatswain refused to join them, both were set upon with sticks and clubs, before their attackers climbed the rigging and dragged Thomas Peterson down. Another group boarded the

---

7 Tars – a common eighteenth century term for seamen.

High Street, 1797, leading to the back of the Exchange, part of the route taken by striking seamen in 1775 (Herdman Collection 1266, LRO)

Jane and escorted the crew to the Ladies' Walk. At midday the sailors again marched en masse to the Exchange to ask for support from the mayor and magistrates, but their plea fell on deaf ears and the men were ordered back to work. Seething with discontent, the crowd drifted off, some towards the docks, where their anger was vented on the rigging of several more ships. Others wandered around the town in gangs, calling at merchants' houses and soliciting contributions towards a sailors' levy. To the town's more prosperous inhabitants, the atmosphere now became more menacing, and some sent wives and children away to take refuge with their more valuable possessions for safekeeping. But for the majority, with little means of transport, safety lay indoors with shutters firmly closed. For the most part, however, the seamen remained reasonably peaceful. When one group called at merchant William Leece's house in Whitechapel, his daughter courageously answered the door and asked nervously about the purpose of their visit. The gang's spokesman saw she was frightened, and so removed his hat in deference before respectfully asking for a contribution. On receiving her offering he thanked her politely, and the sailors moved on. Predictably, as day turned to evening, much of the money collected on such visits was frittered away in alehouses across the town.

The following day was a far more eventful affair. Meeting first at the Ladies' Walk to discuss tactics, the seamen set off late in the morning towards the Exchange to press their case once more. While they crowded into the corn market, their leaders met a group of merchants and came away believing that normal wages would be restored. Jubilant at this news, the gathering dispersed in festive mood and made for the taverns to celebrate. As they did so, however, the magistrates were busy hiring special constables to make arrests so that the dispute could be ended without any settlement. Offered ten shillings a day, the rate of pay was indeed tempting to those willing to risk retribution, but the mood of the revellers soon turned sour as news of this treachery became known. Clearly, the merchants had no intention of restoring seamen's wages, yet they were willing to put their hands in their pockets and pay their stooges handsomely. Celebration turned to violence as sailors rallied to support anyone threatened with arrest. Word went round to return to the Exchange, and by nine o'clock that evening many hundreds had surrounded the building with the intention of wrecking it if their claim was not met. In the meantime, 120 armed constables had been garrisoned within to join the merchants and magistrates who had taken refuge there, having had news of the sailors' threat to "pull the 'Change down". Together, they set about barricading themselves within the building and preparing their defence.

Liverpool Town Hall, or Exchange, 1773 (LIC 508, LRO)

The discipline of the mob outside quickly broke down, and some began pelting the building with stones. After several windows had been shattered, the Riot Act was read from behind the safety of a Doric column on the balcony of the upper floor. But little was heard amidst the noise and chaos below. As more windows were broken, and frames prised open to force entry, a volley of shots split the night air. Three men fell dead and fifteen were wounded, and many a stray musket ball was embedded in woodwork in nearby Castle Street. The attackers scattered in terror, leaving behind them the dead and injured.

Few of Liverpool's inhabitants slept much that night, as they thought about the following day either with dread or the urge for vengeance. Many fled with their most precious and portable possessions, securing their houses as best they could and with good reason. On Wednesday 30th the rioters returned to wreak their revenge directly on the merchants who they believed responsible for the casualties of the previous night. First to be visited was Thomas Ratcliffe, a Guinea merchant who lived in Whitechapel, who some said had fired the first shot. Armed with pistols, blunderbusses, cutlasses and clubs, dozens of seamen marched under a red flag to the sound of a drum. As they reached his house at the corner of Richmond Street they fired a volley of shots, shattering all the windows and splintering the frames. Removing what was left using iron bars, they climbed in. One of them spotted Ratcliffe's son, Jonathon, who turned and fled in terror. As he did so, a shot rang out but narrowly missed, enabling him to make his escape through the back of the house. The intruders now set about ransacking the property, smashing the furniture and throwing it onto the street. Feather beds and pillows were torn open, their contents scattered to the wind. Clothes, lace, linen, parchments, china and glassware, and even the iron stoves, - all were ripped, shredded or smashed in a frenzy of hatred and contempt. The next victim was William James, whose fine Georgian house in Rainford Gardens was just yards away. Wisely or not, the James family had escaped to their country home during the night. Fuelled by a quantity of wines and spirits discovered in the cellar, the mob hurled the rich possessions into the street, destroyed James's accounts and letters, and took away what booty they could carry. During the mayhem, a clock case was opened to reveal James's black servant hidden inside, who fled in terror, much to the amusement of the revellers.

Meanwhile, there were others at large wearing red ribbons on their hats. Some broke into Mr. Parr's gun shop, and others into an arms warehouse, gathering between them a hundred or more muskets and pistols, with supplies of powder and lead balls. Then they paraded through the town, threatening and demanding money from its more prosperous inhabitants. Others visited the South Dock, removing three cannon from the *Essex* and harnessing the gun carriages to horses before hauling them to the Exchange. As one was placed between Mr. Warren's goldsmith shop and Mr. Cordeux's hosiery business in Castle Street, someone pointed to the 'Liver' bird in the armorial painting of the pediment and quipped "aim at the goose." Another was placed near the *Golden Fleece* in Dale Street to blast away at the east side. By one o'clock all the rioters had once more surrounded the building. When the red flag was hoisted the firing began, shaking buildings and shattering windows with each blast. As cannon and musket balls slammed into the Exchange, pistol and musket shot was returned from within, where the stonework offered the better protection. But the disorderly rioters, many of them drunk, were far more vulnerable. By late afternoon four more had been killed and many wounded, and it was clear there was little prospect of destroying the building. With this in mind, some of the rioters resumed their ransacking, setting off next to visit none other than *Derby* owner John Yates in Cleveland Square, followed by John Simmons in St. Paul's Square and several others. Some got off more lightly with the threat of return visits if grievances were not met. Meanwhile, the assault on the Exchange continued well into the night, but still with little effect.

Gripped in terror, a witness to the initial ransacking put her fears on paper. "This day I have been so frightened as hardly to be able to do anything. Such scenes of distress as I have been witness to, with the clattering of swords and cannon, have so terrified me, that I hardly know what I say or do." Describing the attack on property, she added, "…our poor Debby would go to see them, and has got an eyelash [brow] cut with a candlestick." She continued, "It is not possible to form any idea of the distress this place has been in all this day. The merchants get to the corner of the streets, where, methinks, I yet see them standing with fear painted in their faces. The 'Change has all its windows broke, and frames forced quite out. They have also been firing at the walls the greatest part of this day, and are now gone to Cleveland Square. I suppose there is not a merchant who has wanted to lower their wages but will be visited by them; and God knows how long these riots may continue. You will not wonder after reading this that I was terrified. I am a coward its true, but I think this would have alarmed anyone. They read the Riot Act last night, and then began to fire on them, when they killed three and wounded fifteen. This has made them so desperate. I could not help thinking we had Boston here, and I fear this is only the beginning of our sorrows." [8]

As the rioting continued, however, steps were being taken to quell the mob once and for all. By three o'clock that Wednesday afternoon, a dispatch rider had reached the Royal Regiment of Dragoons in Manchester with an urgent message from Mayor Peter Rigby requesting speedy assistance. Two magistrates arrived later that evening, suggesting hysterically that Liverpool would be laid in ashes and every inhabitant murdered if the response was not immediate. Given this prospect, a hundred cavalrymen and six officers were mustered, although they did not get underway until three the following morning of the 31st August. Riding through heavy rain, they eventually rested at Prescot, six miles from Liverpool, where the mayor awaited them with news that the rioters were preparing to attack them upon their arrival.

---

[8] Printed in the *Morning Chronicle and London Advertiser*, 8th September 1775, quoted in Brooke, op. cit., p331-332.

At this point, they carefully dried and loaded their weapons before pressing on to Liverpool. Meanwhile, Mayor Rigby had arranged for a delegation to meet with the sailors that morning to offer them wages of two shillings a day. At sixty shillings a month, this was obviously a ploy to buy time and calm the situation before the arrival of the soldiers. However, most of the seamen were attending the funeral of Tuesday's victims, but the delegation was left in no doubt by London sailor George Hill of the rioters' intentions to destroy the Exchange come what may. By four that Thursday afternoon, the weary dragoons had reached the town, greeted by hundreds of townsfolk anxious for relief from their oppressors. Encouraged by the reception, they proceeded at a gallop towards the centre, where further acts of rioting were unfolding. As they converged on the mob, brandishing swords and pistols, there was a panic dispersal into cellars, garrets, and every available place of concealment. Throughout the day, the men of the Light Horse roamed the troubled town, rounding up suspects and gathering information. On 1st September, tipped off by informers, they swarmed through the docks and poorer quarters, rounding up the main activists and ringleaders. By the end of that Friday around fifty men were under lock and key in the Old Tower, protected by a heavy guard. The riot was now quelled and the seamen were well and truly beaten.

The dragoons remained in Liverpool throughout most of September, and were billeted in several taverns and public houses, including the *White Lion* in Castle Street and the *Angel Inn* in Dale Street. Order was maintained while witnesses were questioned about the involvement of the various prisoners, and the town returned to normal. A special council meeting voted to pay the regiment's expenses from local parish taxes, and the freedom of the borough was granted to the captain and officers. They were welcome to visit the Theatre Royal in Williamson's Square, where Shakespeare's comedy *All's Well That Ends Well* was being staged. At the end of the performance the audience was to be treated to a "new dance" entitled *The European in America*, in which Mr. Dagville played the part of "first savage". There was also a musical entertainment, *The Lady's Frolick,* the principal part being played by Mrs Mattocks. Tickets sold at 3s 6d for boxes, 1s 6d for the pit, and a shilling for the gallery. [9] Clearly, the officers of the dragoons enjoyed their privileges. Second Lieutenant Garrick stayed at *St. James' Coffee House* in Castle Street, where he consumed wine, beer, porter, punch, cider, and spiced port wine costing £1 14s 6d in total, while his consumption of tea and coffee amounted to £1 12s 5d.[10] Clearly, Garrick intended to get the most out of his stay.

By late September investigations into the roles of the prisoners during the riots were complete, and the magistrates had made their decision as to which

---

[9] Williamson's Advertiser, Friday 15th September 1775.
[10] Brooke, op. cit., p345. Garrick's bill for alcohol, tea and coffee would amount to about £300 today.

should be committed to trial. Fourteen ringleaders were taken to Lancaster on the 26th, where they were incarcerated in the castle gaol and supported by contributions from Liverpool. At the Lent Assizes the following year only eight of the accused were found guilty, yet all fourteen were treated equally and discharged on condition that they enlisted in His Majesty's navy.[11] This was rough justice indeed, not only for the six against whom charges were not proven, but also because the lax conditions of a Georgian prison compared favourably to life on board a man-of-war. This was the long arm of the Admiralty doing its recruitment work, as guilty and not-so-guilty men throughout the country were finding out.

Meanwhile, Liverpool's dignitaries wrote deferentially to their "Most Gracious Sovereign" to assure him they were "truly sensible of the many blessings we enjoy in common with the rest of your people under your Majesty's mild administration and paternal care." They continued effusively, "we, your Majesty's dutiful and loyal subjects, beg leave to approach the throne with all due respects to your royal person, the most steady attachment to the protestant succession, and the firmest zeal for our glorious constitution, to testify our warmest commendations of the wisdom and stability of your Majesty's councils, which have been directed to allay and put an end to the unhappy differences subsisting between Great Britain and her colonies. It is with the greatest concern we reflect, that the measures hitherto pursued to bring our fellow subjects in America to a true sense of their duty and interest have not as yet had the desired effect; but we ardently hope that they will very soon be sensible of their error and return to a due acknowledgement of the power of the British legislature; that the joys of peace and tranquillity may be restored, and the hearts of all your Majesty's subjects be united in the strictest bonds of mutual confidence and affection. We cannot, however, avoid expressing our abhorrence and detestation of all traitorous and rebellious disturbers of your Majesty's peace and government; and assuring your Majesty, that we shall ever be ready and willing to exert our utmost endeavours for the discouragement of such illegal proceedings. And we pray, that your Majesty may long reign in the hearts and affections of all your subjects, and that the crown of these realms may descend to your latest posterity." [12]

---

11 *The General Advertiser,* 5th April 1776 lists Thomas Locket, John Hipsley, James Hamilton, George Hill, Thomas Williams, George Oliver, Joseph Black, Bernard Handwright, Robert Peat, Abraham Place, John Fisher, James Rosthorn, John Sparks and Thomas Pearson.
12 *Williamson's Advertiser,* 22nd September 1775.

By the end of September news was reaching Liverpool about the siege of Boston and how events had been unfolding. *Williamson's Advertiser* reported that "Letters from Boston say that General Gage and General Burgoyne will be in England by the time the parliament meets, in order to lay before the House an account of their whole proceedings since the army has been at Boston, with the situation the troops are in, and their improbability of subduing the Americans without a reinforcement of 50,000 men, a strong train of artillery, and some small field pieces to traverse the woods with, where the riflemen cannot do that mischief they can do in a pitched battle; and the letters further add that without the above is granted, the Generals are determined not to return on that service." The report added that the government had contracted to supply the troops with ten thousand butts of strong beer, five thousand 'chaldrons' of coal, a large consignment of potatoes and a quantity of faggots, to be shipped on board several transports at Deptford. There was also a report that "A fleet of transports, which have been out in search of livestock, is just returned with about eighteen hundred sheep and above one hundred head of oxen, which will be some relief to the troops in general and of great benefit to the hospitals." As to military hardware, the paper reported that, "Among other new constructed implements of war at Woolwich, designed for America, is a spreading mortar, which at one explosion discharges at least one hundred balls, all of which burst and extend to an amazing degree." [13]

Further news of the siege was revealed in letters from General Washington's personal secretary and aide de camp in Cambridge, near Boston, to a friend in Philadelphia. One noted that, "The last three weeks have afforded no occurrences in either camp. Our army has been strengthening their lines, forming their redoubts, and drawing down cannon to make any attack upon this town, or penetration into the country this way, impracticable. The enemy has done the same on the other side, and in this condition the armies of both sides are looking at each other...[our] men are healthy and in good spirits, so that we have nothing to fear but a surprise, which is guarded against by the utmost vigilance. The enemy, on the other hand, are sickly, totally destitute of fresh provisions and vegetables; the scurvy, fevers and fluxes carry off numbers every day, and most of their wounded die from their bad habit of

[13] *Williamson's Advertiser*, 29th September 1775.

body. Four deserters as have come out within these 24 hours; all of them agree in the account of their sickness and mortality."[14] The following day, further details were sent about British losses, their lack of adequate supplies, soldiers' complaints about lack of pay, and the deprivations suffered by Bostonians. It was also revealed that one of the deserters had provided the rebels with a plan of British defences.

The conflict soon gave rise to accusations of the mistreatment of prisoners on both sides. A letter from General Washington to his British counterpart, Gage, complained that "that no consideration has been had for those of the most respectable rank when languishing with wounds and sickness; that some have even been amputated in this unworthy situation." He warned, " My duty now makes it necessary to apprise you that, for the future, I shall regulate the conduct towards those gentlemen, who are or may be in our possession, exactly by the rule which you shall observe towards those of ours who may be in your custody. If severity and hardship mark the line of your conduct, painful as it may be to me, your prisoners may feel its effects; but if kindness and humanity are shewn to ours, I shall with pleasure consider those in our hands only as unfortunate, and they shall receive the treatment to which the unfortunate are ever entitled." [15] Gage retorted that "Britons, ever pre-eminent in mercy, have out-gone common example, and overlooked the Criminal in the captive." He added, "My intelligence from your army would justify severe Recrimination. I understand there are of the King's faithful subjects, taken some time since by the rebels, labouring, like negro slaves, to gain their daily subsistence, or reduced to the wretched alternative, to perish by famine, or take arms against their King and Country." He warned, "Should those, under whose usurped Authority you act, control such a disposition, and dare to call severity retaliations, to God, who knows all hearts, be the appeal for the dreadful consequences." [16]

Meanwhile, despite the rapid rise in unemployment amongst its seamen, life in Liverpool continued much as it had before the disturbances at the end of August. At the opposite end of Castle Street to the Exchange, overlooked by St. George's church, market stallholders sold vegetables, fish and pigs, and a variety of produce was sold under the arches of an arcade along the southern perimeter of St. George's terrace. At either end of the arcade were two

---

[14] Letter dated 27th July 1775 and printed in *Williamson's Advertiser*, 29th September.
[15] Dated 11th August and printed in *Williamson's Advertiser*, 29th September 1775.
[16] Letter dated 13th August, printed in *Williamson's Advertiser*, 29th September 1775.

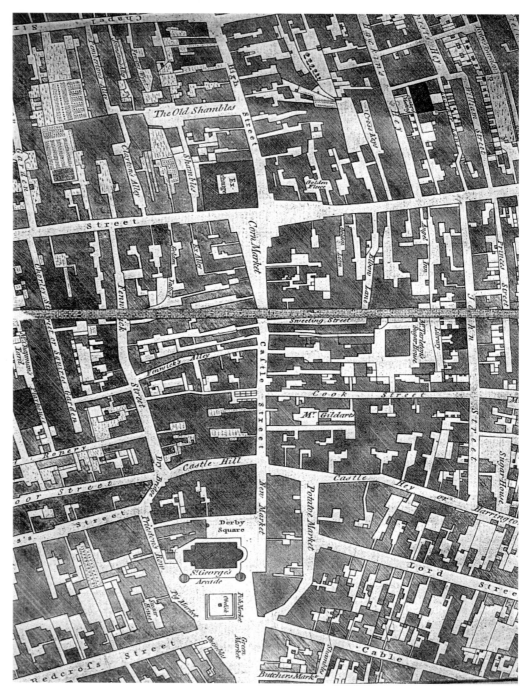

A detail from George Perry's Map of Liverpool, 1769 (LRO) showing the area around Castle Street.

octagonal domed structures, one being the office for the clerk of the market, the other serving as the watchmen's base and temporary prison lock-up, which was topped by a fire bell. Nearby, at the foot of a tall obelisk, was the water cistern for the fire engines that were stored under the arcade. Nearby, too, were the public stocks and pillory for the punishment of petty offenders. Replacing the castle that had been demolished fifty-four years earlier, St. George's was an elegantly decorated, neo-classical building of pale limestone, its steeple watching proudly over the market place. Less elegant, however, were the warehouses of Prieston's Row skirting its western perimeter. [17]

Looking down Pool Lane from St. George's Church towards the Old Dock, 1798. The foreground area was used for the green market (Plate 9, Pictorial Relics of Ancient Liverpool, W.G.Herdman, Hf942.7214 HER, LRO)

Leading up to St George's from the docks nearby were James Street, Redcross Street and Pool Lane, each a jumbled collection of the old and new. Some properties reflected an earlier age, with their stone construction, attic rooms and dormer windows, and were squat in appearance when nestled between taller, three-storied, brick-built Georgian town houses. Old or new, all had cellars, whether used for storage or rent. And amongst these dwellings were the warehouses, some small and narrow, others five or six floors high and more imposing. Each building told its own story of Liverpool's developing wealth and status, adding to a scene without any notion of uniformity or design. These streets were filled with the hustle and bustle of trade, the sound of cartwheels

---

[17] W. G. Herdman, *Pictorial Relics of Ancient Liverpool* (1843) LRO, Hf 942.7214, plate 18.

rumbling over rough cobblestones, and the smells of horse manure and human excrement. Most obvious to the eye at the bottom of these streets were the masts, yards and sails of vessels that were loading or unloading, attended by an army of cartmen. Attending, too, were the merchants, anxious to check that their goods were not pilfered between ship and storage. Merchants Francis Ingram and William Crosbie lived in Pool Lane, while William Earle and Thomas Golightly resided in Redcross Street, each at the heart of where their business interests lay. Looking up to these men of wealth were lesser traders such as grocer William Ankers, butcher Richard Cropper, saddler Anthony Tristram, and Robert Corran, barber and wig maker, all of Pool Lane. There, too, was milliner Ann Dewhurst, clock maker and silver smith Hannah Hadwen, and bookseller Margaret Eyres, each of whom, like many Liverpool women, ran thriving businesses. In addition, Pool Lane boasted the services of one Egerton Smith, mathematical instrument maker and lecturer on philosophy. He lived at number seventeen and named his residence Newton's Head. In Redcross Street there was a mug warehouse, a shoemaker, a jeweller, and wine merchants Golightly and Broster, while tallow chandler and soap boiler Robert Davison added to the pervasive odours of the neighbourhood. Among those trading in James Street were a cabinetmaker, a tailor, an ironmonger and surgeon William Pickering. [18]

James Street, 1823, looking down to Georges Dock, and virtually unchanged from fifty years earlier (LIC 268, LRO)

[18] All details of traders in this chapter are from *Gore's Liverpool Directory*, 1774. No directory was published for 1775 or '76.

Between the fish market at the bottom of James Street and the Old Dock was Strand Street, which traced part of the original shoreline before men of enterprise had built the docks.[19] It was here that Mary Catherwood played hostess at the *Three Tuns*, where nightly meetings of a homely fireside club were held. This was a favourite haunt of Liverpool captains, where they claimed in humour to be empowered by the ancient Greek god Aeolus to sell favourable winds to any who were due to sail. Needless to say, the purchases bought ale and good cheer, and each was recorded. One note showed that "Captain Nehemiah Holland hath bought a fair wind this 25th Jany. 1776 on his voyage to Jamaica," and hoped he would prosper. Success was offered to the *Jenny*, whose Captain Eastham paid a shilling for "a fair wind for his present voyage to Guinea," while Charles Wilson paid 2s 6d for a fair wind to carry the *Lydia* to Barbados. However, drinking funds were also raised in other ways, particularly by fines imposed for wearing new suits of clothes, or for having them turned inside out and re-tailored out to provide a new lease of life. Captain James Fazakerley paid one shilling for "his suit of chocolate coloured cloaths with guilt buttons," while others paid for brighter, more adventurous outfits. These included a suit of blue clothes with yellow oval buttons, a purple coat and green striped waistcoat, green and orange clothes with buttons to match, a "thunder and lightning coat and hell-fire waistcoat," and "damned ugly green clothes." Besides the paying of fines and the buying of winds, members paid to celebrate birthdays, births and marriages. Peter Allen paid to celebrate his brother's marriage, hoping he would "have the comfort of a son in nine months," and George Bates paid "one shilling in ale for ye honour of having a daughter launched at half past eleven o'clock last night." Members also took a close interest in the American War and laid various bets on its progress, including a barrel of ale on the fate of military campaigns for the control of New York and Philadelphia. [20]

Among the many ships moored in Liverpool's docks in late September 1775 was the *Waddell* from New York, laden with ninety tons of iron and nearly nine hundred oaks planks. The *Endeavour* had arrived from Newfoundland with a catch of codfish, nearly two hundred casks of fish oil, two pipes of wine, and twelve bundles of wood hoops and staves. The *Friendship* brought over nine hundred quarters of wheat from Danzig, while the *William* brought three hundred quarters of barley from Strangford. Three ships had arrived from Drogheda, two bearing limestone, the other with nineteen packs, thirty

---

[19] The Old Dock was built in a tidal inlet known as the 'Pool,' from which the town partly derives its name. The Pool opened out to the Mersey roughly opposite the site of the later Canning and Salthouse docks. It ran inland along the line of Canning Place, Paradise Street and Whitechapel.

[20] C. Birbeck Wilson, *The Records of a Liverpool Fireside, 1775-81*, Historic Society of Lancashire and Cheshire, Vol. 79 (1927) p136-148

trusses, and one bundle of linen. The *Margaret* and *Mary* from Belfast brought twelve hundred firkins of butter, seven hogsheads of tallow fat, and ten tierces of beef, while wheat had come from Dublin, slates from Caernarfon, and sailcloth from Preston.[21] Typical of the proceeds of the slave trade was the cargo of the *Thomas*, which had arrived from Jamaica with fifty-one elephant teeth, forty-nine puncheons of rum and two of beeswax, twenty tierces of coffee and twelve of sugar, fifty-three bags of cotton, and nine barrels of indigo dye. During the second week of October, the *Toms* came in with bales and bundles of linen, hemp yarn, flax, and bags of linseed from Koningsburgh on the Baltic. Nearly three thousand iron bars were brought from St. Petersburg aboard the *Heywood*, and over four hundred hogsheads of tobacco arrived from Virginia. The *Roberts* brought butter, barley, cowhides and calfskins from Belfast, while barley and oats were brought in from Dungarvan on the southern coast of Ireland. Meanwhile, sugar, rum, cotton, and ivory arrived aboard the *Freeholder* and the *Valiant* from Tortolla and Antigua, bringing further proceeds from the African trade.

A detail from Williamson's Liverpool Advertiser, 29th September 1775, showing some recent imports (LRO)

GOODS *Imported at* LIVERPOOL,

From the 22d to the 29th of SEPTEMBER 1775.

JOHN *Roberts and co* 193 *casks oil a parcel codfish* 2 *pipes wine* 12 *bundles wood hoops* &c *hhd staves Thomas Ryan* 3 *pipes wine Earle and Woodhouse* 2 *pipes wine In the Endeavour William Power from Newfoundland*

Haliday and Bamber 896 *oak planks* 150 *pipe & hhd staves* 100 *heading* 30 *oak knees Rawlin sons & Chorley* 74 *tons pig iron Robert & Nathaniel Hyde* 8 *tons and a half bar iron Benjamin Bower* 7 *tons and a half ditto Thomas Earle* 5 *tons pig iron* 3 *tons and a half bar iron Said Master* 1 *ullage puncheon rum In the Waddell, Wm. Scott from New York*

John Dobson & co 925 *quarters wheat In the Friendship Wm. Stancliffe from Dantzick*

James Clemens 51 *elephant teeth* 17 *seamorse teeth* 2 *puncheons bees wax* 20 *tierces coffee* 49 *puncheons rum* 12 *tierces sugar* 53 *bags and pockets cotton* 9 *barrels indigo In the Thomas John Bone from Africa and Jamaica*

Mason and Bourne a parcel wheat and oats 11 *half barrels tongues* 12 *quarter barrels pork In the Hawke Roger Heas from Dungarvon*

William Wallace 313 *quarters barley In the Two Brothers Alexander M'Mullian fr. Strangford*

Trotter & Myers a parcel barley In the Bounty Henry Tomilty from Strangford

Castle Street, between St. George's church and the Exchange, was where Mr. Warren and Mr. Cordeux had recently witnessed the riots in fear from their premises. So too had John Gore on the corner at number 1, where he printed *The General Advertiser* and the *Liverpool Directory*. Confectioner Fanny Patten kept shop at number 13, and Acton Fox had his shoe warehouse nearby. These, and many others at the north end of the

---

21 *Williamson's Advertiser*, 29th September and 13th October 1775. Most goods arrived in various types of cask or barrel. Puncheons varied in size from 72 to 120 gallons. A pipe contained 105 gallons, twice as much as the 52.5 gallons in a hogshead. A tierce contained 35 gallons, or one third of a pipe. A modern barrel contains 36 gallons, but it seems unlikely this was so in the 18th century, given the capacity of the tierce. The baby of them all was the firkin, which held 9 gallons. All were watertight and could easily be moved about by rolling.

street, had suffered broken windows, splintered frames, and damage to brickwork and rendering caused by muskets balls and the concussive effects of cannon. Although it fanned out near the Exchange, Castle Street was indeed narrow for a main thoroughfare, with just enough room for two carriages to pass each other in safety along most of its length. Most of its buildings were of three storeys and had shops beneath the living quarters, their leaded windows displaying a variety of wares to passers-by. On either side of the narrow slab-stone road were pavements of sharply rounded cobblestones that were ill-suited for purpose, as was the case throughout Liverpool. Castle Street was dimly lit at night by oil lamps and tallow fat torches, but some had no lighting of any description. [22] When darkness descended there was almost total blackness, so that no one could venture out at night without a lantern to light their way.

Castle Street, 1786. (Herdman Collection, 1268, LRO. This is a detail from the original showing the wider, north end of the street near the Exchange.)

22 Brooke, op. cit., p119 & 451. Herdman Collection, LRO, 1267A, 1268.

Somewhat oddly, it was only as Castle Street led into the corn market that the Exchange came into full view.[23] This was the centre of Liverpool's political life, which was dominated by a clique of about forty men of wealth and status chosen from within their own ranks. It also contained the magistrates' courtroom, the treasury and surveyor's offices, an assembly room, and others for entertaining dignitaries on grand occasions. The Exchange was a moderately grand building built of stone, with arched windows, Doric columns, and a dome crowned with a smaller cupola. The columns supported a pediment, on which was painted a fanciful scene showing Neptune holding a trident, a shield emblazoned with the Liver Bird, and various other figures representing the commerce and success of Liverpool.[24] However, the full effect of the building was lost to any not standing directly in front. It also backed onto a jumble of ancient, untidy streets and buildings known as the Shambles, where many of the town's butchers were concentrated. Some operated from the front rooms of ramshackle houses that were open to the street. Their wooden shutters opened upwards to form awnings, and downwards to display the meat. [25] In amongst the shabbiness, Isaac Scotson sold both clocks and 'victuals' at *Merlin's Cave*, and widow Alice Taylor entertained customers at *Neptune's Coffee House* and tavern, with its skittle yard attached.[26]

Dale Street led east from the Exchange towards the furthest part of the town and away from the river. Near the corn market it was broad and spacious, but it soon narrowed like a furred artery, and cattle and sheep were frequently driven along it towards the Shambles.[27] It boasted many public houses, including the *Angel Inn, Cross Keys, Bull* and *Punch Bowl, Millstone, White Bull* and *Woolpack*. But perhaps the finest were the *Golden Fleece* and the *Golden Lion*, much frequented by gentlemen from the Exchange. Supplying some of their needs were distiller John Houghton and brewers Ormered, George and Company, both based in Dale Street. Here, too, lived William Stringfellow, Overseer to the Poor, and Miles Timons, surgeon and operator for the ears, but just about every trade and profession was represented amongst the residents of Dale Street.

Between Dale Street and Whitechapel, and beyond Mr. Tarleton's sugar refinery, an iron foundry, coal yard and distillery, was Crosshall Street, where Dr. Weale practised at number 59. Weale offered "Specific drops for the Venereal Disease, the Scurvy and Rheumatism," claiming that his was well

---

23 See details from Perrys map of Liverpool 1769, page 30.
24 Brooke, op. cit., p71-2 & facing p195.
25 Herdman Collection, LRO, 1182A.
26 Victuals could mean any form of food or drink, but Merlin's Cave was both coffee house and tavern, as well as an outlet for his clocks. Those described as victuallers were generally public house keepers.
27 Herdman Collection, LRO, 1113 and 1269.

Dale Street from the Exchange, 1790. The Golden Lion is shown third from right behind the coach (Herdman Collection 1113, LRO)

known to be the only absolute cure. This would occur within just a few days "without any ill-conveniency to the Patient, restraint of diet or hindrance of Business, and with such secrecy, even without the knowledge of a bed-fellow." He claimed his cure had "antidotal qualities, dilutes and tenuates the blood and juices, and makes immediately to the offending impurities, which they suddenly dislodge and expel by washing away from its habit its virilency by the most gentle evacuations." Furthermore, the drops would not deteriorate or suffer any ill effects from changes in climate, therefore being well suited to the needs of seafaring men. Bottles cost 2s 6d, and he would throw in a copy of his treatise on venereal disease for good measure. Weale also advertised that he took out "all corroded rotten stumps or hollow teeth, and puts in artificial ones in their head, which will be of the same service as any of the rest, and what other dentists deem impracticable performs with ease, and cures the tooth ache instantly; and performs bleeding of any part of the body, on children as well as adults, with the utmost care and safety, at his house."

However, a rival named Molineux offered dental services for the relief of "the most violent Toothache Cured in a few Minutes without Drawing, by a tincture which gives immediate ease in the Tooth Ache, and cures all disorders

One of several potteries in the neighbourhood of Shaw's Brow, now William Brown Street (Herdman, Pictorial Relics, plate 48, undated, LRO)

whatever in the Mouth or Gums." He also promised "in a few days using will fasten the Teeth if ever so loose....prevents scurvy in the gums and prevents teeth from rotting." Molineux also sold "Smelling Medicine, For the Cure of the Scurvy, Itch, pimpled Faces, Scald Heads, Films in Children, Rheumatic Pains, and all cutaneous Eruptions (by Smelling only)". He added that his remedy "...is also of the utmost Service to the Female Sex, either Coming at Age, or the Decline of it (which often proves very fatal) at Spring and Fall, Without Bleeding, Bathing, taking Physic, anointing the Body, changing the Bed, Cloaths, or wearing Apparel." [28]

Near the junction of Dale Street, Shaw's Brow and Whitechapel were a number of potteries and tanneries, a silk weaving workshop, and the hay market.[29] At the bottom of Shaw's Brow (now William Brown Street) was a row of almshouses intended chiefly to house seamen's widows and their families. At the top of the brow, by Lime Kiln Lane (now Lime Street) and the Townsend Windmill, stood the Liverpool Infirmary and the Seamen's Hospital, the latter supported by compulsory monthly contributions of six pence from seafarers' pay. Here, elderly sailors and their wives lived out their remaining lives.[30] Across the fields, overlooking the town from Brownlow Hill, some six hundred inmates languished in the new workhouse. Opened in 1771, and supported from parish rates, it brought together under one roof the most destitute of Liverpool's population. It was intended to prevent abuses of charity by ending the previous system of outdoor relief, or doling out money to the poor in their homes. It also aimed to instil a proper work ethic by making inmates earn their keep by manufacturing clothing and bedding.[31]

[28] Both advertisements in various editions of *Williamsons Advertiser*, 1775.
[29] Perry's map, 1769, LRO.
[30] Ibid, and Brooke, op. cit., p62-67. St. George's Hall was later built on the same site.
[31] H.Peet, *Liverpool Vestry Books*, Vol.1 (1912) pXLV. This is now the site of the catholic Metropolitan cathedral.

The workhouse replaced the old Poor House that had stood next to the Blue Coat Hospital and the Free School for orphans. This was supported by a private charity, which also fed and clothed the children until such time as they could be indentured as servants or apprentices to earn their keep until reaching adulthood.[32] Yards away, at 5 School Lane, Cannel and Jones pandered to the more fortunate. Newly established as hairdressers, they thanked their customers and looked forward to "the future favours of the Ladies and Gentlemen, which will ever be greatly acknowledged by their most obedient humble Servants." They also offered "all Sorts of Hair Powder, hard and soft Pomatum, &c all Sorts of False Hair, as neat in London, Cushions and Pads of the newest Fashion."[33] Many of their customers attended the church of St. Peter's nearby, and perhaps had occasion to visit apothecary and surgeon Richard Gerrard in Church Street. John Marsden, surveyor of customs, also lived in Church Street, as did John Renshaw, who owned a ropery close by. Merchant John Backhouse lived at 45, and may have insured his shipping ventures with George Bowden at number 5. Several captains also lived in Church Street, including Samuel Kirkpatrick, Joseph Caton, and the aptly named Thomas Seaman.

The town was surrounded by orchards, pastureland, and fields of hay and barley, all ripe for development. Among the major landholders were the Earl of Derby, Thomas Cross, John Colquitt, Thomas Seel, Foster Cunliffe, and the corporation. To the north and south of the town, by the docks and small industries, land was reserved for modest housing and cheap back-to-backs. Houses of greater distinction were rising on gently sloping ground to the east of the town, where there was refuge from the hustle and bustle, and easy access to fresh air and open spaces. Beside the upper end of Duke Street, between fields belonging to Mrs. Hardman and the Reverend Wolstenholme, was an avenue of trees that led towards St. James's Walk overlooking the town. This provided a fine vantage point from which to view Liverpool, with its church spires and forest of ships' masts, and the wild landscape across the Mersey. But the Ladies' Walk by the north shore and public baths offered a more intimate view of the river and its sailing vessels. On Sundays and fine evenings especially, the townsfolk promenaded between four neat rows of trees, their dress a testament to their status. The best-attired gentlemen wore broad-skirted coats, embroidered waistcoats, satin breeches, silk stockings, gilt-buckled shoes, braided tricorne hats, and carried ebony canes topped with gold, silver, or ivory. Many a dandy wore a sword at his side, and it was not unknown for young-bloods to draw them in sport or anger, perhaps mindful of

---

32 Brooke, op. cit., p64-65.
33 *Williamson's Advertiser*, 3rd November 1775. Pomatum was a scented oil for dressing the hair.

female admirers for whose attention they competed. Meanwhile, the gentler sex wore high curled wigs, hooped silk dresses, satin shawls, high-heeled shoes, and carried decorated fans to shield their tender faces from the sun while gently cooling themselves.

Those at the lower end of society made do in their best slops - cheap ready-made or second-hand clothes, much faded and patched. The labouring classes viewed their wealthy neighbours with envy, and dreamed of following in their footsteps by setting up small businesses or working their way up through the ranks of seamen to become ships' masters in their own right. But for the majority this was a forlorn hope. Most had little or no education, and many lived in the darkness of cold, damp cellars once intended for storage. Those along Paradise Street and Whitechapel were especially liable to flooding, since they were built along low-lying land that had been reclaimed from the tidal inlet earlier in the century. During wet weather, rainwater seeped down through ash pit privies and waste middens on either side, leading to many occasions of sewage oozing through cracks in cellar walls.

Life held few pleasures for those on the margins, when even the cost of a few tallow candles was often beyond reach. Life could be truly dark, in more ways than one, leading some to petty crime. Punishments for theft were especially severe. Standing before magistrates in 1776, Robert Jolly and Phillip M'Ginnis were sentenced to be severely whipped in the gaol yard for stealing scraps of ironware. So too were Ellen Berry and Ann Melling, one for stealing two hand towels, the other for the theft of a guinea. William Montgomery was found guilty of stealing wheat, and was sentenced to a whipping and imprisoned for fourteen days. Mary Bramwell was convicted for stealing a piece of stamped muslin cloth, imprisoned for a month, and ordered to find sureties for her good behaviour for twelve months. Among other items of petty theft were a single piece of black ribbon, a pair of silk stockings, a pair of sheets and a blanket, a hat and silver buckles, and various small quantities of money. However, William Dennin was acquitted of stealing ten gold pieces from Thomas Weale, which must have been gratifying to those who had bought Weale's dubious cures and found them wanting. There were also two assaults on night watchmen, resulting in small fines and brief periods of imprisonment, but in neither case was the offence considered serious enough for a whipping.[34]

Situated at the bottom of Water Street, the Tower prison was considered by philanthropist John Howard to be filthy and in need of repair. In addition to seven subterranean cells, each about six feet square and holding three or more inmates, there was a larger dungeon, with an iron grated opening looking up to the street. This, too, was overcrowded, sometimes by as many as forty people.

[34] Quarter Sessions of the Peace, reported in *Williamson's Advertiser*, 2nd February and 2nd August 1776.

Prison Weint, looking towards St. Nicholas Church, c.1810. The Tower Gaol is on the right (Herdman Collection 184, LRO)

Debtors were held in the tower above, and were allowed to share a bed at the cost of a shilling a week. However, prisoners were only locked up at night, and were allowed to "mix promiscuously" in the courtyard by day, sharing this small area with a dunghill.[35] It was now clear, however, that Liverpool had outgrown this ancient gaol, a situation made worse by the desperate shortage of work brought about by the war. In February 1776, the parish committee agreed that a "House of Correction for the punishment and setting to work of vagabonds and idle disorderly persons within this town… shall be forthwith erected upon Brownlow Hill, near the present Poor House." The Corporation agreed to pay five hundred pounds towards the building, and the running costs were to be funded from the parish rates.[36]

35 Brooke, op. cit., p77-79.
36 Special Vestry Meeting, 9th February 1776, in Peet, op. cit., p246.

The country shivered during the winter of 1775-6, but none more than the poor and destitute, for whom the price of a bucket of coals was often beyond reach. The River Thames froze over and Londoners held impromptu fairs on the ice, while the people of Liverpool were advised to attach felt to their shoes to avoid slipping on treacherous pavements.[37] By April, however, the ice and snow had long since cleared, and Mayor Clemens was publicly complaining that "the Drivers of Carts, in and through the streets, frequently are found Riding thereon, and Driving their Horses at a furious Rate, to the great Terror and Danger of his Majesty's Subjects."[38] By summer, Clemens was complaining about excessive quantities of gunpowder in houses, shops and warehouses, and implored people to limit stocks and store them "in the uppermost Rooms, that in the Case of any accidental or sudden Explosions thereof, the same may from thence be attended with the less effect."[39] Notice was also given of additional taxes due to take effect. All coach drivers, except those of hackney carriages, were to pay an extra twenty shillings per year, while stagecoaches would add five pounds to government coffers. There would also be additional duties of six pence on new packs of playing cards, 2s 6d for new pairs of dice, and an extra halfpenny on every sheet of paper.[40]

People complained about taxes, but they were happy to buy a stake in the annual state lottery, which the government had started twenty years earlier to fund the building of Blackfriars and Westminster bridges on the Thames. Whole tickets typically cost about thirteen pounds, but were usually bought up by agents and divided into shares - halves, quarters, eighths, sixteenths, thirty-seconds, and sixty-fourths – each endorsed and stamped on the back.[41] Agents bought up whole tickets and sold shares at a profit. Prices for punters varied, but a sixty-fourth share was within the reach of the better off at about four shillings. There were two top prizes, each worth £20,000, with an increasing number of lesser ones, down to nearly 19,000 prizes worth £15 each. In total, 20,000 tickets were drawn from two giant lottery wheels over a period of days under careful scrutiny at the London Guildhall, their value depending on the order in which they were drawn.[42] For two Liverpool merchants there was a lucky windfall at the end of 1776, when Dillon and Leyland won a top prize that enabled them to set up a new bank.[43]

Among the more tangible entertainments enjoyed in Liverpool were horse racing and cockfighting, but the latter was more popular and attracted people of

---

37 *Williamson's Advertiser*, 9th February 1776.
38 Ibid, various editions, including 26th April 1776.
39 Ibid, various, including 31st May 1776.
40 Ibid, 31st May 1776.
41 £13 would be around £1170 in today's money.
42 Advertisements appeared in *Williamson's Advertiser* each week from about August.
43 Birbeck Wilson op. cit., p144.

all classes to contests at various cockpits throughout the year. The major event coincided with the Crosbie Races and was fought "between the Gentlemen of Lancashire and the Gentlemen of Cheshire, on Monday, Tuesday, and Wednesday in the Race Week at Four O'Clock in the Afternoon each Day at the North Shore Coffeehouse." Winners of each "battle" received ten pounds, but the prize for the main event stood at fifty.[44] However, although it was usual to set one bird against another, there were popular variations. In the fields above Lime Kiln Lane, where many of the rougher elements congregated, it was common for boys to enter the cockpit with their hands tied behind their backs. This was followed by a scramble, as each contestant tried to throw himself onto a bird to pin it down and seize it between his teeth to claim his prize money. But, just as popular were dogfighting and bear-baiting contests, which, along with cockfighting, were regular features of market days and fairs.

Of all the people on Liverpool's streets the seamen were the toughest. Their complexion and style of dress made them recognisable from a distance, and their language set them apart from landlubbers. The typical seaman wore baggy breeches cut a few inches above the ankle, which were made of thick flannel or linen and were brightly coloured. Over his coarse checked or striped linen shirt, the seaman wore an oiled jacket to protect him from the weather. He was adept at clothing repairs, just as he was in using a needle and thread to mend sails. Seafarers were invariably tanned and weather-beaten due to exposure to the elements, and the constant hauling and climbing of ropes fashioned powerful hands and muscular frames. They were heavily tattooed, using a needle to prick the skin and gunpowder for pigment. Their gait also gave them away, as they swung their arms and took broad strides as though they were still countering the pitch and roll of a ship. Seamen also had a distinctive style of language that had less to do with their place of origin than their belonging to an international community that understood a world of wind and water, timber and rigging. As for cursing and swearing, they had no equals.[45]

Across the Atlantic, the port of Boston shared much in common with Liverpool in its dependence on the sea, the nature of its people, and the size of its population. Many Bostonians, too, were seafarers, shipbuilders, dockworkers, and allied tradesmen, mostly in the pay of wealthy merchants. They were well

44 *Williamson's Advertiser*, 4th July 1776
45 Rediker, op. cit., p11-12 & p165-166.

Sketch map of the Boston area, 1775.

Please note: # lines on map indicate Boston Streets.

used to rioting, drinking, cock fighting and bear baiting, and some were no strangers to the Queen Street prison or the Fort Hill poorhouse. Boston had some well-paved streets and elegant houses, but many of its population lived in cramped conditions in small wooden shacks. Unlike Liverpool, Boston was built on a peninsula connected by a narrow neck to the mainland. Its natural harbour provided good shelter, and ships were able to load and unload their cargoes with ease at the many wharves. Long Wharf was Boston's pride, stretching out a quarter of a mile from King Street.[46] But reaching or leaving the harbour called for steady handling, as many rocky islands and shallows stood between it and the open seas.[47]

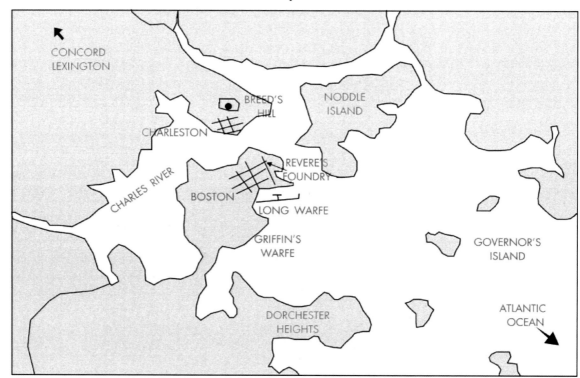

This was the scene that Washington surveyed from the Dorchester Heights early in 1776, as he took delivery of sixty pieces of artillery. These had travelled three hundred miles from Fort Ticonderoga, dragged by ox-drawn sledges over the snow and ice-covered Appalachians, and now overlooked Boston and the ships in the harbour below. With the hinterland under rebel control, and his troops and warships under serious threat from cannon and mortars, General Howe found he had little choice but to negotiate a safe withdrawal

---

[46] Rediker, op. cit., p62-65.
[47] Map of Boston and its Environs, 1800, www.earlyamerica.com.

and evacuate his Redcoats from Boston. The entire garrison headed out to sea on 17th March 1776 and set sail for Nova Scotia, taking with them a thousand loyalist Bostonians.

By now the conflict had spread from Canada down to Georgia. The rebels had taken control of Montreal that winter, hopeful of support from French Canadians, but none was to come.[48] Meanwhile, Benedict Arnold's soldiers had struggled across the Appalachians towards Quebec in freezing winter conditions, eating their dogs and chewing leather to ward off starvation. An attempt to storm the fortress with a small force during a heavy snowstorm ended in disaster, and the survivors sat out the dreadful winter conditions south of Quebec, starving and demoralised. By the spring of 1776, all remaining American forces were retreating from Canada, with the British and their allies in pursuit. Lieutenant George Turnbull provided gruesome news of the rout. "We have just heard that General Carleton has this day a meeting with five hundred Indian chiefs, friends to Government. They have brought in four rebel scalps with them, so you find that work is begun, which is horrid, but must have a vast effect on the Provincials. You may with safety inform your friends that the rebels are drove quite out of Canada. I wish we might be successful to the Southward."[49]

However, rebels in the south were preventing ships from leaving the Savannah River in Georgia and harassing loyalists. Captain Fletcher wrote from his brig *Nelly* that "we are now near half loaded with timber, and shall load out with rice and indigo, and expect to sail about Christmas for Liverpool. Several ships are loaded and loading, but cannot sail for want of people, as many of the sailors have died [or] are sickly. Our hands are all well. The people here are very rebellious; they have fitted out several privateers out of different parts of America, and have taken a snow belonging to Bristol with 2000 barrels of flour that was bound to Boston for the use of the forces."[50] But the *Nelly* did not sail that Christmas, and the situation deteriorated. On 3rd March the *Nelly* and four other ships were burned, although Fletcher managed to escape. If reports were true, the rebels were also attacking loyalist communities, burning houses and committing atrocities.[51] In the West Indies, meanwhile, American privateers were cruising Caribbean waters and threatening British ships with

---

[48] Although the word patriot may be preferred by many American readers, the word 'rebels' is used here in a non-pejorative sense, and is intended to distinguish them from those who remained loyal to the crown.

[49] Letter from Trois Rivieres, dated 24th June, in *Williamson's Advertiser*, 9th August 1776. Reference to five hundred *chiefs* was doubtless a mistake. All chiefs and no Indians?

[50] Letter dated 5th December 1775 published in *Williamson's Advertiser*, 9th February 1776. Privateers were merchant ships authorized to attack and seize enemy vessels. A snow was a two-masted ship similar to a brig.

[51] *Williamson's Advertiser*, 17th May 1776, details of a letter from Georgia describing events during March.

their supplies of produce and slaves. A letter from Jamaica stated that, "The rebels have carried matters to a great length, encouraged by foreign powers, that their privateers cruise publickly round this island."[52]

All seemed calm in New York, however, as the East River wharves heaved with timber, furs and foodstuffs being loaded onto ships alongside. From here, too, many a privateer or slave ship set sail. Nestled at the southern tip of Manhattan Island, New York was protected by Fort George and its battery of fifty-six cannon. Many of its houses were of the Dutch style, with their gable ends set towards the cobbled streets. Its finer houses stood along Queen and Dock Streets overlooking the waterfront, and were occupied by merchants and other dignitaries. But behind these were many narrow crooked streets, where labourers and their families lived in cramped wooden shacks. New York boasted many taverns and coffee houses, including the *Blue Anchor*, the *Long Room*, the *Bunch of Grapes*, and the *Sign of the Dog's Head in the Porridge Pot*. Of its 20,000 people or so, about a fifth were black slaves, toiling alongside their fellow white dockworkers, carters, and warehousemen.[53]

It was to New York that Washington's army repaired in March 1776, now that Boston had been cleared of British Redcoats. With its largely loyalist population, its importance as a port, and its command of the Hudson River, Washington guessed that this would be the next focus for General Howe and his Redcoats. Defences were soon erected around the town, and on the Brooklyn Heights on Long Island across the East River.

Meanwhile, America's politicians were debating their options. By May, John Hancock, the radical Bostonian and President of the American Congress, had given notice "That it be recommended to the respective Assemblies and Conventions of the United Colonies.... to adopt such government as shall, in the opinions of the Representatives of the people, best conduce to the happiness and safety of their constituents in particular, and America in general." [54] Yet, when the Declaration of Independence was finally signed and sealed on 4th July, Americans remained as divided as ever. As one Virginian wrote, "the Convention of this once happy Colony has declared themselves *independent of Great Britain* and have passed some resolves for confiscating the estates of *the deserters of their country's liberties* (as they call those gentlemen whom they obliged to leave the Colony)....It is astonishing to what amazing heights of madness they have arrived."[55] True to expectations, the arrival of British forces to the New York area came at

---

52 Letter dated 18th June, printed in *Williamson's Advertiser*, 9th August 1776. 'Foreign powers' refers chiefly to France.
53 Rediker, op. cit., p67.
54 American United Colonies in Congress, 15th May, in *Williamson's Advertiser,* 12th July 1776.
55 Ibid, 9th August 1776.

the end of June. Sailing from Halifax, they headed for Staten Island, where they established their base and awaited further reinforcements, including eight thousand mercenaries from Hess in Germany. After several weeks, over thirty thousand men stood ready for their encounter with the rebels. Most were soon being transported to Gravesend Bay on Long Island, while naval ships exchanged fire with the gun batteries in New York. Awaiting them were ten thousand Americans dug into fortified positions in the hills. Under cover of darkness, British and German troops moved close upon their enemy, enabling a surprise attack on the morning of 27th August. The beleaguered Americans fled in the face of an overwhelming force, eventually to make their escape across the East River in a flotilla of river craft under cover of a thick fog. British forces followed two weeks later, forcing Washington's soldiers to evacuate New York and take refuge in the Harlem Heights at the northern end of an otherwise almost deserted Manhattan Island.

But, by the early hours of 21st September, much of New York was burning. Starting perhaps at the *Fighting Cocks* tavern in Whitehall, the flames spread quickly through the tightly packed houses and businesses, fanned by strong winds. Many of the fire bells were found to be missing when the alarm was raised, and fire fighters were soon discovering that cisterns had been emptied and fire buckets vandalized. As citizens struggled to douse the flames, accusations and acts of savagery against rebel sympathizers were creating a different sort of conflagration, as suspects were given summary justice and cast into the burning wreckage. By late morning the fire was brought under control, but a quarter of New York now lay in ashes.

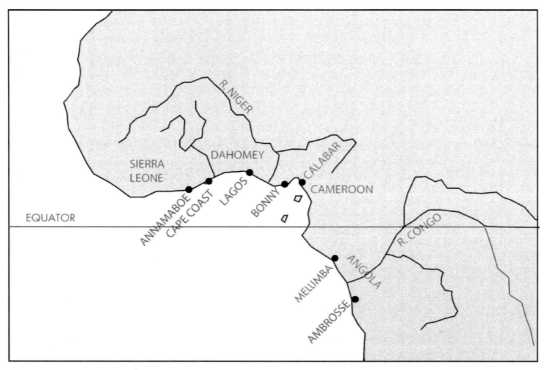

Sketch map of West Africa, showing the slave trading ports and regions featured in this book.

Chapter Three

On a pitch-black night in June 1776, four hundred miles off the Guinea coast, the *Badger* was struck by a sudden violent squall that tested every sail and piece of rigging to the limit. As the night watch called out to those below, whose hammocks swung in sympathy with the storm tossed sea, the sleeping crewmen were quickly roused and all hands set hurriedly to work. They were just getting the sails down when the foremast snapped eight feet below the top, taking with it the foretop and foretopgallant masts, the main topgallant mast, and all their yards and sails. When the squall subsided, as quickly as it had appeared, Captain Peter Potter peered into the darkness around him and wondered what to do with the wreckage, realising "through the Darkness of the Night, which was so Excessive, that we could not find beginning or ending, as it all Lay in such a mangled condition & most or all over the side in the Water." Since there was "no grate swell going", Potter "let all be till day Light", allowing his crew to rest, soaked and exhausted. Next morning, all hands got to work retrieving the wreckage, with Potter "not suffering any body to cutt even the smallest Rope", and over three days a jury mast was set up and rigged to allow the *Badger* to get under way.[1]

But, while the *Badger's* crew had been battling with the passing storm, a much greater devastation was being played out across West Africa from Senegal to Angola. Night after night, raiding parties attacked sleeping towns and villages, setting fire to houses, and seizing terrified occupants as they fled the flames. Victims were netted, clubbed, whipped and beaten into submission, before being bound together in chains of misery. Chains formed into human caravans of many dozens or hundreds at a time, snaking their way on long, tortuous, miserable journeys that ended on the coast. Most went by way of busy inland markets, where they were sold on to African brokers and traders, along with others enslaved as punishment for crimes or debts unpaid. Some continued overland on journeys hundreds of miles long, the men shackled to wooden yokes to weigh them down. The weak and sick were left to die or killed along the way, and any attempt at escape was treated brutally as a warning to others. But most continued their journeys by river in long convoys, having been bundled twenty or thirty at a time into large canoes with their hands bound behind their knees. Either way, their first destination was to one

---

[1] Letter from Captain Potter, on board the Badger from Cameroon, to William Davenport & Co., 15th October 1776, Davenport Collection, D/DAV/10/1/1, Merseyside Maritime Museum. A jury (or injury) mast was a temporary mast set up to enable a ship to continue sailing. Presumably, the crew would have rigged what was left of the foremast.

of the many 'factories,' or coastal trading stations, where captives were oiled, fed, and prepared for sale [2] Some African factors operated independently, but most acted on behalf of kings and chiefs, and it was these who sanctioned the largest raiding parties and governed most of the trade. The process provoked tribal wars and acts of pillage, providing excuse for acts of retribution and further kidnapping, fuelled by demands for cheap labour in the Americas and manufactured goods in Africa.[3] The ancient African custom of sentencing prisoners to limited periods and conditions of domestic slavery was thus transformed into a trade in human flesh, driven purely by greed.

It was greed that led men like William Davenport to invest their money in such ventures, despite the risk of financial ruin. One month after the storm, his ship reached Cameroon under much reduced sail, and it was now up to the captain to organise a replacement mast. This proved problematic. Having bought a suitable tree, Potter had the timber fashioned to the correct length and thickness, all of which took ten days. Fortunately for Potter, "Capt. Smale assisted me greatly with his Carpenter, as mine was Sickly & not able to do much. We have been very agreeable Neighbours." Two boats were used to transport it from shore to ship, and the crew brought the new mast alongside the *Badger* with the help of four Africans. Having lashed up the mast, the crew began to raise it, when the lanyard snapped and it sank like a stone into the water. The next tree Potter bought turned out to be "quite hollow from End to End." However, third time proved lucky, and after another eight days a new mast was on its way from shore to ship with the help of twenty local hired hands.

Potter was concerned that he would be short of trading goods, and that insufficient allowance had been made for 'dashes', or payments to the local chief for permission to trade. He was also concerned about the price of slaves, as he could not buy any for less than "nineteen or twenty Barrs" of iron, which was valued locally for its purity. In addition, two of the slaves had died of sickness. Although a third had recovered, "he ran immediately to the Gangway & jumpt Streight overboard, & tho' we were instantly in both Boats after him, yet before either could reach him he went down & we saw him no more." However, the mortality rate among Potter's crew was higher still, with six of them dying between early August and mid-September, and a seventh some months later.[4] This was not unusual, since Europeans were particularly

---

[2] R. Oliver & J.D. Fage, *A Short History of Africa* (1978) p123. The original use of the word factory was as a merchant company's foreign trading station, where agents, or factors, did their trade.

[3] G. Williams, *History of the Liverpool Privateers and Letters of Marque, with an Account of the Liverpool Slave Trade* (1897) p583-584. Also, M. Johnson, *The Atlantic Slave Trade and the Economy of West Africa,* in R. Anstey & P.E.H. Hair, *Liverpool, the African Slave Trade, and Abolition,* Historic Society of Lancashire and Cheshire, Occasional Series, Volume 2 (1976) p24-27.

[4] Letter dated 11th June 1777, Davenport Collection, Merseyside Maritime Museum, D/DAV/10/1/3.

vulnerable to tropical diseases such as malaria and yellow fever, and many seamen refused to work on slaving voyages because of the enormous risks. As for his officers, Potter was "not so happy in Mr. Anderson as I could wish. Whatever he might have been when Master he makes but an indifferent Mate. My Doctor is a very clever sober young Man and behaves Exceeding well, as does my second Mate Mr. Evans."

By mid-October Potter had bought eighty-one slaves and nearly two tons of ivory.[5] Although Potter regarded trading conditions as "very Slack", the process was never a simple matter of buying large numbers of slaves in a short period of time, especially when several ships were competing for business. Every deal involved haggling over quantity and quality, whether of merchandise or slaves, as each trader, black and white, tried to maximise profits. Slaves tended to be brought on ship in small numbers, sometimes one or two at a time. Once on board, the men were kept shackled together by their wrists and ankles and tethered to the timbers, either on the deck floor or on wooden platforms built half way up the ship's sides. However, Potter would have followed normal practice by allowing women and children greater freedom to remain unfettered, the only escape route being through a hatch that was secured by a heavy iron grating. No bedding was provided, and the captives were forced to lay in great discomfort on bare boards. Each had about thirty inches of headroom above them, the height between decks being less than six feet and divided by the platforms. Although fresh air passed through the open portholes and the hatch, ventilation was limited and temperatures frequently stifling. Sleep was extremely difficult, and disease spread like wildfire. The ordeal was greatest for those who arrived first, for it was they who had to endure it longest. Ahead of them lay several months of waiting, and beyond that a further two months at sea. With every new arrival there was less space, less clean air, more heat, and more despair. And for rebellious slaves there was either the cat-o'-nine-tails or the torture of the thumbscrew.

In fine weather, slaves were taken onto the main deck during the day, and fastened by their ankles to chains running through ringbolts in the main deck. This helped to keep most in reasonable health, and also allowed the vacated areas below to be scrubbed clean. Given the high incidence of 'the flux', this could mean cleaning up the excrement, blood and mucus that resulted from cases of dysentery. While on the main deck, the slaves were doused with salt water to clean them, and made to dance to drum rhythms to give them exercise. Given the painful rubbing of iron shackles against ankles, this required the use of the cat-o'-nine-tails. The slaves were

---

[5] Letter of 15th October 1776, Davenport Collection, Merseyside Maritime Museum, D/DAV/10/1/1.

given a pottage of rice, corn, beans, yams and corn oil, but if they refused food, preferring starvation and death to captivity, their mouths were held open with the speculum oris and they were force-fed. During bad weather, however, slaves had little or no time above, their 'quarters' remained dirty, portholes were closed, and the hatches covered over with a waterproof tarpaulin. Under such conditions, the lack of ventilation led to unbearable temperatures, sickness and overpowering stench.[6]

For their oppressors, however, trading was a complex business that required an understanding of local customs called 'dashes'. First and foremost was 'comey,' or tribute paid to the king or chief for permission to trade, after which further dashes were expected by wives and a variety of officials.[7] No records of these exist for Potter's voyage, but captain Ambrose Lace provided guidance a few years earlier to captains trading at Whydah in the kingdom of Dahomey.[8] Most expensive was the king's comey, which amounted to eight slaves, "after which he gives you two small children of 7 or 8 years old which the King sends as a return for the Customs." Lesser payments were made either in cloth, brandy or cowrie shells, which were widely used as currency.[9] For example, the king's messenger, "for Carring [carrying] News of the ships Arrivell and Captain's compliments to the King," received ten Gallinas, worth two hundred cowries each. The king's "Vice Roy, who go's with his people to Compliment the Capt. at his arrivell and Conduct him to the Fort," was to receive two flasks and an "anchor" of brandy, fifteen yards of silk, one cask of flour, and one of beef. Two brokers, "which are obliged to go to the traders houses to look for slaves and stand Interpiter for the Purchas," were both to be paid two tokees of cowries a day, amounting to eighty cowries each. In addition, they were to be given one flask of brandy every Sunday, and at the end of the trade both were to receive an anchor of brandy and a length of cloth. Lesser underlings included, "One Boy to Serve at the tent water side," and "One Waterwoman for the factory", each earning two tokees, or eighty cowries, per day. The washerwoman was to receive two tokees per day and "six Tokees every

---

[6] A. Falconbridge, *An Account of the Slave Trade on the Coast of Africa* (1788) p19-25. Williams, op. cit., p532-533 and p586-589.

[7] B.K. Drake, *The Liverpool-African Voyage c.1790-1807: Commercial Problems*, in Anstey & Hair, op. cit., p143.

[8] Dahomey is now part of modern Benin.

[9] In many parts of Africa cowrie shells were standard currency. The Cypraea moneta species was harvested in abundant quantities around the Maldive Islands. Small and beautiful, the shells are almost unbreakable, and large quantities could be heaped, poured, shovelled, bagged, and emptied down chutes into ships' holds to be used as ballast, all without damage. They could not be clipped or counterfeited, and since every shell is virtually identical to another, they could be traded by weight (about four hundred to the pound). By the 1770s, slaves were valued between 160,000 and 176,000 cowries each, although actual commodities made up most of each trade (J. Reader, *Africa: A Biography of a Continent*, 1997, p387-388).

time you give her any Linnen to Wash and one ps [piece] of cloth at ye end of trade." Among others to receive payment were a doorkeeper, the captain of the waterside, canoe men, six rowers, and "the Captn, Gong Gong that looks after the house at night, one bottle a day and one ps Cloth if your content."[10]

Off the coast of Cameroon, however, Captain Potter was finding the trading conditions increasingly tough. He wrote to Davenport and Company on 22nd November in exasperation. "Gentlm., the Inclos'd is copy of my Last by Capt. Smale,[11] since which I have had but one intire stillstand of Trade for a whole Month. They would not so much as let a bunch of Plantins Corn on board to me.[12] They even made a law amongst themselves that if any of them offered to sel me a Slave the others would emmediately take all his goods from him, destroy all his plantin trees & pul His Houses down. This was on account of my not giving them Cowries enough, so that I was at last obliged to give them thire full prise, else I might have Layn here God knows how long. It is only a week since I got settled with them and have made up my number to one hundred & forty. I have had the misfortune to bury two more Slaves since my last, which makes now Five Dead. My White People is as before in pritty good health. I likewise have on board four thousand & thirty pound weight of Ivory. The Brig Indeavour, Capt. Dwyr, Arrived here Nov. 5th in great Distress, ocationed through himself & all hands but two being sick. I assisted him with my People & Doctor all the time he was here and cutt all his firewood." Potter added, "we have from ye first of our arrival here been troubled with the Feavour. First it was amongst the white People, & since till of late it as been amongst the Slaves, but with some difficulty & smoking the Rooms, Hold & everywhere with Tarr, we have got our selves now pritty clear of it. We also made a spike hole in the Ship for to let frish water come continuously in the hold as she is so tite that I though the Bilge water was one thing that created the feavor. There is only three on board now that ails anything, & even those ye have now no feavour."[13]

10 Williams, op. cit., p551-553.

11 Ships' masters relied on each other for the delivery of letters. Captain Smale would have taken letters from the *Badger* as he sailed from Africa ahead of Potter. Once Smale got to the West Indies he would have arranged for another ship bound for Liverpool to take the *Badger's* letters.

12 Plantain is a type of banana that is harvested green and used as a cooked vegetable.

13 22nd November 1776, Davenport Collection, Merseyside Maritime Museum, D/DAV/10/1/2.

While Peter Potter was anxiously bartering for his human cargo, a different encounter was taking place thousands of miles away in mid-Atlantic, as Captain Elisha Hinman prowled the ocean in search of enemy ships. His fourteen-gun brig *Cabot* was now carrying eighty prisoners, having taken five British merchant vessels in recent weeks. On 2nd October Hinman's lookout spotted the *Watson* on the horizon, and the American privateer gave chase. On board the Liverpool bound vessel was her owner, James Bier, returning on business from Jamaica. Out-manoeuvred, out-gunned, and out-manned, Bier had no choice but to surrender his vessel without a fight. His crew was taken on board the privateer, but Bier, Captain James Brison and a passenger, were allowed to remain on board the *Watson*, together with the ship's boy. Their ship was now taken as a prize with a new American crew of eight. Writing two months later, Bier recalled, "In about three weeks we got into soundings off Boston, but that night I had determined to re-take her, having brought over to my party two of their people by promising them £100. Accordingly, at 8 o'clock they sent me a pistol by the boy, on which I immediately jumped upon deck, clap'd it to the prize-master's breast, and demanded him to surrender the vessel, which he instantly complied with. At the same time, the captain and boy secured the lieutenant of marines in the cabin. We then secured the hatches till I got all the arms, which compleated the business. I bore away for Halifax, but the wind being fair, stood on for Newfoundland. The wind still continuing favourable, stood on for Ireland, where I struck soundings in 27 days. We had but two barrels of beef and three of bread when I bore away, but fortunately had two turtles about 600 lb. weight, which served us three weeks. We ran in here in a hard gale of wind, where we lie in safety, having (thank God) received no damage, except one boat washed overboard with studding sails and some spare ropes. Our fire and candles were intirely exhausted. I hope this will be agreeable news, and remain &c., J. B."[14]

By now, there were estimated to be 170 American cruisers at sea, all intent on seizing British shipping and destroying the economic lifeblood of the country. The West Indies were especially vulnerable, as many a Liverpool crew were to testify. Towards the end of January the *Thomas* was approaching Barbados when it was attacked by the *Revenge*. The American sloop drew alongside, and its crew boarded the *Thomas* with swords and pistols, killing the captain and two of the crew before seizing the vessel. The sloop then attacked the *Sarah* nearby, which fortunately managed to escape. Next day, however, the *Sarah* was attacked again, this time by a large schooner. The schooner's crew attempted to board, but were prevented by booms rigged out on each side of the Liverpool vessel. Both ships were badly damaged, with sails and rigging

---

[14] Letter dated 3rd December 1776, quoted in Williams, op. cit., p189-190.

cut to pieces and gaping holes above the waterline. Among the casualties was Captain Frith, who died on Barbados from two musket ball wounds.[15] Other losses included the *Sisters*, captured in Atlantic waters and taken to Martinique with a cargo of 163 slaves, and the *Lydia*, taken on its return from Jamaica and sold with its cargo in Maryland for £20,000. The *Fly*, an American sloop of fourteen guns and over 100 men, attacked the *Elizabeth* in June 1777. Guns blazed for over an hour before the privateer ran alongside and its crew boarded their quarry, killing three and wounding thirteen in a bloody encounter.[16]

An extraordinary encounter involved the notorious ship *Brooks*, whose captain took the decision to arm some of the slaves on board to help repel an attack. Writing later from Montego Bay on 26th April 1777, Captain Noble gave these details. "I can with a good deal of pleasure inform you that your ship Brooks has been the destruction of one of the American privateers. The next morning after we left Barbados, we were chased by her and made all the sail we could to get from her, but to no purpose, for she came up with us very fast, and a little afterwards we saw another privateer right ahead, so that we had then nothing to do but either fight or be taken. We therefore, to prevent being engaged by them both at once, took in all our small sails and made ready for an engagement. She came up right astern; would shew no colours till we fired two shot at her, which did great execution; upon which she hoisted American colours and gave us a broadside, which we returned with our two stern chasers, which never missed raking them fore and aft. After engaging her about an hour, we were so lucky as to shoot away her mast just above the deck, by which time the other was almost up with us, but seeing the sloop's mast gone, she hauled away from us as fast as possible. The sloop and us exchanged many shot after her mast was gone, but I thought it the most prudent way not to attempt taking her for fear of the other (which was a schooner) altering her mind and coming back. Upon which we bore away in a tattered condition, our sails and rigging being very much torn to pieces, and a great many shot in the hull, but miraculously nobody killed or wounded on board us except the Doctor, who received a musket ball in his belly, but has got the better of it already, as it came through the stern before it hit him. We killed a great number on board the privateer, as they stood quite exposed to our shot. She was a sloop of ten or twelve guns, a great number of swivels, and as full of men as she could stow. I believe the greatest part Frenchmen by their appearance. I had fifty of our stoutest slaves armed, who fought with exceeding great spirit. After I left the sloop, the schooner came to her, and I suppose took the people out of her. She sunk about an hour after I left her.

---

15 Williams, op. cit., p195-198.
16 Ibid, p201-202.

The engagement was within two miles of St. Vincent, on the S. E. part of the island. I went into Kingston Bay, and went on board the Favourite sloop-of-war to beg some powder, which they supplied me with very readily, and that evening made sail for Jamaica, kept a great way to the southward, and then hauled right over for Jamaica, by which means (I dare say) we escaped a good many of the Americans. We saw several small sail on our way down, but what they were, I cannot tell."[17]

In Liverpool, meanwhile, tension was building as press gangs went about enslaving seamen. They were sanctioned by the navy to impress seamen by force and hold them in captivity, before handing them over for service on one of 'His Majesty's ships.' This led to frequent violent conflict, and the authorities tried to calm the situation by offering a bounty of two guineas to able seaman, or one guinea for ordinary seamen, who volunteered to enter the navy.[18] Although this offer attracted some, especially the unemployed, the harsh discipline on board a man-of-war was uninviting to those who preferred the conditions of service on merchant vessels. In November 1776 a press gang member forced his way into a seaman's house and was shot dead on the spot.[19] Two months later a mob gathered outside a woman's house in Frederick Street, angry that she had "given information to the press-gang against a sailor, who had lately married her in the north, had brought her here, where he had a former wife, and refused to give her two shillings to carry her home again." The mob dragged her from her house to the nearest dock, stripped her, and ducked her in the water several times. The woman ended up at the infirmary.[20]

During that same month of January 1777, several recent attempts to burn ships and warehouses in Bristol and Portsmouth led magistrates and merchants in Liverpool to increase their vigilance by enrolling extra volunteers as watchmen and special constables. A virtual curfew was now established, but with a specific class of person in mind. "All riotous, disorderly, and idle persons," said the official order, "are hereby cautioned to forbear their wicked courses, and to be early in their houses or places of abode at nights; and all strangers are desired to keep in their inns in due time, and not be strolling about the town at unseasonable hours, to prevent the inconvenience of being taken up

---

17 Quoted in Williams, op. cit., p560-561.
18 *Williamson's Advertiser*, 22nd November 1776. (The bounty was increased to ten and five guineas in June 1779).
19 Ibid, 22nd November 1776.
20 Ibid, 17th January 1777.

by the constables on the watch, the mayor and magistrates being determined rigorously to put the laws in force against all offenders. And the gentlemen, merchants, traders, and inhabitants in general of this great commercial town and port will heartily concur, and diligently assist in their guard, care, and watching for the safety and preservation thereof."[21]

When the *Badger* left Cameroon in the middle of March 1777, 415 slaves were crammed together with nearly three tons of ivory. By the time she neared the West Indies two months later, twenty-five had died, two having jumped overboard, which was a mortality rate of about six per cent.[22] The Middle Passage was the greatest torment for any human cargo. Some had already been confined on board for eight months before leaving the coast, and none was used to the motions of the sea, especially during storms. Violent sickness added to their ordeal, made all the worse by the sheer lack of physical space, privacy, or effective medication. Crammed into every available space, the captives lay shoulder-to-shoulder, head-to-toe, with barely an inch to move. Painful sores and ulcers developed, as flesh lay heavy on unforgiving timbers and skin was chaffed by iron shackles. Indeed, two thirds of deaths were among adult males, since it was they who bore the greatest physical and psychological constraints.

The *Badger* first arrived in the Virgin Islands, having managed to evade the privateer *Rattle Snake*, which had been in pursuit nearly all the way from Africa. On the small island of St. Thomas, Potter had the hull of his ship scraped and cleaned, while he bought in provisions using the money from the sale of two slaves. Three weeks later, the *Badger* joined a convoy of merchant ships under the protection of the naval ship *Southampton* bound for the Windward Islands. On hearing of where his competitors were headed, Potter decided to pull in at Dominica in the belief that he would fetch his best prices there. But he soon learned that enemy privateers were flooding the markets of nearby Martinique with slaves from captured British ships. His first sales went well for him and his employers, and by 10th June Potter had sold seventy-nine Africans at an

---

21 *Williamson's Advertiser*, 24th January 1777.
22 Figures given by H.S. Klein and S.L. Engerman, *Slave Mortality on British Ships, 1791-97*, in Anstey & Hair, op. cit., p118, show that mortality rates for voyages from most areas of West Africa averaged about 3.5 per cent. But for the Bight of Biafra, which included Cameroon, the rate was far higher at 10.56 per cent. These figures apply to a period after legislation in 1788 that placed limits on the number of slaves allowed per ton of ship. The Badger voyage would have exceeded this limit for a 250-ton ship by 31 slaves, which indicates that they were tightly packed.

average of £33 each. However, prices slumped, and by the time he had sold all his slaves, less two more that died of small pox, the average had fallen to a little under £26 each. Besides the death of thirty-four people, black and white, no less than eight of his crew were discharged for indiscipline, five on one day, and three more had "run" or simply left the ship's service. However, without its human cargo, which was now bound for sugar plantations throughout the Caribbean, Potter had less need of hands.

Sketch map of the West Indies.

By mid-July Potter was on the horns of a dilemma. He would normally expect to use some promissory notes from his sales to buy sugar, rum and other produce to add profit to the venture in Liverpool. Although freight had been arranged in advance, as was the normal practice, the agent had reneged on the deal and sold the agreed goods to another venture. The *Badger* had now been out from Liverpool for fourteen months, and the return could add another two, when the normal round trip could be done in less than a year. The hurricane season was fast approaching, and Potter reckoned he would be risking disaster if he stayed in Caribbean waters much longer buying in cargo. With another large convoy of merchant ships due to head across the Atlantic, Potter had little choice but to return safely and intact. And so, by 1st August, the *Badger* had joined over a hundred vessels under the protection of the naval ship *Cammel*. Potter had an empty hold, except for the ivory and several tons of stone ballast, plus he had a bundle of promissory notes to be redeemed by Davenport and Company on their next venture.[23] When the accounts were finally totted up, the venture showed a profit of just over seven per cent.[24]

While Potter was preparing to head home, Captain Edward Forbes was heading for Jamaica in his 300-ton ship *Sparling*. John Sparling had taken no chances in arming his ship with ten 6-pounders, four 4-pounders, and eight swivel guns, leaving it well able to hold its own, as Forbes was able to show. "I arrived here safe, after a passage of six weeks. In crossing the Bay, I saw several ships, but passed none without bringing them to, boarding and examining them. Off the Western Islands saw a brig privateer, who, on my giving chase, thought proper to alter his course and make the best of his way. I saw nothing more until I was within fifteen leagues of this island, where I was attacked by a large privateer sloop of 12 guns, a number of swivels, blunderbusses, and full of men. They attacked me at four o'clock in the afternoon, with a great deal of vigour for an hour and-a-half, and then sheered off. I attempted to give chace, but soon found she could sail two feet for my one. She then got her graplins out for boarding when dark, and attempted it three times, but perceiving his intentions, disappointed him, and threw him off his guard, by which means I got our guns to bear, which made him sheer off to refit. This I was not sorry for, as it gave us an opportunity to do the same, for our braces and running rigging were often shot away. The engagement lasted six hours. Getting all my guns to bear, in less than a quarter of an hour I lost sight of him. The ship is a good deal damaged in her rigging, sails and hull, but no lives lost, which is owing to the good shelter we had on deck, as she constantly fired small arms. I found the sloop had great advantage over us, we being square rigged, she always kept on my quarters. The Sparling's sides are hard, but the yankies found means to shew daylight through her in several places, but hope to repair her at a small expence. There is three feet of the starboard quarter entirely knocked out, and some shot in the bends. My

---

23 Davenport Collection, D/DAV/10/1/3 and 10/1/4. Promissory notes were a form of cheque.
24 D. Richardson, *Profits of the Liverpool Slave Trade: The Accounts of William Davenport, 1757-1784*, in Anstey and Hair, op. cit., p82-83.

men behaved during the action with the greatest courage and very attentive to command."[25]

Another Liverpool slave ship, the *Will*, was attacked by a well-armed sloop ten weeks later in Caribbean waters and fought for five hours. When the sloop drew up alongside, twelve of her crew tried to board but were all killed. It then pulled away, but the *Will* gave chase and managed to fire three broadsides into the assailant before giving up the fight. Captain James Collinson reckoned his crew had killed forty or fifty of the 120 Americans on board the privateer. Later that day, the *Will* was challenged by a 14-gun schooner and fought for another six hours. The schooner had stinkpots ready for boarding, but was beaten off. Collinson claimed not to have a single man killed or wounded, but narrowly missed injury himself when a swivel ball lodged itself in a speaking trumpet he was holding in his right hand.[26]

In the year following the struggle for New York and the subsequent fire, the two main armies had continued to clash in the region. The rebels had managed to repel a British attack on their refuge at Harlem Heights, but were later forced to retreat from the battlefield at White Plains. Then they lost control of two strategic forts at the mouth of the Hudson River, and retreated across New Jersey and into Pennsylvania. General Washington was frustrated by the lack of a professional full-time army with trained officers, and was forced to play a cat and mouse game with the British by retreating whenever he was confronted by the prospect of a decisive defeat. By the end of 1776 his army was in danger of melting away, but his opponent, General Howe, failed to take the initiative, and withdrew the bulk of his troops to winter quarters near New York. On 26th December 1776 Washington brought about his first major victory by mounting a surprise attack on a garrison of German mercenaries at Trenton, taking nine hundred captive. Howe sent General Cornwallis with a large force to settle the matter with Washington. The American general mounted a deception by making it appear that defensive earthworks were being built in readiness for a decisive battle. In fact, the bulk of his army evacuated their position, circled round the British, and attacked a smaller force at Princeton, before making their way to winter quarters to the north of New Jersey. Washington had shown that

[25] Letter from Kingston, Jamaica, 23rd July 1777, quoted in Williams, op. cit., p210-211.
[26] Letter from Dominica, 13th October 1777, Williams, op. cit., p211-212.

his force was far from beaten and could strike a blow wherever he chose.

General Howe now asked Parliament for reinforcements of 20,000 men, but received little more than two thousand. Concerns in London about the cost of the war meant that it was being fought on the cheap. There was also a reluctance to send more ships, because the French were increasingly aiding the rebels and could strike a blow closer to home. With limited resources, the British were unlikely to win control over such vast distances. Besides those who fought with Washington, there were rebels well versed in guerrilla tactics throughout all the colonies. Strongholds became targets, and once a British force was on the move the territory left behind was exposed to attack. In order to try and bring a speedy end to the war, the British Secretary for America, Lord George Germain, devised a plan to end the rebellion in the northern colonies of New England before mopping up the resistance further south. It was intended to trap the northern rebels between two separate forces brought down from Canada under General Burgoyne and Colonel St. Leger, and Howe's army moving up from New York. These armies were finally to meet at Albany.

But Howe had other plans. He was determined to deal a blow to General Washington by capturing Philadelphia, the American capital, and gaining control of the eastern seaboard. He believed that would still leave time to move north to meet the rendezvous. During July and August 1777, he transported fifteen thousand troops southwards by ship to Chesapeake Bay and up to the head of the Elk River. The troops suffered miserably with the heat, seasickness, and cramped conditions, before finally making land again after a month at sea. They now made their way across Delaware through torrential rain towards Pennsylvania. They met the Americans at Brandywine Creek, where they attacked and overwhelmed Washington's army, forcing it into a retreat towards Philadelphia. The General gave his account to the president of the Congress in the following terms: "I am sorry to inform you that in this day's engagement we have been obliged to leave the enemy masters of the field. Unfortunately, the intelligence received of the enemy's advancing up the Brandywine and crossing the ford about six miles above us was uncertain and contradictory, notwithstanding all my pains to get the best. This prevented my making a disposition adequate to the force with which the enemy attacked us on the right, in consequence of which the troops first engaged were obliged to retire before they could be reinforced… yet the loss of men is not, I am persuaded, very considerable; I believe much less than the enemy. We have also lost eight pieces of cannon….the baggage having been previously moved off is all saved….. I have directed the troops to assemble behind Chester, where they are now arranging for this night….I am happy to find the troops in good spirits, and I hope another time we shall compensate for the loss we now sustain."[27] But Washington lost the next two engagements and Congress was soon forced to flee, leaving Howe's forces to take control of Philadelphia.

While the British commander-in-chief was pursuing his personal aims, Burgoyne's army of British, Canadians and German mercenaries had recaptured Fort Ticonderoga. From there they had struggled south to reach Saratoga, traversing thick forests with heavy cannon, inadequate transport and few supplies. Now encamped, Burgoyne received a letter from Fort Stanwix, where Colonel St. Leger had been held up on his way to Albany via a different route. The letter brought news that, "After combating the natural difficulties of the river St. Lawrence, and the artificial ones the enemy threw into my way at Wood Creek, I invested Fort Stanwix the 3rd instant. On the 5th I learnt from discovering parties on the Mohawk River that a body of one thousand militia were on their march to raise the siege. On the confirmation of this news, I moved a large body of Indians with some troops the same night to lay in ambuscade for them on their march. They fell into it; the compleatest victory was obtained, above 400 hundred lay dead on the field, amongst the number of whom were all the principal movers of rebellion in that country."[28]

But this victory, and Howe's successes, soon proved hollow. While Howe was conducting his New Jersey campaign, Burgoyne's soldiers were awaiting news of Howe's forces supposedly moving north to meet them. They were desperately short of food and supplies, and in mid-August Burgoyne dispatched a detachment of troops to the Connecticut Valley hoping to find horses, carriages, cattle and corn. They were met at Bennington by a large force of New Hampshire militiamen and Green Mountain Boys, in a rout that cost them more than 800 dead, wounded or captured, and the loss of much needed supplies. On 20th August Burgoyne sent a dispatch to Quebec, from where it left for Britain on 7th October via an armed transport ship. News of his army's trials reached the government early in November, when Lord Germain learned that, "...every possible measure was employed to bring forward bateaux, provisions and ammunition from Fort George to the first navigable part of the Hudson river; a distance of eighteen miles, the roads in some parts steep and in others wanting of great repair. Of the horses furnished by contract in Canada, not more than a third part was yet arrived. The delay was not imputable to neglect, but the natural accidents attending so long and intricate a combination of land and water carriage. Fifty team of oxen, which

---

[27] Letter from George Washington to John Hancock, President of the Congress, *New York Gazette*, 22nd September 1777, reprinted in *Williamson's Advertiser*, 7th November.
[28] Letter dated 11th August 1777, Ibid.

had been collected in the country through which I had marched, were added to assist the transport; but these resources together were found far inadequate to the purposes of feeding the army and forming a magazine at the same time. Exceeding heavy rains augmented the impediments." Burgoyne explained, "For the fifteen days above stated there were not above four days provision," and then concluded with details of the disaster at Bennington.[29]

By mid-September Burgoyne had decided to push on towards Albany, aware that a large American army was in the area. However, his troops were held up on the road following the Hudson River. General Gates, the American northern commander, had set up fortifications on Bemis Heights overlooking the route to block the British advance. On the 19th the British and their allies attempted to dislodge the Americans from their commanding position, which resulted in "a very rigorous attack on the British line, and continued with great obstinacy till after sunset."[30] Heavy losses were suffered on both sides. Believing that help was forthcoming, Burgoyne noted, "I continued fortifying my camp and watching the enemy, whose number increased every day," but he soon had to reduce his soldiers' rations. He believed "the difficulties of a retreat to Canada were clearly foreseen, as was the dilemma, should the retreat be affected, of leaving at liberty such an army of General Gates to act against Sir Wm. Howe." Little did he know of Howe's campaign hundreds of miles further south, and was therefore determined "to abide events as long as possible."[31] With this in mind, Burgoyne decided to try a fresh attack on 7th October to dislodge his enemy, but this was overwhelmed and a retreat forced under continuous fire.

The next day, Burgoyne decided on a retreat to Saratoga, but was forced to leave 528 sick and wounded behind, under pressure from constant attacks. By now, news had reached him that reinforcements were unlikely to reach him from New York, making his position untenable. His soldiers were starving, all morale had ebbed away, and his much-diminished army was totally hemmed in by a superior force. The enemy's strength was now thought to be 16,000 and growing daily. All escape routes were closed, and the encampment was under constant attack. Burgoyne waited until 13th October, but following "hard toil, incessant effort, stubborn action," and "disappointed in the last hope of any timely co-operation from other armies" he "called to council all the generals, field officers, and captains commanding corps, and by their unanimous concurrence and advice…was induced to open a treaty with Major General Gates."[32]

[29] Letter from General Burgoyne at his "Camp, nearly opposite Saratoga, Aug 20, 1777" to Lord George Germain, printed in *Williamson's Advertiser*, 7th November 1777.
[30] Letter from General Burgoyne to Lord George Germain, Albany, October 20 1777, printed in *The General Advertiser*, 26th December 1777.
[31] Ibid
[32] Ibid.

The treaty led to an inevitable surrender, and allowed nearly 6000 disarmed soldiers to return to Britain, Germany or Canada on the simple promise of their not returning to America. Nearly 3,500 allied soldiers had been killed, wounded, taken prisoner, or deserted since they had started off from Canada. The remaining forces were now marched to Boston, where they were detained in camps for several months before being transported abroad. When news of the surrender reached Britain, and was debated in the House of Commons on 3rd December, the government's leading opponent, Charles James Fox, rounded on Lord Germain with "rage and indignation". He retorted, "Burgoyne's orders were to make his way to Albany, there to wait the orders of Sir William Howe, and to co-operate with him. But General Howe knew nothing of the matter, for he was gone to a different country, and left the unhappy Burgoyne and his troops to make the best of terms for themselves in a country that was by nature so defended, that strongholds were to be met at almost every mile, and every hour's march presented almost insurmountable obstacles to his progress."[33] Fox called for an enquiry, suggesting that the Secretary for America and his supporters were guilty of criminal negligence.

The defeat of the British in New England changed the course of the war. Although it was to continue for more than five years, British resolve was crushed, while a new threat lurked. In March 1778 the French government signed a 'Treaty of Amity' with the revolutionary government in America, which effectively meant that it was now at war with Britain. The French had been providing aid for some time, not out sympathy for revolutionary principles, but rather to damage British trade and weaken the country. Rivalries ran deep, and there was a strong desire for retribution for their losses in America and India during their previous war.[34] French commitment had been limited while the rebels enjoyed few successes, but the victory at Saratoga now showed them worthy of greater support. What remained uncertain, however, was the extent to which the French would go, and where and how they might strike. With much of Britain's army in America, George III expressed his "parental care and concern for his people, and his wishes to provide every means in his power for their defence and the defence of the kingdom." And, with these sentiments, the king added his wish to "acquaint their Lordships of

[33] *Williamson's Advertiser*, 12th December 1777.
[34] The war of 1756-63 had been a Europe-wide conflict, but Britain and France had also fought for a controlling interest in both North America and India.

his intention…to call forth and embody the Militia of the kingdom, wherever occasion shall require."[35]

Liverpool was not slow to respond. By late May 1100 volunteers had joined the regiment of Liverpool Blues, helped by public subscriptions and £2000 from the corporation.[36] But, by mid-June, many were on their way to defend Jamaica, where most would meet their deaths due to the ravages of disease rather than enemy action.[37] Temporary defences were installed on the riverfront while a more permanent fort was built. The public was informed that, "There are two grand batteries here of 27 eighteen-pounders, in excellent order for the reception of any mad invader whose rashness may prompt him to attempt to disturb the tranquillity of this town. George's battery is commanded by the Mayor, and the Queen's by Captain Hutchinson, both of them accustomed to the thunder of cannon, as are also the several captains and assistants stationed to each gun, which are shoted, etc. Centeries are fixt, and all the requisites so regulated as to be ready for action at the shortest notice. The King's battery for thirty-two-pounders is preparing with expedition, under the direction of Lieutenant-Colonel Gordon, an experienced engineer. To these securities will be added the Hycena frigate, a King's ship built here, which in a day or two will be fit for sea, and will be moor'd in the river. For our security by land we have two companies of Veterans, and four companies of the Liverpool Blues, commanded by General Calcraft, who resides in Liverpool."[38] That the threat was real was not in doubt, given the recent attack on the northern port of Whitehaven, when eleven French ships had opened fire on the town.[39] By the late summer, however, concerns were raised that some of the arms for the remaining volunteers had been stolen from caches concealed around the town. Lieutenant Surman thought it proper "to acquaint the public, that whoever conceals or embezzles his Majesty's stores, are liable, on conviction, to the penalty of five pounds, three months imprisonment, or to be publicly whipp'd, at the discretion of the Magistrate."[40]

The Franco-American treaty unleashed hostilities between French and British ships, creating new opportunities for Liverpool merchants and seamen. The first Letters of Marque were issued in July 1778, granting licences for eighteen ships to refit and sail as privateers. For a small fee, these enabled merchant vessels to become private 'men-of-war', allowing them to challenge and seize enemy vessels, and take them to a friendly port if successful. Once

---

35 *Williamson's Advertiser*, 27th March 1778.
36 Ibid, 22nd May 1778, and Brooke, op. cit., p359.
37 Williams, op. cit., p264.
38 Quoted in Williams, op. cit., p223-24.
39 *Williamson's Advertiser*, 22nd May 1778.
40 Ibid. 31st July 1778.

it was verified by admiralty officials that the prize ship and its cargo belonged to the enemy, both could be sold. Within weeks, £100,000 worth of ships and cargo had been brought into port and sold [41]. The *Lady Granby* captured the *Lady Louisa*, bound for Bordeaux with a cargo of fish. The *Sarah Goulburn* took the *Minerva* with its cargo of tobacco, and a week later captured the *Amiable Magdalaine* with a cargo of sugar, coffee, cotton and ivory. But it was not only French ships that risked heading for French ports. The *Santa Maria* from Barcelona was bound for Honfleur with a cargo of brandy when it was captured by the *Wasp* and taken to Liverpool.[42] In October, however, a greater prize was brought into port by the *Mentor*, its mission being to challenge French ships bound for the East Indies. The reward was the *Carnatic*, with a box of diamonds valued at £135,000.[43] Captain John Dawson joined Baker & Co. to create the new firm of Baker and Dawson, and was soon married to Peter Baker's daughter. The partners also went on to buy the manor of Garston five miles south of Liverpool, and later bought a large estate at Mossley Hill.[44] An even greater prize was almost won by the *St. Peter* when it captured a French East Indiaman valued at over £200,000, but the Liverpool ship was itself then captured by a French frigate of 74 guns and taken into Port L'Orient. Ships sometimes sailed in pairs, as did the *Two Brothers* and the *Young Henry*, when they sailed from Liverpool in 1778. They captured *La Gaston* on 29th September on its return to France with a valuable cargo of cloth, cotton, coffee, tortoise shells, and a large quantity of ebony from India. The French ship was frigate built and was pierced for 32 guns but only carried six, leaving it poorly defended against the broadsides of her attackers.[45] When Captain Fisher of the *Two Brothers* returned to Liverpool the following year, he called at the *Three Tuns* and donated five shillings for ale to celebrate the prize.[46]

The dangers of the Mersey estuary were, however, a constant threat to shipping. In December, the *Mary* approached Liverpool in heavy weather with a prize bound for Bordeaux from St. Domingue carrying sugar, coffee, cotton and indigo. *L'Equite* had followed the Mary through the Rock Channel, and was just rounding the Perch when the rudder struck rocks below and was washed away. The strong winds prevented any assistance to tow the ship up river and into dock. Eventually, after running aground several times and being swept back into the river, *L'Equite* was run ashore near the New Ferry, where she was finally secured with anchors and cables. Several lighters were organised to take

---

[41] *Williamson's Advertiser*, 25th September 1778.
[42] Williams, op. cit., p224.
[43] Worth about £12,000,000 in today's money.
[44] Williams, op. cit., p239-240.
[45] Ibid p230-231.
[46] Wilson, op. cit., p147.

out the cargo, while word spread throughout the isolated Wirral communities. Hundreds of wreckers arrived the next day, then overpowered the crew and lightermen and carried off all they could. The *Mary's* owners then asked for help from the local militia, but this was denied on the grounds that they had no jurisdiction in Cheshire. The wreckers returned the following night to renew their plunder, despite there now being four armed guards to deter them. The guards fired first above their heads, but then fired into the crowd, killing one. This unleashed the mob's fury, leaving the guards with little option but to make their escape by boat and abandon the remaining cargo to the looters.[47]

The mobs across the river were fighting injustice, as press gangs roamed Liverpool's streets in search of prey. However, the authorities saw the matter differently. At the close of 1778, Mayor William Pole complained that "numbers of seamen and others engaged and entered on board the several privateers…go armed in a riotous and unlawful manner through the town and its environs, as well in the day as in the night time, without any commission or other officer being in company or to command them, to the great annoyance of the inhabitants and others, and who have committed several outrages thereby against his Majesty's peace, and the laws of our country in particular, in forcibly breaking open, and rescuing several impressed seamen out of the houses for the reception of them." He then warned "I shall be under the most disagreeable necessity of calling unto my assistance, for the preservation of the lives and property of his Majesty's peaceable subjects in this town, the military stationed here, of which I hereby require all such persons to take notice at their peril."[48] Clearly, officialdom did not wish to consider the rights of seamen to fight against virtual enslavement, just as it argued, particularly in Liverpool, against the rights of tens of thousands of Africans shipped yearly across the Atlantic.

By April 1779, 120 ships had been fitted out to chance their luck upon the enemy, which by this time included not only America and France but also Spain. Liverpool's merchants and seamen were positively encouraged to plunder ships at will, and had even been tipped off by the Admiralty that a huge convoy of French ships was preparing to leave St. Domingue, "a promising harvest for our spirited privateers," but none dared risk that encounter.[49] By September 1779, the *Enterprize* was ready to undertake three voyages as a privateer under the new ownership of Francis Ingram and Company, involving the collaboration of eleven partners. The *Enterprize* carried twenty-two guns and 106 crewmen, which was well in excess of the peacetime norm of perhaps twenty men for a ship of 250 tons. Apart from the captain, they included a

---

[47] Williams, op. cit., p232-233.
[48] Ibid, p237-238.
[49] Ibid, p246.

sailing master and two mates, three lieutenants and a captain of the marines, a surgeon, and two prize masters to command any seizures. Less senior specialists included carpenters, coopers, stewards, boatswains and gunners, each with one or more mates, plus an armourer, sail maker, cook and four quartermasters. There were also forty-eight sailors, many ranked as three-quarter, half or quarter seamen, depending on their experience, plus three boys and three apprentices. Finally, there were eighteen landsmen with no seafaring skills to act as marines.[50] Unlike the normal merchant venture, the privateer required high manning levels for encounters that were expected to take place, and to crew any prize ships adequately as they were brought into port.

In view of the dangers, wages were much higher than peacetime rates. Full seamen now earned around £3 5s per month, while three-quarter seamen averaged £2 15s and half seamen £2 3s. Landsmen earned about thirty shillings, which was what sailors had fought to retain four years earlier. Wages for specialist crewmembers ranged from £4 10s down to £3 for the captain's clerk and two stewards, and many received two months advance wages. Some of the men came from Whitehaven and Chester, and were recruited by 'crimps' or agents, as labour in Liverpool was now in short supply. Indeed, Captain James Haslam himself visited Whitehaven with several seamen, paying over £200 on inducements and other recruitment costs. While this was underway, the *Enterprize* was being fitted out by riggers, sail makers, carpenters, coopers, and many more. Provisions included beef, pork and fish, most of which was dried or salted, and vast quantities of bread, potatoes, peas, brandy, rum, beer and water.

The first voyage was intended to last six months, during which time Haslam was to follow specific instructions. He was to begin his cruise about 400 miles south west of Ireland, head south towards the Azores, and then return northwards again, always remaining well away from the coast of Europe and enemy naval cruisers. Any prize ships were to be escorted to the nearest Irish port, from where the *Enterprize* could resume its activities in the Atlantic. Haslam was also advised that "the prisoners be not plundered of their Clothes and Bedding, but that they may be used with all tenderness and Humanity consistent with your own safety." However, five weeks after leaving, the *Enterprize* captured *L'Adventurier* bound for Bordeaux from Martinique with a cargo of cotton, sugar, tobacco, coffee and cocoa. Due to unrest amongst the crew, Haslam chose to return directly to Liverpool with the prize, but he was retained for the next voyage with a rebuke for disobeying orders. His new instructions were to cruise off the coast of France in the Bay of Biscay for five months, which was quite contrary to the more cautious approach of the first voyage. Haslam was told, "do not return to Liverpool on any account or

---

[50] Williams, op. cit.., appendix II.

pretence," and that the owners depended upon him and his officers to "prevent any Disobedience or further attempts to Mutiny." He was also instructed to "keep a good look-out on all occasions, and make short work of any actions you have by running close alongside before you open fire." Despite having a reduced crew, the *Enterprize* went on to capture five more ships. However, one of these went aground on Burbo Bank at the mouth of the Mersey with the loss of all but one of the crew, although much of the cargo was eventually recovered.[51]

Arming privateers required large quantities of gunpowder. This was meant to be stored at the Liscard magazine a mile or so down river from Liverpool on the Cheshire coast so as to minimise the risk of explosion. Ships entering or leaving the port were expected to deposit or load their powder kegs, which were stored in cells or compartments built below ground. However, various private stocks were kept throughout the town, which the authorities found difficult to control.[52] Adding to the risk were the stockpiles needed for the defensive batteries, and the completion of the new fort at the northern edge of the town compounded the problem. The council received news in September 1779 that the American corsair John Paul Jones was in the Irish Sea with several privateers and hundreds of marines. It was now proposed to move a quantity of gunpowder from the Liscard magazine in readiness for an attack. The council also proposed asking the government for "a Thousand stands of Arms, for the use of such Gentlemen and private men who may offer themselves to serve as independent Volunteer Companies in case of the enemy's landing upon this coast, which is now much to be feared."[53] Further precautions were to be taken by stationing boats in Liverpool bay to provide warning of an attack. Warning would also be provided by signals from Bidston and Hoylake lighthouses. Enemy ships entering the bay would be at considerable risk, since the channel marker buoys would have been sunk, and the lighthouse braziers extinguished, making an attack by day or night highly liable to running aground on sandbanks or rocks.

It was perhaps the difficulties of navigating the river entrance that deterred any would-be attackers, and Liverpool was spared. For the crews of privateers, however, earning a living meant living with constant risk, as the crew of the *Nanny* discovered in May 1779. Their ship carried fourteen guns and fifty men, but proved no match for the American privateer *General Arnold*, with eighteen 6-pounders and 100 men. Captain Benyon provided the following account. "On the 20th of May, off Cape Finisterre, saw a ship in chace of us. Being resolved to know the weight of his metal before I gave up your property,

---

51 Williams, op. cit., p18-31 & 661-664.
52 See p42.
53 Brooke, op. cit., p365-366.

I prepared to make the best defence I could. Between eight and nine o'clock, he came alongside with American colours, hailed, and told me to haul my colours down. I desired him to begin and blaze away, for I was determined to know his force before I gave up to him. The engagement began and lasted about two hours, our ships being close together, having only room to keep clear of each other. Our guns told well on both sides. We were soon left destitute of rigging and sails, as I engaged him under my topsails and jib. We were sadly shattered below and aloft. I got the Nanny before the wind, and fought an hour that way, one pump going, till we had upwards of seven feet water in the hold. I thought it then almost time to give up the battle, as our ship began to be waterlogged. We were so close that I told him that I had struck, and hauled my colours down. The privateer was in a sad shattered condition. By the time we were all overboard the Nanny, the water was up to the lower deck. When Captain Brown heard the number of men I had, he asked me what I meant by engaging him so long? I told him, as I was then his prisoner, I hoped he would not call me to any account for what I had done before the colours were hauled down. He said he approved of all I had done, and treated my officers and myself like gentlemen."[54] The crew were later taken to Cadiz, where they were held as prisoners.

As the war continued the numbers of prisoners grew on both sides of the Channel and across the Atlantic. Several hundred foreign prisoners in Liverpool were confined in a converted gaol on Brownlow Hill, which was much visited by the Reverend Gilbert Wakefield. He complained of being "much mortified and ashamed at their uniform complaints of hard usage, and a scanty allowance of unwholesome provision."[55] However, British captives of Fougeres Castle, Ille-et-Vilaine, fared no better. They complained of bad bread, beef barely suitable for dogs, and peas "so bad that one half of them are as hard when they come out of the furnace as when first put in." Bedding had been removed, and prisoners were left to lie on vermin-infested straw. Worse still, if rumours were true, 1600 prisoners had died at a French prison at Dinan during the winter, thirty of them in one day. The dead were loaded onto a cart and thrown into a pit like dogs.[56] As the war continued, so the numbers of prisoners grew, and many of those at Liverpool had to be transferred to castle gaols in Chester, Lancaster and Carlisle. Yet, as Europeans and Americans fought over issues of liberation and plunder, Africa was given some respite, as the number of slaving voyages slumped and many were spared captivity.[57]

[54] Quoted in Williams, op. cit., p244.
[55] Ibid, p283.
[56] Ibid, p260.
[57] D.P.Lamb, *Volume and Tonnage of the Liverpool Slave Trade, 1772-1807*, in Anstey & Hair, op. cit., p92. The average annual clearances of Liverpool ships to West Africa between 1772-75 was 95, dropping to 35 between 1776-82. London figures dropped from 40 to 17, and Bristol from 22 to 6.

Chapter Four

By the end of the 1770s Liverpool was in decline, as the attacks on its shipping took their toll. With fewer cargoes to handle, there was less work for seamen, carters, warehousemen, ship fitters and others, and people were drifting away. Nearly two ships a week had sailed for Africa before the war, but now there were barely three a month,[1] and many a Guineaman had been converted to privateer. Now Liverpool depended on its seamen waging war to bring in wealth, but for every prize taken a ship was lost, and with every sea battle came death, maiming and widowhood. Nearly a third of the population was now supported by parish relief or charitable donations.[2]

The character of Liverpool's people, and the nature of its trade, was described many years later to a local historian by a nonagenarian looking back to the time of his youth. James Stonehouse did not reveal the old man's name, but included in his many reflections was this illuminating account. "My father was owner and commander of the *Mary Ellen*. She was launched on the 4th June, my birthday, and also the anniversary of our revered sovereign, George III. We used to keep his majesty's birthday in great style. The bells were set ringing, cannon fired, colours waved in the wind, and all the schools had a holiday. The *Mary Ellen* was launched on the 4th of June 1775. She was named after, and by, my mother. The launch of this ship is about the first thing I can remember. The day's proceedings are indelibly fixed upon my memory. We went down to the place where the ship was built, accompanied by our friends. We made quite a little procession, headed by a drum and fife. My father and mother walked first, leading me by the hand. I had new clothes on, and I firmly believed that the joy bells were ringing solely because our ship was to be launched. *The Mary Ellen* was launched from a piece of open ground just beyond the present Salthouse Dock, then called the South Dock. I suppose the exact place would be somewhere about the middle of the present King's Dock. The bank on which the ship was built sloped down to the river. There was a slight boarding round her. There were several other ships and smaller vessels building near her; amongst others, a frigate, which afterwards did great damage to the enemy during the French war. The government frequently gave orders for ships to be built at Liverpool. The view up the river was very fine. There were few houses to be seen southward. The mills on the Aigburth road were the principal objects.[3]

[1] D. P. Lamb, *Volume and Tonnage of the Liverpool Slave Trade, 1772-1807*, in Anstey and Hair, op. cit., p92.

[2] Figures given by Williams, op. cit., p301 show that between 1775 and 1780, following years of continual growth, the total tonnage of Liverpool ships fell by about 6.5%, customs revenues dropped by nearly a third, and the population declined by about 4% from 35,600 to 34,107. By the end of the war in 1783 nearly 30% of the town's population received parish relief or charity.

[3] This refers to the present Mill Street.

It was a pretty sight to see the *Mary Ellen* launched. There were crowds of people present, for my father was well known and very popular. When the ship moved off there was a great cheer raised. I was so excited at the great 'splash' which was made that I cried, and was for a time inconsolable because they would not launch the ship again so that I might witness another great splash. I can, in my mind's eye, see the splash of the *Mary Ellen* even now. I really believe the displacement of the water on that occasion opened the doors of observation in my mind. After the launch there was great festivity and hilarity. I believe I made myself very ill with the quantity of fruit and good things I became possessed of. While the *Mary Ellen* was fitting up for sea I was often taken on board. In her hold were long shelves, with ringbolts in rows in several places. I used to run along these shelves, little thinking what dreadful scenes would be enacted upon them. The fact is that the *Mary Ellen* was destined for the African trade, in which she made many very successful voyages.[4]

In 1779, however, she was converted into a privateer. My father, at the present time, would not perhaps be thought very respectable, but I assure you he was so considered in those days. So many people in Liverpool were, to use an old and trite sea phrase, tarred with the same brush, that these occupations were scarcely, indeed were not at all, regarded as derogatory to a man's character. In fact, during the privateering time, there was scarcely a man, woman or child in Liverpool of any standing that did not hold a share in one of these ships. Although a slave captain, and afterwards a privateer, my father was a kind and just man - a good father, husband, and friend. His purse and advice were always ready to help and save, and he was consequently much respected by the merchants with whom he had intercourse. I have been told that he was quite a different man at sea, that there he was harsh, unbending and stern, but still just. How he used to rule the turbulent spirits of his crews I don't know, but certain it is that he never wanted men when other Liverpool ship owners were short of hands. Many of his seamen sailed voyage after voyage with him. It was these old hands that were attached to him who I suspect kept the others in subjection. The men used to make much of me. They made me little sea toys, and always brought my mother and myself presents from Africa, such as parrots, monkeys, shells, and articles of the natives' workmanship...."

"As a young boy and an old man I have seen my native town under two very diverse aspects. As a boy, I have seen it ranked only as a third-rate seaport. Its

---

[4] Although there is no record of a *Mary Ellen* in *Lloyd's Register* for that time, there are two entries for ships named *Mary*. One was a 40-ton sloop owned by Thomas Tarleton. Although very small for a slaver, it is listed as such ("Li Africa"). Sloops were quick in the water, which may have given it some advantage as a privateer, despite its size. The other was a 160-ton ship, which was built in 1771, but was lengthened in 1772 and repaired in 1775, and also sailed to Africa. It could be that the event described refers to re-launching following its repair. As for the name, Lloyd's was not always fully accurate.

streets tortuous and narrow, with pavements in the middle, skirted by mud or dirt as the season happened.[5] The sidewalks rough with sharp pointed stones that made it misery to walk upon them. I have seen houses, with little low rooms, suffice for the dwelling of the merchant or well-to-do trader - the first being content to live in Water Street or Oldhall Street, while the latter had no idea of leaving his little shop, with its bay or square window, to take care of itself at night. I have seen Liverpool streets with scarcely a coach or vehicle in them, save such as trade required, and the most enlightened of its inhabitants at that time could not boast of much intelligence, while those who constituted its lower orders were plunged in the deepest vice, ignorance, and brutality.

But we should not judge too harshly of those who have gone before us. Of the sea savouring greatly were the friends and acquaintances of my youth. Scarcely a town by the margin of the ocean could be more salt in its people than the men of Liverpool of the last century; so barbarous were they in their amusements, bull-baitings, and cock and dogfightings, and pugilistic encounters. What could we expect when we opened no book to the young, and employed no means of imparting knowledge to the old - deriving our prosperity from two great sources - the slave trade and privateering? What could we expect but the results we have witnessed? Swarming with sailormen flushed with prize money, was it not likely that the inhabitants generally would take a tone from what they daily beheld and quietly countenanced? Have we not seen the father investing small sums in some gallant ship fitting out for the West Indies or the Spanish Main in the names of each of his children, girls and boys? Was it not natural that they should go down to the Old Dock or the Salthouse, or the New Dock,[6] and there be gratified with a sight of a ship of which they - little folks as they were – were still part owners? We took them on deck and showed them where a bloody battle had been fought - on the very deck and spot on which their little feet pattered about. And did we not show them the very guns, and the muskets, the pistols and the cutlasses, the shot-lockers and magazines, and tell them how the lad, scrubbing a brass kettle in the caboose, had been occupied as a powder-monkey and seen blood shed in earnest? And did we not, moreover, tell them that if the forthcoming voyage was only successful, and if the ships of the enemy were taken - no matter about the streams of blood that might run through the scuppers - how their little ventures would be raised in value many hundred-fold - would not young imaginations be excited and the greed for gain be potent in their young hearts? No matter what woman might be widowed, parent made childless, or child left without protector. If the gallant privateer was successful, that was all they were taught to look for."[7]

---

5 This refers to the paving of roads with rough stone slabs.

6 George's Dock, now the site of the Liver Building and its neighbours.

7 James Stonehouse, *Recollections of Old Liverpool by a Nonagenarian* (1863) p8-11 & p251-253.

Across the River Mersey, the village communities on Cheshire's Wirral peninsula were involved in quite a different form of enterprise. Here, between the Mersey and Dee, they were favoured by the occasional rich harvest that was bound for Liverpool, but which ended up being driven aground in the darkness of night during misty or stormy weather. Yet some folk had their own way to lure ships off course as they approached the Mersey by night. As their helmsmen steered to bring in line the dim light of braziers on the Bidston and Mockbeggar lighthouses, two further lights at Hoyle Lake came into view and guided them towards a safe overnight anchorage. But when mist obscured the lights, wreckers lit false beacons to guide unwary crews onto the sands. News spread like wildfire when a ship ran aground, and the locals poured from every direction to carry off whatever they could carry or cart away. Although a well-defended crew might fend them off, the ruthlessness of the locals was something to be feared, as this account shows. "The inhabitants were nearly all wreckers or smugglers. They ostensibly carried on the trade and calling of fishermen, farm labourers and small farmers, but they were deeply saturated with the sin of covertness, and many a fierce fire has been lighted on the Wirral shore on stormy nights to lure the good ship on the Burbo or Hoyle Banks, there to beat and strain and throb until her timbers parted and her planks were floating in confusion on the stormy waves. Fine times then for the Cheshire men. On stormy days and nights, crowds might have been seen with carts, barrows, horses, asses, or oxen even, which were made to draw timber, bales, boxes, or anything that the raging waters might have cast up. Many a half-drowned sailor has had a knock on the sconce, whilst trying to obtain a footing, that has sent him reeling back into the seething water, and many a house had been suddenly replenished with eatables and drinkables and furniture and garniture, where previously bare walls and wretched accommodation only were visible. Then for smuggling. Fine times the runners used to have in my young days.[8] Scarcely a house in North Wirral that could not provide a guest with a good, stiff glass of brandy or Hollands. The fishermen used to pretend to cast their nets to take the fish that then abounded on our coasts, but their fishing was of a very different kind."[9]

Whenever a ship was wrecked, whatever the cause, notices were placed in the local press, such as this one in *Williamson's Advertiser*. "The ship Reginald, being unfortunately stranded on Hoyle Bank, on Saturday last. This is to inform all persons who may have already taken, or may hereafter take up any part of the said ship's cargo, consisting of Barwood, Ivory, Tortoise Shell, &c, or any of her materials or stores, that, upon giving in an account of the same to George Dunbar in Exchange Alley, they will be cheerfully paid any

---

[8] Runners was another term for smugglers, ie. those who ran contraband.
[9] Quoted in Stonehouse, op. cit., p60-61.

charge they may have incurred in saving the same, and the customary salvage. And this is likewise to caution dealers in the above articles from purchasing, from any person, goods of that description, and so request they will stop the persons offering them for sale, and give information as above."[10] But, given the scarcity of 'preventative officers', or customs and excise men, there was little chance of retrieving any wreckage. Some of the spoils were taken directly to the wreckers' cottages and quickly consumed or hidden, but much of the plunder was concealed in sandhills between the Mersey and the Dee to be smuggled away. There were also several smugglers' caves in sandstone rocks known as the Red Noses at the northeast corner of the peninsula. One of these was called the Wormhole, which was reached from the sea by a long tunnel. This led into the main storage area, complete with its own supply of water from a well. At over twelve feet high and thirty-three long, there was plenty of space to store casks and cases until it was safe to move them.[11] This was a well-organised business, involving a network of smugglers who understood the advantages of the local terrain. This part of the Wirral was cut off from the rest of the peninsula by a tidal inlet that opened onto the Mersey opposite Liverpool. The treacherous, low-lying bog known as Bidston Moss was flooded at high tide, and was impossible to cross without an intimate knowledge of its labyrinth of pools and morasses.[12] The only safe crossing point was via the 'Jaw Bones', where indeed a pair of whale's jawbones was laid on top of wooden beams to form a bridge across a stretch of water. The smugglers encouraged a rumour that the crossing was haunted by the ghosts of people who had drowned nearby, and this kept most at bay. Once they had taken their loads by packhorses across the bog, the smugglers followed a track up onto Bidston Heath and to the *Ring-o'-Bells* tavern, where there were places of concealment nearby. From there, contraband was taken southwards over Storeton Heath and the Clatter Bridge, before finally ending up in Chester or beyond.[13]

Smugglers also frequented *Mother Redcap's* tavern near the gunpowder magazines on the edge of Liscard Moor. This was an isolated sandstone cottage built just above the high water line of the River Mersey. *Redcap's* was much favoured by sailors, partly for its strong, dark, home-brewed ale, and also for

---

10 *Williamson's Advertiser*, 22nd January 1784.

11 The cave still exists, although the tunnel on the seaward side has been bricked off. However, there is still access to it from the back garden of a house overlooking Liverpool Bay.

12 The tidal pool was utilised to build the docks at Wallasey and Birkenhead in the mid-19th century, and ditches were dug to drain Bidston Moss. The area now supports a retail park, a supermarket, and other businesses, and two railway lines cross the area on embankments. The M53 motorway, which starts at Wallasey, also crosses the Moss, but the fly-over at Junction 1 has been subject to continual subsidence and repairs.

13 E.C. Woods and P.C. Brown, *The Rise and Progress of Wallasey* (1960) p126-127

the hospitality of its large, but comely hostess. They had every confidence in her, and frequently entrusted wages and prize money to her safekeeping, which she later concealed in hidden cavities contained within the thick walls and chimney breasts of its two drinking rooms. At high tides, contraband ships could lay a short way in front of the tavern at an anchorage known as Red Bett's Pool, from where they could observe a false weather vane. This signalled all was clear when it pointed towards the tavern, and their boats were sent to off-load at the quayside in front of *Mother Redcaps*. Contraband was lowered through a trap door to the cellar, which was directly behind a thick, studded oak door at the front of the tavern. If this was full they were concealed in a second cellar that had been excavated behind the building. This was roofed over with wooden planks, and these supported some of the flagstones that paved the yard. One of these could be lifted to reveal a steep set of steps leading to one end of the cavity. At the other end was a narrow underground passage that led up the hill behind the tavern to a concealed opening by a large willow tree. This was ideal for a lookout to spy the surrounding area so that contraband could be moved safely over Liscard Moor, and then over Bidston Moss via the Jaw Bones.[14] Indeed, the public's demand for smuggled goods was insatiable, and there were few who were unwilling to buy tea, tobacco, spirits, or fine cloths at more affordable prices.

Those convicted of serious cases of wrecking or smuggling could expect to end up dangling on a rope, to be launched into eternity at a public hanging outside the county gaol. Others might count themselves lucky to be sentenced to seven years transportation to work alongside Caribbean slaves. Liverpool's petty criminals could expect a whipping, followed by a spell at the Tower Gaol or the House of Correction. The former was now reserved for male prisoners owing to its previous licentious conditions, while the latter held both sexes in separate areas, although a majority of its inmates were female. Prisoners lived on a daily diet of bread, potatoes and a little salt, but there were larger cells with beds, and a workroom where they picked oakum for sealing gaps in ships. Although the House of Correction was considered an improvement on the old gaol, there was regular abuse of women for the men's entertainment. Dressed only in a flannel shift, victims were taken by a gaoler to the men's yard once a week, where they were tied to the water pump and thoroughly soaked. An alternative form of cruelty was provided by the ducking stool, a device with a long history. This consisted of a chair attached to the end of a

---

[14] Woods and Brown, op. cit., p113-117, and E.C. Woods, *Smuggling in Wirral*, Historic Society of Lancashire and Cheshire, Vol. 79 (1927) p125-131. Liscard Moor is now entirely built over, and Mother Redcaps is the site of an old people's home. It displays the legend that was written on a hanging sign outside the tavern, "All ye that are weary come in and take rest, Our eggs and our ham are of the best, Our ale and our porter are likewise the same, Step in if you please and give 'em a name."

pole or beam, which rested on a supporting fulcrum. Victims were strapped into the chair and lowered into a large open-air bath, which was otherwise intended for purposes of cleanliness. Although this practice was stopped after philanthropist John Howard's 1779 visit, the use of the pump continued into the next century.[15]

The gaols were financed by the parish, which also administered a public dispensary that had opened in 1778 to provide free medical treatment for the poor. Over two thousand patients were treated during the first eight months, of which around four hundred had fevers, mostly from typhus. Sore throats, coughs and asthma accounted for 324 cases, while 221 suffered from "itch and other eruptions", and 175 from tumours, abscesses and ulcers. Ninety-six had worms, while hysteria and "convulsive affections" accounted for thirty-eight. Fifty-nine had small pox, and there were thirty-four venereal complaints, while fifteen suffered from cholera. Other conditions included dysentery, "ophthalmy", "gravel" and "insanity". By the end of March 1779 the dispensary claimed to have cured nearly three-quarters of its patients, and only seven had been turned away on account of their ability to pay privately. Some remained on the books or had merely been relieved, while twenty-four had been taken to the infirmary, and 115 had died.[16] Having been built from parish rates, its running costs came mostly from donations, but by the end of the first year the dispensary was a mere £4 11s 6d in arrears. During its third year of operation, the dispensary dealt with 10,000 patients, and a decision was made to open a much larger one in Church Street. This was soon dealing with 14,000 cases a year, with six physicians and three surgeons working on a rota basis.[17]

Across the Atlantic, meanwhile, the war had ground almost to a halt. On the one hand, rebel commanders were finding it increasingly difficult to clothe, feed and pay their militias, and inflation was rampant. On the other, the will of the British government to continue the war was being sapped by the sheer magnitude of the task. Indeed, its most ardent supporter was George III, who argued that the loss of the American colonies would lead to the loss of the lucrative West Indies. Now that the French and Spanish were allied to the rebels, much of the British effort was focused on defending its Caribbean colonies, and

---

[15] Brooke, op. cit., p354-356.
[16] Ibid p364.
[17] Peet, op. cit., pLV.

also in guarding against an invasion at home. Early in 1780, however, General Clinton, William Howe's replacement as British commander, decided to move on South Carolina to support American loyalists in their struggle against the rebels. By April they were preparing to besiege Charleston, and a dispatch was sent to the rebels, "regretting the effusion of blood, and the distresses which must now commence…to warn the town and garrison of Charles Town of the havoc and desolation with which they are threatened from the formidable force surrounding them by land and sea. An alternative is offered at this hour to the inhabitants of saving their lives and property (contained in the town) or of abiding by the fatal consequences of a cannonade and storm. Should the place in a fallacious security, or its commander in a wanton indifference to the fate of its inhabitants, delay the surrender, or should the public stores or shipping be destroyed, the resentment of an exasperated soldiery may intervene; but the same mild and compassionate offer can never be renewed."[18] The reply from General Lincoln, who commanded the southern rebels, was that he would defend Charleston "to the last extremity", but after several day's siege he was forced to surrender, along with nearly six thousand troops and a thousand seamen.

The British soon began mopping up any remaining resistance in the region. Colonel Banastre Tarleton was sent with a small cavalry detachment to intercept an American regiment that was escorting Governor Rutledge and others who had escaped the siege of Charleston. They met at Waxhaws on the Carolinas' border, and although Tarleton's dragoons were heavily outnumbered, he sent terms of surrender to the Americans with a claim he that he had nearly three times the 270 troops actually under his command. The American commander replied, "Sir, I reject your proposals, and shall defend myself to the last extremity," but his orders to hold fire until the opposing cavalry were within ten yards proved a disaster.[19] His men were quickly routed and began to surrender, but the ruthless treatment they received earned Tarleton a reputation for brutality. Two months later, Saratoga victor General Gates marched six thousand troops to put down a loyalist uprising in North Carolina. His men were met at Camden by British troops under Lord Cornwallis, and two thousand rebels were killed or captured in a bloody encounter. Tarleton's reputation as 'Bloody Ban the Butcher' was soon sealed, as his Green Dragoons harried the remaining rebels in the Carolinas, burning their houses and giving them no quarter. News of Tarleton's military successes soon reached his hometown of Liverpool, where he was hailed as a hero.

---

[18] Copy of the Summons sent to Major General Lincoln, 10th April 1780, printed in *The General Advertiser*, 23rd June 1780.

[19] R.D. Bass, *The Green Dragon: The Lives of Banastre Tarleton and Mary Robinson* (1958) p80. The decision to delay firing meant that the rebel troops had no time to reload before their attackers were upon them.

While Tarleton was harassing the Southern rebels, Liverpool was preparing for its first parliamentary election contest in nearly twenty years. Although a single constituency, the town was represented by two MPs. Since there had only been two candidates at the previous two elections, the matter had been a mere formality, and on each occasion both men were sent to Westminster. It was in this manner that Richard Pennant had twice become MP, but had since lost much local favour with his opposition to the government's American policies and the subsequent damaging war. Yet Pennant still had the backing of like-minded supporters, and was urged to stand again for the election of September 1780. Opposing him were two corporation nominees, successful merchant Henry Rawlinson, and the twenty-two-year-old Bamber Gascoyne junior. Young Gascoyne had just finished at Oxford, and lived four miles from Liverpool at Childwall Hall. Bamber senior had been MP for distant Truro, and held government sinecures as Receiver General of his Majesty's Customs and as a Lord Commissioner of the Admiralty. Bamber Gascoyne senior was a wealthy man of influence indeed.

Only freemen burgesses were qualified to vote, and membership of their ranks was controlled by the powerful local council.[20] At the start of the century, when Liverpool's population stood at roughly 6,000, most of its adult males had been burgesses. This privilege had passed down through family generations, but successive councils had restricted new admissions as migrants swelled the population. By 1780 there were little more than two thousand voters, much as there had been eighty years before.[21] This left a curious situation whereby most were men of little means, whereas many a merchant or professional man was denied the vote. Being freemen, burgesses were absolved from payment of town dues and half the market tolls. Perhaps most importantly, however, being a freeman meant benefiting from bribes of free drink, food and entertainment in return for pledging their votes at elections. Past candidates had spent small fortunes touting for votes, and the present ones were unlikely to win now unless they did so lavishly. There was also the cost of bunting and

---

20 The Oxford Dictionary of English defines a burgess as the inhabitant of a town, or borough, with full rights of citizenship. The word derives from the Anglo-Norman French 'burgeis' and the Latin 'burgus,' meaning castle or fort, and also relates to the Middle English 'burgh,' or town, and 'burgher.'
21 The situation in some constituencies was far stranger. Old Sarum by Salisbury was an example of a 'rotten borough,' having only one voter yet returning two MPs, as did Newton. Marlborough had three voters and Grampound nine, yet both had two MPs.

banners, the hiring of canvassers and bands, the printing of election materials, and additional expenses for coach tickets and lodgings for 'outvoters' who had moved away, but who were still eligible to cast their vote in Liverpool.

Although Liverpool was predominantly a Tory town and Whigs were a small minority, such labels meant little, either locally or nationally. When contests were held, most voters cared little for the issues, and since the majority were men of humble origin, they felt no allegiance to the candidates. Each freeman had two votes, and could either cast both to gain from two lots of bribes, or could 'plump' for a single candidate by using one and withholding the other. Winning over 'plumpers' meant giving additional bribes in compensation, but the extra expense could make all the difference by depriving the opposition of votes. However, those who depended on the council for work or lived on council-owned land were unlikely to oppose its candidates for fear of reprisal, while others felt bound by their employers' wishes.[22] Freemen voted in full public view in tallies, or groups of ten, and their choices were recorded against their names; indeed, it would be another ninety years before the introduction of the secret ballot. Few cared to question the morality of the occasion, or the oath sworn by every voter, "I do swear I have not received, in trust for me, or for my use and benefit, directly or indirectly, any sum or sums of money, office, place, or employment, gift or reward, or any promise or security for any money, office, employment, or gift, in order to give my vote at this election; and that I have not before been polled at this election."[23] In practice, elections were an occasion for binge drinking, rowdyism, and brawling between rival groups. Candidates complained bitterly about the bribery of their opponents, while forking out large sums to lure voters and protesting their own innocence.

In the run up to the election, hired hands distributed pamphlets, songs and squibs that praised their paymasters and ridiculed opponents, although some raised more serious concerns about the war. Writers posed under the guise of such pseudonyms as *Sting, The Old Watchman, Veritas, Tom the Tinker* and *Old Carpenter,* but avoided naming the candidates directly in case of legal reprisal.[24] With Gascoyne's youthful inexperience, and his father's lucrative government benefits, their critics had a field day. Leading the attack was *Varro*, who wrote on 8th September, "Let us look on Mr. G. Senr. in his public capacity. He is by profession a courtier, that is, the most infamous of all professions; the traffic is the vices, money, and liberty of

---

[22] F.E. Sanderson, *The Structure of Politics in Liverpool, 1780-1807,* Historic Society of Lancashire and Cheshire, Vol. 124 (1972) p75
[23] Ibid., p74-75
[24] Liverpool Poll Book, 1780, including *'A Collection of Papers, Addresses and Songs &c. Printed on all Sides, During the Contest for Representative in Parliament for the Borough of Liverpool.'*

the people. These are bought with fair promises and flattering addresses, and exchanged for ministerial gold, and for lucrative places for themselves and families." The vitriol continued, "As it is not to be supposed that a boy can have any services of his own to tell of, Mr. G. Junr, I am inform'd, leans entirely on his father's merit…to him and the rest of our wise and upright ministers we owe all the blessings of the American war. To them we owe the decline of our trade, the neglect of our navy, and the hateful superiority of the fleets of the house of Bourbon.[25] These we have to thank for our burdensome taxes, for the cruel necessity and inhuman practice of impressing seamen, and for our blood and treasure fruitlessly squander'd away. In a word, Mr. G has never swerve'd from the side of any of those ministers." Next day, *Varro* continued his diatribe against father and son, exclaiming, "Curses, diabolical, abandoned, all in one breath! The thief who runs foremost is the loudest to cry 'stop thief.' I hate faction as well as you; but who, my honest botching friend, pass'd the acts that provok'd the Americans without a soldier to support them – and then complain'd of wrong information? Who refused to hear the petitions of the Colonists, and afterwards offered concessions more derogatory to the honour of Britain than they themselves demanded in the beginning? Who left the West Indian Islands defenceless, who suffered our navy to go to ruin? Who planned all the schemes that have repeatedly miscarried? Who prevented the bill to prevent the impress of seamen? Who voted for all these blunders? Not Mr. P but such hireling slaves as the little tyrant of Childwall Hills."

As *Varro* put out his second missive, one bold *Cassandra* ventured into the field in Gascoyne's defence. "Enough of broils, elsewhere, all mobbing hence, censure none but the deserving. Let each candidate exert his power with freedom and honour; let every freeman poll merrily, drink moderately, vote heartily, without anger, scorn or envy." *Cassandra* considered the candidate's merits, starting with Pennant, who had represented Liverpool for thirteen years, and who she felt "we have found little harm in, little good, no orator, no knowledge of our trade and constitution, no influence to procure friends in the House." *Cassandra* gave bold advice that, "cou'd a Woman vote," she would espouse the cause of Gascoyne and Rawlinson. This prompted *Davus* to complain about the woman who dared "take up the cudgels in an electioneering squabble, and so divest herself of all sense of decency." He retorted, "I blush for the sex, and am led to think that Bedlam, or some other Madhouse, is certainly broken loose, and that Cassandra, after a close confinement, is let out amongst the rest without her keeper." He concluded, "From your speaking with such confidence of the Abilities of the different Candidates, it should

---

[25] The house of Bourbon was a reference to the French royal family line.

seem that your ladyship has had more to do with ALL the three Gentlemen than we are aware of. Your ladyship knows the Best."

During the five days of polling, from Tuesday 12th to Saturday 16th September, invitations went out to potential supporters to partake of hospitality. One read, "The Friends of Mr. Rawlinson desire the Freemen in his Interest to meet them To-morrow Morning by Eight o'clock, at the Talbot, at the White Lyon in Castle Street, at the Black Horse and Rainbow in High Street, or at the Peacock in the Old Shambles." Gascoyne's 'friends' had a choice between the *Fleece, George's Coffee House,* or the *Neptune,* while Richard Pennant's invitation was limited to *Forshaw's Great-room* at the *Golden Lion* in Dale Street, albeit the most prestigious venue in the town. This was when the real expense began. As the gatherings were plied with free food and drink, canvassers wandered streets and alleys to entice additional supporters to join them. Meanwhile, between visits to their chosen venues, the candidates were busy lampooning their opponents from their platforms, attended by bands of musicians and entertainers. Banners, bunting and ribbons everywhere displayed the candidates' colours, and the streets were soon littered with debris and drunken revellers. As the contest heated up, business came almost to a stand, as the whole town was drawn into the excitement of the occasion and the lure of the taverns. As colourful parades competed through the town, everyone was infected by the air of festivity. Normality was abandoned, and would not return until some time after the last votes were cast.

Voting on the first day was somewhat slack, but picked up the following day. Each candidate sought pledges of support from the privileged freemen with bribes of food and drink, and was especially generous to any who promised to plump for him. But with two votes each, and so much fare on offer, such loyalty could not be depended on, and many split their votes between two candidates. When each had had his fill, voters were organised and led before the magistrates in front of the Exchange, but by late afternoon the parties had to root out stragglers to make up the final tallies. After reciting the convoluted oath with difficulty and confusion, they registered their individual votes, which were recorded in the poll book while on-lookers watched and cheered. No matter that a man slurred his words or could barely stand; all that counted was his vote. At the close of each day's poll the votes were counted, and the results announced to the crowd.

By the end of Wednesday 13th it was clear that young Gascoyne was heading the poll, due largely to his corporation backing and the extent of his purse. Pennant trailed in third place, having hit raw nerves with his stance against the war when so many were in favour. His friends continued their attacks on his opponents, prompting *Candour* to jump to Gascoyne's defence with lofty invective. He cautioned, "Be not led astray from your real interest by the base and villainous insinuations of character stabbing; wretches, hirelings, who, for pecuniary reward, would strive to blacken the fairest character. 'Tis obvious their cause is in a dangerous situation, who permit such foul methods to be made use of to raise themselves in public favour. But regard not these lurking serpents, who hide in holes, send forth their contagious breath to poison your mind against a gentleman, whose only study is, and will be, to deserve the great encouragement he has already met with amongst you. Do then, like freemen, nourish the young plant, which in time will flourish like your native oak, and by a power of oratory, unknown to any that has yet represented you, support the cause of this flourishing town and shield it from oppression." A reply came next day describing Gascoyne as "a son to a wretch who …does not enjoy one single virtue, public or private," while his father was mocked as "bold enough to offer us his unthinking, illiterate boy as a candidate."

Some voters held back until the final day in the hope of even heftier bribes, but when the final poll was closed and the result announced it was clear that Richard Pennant had lost his parliamentary seat.[26] Gascoyne topped the poll, followed closely by Rawlinson, who, as a leading merchant, many felt had "rendered this town essential service, especially in preserving our Guinea trade." They were now carried aloft on triumphal seats, followed by their still thirsty supporters. Toasts were drunk in profusion, while whole roast sheep and pigs, and sides of beef, were stacked onto sagging tables in gratitude. The celebrations went on well into the night, accompanied by the sounds of pipes, flutes, fiddles, trumpets, drums, and accordions.

Next Monday morning word went round that Gascoyne's voters were invited to Childwall Hall, where an ox would be roasted and shared among them. Gascoyne's party assembled early with their coloured banners and musicians in School Lane, and started off on their four-mile walk. The procession was soon swelled by the ranks of the multitude, joined by more along the way. By the time they reached the family residence it was difficult to maintain order, and stewards were given poles to hold people back and prevent them from wandering over the well-tended lawns and gardens. Tensions rose as the food was distributed, since the hangers-on expected a great feast. Clearly, one animal was insufficient to meet the challenge, and some who were lucky enough to get a slice complained that it was merely a tough old bull. There was discontent over the vegetables too, and rumour had it that they were being fed on cabbage stalks. Fortunately for Gascoyne and his father, the disappointed crowd melted away in disgust, although the event remained a legend for many years to come[27]

[26] Gascoyne received 608 votes, Rawlinson 572, and Pennant 462.
[27] Brooke, op. cit., p370-371.

A few weeks after the election, James Finlow was recruiting on behalf of William Davenport and Company for a voyage to Africa and the West Indies on board the *Hawk*. Thomas Johnson signed up as cook on 13th October, and was given £12 in advance to help support his family during a year or so of absence. Finlow noted in his wages book, "Three Months after the Ship Hawk sails from the Black Rock, I promise to pay Thos. Johnson or order the sum of One Pound Monthly, so long as he may continue on board the said vessel to Africa – as Witness my Hand for William Davenport & Co, James Finlow." Robert Hare was taken on as the carpenter two weeks later and received an advance of £11 10s. Unlike cooks, carpenters were regarded as skilled members of the crew, so his wages were thirty shillings a month, payable two months after passing the Black Rock at the entrance to the Mersey. Among others taken on were gunner James July, armourer Richard Walpole, steward Francis Young, doctor's mate John Jenkins, sail maker James Manuell, and seamen John Webb and John Brown. Each received around a third of their expected total wage in advance, and most signed for the receipts with the mark of a small cross between their fore and surnames. James Manuell made arrangements for part of his wages to be paid directly to his wife, as did Walpole, Young and several others.

While Davenport and Company were preparing the *Hawk* for her transatlantic voyage, Liverpool's shipyards were once again working at full stretch, due largely to recent government orders for naval frigates. Recent launchings from Liverpool had included the *Nemesis*, *Adamant*, and *Daedalus*.[28] The largest of these was the *Adamant*, a fifty-gun frigate of just over a thousand tons built at Peter Baker's yard, which soon started work on a sister ship, the *Assistance*. The *Alligator*, a 14-gun sloop of 300 tons, was launched that November from John Fisher's yard, while work had also begun on the *Phaeton*, a 38-gun frigate that would only later see action against revolutionary France. Meanwhile, despite the damaging effect of the war on trade, some merchants like Francis Ingram, whose ship *Blayds* was built during 1781, were still placing new orders. Some yards specialised in building smaller boats, and an increasing number of orders were being placed for barges for the developing network of canals.

Liverpool's shipyards were concentrated along the waterfront south of the town, and there could be a dozen vessels under construction at any one time.

---

[28] R. Stewart-Brown, *Liverpool Ships in the Eighteenth Century* (1932) p89.

Stacks of timber lay all around, some ready to use, others in seasoning, while tree trunks and boughs still awaited sawing. Some were supplied from around Speke, Halewood and Woolton, and from Lord Sefton's Lancashire estates, but builders had to look further for most of their supplies. Suitable trees were becoming scarce, and the price of timber was rising sharply, with oak now selling at between four and six shillings per foot. Since the start of the century some three-quarters of Britain's woodlands had been cut down, much of it for shipbuilding, but also for use in the rapidly growing iron industry. Many of the forests of Lancashire, Cheshire, Shropshire and Staffordshire were nearly depleted, and Liverpool was now relying heavily on supplies from Wales, while some were brought from overseas.[29]

Sales of timber were frequently advertised in the newspapers. In January 1781, 470 trees were advertised for sale in Knowsley, about eight miles from Liverpool.[30] On 8th February, *Williamson's Advertiser* printed an advertisement for "Oak Timber, to be sold to the highest bidder on Saturday 3rd March next, between the Hours of Three and Six o'clock in the Afternoon, at the House of Mr. Jackson, the Sign of the Talbot, in the City of Chester…1426 full grown Oak Trees. This timber is now growing in the township of Edge, in the County of Chester, within four post miles of the River Dee at Farndon … is fit for all the purposes of shipbuilding, and amongst it is a considerable Quantity of crooked Timber." Two weeks later another advertisement appeared for "1988 oaks to be sold at the King's Arms in Middlewich on Tuesday 13 March 1781 between 3 and 5, marked and numbered, growing on several farms in Kinderton and Sproston near Middlewich – the respective tenants will shew the timber." Oak was preferred for most of the main timbers due to its great strength and durability. Wood from the main trunk provided straight timbers, whereas 'crooked timber', the curved sections also known as compass oak, came from the natural bends provided by the branching of main boughs. Elm was also used, especially for the keel and lower sections of the hull, due to its resistance to seawater. Beech and pine were sometimes used for inner planking and decking, whereas pine and fir were particularly suited for the masts and other spars. While Britain was at war with America, supplies of long, straight coniferous woods relied heavily on the Baltic region and Russia.

Trees were felled by woodsmen towards the end of the year, when their sap was no longer rising and the leaves had dropped. Only mature trees were selected, since younger specimens had yet to yield up the full value of extra growth to come. Those with the most boughs and thick bending branches were

29 Stewart Brown, op. cit., p56-57.
30 *Williamson's Advertiser*, 11th January 1781.

highly favoured for the curvature they helped bring to a ship. Once they were felled, and their smaller branches removed, the trees had to be transported over land, and where possible by water. Trunks and branches were raised with blocks and tackle onto large wagons, and these were hauled by up to ten pairs of oxen or heavy horses. A 50-gun frigate might require as many as two thousand loads, while even a 200-ton merchant vessel may need three or four hundred. Since the roads were in such a poor state, many little more than a quagmire in wet weather, loads were transferred onto barges or single-masted hoys, and taken on by navigable rivers and canals wherever possible.[31] When 160 oaks were advertised for sale in Holywell, North Wales, the advertisement stressed "just one mile from the sea."[32]

Once a vessel was ordered, its plans were drawn up, unless existing ones were to be used. Either way, these were generally on a scale of one to forty-eight.[33] Each set consisted of a set of lines that showed the contours of the ship and the extent of its curvature. The convention was to show just one side elevation, and half of the underside from the keel, since both halves of a ship were symmetrical. A further drawing combined two views in one plan. The right side showed the contours leading forward from the bow, while the left showed those from the stern.[34] For larger vessels, a final drawing showed the design of the elaborate upper stern section. The main difference between naval and merchant vessels, other than size, was in the shape of the hull. Naval ships curved inwards above the waterline, which gave them great stability and manoeuvrability, and allowed for batteries of heavy guns to be mounted high up in the vessel. Merchant vessels, however, were designed for maximum freight-carrying capacity rather than agility, and therefore had more box-like hulls. Whichever the case, once the plans were produced, it was necessary to translate the drawings for practical use. Draughtsmen's skills were seldom highly developed, and much depended on the shipwright's experience and rule of thumb.[35] Most commonly, the plan of the ship and its individual timbers were chalked out full-size on the smooth floor of the mould loft situated above a large shipwright's shed. Using these patterns, moulds or templates were cut from thin wooden battens, which could then be transferred to pieces of timber to act as guides for cutting and shaping.[36]

First to be laid on its supporting blocks was the keel. This was the backbone that ran the full length of the bottom of the ship. It was joined to the stempost at the bow, and the sternpost at the rear, each of which formed an extension

[31] P. Goodwin, *The Construction and Fitting of the Sailing Man of War, 1650-1850* (1987) p3.

[32] *Williamson's Advertiser*, 8th February 1781.

[33] P. Cordingly, *Billy Ruffian: The Bellerophon and the Fall of Napoleon* (2003) p21

[34] A. McGowan, *The Ship: The Century Before Steam* (1980) p8 and frontispiece.

[35] Goodwin, op. cit., p6.

[36] Cordingly, op. cit., p21.

of the backbone that rose up to main deck height. A false keel was added to the underside of the keel, and could easily be replaced if damaged, unlike the keel itself. An inner keel, or keelson, was attached above the keel, and further components were added to strengthen this assembly and provide rigidity for the rest of the structure. None of these was made from a single length of timber. They were all made from sections that were joined together using scarph joints, whereby the ends were cut away like wedges, but incorporated various smaller joints that were chiselled out so that opposing sections fitted together snugly and securely. This method was used on all the major timbers, and all were bolted together for extra strength. The keel and posts of a 28-gun frigate of nearly 600 tons measured about thirteen inches square in cross section, but these dimensions varied with the size of the vessel, and could reach well over two feet in thickness.[37] Once this foundation had been built, the frame or ribs of the vessel were added. These were fitted at right angles to the keel at intervals, and were built up in sections of curved timbers, each jointed together, so that the underlying shape of the vessel was established. This skeleton was supported by planks, and the shipwrights built up a wooden scaffold from which to work as the structure rose in height. Gun ports were framed between the ribs, after which further construction was delayed to allow time for additional seasoning of the wood.[38]

When building resumed, crossbeams were attached to each side of the frame to support the decking, which was added later. These were given extra support using brackets of timber or iron known as knees, which were attached to both beams and ribs. Two layers of planking were then fixed to the ribs. The outer oak or elm planking, and the inner planks of pine, ran the length of the ship in sections that were scarphed and bolted together using wooden trennels (hence, tree nails). These were preferable to metal bolts because they did not corrode, and as they swelled in water the joints became tighter. Planks measured about four inches in thickness and around fourteen in width on average, although these dimensions varied according to which part of the hull was being assembled and the shape of the ship. Lengths also varied, the larger ones being about twenty feet in length. Once the external planking was in place, further bands of timber called wales were added to the outer hull to provide extra strength and protection. The whole structure was given additional stiffening and bracing with various beams and trusses, after which the decks planks were laid down using oak or pitch pine. The number of decks depended on the size of the vessel. Smaller ships had two decks, the main and lower, with a hold for storage at the bottom of the ship. Mid-range merchant ships also had a middle

---

[37] Goodwin, op. cit., p7.
[38] Ibid., p13-18. Further information on shipbuilding is based on various pages from the same source.

deck, while the largest also had an orlop below the lower deck. Frigates such as *Adamant* had an orlop deck, followed by the lower, middle and main gun decks, and two partial decks above – the forecastle (or fo'c'sle) at the bow, and a quarterdeck at the stern. Guns would eventually be mounted so that the heaviest were on the lower deck and the lighter ones above.

Now that the basic shell was complete, all the planks of the hull and the decks needed to be made watertight. This was done by hammering untwisted, tar-soaked rope into the gaps, a process known as caulking. Drainage was provided by means of scuppers, which were lead or wooden channels fitted to where the deck and side planking met, and these led to gutters in the hull. By the 1780s, most ships were sheathed in copper plates, which prevented Teredo navalis, or sea worm, from burrowing into and rotting the timbers. Sheathing also reduced the build up of marine growth, and therefore cut down on the need for scraping, cleaning and re-tarring the hull, a process known as careening. Plates measured about four feet by fifteen inches, and were fixed by copper nails so that they overlapped at the upper and after edges.

The ship was divided into a number of compartments, which depended on the size of the vessel and the requirement for specialist crewmembers. These included cabins for the captain, surgeon and steward, and storerooms for the carpenter and boatswain. There were also food stores for bread, grains, pulses and other provisions, in addition to a sail locker, rope room, clothing store, and so on. The magazine was always well below the waterline deep within the hold, where it could not be penetrated by enemy shot, and was built on a raised platform so that water could not seep in and damp the powder. There were three main parts – the powder room for storage, a filling room to load the cartridges, and a separate sealed light room with windows that allowed lanterns to illuminate the magazine. The whole area was sheathed with either copper or lead, and felt slippers had to be worn inside to prevent sparks from shoe nails. During action, cartridges were passed to boys known as 'powder monkeys' from the filling room through a hatch above.

All wooden ships were fitted with pumps, since all were liable to some leakage. Water collected in the bilges at the bottom of the vessel which had to be pumped out and discharged overboard. However, pumps could also be used for washing the decks or fire fighting. There were two main designs, the chain pump and elm tree pump, both of which were fitted in combinations of two or four depending on the size of the vessel. The chain pump consisted of two tubes set apart at an angle, through which passed a series of copper washers attached to a chain, each with a flap valve. The assembly passed down one tube as the winch handle was turned, scooping water at the bottom, and raising it up the second tube. As each washer approached the top of the upward tube, the water was discharged into a sluice that led overboard. Such pumps could raise a ton of water a minute. Elm pumps were less efficient, raising only twenty-five gallons per minute, but were easier to maintain with few moving parts. These were made from the two halves of an elm tree that were hollowed out and fitted tightly back together with heated iron hoops that shrunk when cooled. As the pump handle was operated to raise the piston, water was drawn by vacuum through a leather flap-valve in a tight-fitting assembly further down the tube. When the piston returned down the tube, another valve allowed water to pass through, which was then raised on the next stroke. Meanwhile, water was again drawn by vacuum from below the piston, and the process repeated with each action of the pump handle. The water was discharged into a sluice near the top of the tube and over the ship's side.

Food preparation was essential to the proper functioning of a ship, since no crew could operate on an empty stomach. Indeed, the standard of food was directly related to the attitude of the men, despite the low status of cooks. Their work was done in the galley below the main deck, and by the late eighteenth century iron stoves mounted on a brick base were in general use. Designs varied, but most consisted of a fire hearth, with a roasting spit mounted in front, a water boiler above, and an oven to one side or behind. A flue was also mounted over the hearth to carry away fuel smoke, and some incorporated a ventilation duct leading from the lower deck to draw stale air up as the hot fumes were expelled. By the end of the century ships were also beginning to distil seawater to ensure some fresh supplies were available. The toilet facilities were as basic at sea as they were on land. Pissdales were half bowls or basins that were attached to the side planking, and incorporated a lead waste pipe draining out through the ship's sides. Seats of ease were placed at the bow, where there was some overhang to allow waste to clear the ship and be carried away by the wash. These latrines accommodated two or three people, either side-by-side or one behind the other. Often they were located on either side of the bowsprit on the small prow deck, or in the prow below the main deck. Either way, they offered little or no privacy.

Now that the vessel and its deck fittings were complete, a rigid cradle was constructed to keep the ship upright on its launch down the slipway on which it had been constructed. After greasing the slip with tallow fat, the vessel could be eased down the gentle gradient to the river, and then towed to a graving dock to have the masts, yards, sails and rigging fitted. [39]

---

[39] Although some ships seem to have had their lower masts fitted before launch, it would seem likely that in Liverpool this operation was best carried out in one of the dry docks.

The slave ship *Rose* was approaching Jamaica in April 1781 when it was attacked by a French privateer. After exchanging broadsides and small arms fire, the crew of the privateer attempted to board the *Rose*. Captain Stevenson explained how his crew was assisted in fighting off the attack by some of the slaves: "He at last came up on our starboard quarter, with a stinkpot fast to the end of his gaff, thinking to swing it on board, but one of the Trantee slaves shot it away with his musket. He then grappled our main chains, and we lay together yardarm and yardarm for above one glass, when he thought proper to sheer off, having got his belly full. I had about fifty men, black and white, on deck at great guns and small arms, halfpikes, boathooks, boat oars, steering-sail-yards, firewood, and slack ballast, which they threw at the Frenchmen in such a manner that their heads rattled against one another like so many empty calabashes. My people all behaved very well, both white and black. We lost a white man named Peter Cane; myself wounded, and five other white people, as likewise seven blacks, one of which is since dead. The other six I am in hopes will recover. The Frenchmen hove such a large quantity of powder flasks on board us that the ship abaft was all in a blaze of fire three different times. This hurt the blacks much, having no trowsers on them. I had my own shirt burnt off my back. After that, I received a ball through my right shoulder, but, thank God, it was in the latter part of the action, so that I did not lose much blood. On the doctor's examining my wound, he found the ball was gone clean through my shoulder."[40]

Meanwhile, Captain John Small was on his way to St. Lucia, with a cargo of slaves on board the *Hawk*, but had also hired several Africans as additional crew. They were described as 'Fantye men', and were known as Lancelots Hey (after the Liverpool street), Liverpool, Ackway, Cudjoe, Quashey, and Joe Dick.[41] The cook, Thomas Johnson, had died shortly before leaving Cameroon, where the *Hawk* had finished off trading for slaves. Several of the crew had bought items of Johnson's clothing, and the money would later supplement the wages his widow received to the day of his death. The usual practice was for the crew to gather round the main mast several days after the crewmate's burial at sea, when his clothes and other belonging were auctioned off.[42] The men were given instalments on their pay when they reached St.

---

[40] Quoted in Williams, op. cit., p564-565.
[41] The Fante tribe were located along the western part of the Gold Coast, now part of Ghana. It is probable that the Hawk began trading there, and that the men were hired to help manage the slaves.
[42] Rediker, op. cit., p197.

Lucia in June, where, no doubt, they made good use of their time. Since leaving Liverpool many had also bought items of clothing, tobacco, or liquor from the captain, as was also common practice. Robert Hare the carpenter was a heavy drinker, having got through five gallons of brandy over eight months. Each half-gallon instalment at five shillings each had been recorded on his account, costing him £2 10s, and he also took £12 wages on reaching the island. Armourer Richard Walpole had bought three gallons, and was paid £8 in St. Lucia. Gunner James July was more temperate, having bought only half a gallon. He also bought a pair of shoes and a hat for the vastly inflated sum of fifteen shillings, and paid 1s 3d "to Cloaths Bought Belonging to ye Deceased Cook". By the time ordinary seaman John Brown had reached the island he had smoked or chewed his way through about seven pounds weight of tobacco at four shillings a pound. He also bought several pairs of trousers, a pair of shoes, several items of Johnson's clothes, and more besides. Steward Francis Young was less profligate, and was one of those who had ensured that some of his wages were paid directly to his wife while he was away. His only purchases were two check shirts, one pair of shoes, and one of trousers, but these cost him dearly at £1 9s, which was over half his monthly wage of about £2 15s.[43]

When they eventually reached Liverpool, after a voyage of nearly eleven months, the crew were paid their remaining wages. Captain Small had kept a careful account of every item of credit, and also deducted monthly contributions to the seamen's hospital. Robert Hare received his balance of £11 14s 10½d, making his total wage for the voyage £38 3s 2½d.[44] The gunner and armourer's total wages were slightly less, while able seaman John Webb had earned a little over £31. By the time John Brown was given the balance of his earnings of just over £22, he only received 17s 1d. He had now got through ten pounds weight of tobacco during the course of eleven months, in addition to buying many other items. The Fante men were also paid off, each one receiving £10 11s 8d. Whether they returned to Africa on another voyage is not known, but their receipt of wages shows that they were certainly free men. However, the legal status of slaves brought to Liverpool and other towns to work as servants in wealthy households was unclear. A decade earlier, Lord Mansfield had delivered a judgement that any slave setting foot on British soil became free. Yet, despite this decision, *Williamson's Advertiser* published a notice in 1780 which read, "Run away, on the 18th of April last, from Prescot, A Black Man Slave, named George Germain Foney, aged twenty years, about five feet seven, rather handsome; had on a green coat, red waistcoat, and blue

---

[43] His purchases equate to around £130, and his wages to about £250 in today's money.
[44] This would be equivalent to about £3500 in today's money. His monthly wage worked out at about £3.20p, or £288 today.

breeches, with a plain pair of silver shoe buckles; he speaks English pretty well. Any person who will bring the black to his master, Captain Thomas Ralph, at the Talbot Inn, in Liverpool, or inform the master where the black is, shall be handsomely rewarded. All persons are cautioned not to harbour the black, as he is not only the slave, but the apprentice of Captain Ralph."[45]

Soon after the return of the *Hawk* to Liverpool, the slave ship *Zong* was approaching Jamaica, having left Africa ten weeks earlier with some 470 captive souls.[46] The *Zong* had been 'tight packed', which meant the slaves were chained in pairs as close as books on shelves, leaving each one no more room than a body in a coffin. By late November 1781 disease was spreading like wildfire, having claimed the lives of over sixty Africans and seven seamen while threatening hundreds more. On top of this, the *Zong* was some way off course in the Caribbean due to the inexperience of the ship's master, and the supply of fresh water was running low. Captain Collingwood had served as surgeon on previous voyages, but now, as men, women and children lay vomiting and groaning, too ill to reach the wooden tubs, he callously called his officers together on the 29th and suggested throwing the sick and dying into the sea. He explained that if they died a natural death the loss would fall on the owners and ruin the venture, whereas if they were drowned in order to preserve the rest of the human cargo the loss would be borne by the underwriters. Clearly, Collingwood had no scruples, but if he also wanted to preserve the life of the majority he was doubtless mindful of his commission on the number of healthy slaves delivered to Jamaica. Chief mate James Kelsall initially objected but eventually agreed, perhaps because his own commission was at stake. After selecting 132 of the most sickly slaves, the crew were ordered to throw fifty-four overboard that day. Forty-two followed them the next, but on the third, the remaining thirty-six put up stronger resistance. After being overwhelmed and heavily shackled, twenty-six were bundled over the side, and the remaining ten threw off their captors and leapt bravely overboard to their deaths.

When the *Zong* returned to Liverpool, owners Gregson, Wilson and Aspinall submitted a claim for the full value of the murdered slaves on the grounds that

---

[45] *Williamson's Advertiser*, 4th May 1780.
[46] This account is based on F. Shyllon, *Black Slaves in Britain*, (1974) p184-187.

the action had been necessary to preserve the lives of the remaining slaves and crew, and thus the value of the ship and its cargo. Indeed, according to insurance law at the time, the insured "takes upon him the risk of the loss, capture, and death of slaves, or any other unavoidable accident to them: but natural death is always understood to be expected. By natural death is meant, not only when it happens by disease or sickness, but also when the captive destroys himself through despair, which often happens: but when slaves are killed, or thrown into the sea in order to quell an insurrection on their part, then the insurers must answer."[47]

When the insurers investigated the circumstances, Collingwood claimed that a navigational error had extended the ship's time at sea as he tried to find Jamaica. He claimed also that his decision to drown the slaves was due to a shortage of fresh water, the remaining two hundred gallons being insufficient for the needs of all on board. However, first mate Kelsall admitted that on the second day of murders there was continuous heavy rainfall, which enabled six casks to be filled. This was enough for eleven days at full allowance, or double this on half rations. In any event, the remaining murders went ahead regardless, and the *Zong* arrived in Jamaica with 420 gallons to spare. With this information, the underwriters turned down the claim on the grounds of Collingwood's negligence and improper conduct. However, without the slightest sense of shame, Messrs. Gregson, Wilson and Aspinall sought legal action to recover their lost profits.

By now, the war in America was reaching its closing stages. Despite taking control of Charleston eighteen months earlier, and the continued support of loyalists, there was still no hope of British troops controlling more than small areas of territory. The rebels were now being assisted by French forces on land and sea, so that defeat seemed inevitable sooner or later. Part way through 1781, General Cornwallis decided to move the bulk of his troops north to Virginia, where Benedict Arnold had abandoned the rebel cause and was now wreaking havoc on his ex-compatriots on behalf of the British. Seven thousand Redcoats were soon stationed at Yorktown on a peninsula near the mouth of the Chesapeake Bay, which now became the focus for General Washington in his quest to deliver a knock out blow. To do so, he created a diversion by feigning an attack on New York before quickly marching his troops south to Virginia. While fourteen British ships of the line were sent to

---

[47] Cited in Shyllon, op. cit., p185.

join an existing force near Long Island, French Admiral de Grasse arrived with a much larger fleet at Chesapeake Bay. Before long, Yorktown was hemmed in by five thousand rebels aided by eight thousand French troops and their fleet, and it was clear the British had been out-manoeuvred. General Clinton sent seven thousand reinforcements by sea from New York to affect a rescue, while Cornwallis's troops held out under siege. But after several days it was clear their position had become untenable, as this dispatch intimates: "Sir, last evening the enemy carried my two advanced redoubts on the left by storm, and during the night have included them in their 2nd parallel, which they are busy at present perfecting. My situation now becomes very critical. We dare not throw a gun to their old batteries, and I expect their new ones will be open tomorrow morning. Experience has shewn that our fresh earthen works do not resist their powerful artillery, so that we will soon be exposed to an assault in ruined works, in a bad position, and with weakened numbers. The safety of the place is therefore so precarious that I cannot recommend that the fleet and army should run great risqué in endeavouring to save us. I have the honor to be, with great respect, Cornwallis."[48] The beleaguered garrison was forced to surrender four days later, and when the reinforcements finally arrived they were forced to retreat and return to New York rather than risk further disaster.

The final encounter took place not on land but at sea, soon after thirty-six British ships of the line and their supporting frigates began searching the Caribbean for the French and Spanish fleets in February 1782. While it seemed likely that the American colonies would eventually be lost, there was further danger to British possessions in the West Indies. The French had recently captured St. Kitts and were now preparing to invade Jamaica. Fourteen major Spanish warships and eight thousand troops were aiming to meet with thirty-three French ships of the line and dozens of support vessels under the command of Admiral Comte de Grasse. British scout frigates spotted the French between Guadeloupe and Dominica on 8th April, and reported their sighting to Admiral Rodney. The British set off in pursuit and caught up with their enemy next day, but both sides were hampered by light winds and contrary breezes that made manoeuvring difficult. Both tried to gain the advantage over the next two days, and gunfire was exchanged at long range. As two French ships collided, severely damaging one, they were attacked by four British warships. This signalled the start of a major engagement, when two opposing lines were formed, each making for the other, and their guns opened fire as they began to drift passed. After an hour the winds started to change, which opened a gap in the French line just in front of Admiral Rodney's flagship, *Formidable*.

---

[48] Dispatch from General Cornwallis to Sir Henry Clinton, Yorktown, !5th October 1781, printed in *Williamson's Advertiser*, 29th November.

Rodney now ordered a change of course to open up the gap, and seven of his fleet were able to isolate six of the enemy, including the French flagship, the *Ville de Paris*. Their guns blasted broadsides for several hours amidst a dense fog of smoke, causing great carnage as cannon shot, musket balls and wooden splinters carried off limbs and tore through flesh and bone. The crew of the French flagship suffered terribly, despite her 112 guns, and was eventually forced to surrender with the other five beleaguered ships. Meanwhile, the remaining French fleet was in confusion, hampered by adverse winds and the rest of the British ships. Seeing the action was lost it eventually scattered, but two of its ships were captured a week later.

Despite this success, support for the war effort continued to wane. When the issue had recently been put to a vote in Parliament, the majority in favour had been reduced to one. Later in the year a preliminary peace agreement was reached between the British and Americans, although it would be a further year before a final settlement was signed in Paris. The last remaining troops withdrew from New York and returned to Europe late in 1783, accompanied by three-quarters of the inhabitants, whose numbers had dwindled to a mere eight thousand.[49] The return to normality was widely welcomed in Britain, and there was great relief that the Caribbean colonies had been saved, none more so than in Liverpool. While the American colonies had been a drain on the British economy, those in the West Indies were a source of great profit. Liverpool's traders could now resume trade with a new America, and refit their privateers for the lucrative slave trade.

---

[49] Letter from New York, 26th September 1783, printed in *Williamsons Advertiser*, 13th November.

Chapter Five

While the peace negotiations were still underway, Francis Ingram was preparing for the maiden voyage of his new ship, *Blayds*. Built by Grayson and Ross, the basic shell weighed 277 tons when it was launched. Once afloat, the *Blayds* was towed into one of three narrow graving docks, which could be emptied as the tide ebbed. As the water level fell, the keel settled onto large wooden blocks, and timber shoring was placed around the hull to support the ship. While the gates remained closed the dock stayed dry, enabling the masts to be hoisted into position using wooden cranes. Each consisted of three sections to achieve the height needed to carry all the sails. Made of pine, each successive stage was shorter and thinner than that below, the lower ones averaging sixty feet in height and eighteen inches in thickness, and reducing in size by about a third for each stage above.[1] The fore, main and mizzenmasts were first to be hoisted, each being seated in a recess within a mast step over the keelson, and braced by extra timbers set into the decks. These were followed by the foretop, maintop, and mizzen topmasts, which were hoisted up and supported by platform 'tops' constructed around the upper reaches of each mast below. Several feet of overlap allowed both sections to be firmly braced together. Then the fore topgallant, main topgallant, and mizzen topgallant masts were each hoisted onto a second platform top, and braced securely to the section below at the overlap. Finally, the bowsprit was set in position above the bow at an angle of thirty-five degrees, attached to which was a jib boom, extending about fifty feet ahead of the prow. With all masts fitted, the *Blayds* now weighed 300 tons.[2]

The graving dock was allowed to flood once the masts were fitted, and the *Blayds* was towed to a mooring in one of the wet docks to have her rigging, spars and sails fitted.[3] The fixed 'standing' rigging gave extra support to the masts, as they were subject to considerable forces under full sail. Taut ropes called shrouds were rigged between the tops of the lower masts and the ship's sides, while the tops of the upper masts were rigged to the mast-top platforms below. While the shrouds provided lateral support for the masts, forestays and backstays helped secure them from forces fore and aft. Cross spars, or yards, were then attached to the masts to support the sails. Each yard was able to swivel around the mast to allow the sails to catch the wind, and was controlled by ropes called braces. Yards and sails could also be raised or lowered using

---

[1] As there are no surviving details for the *Blayds*, these are approximations for a merchant ship of 300-330 tons derived from K.H. Marquardt, *Eighteenth Century Rigs and Rigging* (1992) p45.
[2] *Lloyds Register*, 1782.
[3] Although possible, it is unlikely this stage of the work would have been done in a graving dock. A mooring in a wet dock would have been cheaper, and the work could be carried out just as easily. There would also be demands on the graving docks from other ships.

Part of the list of payments to tradesmen during the fitting-out of the Blayds in 1782 (Tuohy Papers, LRO 380/TUO/4/9)

halyards, and were secured by slings and lifts. However, many procedures were carried out well above the main deck, and needed men of courage to climb the rigging to reach the yards and sails. This they did by means of ratlines, which were tied and spliced across the shrouds as ladder rungs. On reaching the yards, the men made their way along footropes that were slung below, from which position they were able to shorten or lengthen the sails.

The largest foresail was the fore-mainsail, with the foretopsail, foretopgallant, and fore-royal reducing in size above. Aft of these were the mainsail, main topsail, main topgallant, and the main royal above. Nearest the stern were the mizzen and mizzen topsails, while the spritsail and two triangular staysails were rigged from the bowsprit and jib, forward of the prow. They were made for the *Blayds* at Joseph Matthews' premises in College Lane, using cloth made by James Gaskell and Company at a total cost of £435 pounds.[4] Sailcloth was made from hemp, sometimes with the addition of flax or cotton, and there were strict regulations as to its manufacture. A bolt of English sailcloth was two feet wide by thirty-eight yards in length, but different weights of material were made to suit the various types and sizes of sail, the heavier cloths being of double thickness. Cut pieces were sewn together with a double seam of thick twine, averaging 110 stitches per yard. Both sails and twine were treated to protect them from the elements. Twine was treated with a mixture of beeswax and turpentine, sometimes with the addition of hog's lard. Sails were treated either with oil-thinned tar and linseed oil, or a mixture of horse fat, tar and ochre.[5] They were given added strength by stitching tarred 'boltropes' around the edges, which reduced the strain on the cloth produced by the force of the wind. Loops were added to the corners, and at regular intervals between, which enabled the attachment of

---

4 Tuohy Papers, LRO, 380/TUO/4/9.
5 Marquardt, op. cit., p172-173.

rigging to secure or raise the sails. Sails also had several additional seams sewn across their width, to which straps were attached to allow the reefing or shortening of sails. By securing a line of reef straps to the yard upon which a sail was hung, its area was reduced, thus relieving the forces on the mast. With a following wind, each of the sails was set at right angles to the line of the ship, except for the fore and aft staysails and the mizzen sail, which helped to provide steerage against the wind. Whether staysail or main topgallant, fore-royal or mizzen, each yard and sail was controlled using the extensive network of running rigging, aided by hundreds of woodblock pulleys, and an array of knots to suit each load and every change of wind.

Among Ingram's partners was David Tuohy, whose brig *Nancy* had now made many voyages to Africa and the West Indies. Matching his share was Henry Moore, who was also to captain the ship, and Messrs. Baker and Dawson, whose recent prize, the *Carnatic*, had brought them great wealth. John Clemison, the agent on the African coast who was to direct Moore's trade, held a larger share, but Francis Ingram's five-sixteenths made him the senior partner. He supervised the building, fitting, and provisioning of the *Blayds*, which cost nearly £6,500 in total. He also hired the crew, and paid advance wages totalling another £424. Meanwhile, he bought in hundreds of items of cargo worth more than the ship itself, most of which was stored in large butts that would later be filled with water for the slaves.[6]

His instructions to Captain Moore were that, "You, being appointed Commander of the ship Blayds, are to proceed the first fair wind to Cape Coast Castle on the Coast of Africa. On yr arrival there you are commanded to apply to Mr. John Clemison, whom we most sincerely hope you will find in Health and Spirits & with whom you are to consult & be govern'd by his Advice in your future proceedings in Trade. If any unfortunate incident should have happened (which God forbid) that you do not find him there, you will find Letters from him lodged in the Hands of Mr. Miles, or some other Person in the Fort, containing his Instructions to you for your future Operations in Trade, & to which we expect & desire you will pay the strictest Attention. We are in the greatest Expectation that you not only will find him there, but also that he has open'd such a Path for Trade either at Lagos, Porto Novo or Port Agerg as to enable you with your cargo, which amounts to £7147 3s 9d, to purchase better the 650 slaves and some cloths." Ingram suggested that at Lagos "there are two kinds of Slaves, the one equal to the Whydahs, the other little if any better than Benins," and cautioned Moore against confusing the two. Warning was also given against being too generous with brandy and cowries shells, as "it might be the Ruin of your Purchase was you to dissort

---

[6] Tuohy Papers, LRO, 380/TUO/4/9.

Second page of Captain Henry Moore's instructions (LRO 380/ TUO/4/9)

your Cargoe by parting with too many of those Articles at the beginning of your Trade or indeed in any part of it." Moore was also reminded that "it behoves you to be very circumspect in all of your proceedings & very attentive to the minutest part of your Conduct, for be assured the whole of the Purchase greatly depends on the prudent Behaviour of the Person to whom the Care of the whole is entrusted." Moore was advised to have a tierce of bottled porter on board, which he should deliver to Richard Miles, Governor of Cape Coast Castle, with the compliments of the partners.[7] Ingram was confident that this gift would bring "every Assistance in his Power."

Moore was to sail to Jamaica after completing his trade on the African coast. No instructions were given as to the treatment of the slaves, except to "be watchful of your Negroes to prevent Insurrections." Moore was also warned to be "careful of your Spirits to prevent if possible the dreadful Consequences of Fire," which was good advice given that the cargo included a vast quantity of inflammable brandy. Thomas and Robert Hibbert were to act as agents in Jamaica and sell the slaves to "the best Advantage," but Ingram advised Moore to deceive them about the origin of the slaves by suggesting "if possible you must say from Whydah." Moore was also instructed, "Have nothing to say to any Vessel you fall in with but what you are well assured are either French, Dutch, Spanish or Americans. Be cautious of all neutral Vessels or those bound from a neutral Island, for was you to send in one of these the Expense to the Owners would be considerable indeed, & was this to be lost coming in your Owners would have to pay the whole amount of Ship & Cargo. Therefore we again repeat it, be well assur'd you are right before you take Possession of any Vessel….If you are so fortunate as to take a Prize, send her to Lisbon or Ireland as you judge for the safest and best." As to the rewards, Moore was told, "Whenever you

---

[7] A tierce was a measure equivalent to about 35 gallons in total.

Part of the list of Blayds trading goods (LRO 380/ TUO/4/9)

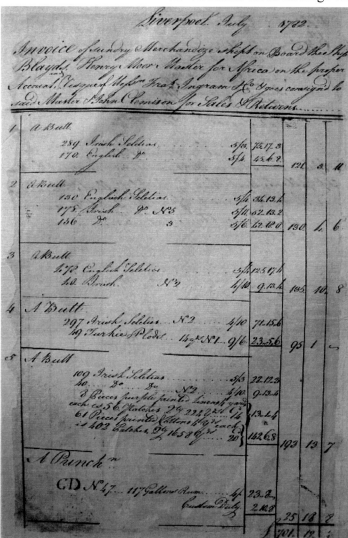

will you are to receive your Privilege & Commissions, & also Mr. Clemison, which is to be as follows – Mr. Clemison is to Draw one sixteenth of the Privilege & Commissions as is usually given, which is 1 slave in 50, sold in the W. Indies on an Average with the Cargo, & 4 on every 104 on the gross Sales & the remaining fifteen-sixteenths of the Privilege & Commission to be equally divided between you & Mr. Clemison. Your chief Mate is to have two slaves on an Average with the Cargo & £5 per month. Your Doctor one Slave on an Average with the Cargo & 20 Guineas paid him in Jamaica & head money of £4 10s per month."

Among the various items of cargo and provisions listed were arms valued at a £135, and nearly £200 worth of gunpowder, most of which was intended for barter. Besides a puncheon of rum for the crew, there were over 14,000 gallons of brandy for trading worth over £1500, and various cloths from Manchester, Ireland, India and Turkey with a combined value of nearly £3000. Peter Rigby and Son provided 300 iron bars, while just over £200 was paid to Tennant and Cust for cowry shells to help smooth the trade. Parry, Corbeth and Afflick provided £45 worth of barley for broths and stews, while John Potter produced the hams. By the time the ship was fully laden and the final bills paid, Ingram and Company had parted with just over £14,000, including their outlay on the vessel.

Added to this were the wages. At the top of the crew list were the captain and his first mate, each on a monthly wage of £5, augmented by their commissions and privileges. James Price also earned £5, given that his skills as a carpenter were considered so vital in keeping the ship watertight. However, at five guineas a month, the highest basic wage went to cooper John Christian. His job was to keep a close eye on the brandy by stemming leakages, repairing casks and barrels, and transferring liquor from damaged containers to new ones he made, thus limiting any chance of a conflagration. The only member of the crew to receive extra payments

Crew list for the Blayds (LRO 380/TUO/4/9)

and privileges, besides the captain and his first mate, was surgeon Beny Walkenson. It was his job to keep as many slaves alive as possible, which had little to do with genuine care and everything to do with profit. Indeed, it was general practice to pay surgeons head money, usually based on the number of slaves taken on board and those actually delivered for sale. Among the other officers and specialists were the second and third mates, a quartermaster and a steward. The boatswain and gunner both had mates, as did the surgeon, carpenter and cooper. Their monthly wages ranged from £4 15s to £3 10s, except for the lowly cook on a mere £3. In addition to these were twenty-seven seamen on wages ranging from £4 down to £2 5s according to experience. Seven landsmen were also taken on at £2 each, their wages reflecting their status as novices to the wooden world. At the bottom end of the wage scale were three boy apprentices, each on around 30 shillings a month.

There is no record of the *Blayds'* voyage, except that she set sail on 12th August 1782, and then left Liverpool almost exactly a year later on her second voyage. By around the time her second cargo of human misery was being traded in the West Indies, the question of liability for the 'loss of cargo' from the *Zong* was being tested [8] The trial was heard on 6th March 1783, when the case of Gregson versus Gilbert was brought before the bench at the Guildhall in London. The jury soon came to a decision against the insurers, who now found themselves liable to pay £30 for each slave drowned. An anonymous writer to the *Morning Chronicle and London Advertiser* gave an account of the trial and noted, "I waited with some impatience, expecting that the Jury, by their foreman, would have applied to the Court for information how to bring the perpetrator of such a horrid deed to justice." There was, however, no such application, and the humanity of the slaves was not considered.

By this time, however, the underwriters were disputing the outcome of the hearing, their case being that the murders had been a fraud on the policy rather than a genuine act of jettison. An application for a second trial was heard on 21st and 22nd of May 1783 before three high court judges headed by Lord Mansfield, whose decision some ten years earlier had declared any black person in Britain to be free.[9] Counsel for the insurers argued that the real motive for the killings was because Captain Collingwood calculated that he would get little for a cargo of sick slaves and would gain more from the insurance. Any pretence that there was insufficient water on board was clearly false, given that the ship could have been taken to any one of the many islands for fresh supplies. Observing that whatever the outcome of the case the killers would be free men, counsellor Piggott asked, "Is it not strange that the parties concerned should be suffered to go out of the kingdom, when they ought to be tried for murder in another place? Is this thing to be justified? Was there such a necessity that every man who hears me will say it was inevitable? Another thing is, was it to be done at all? The life of one man is like the life of another man, whatever the complexion is. Suppose the existency described had existed – I ground myself on the rights and essential interests of humanity – I contend that, as long as any water remained to be divided, these men were as much entitled to their share as the captain, or any other man whatever." Appearing for the owners, Solicitor-General John Lee retorted, "What is all this vast declamation of human people being thrown overboard? The question after all is this, Was it voluntary, or an act of necessity? This is a case of chattel or goods. It is really so; it is the case of throwing over goods; for to this purpose, and the purpose of the insurance, they are goods and property; whether right or wrong, we have nothing to do with it. This property – the human creatures

---

[8] Account below based on Shyllon, op. cit., p187-197.
[9] See p91

if you will – have been thrown overboard; whether for the preservation of the rest, that is the real question."

Summing up at the end of the hearing, the judges unanimously agreed that there had been no proven justification in throwing the slaves overboard, and granted leave for a new trial to settle the matter of liability for the loss of property, but not for the loss of life. This led Granville Sharp, who had witnessed the hearing, to write to the Lord Commissioners of the Admiralty asking that a prosecution of murder should be brought against the crew of the *Zong*, although Collingwood had himself since died. Sharp had long been involved with the anti-slavery cause, and now sent full details of the evidence presented, together with an impassioned plea to serve the cause of justice and humanity. Not only did the Admiralty take no action, but it failed even to reply. Sharp then complained to the Duke of Portland, effectively the prime minister at the time, yet even he ignored him. There is no record of a further trial, and it seems likely that the owners decided not to pursue their claim given that the recent hearing had found so strongly against them. By now, however, the details of the murderous affair of the *Zong* had become widely known, helped by Sharp's recent account published in many newspapers. Although by no means the single seed, the *Zong* case helped give rise to the Society for the Abolition of the Slave Trade, founded four years later by Sharp and others.

There are no other surviving records of the *Zong*, just as the ship's manifest and Ingram's instructions to Captain Henry Moore are all that are known about the *Blayds*. However, the logbook of the *Count Du Nord* does give some insight into the working life of a crew en route to Africa.[10] This ship had been built in France, and had originally been known as the *Oifeau*. At 700 tons, she was large for a merchant vessel, and had probably been taken as a prize in the recent war. The log records details of how the ship was handled in response to changing weather conditions, and sheds light on the daily toil of seamen, regardless of the nature of their voyage. The entries were made by Thomas Dixon, who was first mate to Captain James Penny.

Dixon's record starts on 28th September 1783, when the *Count Du Nord* set off from Liverpool under full sail in clear weather, driven by fresh breezes. These gave way by the start of October to "light airs inclinable to calms," during which time the crew began making rush mats that would later be

---

10 LRO, 387 MD 62.

joined to form a slave enclosure on the main deck. By 3rd October, south of Ireland, a light wind had returned, but was soon developing into fresh gales accompanied by a heavy swell. The crew were now busy hauling ropes, climbing the rigging, and reefing sails to reduce the area exposed to the force of the wind. As conditions became squally, the crew got the topgallant yards down and "struck" the topgallant masts to prevent possible damage. On the morning of the 4th Dixon recorded, "got the T.G masts on deck at 9. Landed the topsail at 10, reeft the F sail, and brought in too the main sail. Employed lashing the boom boats. Strong gales and clear weather." Gales continued into the 5th, and were accompanied by a heavy swell, but the weather then began to calm, allowing the crew to set the top and foresails once more. Later that day, however, the strong gales and heavy swell returned, accompanied by squalls. Late that afternoon Dixon noted, "landed the mainsail, fore and mizzen Ts [topsails]. At 6 struck T.G masts." By eleven that night, however, the crew were once again setting the foretopsail, by which time they were about a hundred miles off the north west coast of Spain.

Over the next five days, as gales alternated with fresh breezes, there was constant activity. Some crewmen worked the tackle to lift or lower loads, while others climbed the ratlines spliced into the shroud rigging, and edged along footropes suspended beneath the yards to reef or strike the sails. This was tough, dangerous work. As the ship pitched and rolled, there was nothing between them and the deck below but the ropes on which they stood. All sails were set when the weather calmed, including the topgallants and royals. At times, additional studding sails were hauled up on extensions to the yardarms to make maximum use of light winds, but these were soon lowered as stronger winds returned. On 11th October the air was filled with thunder and lightning, but by Sunday 12th the weather had once again calmed and all sails were set, including the studding sails, after which prayers were said on deck. By six that evening the *Count Du Nord* was reckoned to be 115 leagues east of Madeira and on her way towards Palma, but a heavy swell was developing "from every quarter of the compass." Dixon wrote on the 13th, "Light airs and cloudy attended with a heavy swell from the westward which caus'd the ship to rowl so much that we could not sett the small sails with safety." By midnight there was "Moderate and clear weather, the moon and starrs very bright at intervals." Next morning Dixon recorded, "People employed about the rigging making wind sails," as once again they set up all available canvass to make best use of the calm weather. By the 17th the *Count Du Nord* had passed east of the Canary Islands, and squalls were developing. The crew were now busy hauling on the ropes, lowering the topgallant, royal and studdingsails, but had to reset them next day as the weather again calmed.

The ship's carpenters were now making the platforms on which the slaves would have to lay.[11] Dixon's entry for 21st October shows "moderate and thick cloudy weather with heavy rain and squalls at times. Employed shifting the provisions in the Mens room &c to make room for the carpenters to fix platforms for the Negroes." He noted on the 23rd, "Squally with shower of rain. Saw a sail …brought too & spoke [to] the sail. She proved to be a Portuguese ship from Africa with slaves, but having nobody on board that could speak the language made sail without further particulars." Next day's entry recorded "Fresh Breezes and Dark Squally wr [weather] with showers of rain. At 3 carried away the Foretopsail yard. Employed getting it down and getting another one up." The carpenters continued building the platforms over the next few days, but were also engaged in making another foretopsail yard, probably as a new spare. Meanwhile, the ship's coopers were making tubs, some of which would be used as latrines for the slaves, and others for serving up their food. By the end of the month the log recorded, "A small bird like a Swallow or Martine has been about the ship for Several Days past and last night lodged in the Cabbin, by which we suppose our Selves to be nearer the land than our reckoning gives us." By now the crew were again weaving mats for the slave enclosure, while the carpenters were busy making bulkheads across the ship to separate the sexes. Dixon wrote on Sunday 2nd November, "this morning i hook'd a Shark, but the line being too small he broke it and made his escape. The small bird still continues about the ship – had prayers perform'd on board."

The next two weeks saw the *Count Du Nord* make steady progress over along the coast of Africa. Depth soundings were taken with a plumb line from 10th November, but even at a hundred fathoms length it did not reach the sea floor, and there was some concern that the ship had been carried off course by a strong current. Heavy rain, thunder and lightning on the 14th broke the relative tranquillity of the previous two weeks, and the crew got soaked as they climbed the rigging and lowered the topgallant, jib and staysails. By Tuesday 18th the carpenters had begun fixing the "barricado", or barricade, across the main deck to separate male and female slaves when they were allowed on deck. On Friday 21st the log recorded, "At 10 a poor Unfortunate Dolphin took the hook, Was Discover'd and Immediately hall'd in," and on the next day, "hook'd a Shark of 11 feet long, hall'd it in and he was Immediatley Cut up and Devour'd." Several days later the crew were busy scraping and cleaning the decks, and the carpenters were still working on the barricado. An entry on the 25th November noted, "from the Course Steer'd & the difference

---

11 Presumably Ingram & Co had decided that to wait for the platforms to be built in Liverpool would have delayed the voyage unnecessarily.

of Lattd. made have reason to suppose that we have had a strong northerly current." Dixon recorded next day, "People employed Scraping and Cleaning the Main deck. Was taken aback with a Squall from the Eastward. Shortened sail occasionally & laid her head the other way."

After two months at sea, and despite fears of drifting, Dixon was pleased to record, "Saw the Isle of Annabona bearing E 10 or 11 leagues." The crew were now employed scraping the quarterdeck and repairing the top and mizzen sails, while the carpenters were busy building a "round house" to provide shelter on the main deck. Meanwhile, it was noted that the sea had turned dark green, indicating shallower waters, but the plumb line still fell short of the bottom. Tensions were exposed during celebrations on the last day of November, no doubt fuelled by brandy or rum, when "A Small Dispute happened with the Scotch part of the Ships Company, being St. Andrews Day, which ended in Boxing." Land was sighted on 3rd December, and soundings were taken showing depths reducing from ninety fathoms at midnight to ten the following noon. Next day, the *Count Du Nord* finally dropped anchor just off Mallimba in seven fathoms of water.[12] However, she was not alone, as Dixon noted the presence of two other British ships and no less than thirteen from France. He added, "At 6 am Hoisted the boats out and sent the Docter on shore." Five hours later a local dignitary was on his way to be greeted, and Dixon noted, "At 11 the Boat Returned with Nambarnsa. Fird 3 saluts, 23 Guns, People Empd [employed] Unbending Sails, getting Goods out of the Houlds, &c." Next day, the pinnace was sent ashore, which later "Return'd with the Mafo and Several Other Black Gentlemen. Fir'd 3 saluts, 21 Guns."[13]

Over the next few days some of the crew were employed in the longboat taking empty butts ashore and returning with fresh water. It was at this point that the structure for the slave enclosure, or "deck house", was completed. First, various yards and booms were lashed between the masts to form a ridgepole, while others were lashed to the shrouds. Yet more spars were lashed between these, eventually forming a lattice structure for the roof and walls. Meanwhile, the mats were fastened together with rope yarn, and likewise attached to the latticework of spars.[14] The completed structure would soon enclose the slaves when they were brought on deck, while several of the crew kept their blunderbusses at the ready. Meanwhile, as others cleaned the ship or worked in the hold, Captain Penny was busy with his trading negotiations.

[12] This is now called Mayumba, which is on the coast of Gabon. It is a sad irony that, two centuries after the British government banned its citizens from trading in slaves, the practice still continues in some parts of Africa, particularly Gabon, where children from such countries as Nigeria, Togo, Benin, and Guinea are trafficked for forced labour (gvnet.com/humantrafficking/Gabon.htm).

[13] Pinnace - a large rowing boat with a single mast and sail.

[14] A description of the construction of deck houses was provided by Falconbridge, op. cit., p5-6.

However, no further entries were made in the log after 8th December 1783 until the end of the following May, when the ship was ready to set sail for the West Indies with 673 Africans on board, far fewer than the thousand or so that Penny had originally intended to buy.[15] Intense competition from the French had only enabled him to buy 701 slaves, but twenty-eight had died, including a young boy that day. Four more died over the next two days, followed by Daniel Broad, the twelfth crewmember to lose his life. Four more slaves died over the next week, each of them in the prime of their lives, followed by another seaman. No records were kept after 10th June 1784, but four years later Penny revealed that an outbreak of measles led to the deaths of about ninety slaves, despite a good stock of medicines and the best efforts of an experienced surgeon and three assistants.[16] Another record shows grim details of the *Count Du Nord's* final trade in the West Indies, when on 20th August Captain Penny "Deliver'd to Mr. Namdrams ship" 110 pairs of leg irons and handcuffs, and a large quantity of iron collars and chains.[17]

On the evening of 21st October 1783, while the *Count Du Nord* was heading towards West Africa, some of Liverpool's most distinguished inhabitants were gathering in Mr. Forshaw's Concert Room at the *Golden Lion* in Dale Street. The ladies were most beautifully attired in full-length dresses of silk or satin, which billowed out below the waist over hoops or pads, and almost obscured their fancy, slender high-heeled shoes. Some had gathered up their long natural hair into elaborately coiffured styles, while others wore their best powdered wigs, replete with ringlets and curls. No less elegant were the gentlemen in their colourful knee length coats, embroidered waistcoats, ruffled shirts, knee-length breeches, silk stockings, and shoes with gilt or silver buckles. Many had plaited their hair at the back, while nearly all wore short powdered wigs with cannon curls at the back and sides.

They took their seats shortly before seven, not for a recital of Bach or Handel, but for a most unusual event. The evening's entertainment was to be

---

[15] Revealed in evidence that was later given by Penny before a Committee of Enquiry, 13th June 1788, Parliamentary Accounts and Papers, Vol. XXIV, p37-38. Penny would have been mindful of the cost of staying longer on the coast to buy more slaves, since delays cut deeply into profits because of factors such as higher wage bills. He would also have wanted to reach the West Indies and sell his slaves before the hurricane season was fully underway.

[16] Ibid. As Penny stated, the deaths could not be attributed simply to overcrowding on this occasion. Nevertheless, any outbreak of disease would have spread like wildfire.

[17] Log of the Mampookata, LRO 387 MD 62. This followed on from the log of the Count Du Nord in the same book. The Mampookata was owned by James Penny.

The Nag's Head, Dale Street, with part of the Golden Lion shown behind the coach (Herdman, Pictorial Relics, Plate 24, undated, LRO)

a lecture about "every late and interesting discovery" concerning electricity, which was considered an "entertaining and important branch of Philosophy." And fascinating, indeed, was the entertainment, as Mr. Long gave one demonstration after another using his "extensive apparatus." Starting with his "amusing experiments on the attraction and repulsion of electricity," he went on to explain Benjamin Franklin's theories using "a number of new, striking, and most decisive experiments," including the best means of applying conductors to shipping, houses and other structures liable to strikes by lightning. The highlight of the evening, however, was Mr. Long's ingenious model of an "ELECTRIC EEL, really swimming in water, which rings bells, fires guns, gives shocks, &c." This was followed by an exhibition of "every mode of applying Electricity medically" using Mr. Nairn's New Patent Medico-Electrical Machine, "perhaps the most powerful and portable of any invented."[18] Yet, as Mr. Long concluded with a discussion about the most recent electrical discoveries, none could imagine how this curious phenomenon would later transform the world.

---

[18] *Williamson's Advertiser*, 16th October 1783. Mr. Forshaw's concert room at the *Golden Lion* was the most prestigious venue in Liverpool at that time.

Of greater concern to most, however, was the matter of health, which likewise awaited a better understanding. While Mr. Long and others promoted the medical potential of electricity, the general wisdom was that illness resulted from an imbalance in four bodily fluids or 'humours' – blood, phlegm, choler (yellow bile) and melancholy (black bile) – based on principles set out by Galen in the second century. Bloodletting was still considered a sound remedy for ridding the body of maladies and for general well-being, but there were no anaesthetics, and surgical instruments were not sterilised. Although there had been some advances, such as Harvey's discovery of the blood circulation system over a century earlier, there was still little understanding of human physiology. Microbes remained a mystery, and both medicine and chemistry were regarded, like electricity, as branches of philosophy. Inoculation against smallpox had become fairly widespread, but as there were yet no syringes, the process involved smearing infected pus into cuts made to the arm. Not surprisingly, many people distrusted the idea, even though it proved effective.

Claims for dubious remedies appeared weekly in the local press. For example, "The most racking tortures of the STONE and GRAVEL are immediately assuaged, and in a short time effectually removed by SWIFEN'S ELECTUARY, the most extraordinary efficacy of which has been proved in the numberless cases, and in long experience.[19] Price 2s 6d the small, and 5s the large pot." Some remedies were seemingly effective for a wide range of unconnected ailments, such as Pullin's Antiascorbutic Pills, which had the "sanction of sixty years experience for being the best purifier of the blood ever yet discovered." They seldom failed "to cure the most inveterate Scurvy, Leprosy, old Sores, King's Evil, Gout, Rheumatism, Piles, pimpled Faces, surfeits, and every other disorder arising from an impurity of the blood." For the gentler sex there were Pullin's Female Pills, which were a "sovereign remedy for the Green Sickness, and complaints peculiar to women. Price 1s the box, containing Forty Pills, sealed up with printed directions." Either product could be bought from druggist Mr. Teasdale, but were also available from stationers Hatton and Sibbald, or from Williamson the newspaper publisher. Likewise, Leake's Genuine Pills seemingly cured a range of diseases too numerous to specify. These were claimed to be "so justly Famous for their superior efficacy in curing every degree and symptom of the Venereal Disease, the Scurvy, &c. without confinement or restraint of diet, in an easy, expeditious, safe and secret manner. One small tasteless pill is a dose, its operation imperceptible, and requires no particular attention. In fifteen days it generally cures those

---

[19] Stone was the term used for gallstones, while gravel described the painful build up and passage of urea crystals in the urinary system. An electuary was a medicine mixed with honey or some other sweet substance (Oxford Dictionary of English).

cruel disorders; and where it fails in that time of perfectly restoring health, the patient has the happy assurance that he or she is at the eve of being so restored; let the malignancy be ever so great. It is an excellency peculiar to these pills to make directly to the complaining part, and enter into contest with the offending matter, which they suddenly dislodge and expel."[20]

Yet, despite the quackery, some remedies must have been effective. Nearly 12,000 patients were treated at the charitable Liverpool Dispensary during 1784, of whom it was recorded nearly 78 per cent were cured. A further ten per cent were given some relief, and only one per cent ended up in the infirmary. Other cases were described as "irregular" or remained under treatment at the start of the following year, but fewer than four per cent had died. During the six and a half years since the dispensary had opened, nearly 65,000 cases had been treated with similar rates of success, perhaps because the dispensary stuck to tried and tested herbal remedies.[21]

Church Street, 1798, showing the dispensary set back behind the railings and the tower of St. Peter's Church in the distance (Pictorial Relics, Herdman, Plate 25, LRO)

[20] *Williamson's Advertiser*, 13th November 1783. The paper ran the same advertisements in most editions.
[21] Percentages derived from raw figures given in *Williamson's Advertiser*, 6th January 1785.

In May 1784 surgeon William Moss published his survey of health in Liverpool, which reveals much about contemporary medical thinking.[22] This illuminating book was largely concerned with the causes of various illnesses, particularly regular epidemics of disease, the last of which had occurred during the previous autumn. He observed that, "Diseases, accompanied with symptoms of putrescency, more or less always occur and become epidemic in the autumn in Liverpool. They commonly commence about the end of August, and continue most urgent through September, or until we have some brisk gales …they are always attended with more or less of fever, sometimes with rashes, and frequently with affections of the stomach and bowels, accompanied with looseness and fluxes, as happened in the autumn of 1783." That particular outbreak produced a much greater number of complaints of dysentery, "bloody flux and agues" than normal, and was in his view linked to the excessive heat and closeness of the previous summer, which affected most of Europe. Moss added, "As this disposition of the fluids is the most unfavourable that can happen in the *small-pox*, the autumn becomes the least eligible season for inoculation." He also observed that diseases tended to be killed off during winter frosts, but were generally renewed during the spring. Moss therefore cautioned against allowing rooms to become too warm and cosy, and he also recommended bloodletting to relieve the effects of disease.

In the absence of any clear knowledge of the causes of infection, one theory was that bad air was to blame. Moss suggested that the town benefited from the westerly winds that cleared the air and limited the incidence of disease, although he also recognised the ill-effects that damp air could have for those with chest complaints such as asthma and consumption. He considered the effects of noxious smells produced by local industries, which many felt were a cause of illness. For example, he regarded the constant smell of pitch and tar to be "remarkable correctors of the air, and particularly calculated to obviate and resist the power and progress of many infectious diseases," as were the fumes from burning spoiled leaves at the 'tobacco house' by the South Dock. Smoke from coal burning, which although very sulphurous and harmful to those with chest complaints, was felt to have antiseptic qualities, and enabled the body "to resist the power, as well natural as accidental, of malignant contagious diseases." While the smell from the oil house, which processed whale blubber, was "in the highest degree nauseous", Moss did not think it injurious to health. The same was felt about the various copper works, kilns, tan yards, soap works, and the breweries that were "very numerous in this town." As for the salt works by the South Dock, which produced "amazing volumes of smoke", Moss believed that few would be affected beyond those

---

[22] *A Familiar Medical Survey Of Liverpool, Addressed To The Inhabitants At Large.*

in the immediate neighbourhood. Indeed, he reserved his ire for the town's numerous slaughterhouses, and suggested "their suppression in the heart of the town becomes an object that claims the attention and exertion of the magistrates."

Moss believed that, "The town is still capable of much improvement in its streets, which in the interior parts are too narrow. The footpaths are in general paved with small pebbles, which all strangers observe are rougher, sharper, and more uneasy to walk on than in other towns; the custom of laying flags not having yet generally obtained, although much to be wished for." However, the unhealthiest district was the area of the former tidal pool, which had since been filled in and built over. As Moss observed, "it lies low; the streets are wet, dirty and damp, and the foundations of the houses are for the most part damp, wet, and of course not very wholesome. Whitechapel and Paradise Street are the lowest situations in this or any other part of town, and are consequently supposed the least healthful on that account…The *common sewer* runs in the direction of these last two mentioned streets, which has generally esteemed an addition to their unhealthfulness. The disagreeable smell, which sometimes issues from it, chiefly creates this alarm; which is more imaginary than real, as the simple decay of any substance, whether animal or vegetable, is not so baneful to the human constitution as is commonly supposed." Moss explained, "A *common sewer*, it is true, is the receptacle of the dirt and filth of a town, and contains a heterogeneous mixture of animal and vegetable substances; chiefly the latter; and which, when confined for some time in hot weather (at which times the sewers are most disagreeable, being seldom or never so in cold seasons), ferment, and occasion the effluvium so offensive to the smell. However, it happens at the same time that a quantity of *fixed air* is in consequence of such fermentation thrown off, which so far from being injurious to the human body might, if conveyed in a more agreeable manner, be desirable and esteemed salutary. The *fixed air*, which is generated and sent off by this process, is of a somewhat similar quality with that which comes from the fermentation of beer or any other fermenting liquid or mixture. Fixed air is esteemed a powerful remedy in putrid diseases, and is introduced into the chambers of the sick, who are even, upon some occasions, suspended in the vapour of fermenting mixtures." This 'fixed air' from fermentation was later recognised as carbon dioxide, but the sewer's contents were in fact rotting and giving off methane, which would have proved even more injurious to the health of the patient.

The limits of understanding of the scientific community were further demonstrated by Moss in his belief that "it does not appear that the inhabitants of *Whitechapel* or *Paradise Street* have ever suffered in a single instance from any general disease that could be said to be occasioned directly by the effluvium from the sewer. *If any complaints or diseases have arisen from this cause, what were they? And what were the symptoms?*" To later generations the answer to his questions lay in the numerous cases of dysentery and fever that afflicted the population. Moss and his colleagues clearly saw no connection between the seasonal rainfall patterns and bad drainage that wreaked havoc on the blighted lives of the thousands who lived in damp, infested cellars. Nevertheless, he did offer one solution. "Could a reservoir of water be obtained at or near the upper part of this sewer, so that a proper stream of water might occasionally (three or four times, or oftner, in a week) in the summer season be forced through it, such means would contribute towards keeping it very sweet and clean."

Given the ability of the town to muster the resources to build a network of tidal docks, and similar investment in the growing network of canals in the region, there was clearly some complacency concerning a proper system of drainage. The same applied to the supply of clean water. As Moss noted, "The water with which the town is supplied for culinary purposes, and which is well-water brought from the east side of the town, is unexceptional in all respects, except the awkward mode of its being conveyed to the inhabitants, being sufficiently soft and pure.[23] The well water which is obtained from the heart of the town and near the river is hard and brackish, and therefore never used for these purposes." But, somewhat obscurely, he went on to suggest, "The native purity of the water contributes a good deal to the health of the inhabitants."

As for the living standards of the poor, Moss felt "The habitations of the poorest class in this, as in all large towns who depend upon daily casual support, are of course confined, being chiefly in cellars; yet the diet of the sober and industrious is wholesome and sufficient." This ignored the realities of living on the breadline in crowded spaces intended for storage that were almost entirely devoid of light or ventilation. Perhaps inevitably, some were unable to keep on the straight and narrow, leaving poorer neighbourhoods blighted by drunkenness and prostitution. As Moss lamented, "Humanity here solicits to draw a shade over the wretchedness of those who, deserting the tranquil prosperous paths of sobriety and virtue, exhibit a variety of misery in themselves and their families. Their children, most particularly, are objects of commiseration, who frequently from inattention and utter neglect droop under the chilling blights of parental inclemency, and are - melancholy reflection! – often entirely severed, thus prematurely, from society; or, which is yet more lamentable, are by the effects of vicious example early initiated and confirmed in habits of immorality and vice."

---

[23] This came from the Fall Well somewhere in the area of the present St. John's Gardens behind St. George's Hall. People could collect their own supplies, or buy it by the bucket load from water carts.

Moss's concerns about the proliferation of alcohol and its damaging effects on the community were shared by the authorities. Owners of inns and taverns on Liverpool's main streets had little reason to fear; it was the myriad of taprooms and alehouses in the poorer quarters that caused concern. Notices appeared each November in the local press when the annual round of licence renewal took place. Licensees were instructed in 1783 to report to the Exchange during early December, "when and where such persons as desire to have their licences renewed are to attend, prepared with sufficient sureties for their good behaviour and authentic testimonials of a fair character, the Magistrates being determined to prefer those persons whose past conduct has met with the approbation of the neighbourhood in which they live, and who shall be able to procure the best security for maintaining peace and regularity in their houses. And to accomplish so desirable a work as the suppression of such as are known to be disorderly, the Magistrates most earnestly call upon the gentry and principal inhabitants of every district of the town, and most strictly charge the Peace Officers to assist and promote their endeavours, by making a candid representation of them as soon as possible of those houses in particular which are not conducted in a regular, orderly manner, and therefore merit not to be again licensed."[24]

At around the same time as Moss published his report, the deplorable state of Liverpool's streets was exercising the minds of the parish vestry committee. A typically long-winded notice appeared in the local press for several weeks reminding people of their responsibilities, as stated by an Act of Parliament passed thirty-six years earlier. Townsfolk were told in no uncertain terms that they must, "sweep and cleanse, or cause to be swept and cleansed, all the streets, lanes and public places before their respective houses, buildings and walls, twice in every week at least, that is to says, every Monday and Thursday in the week, or oftner if occasion be, between the hours of two and five in the afternoon, to the end the dirt and soil in the said streets, lanes, and public places may be heaped for the scavengers to carry away, upon pain of forfeiting five shillings for every such offence or neglect. And no person or persons shall throw, cast or lay any coal ashes, wood ashes, rubbish, dust, timber, dirt, dung, filth, carts, carriages, tubs, or other annoyances to remain longer than the space of twelve hours …and he, she, or they are required to keep such soil, ashes, rubbish, dust, dirt, dung, and filth, or cause the same to be kept in their respective houses, backsides or yards until such times as the scavenger shall come by or near their houses or doors with his cart, wheelbarrow or other vehicle used for carrying away thereof." Inhabitants were also invited to bid for contracts for the disposal of waste, and also to "provide the lamps of this

---

[24] *Williamson's Advertiser*, 20th November 1783.

town with oil and all other materials, and to light, attend, dress, and repair the same."[25]

When the council eventually decided to make improvements to the town it had no plans for Whitechapel or Paradise Street. Despite the primitive sewer,

Castle Street looking towards the Town Hall or Exchange during demolitions in 1786 (Herdman Collection 1267A, LRO)

these streets had some advantage in being wider than the older, narrow streets that gave Moss most concern. The chief aim was to allow freer movement of people and traffic around Liverpool's hub, and so put an end to congestion. Work was begun in the middle of 1786 to widen Castle Street by pulling down the whole west side area to allow redevelopment, while several buildings were demolished to open up the area around St. George's church. No doubt to Moss's delight, the Shambles around the Exchange was also cleared of its butchers' stalls and slaughterhouses, which also allowed this civic building to stand alone in its own square. Some demolition and redevelopment would also take place along Chapel, Water, High and Dale Streets, but this was limited in scope, and further improvements were necessary a generation later. The council also planned to improve water supply and drainage, but its good

---

25 *Williamson's Advertiser*, 3rd June 1784, and other editions.

intentions were not carried through. Nor, too, did it make any improvements to roads and paving until early the next century.[26]

The local contest in the general election of April 1784 was attended by the usual flagrant acts of bribery, drunkenness and public revelry, and the occasional act of violence. Among the contestants was Colonel Banastre Tarleton, who was hoping to capitalise on his local hero status as Liverpool's own veteran cavalry commander in the recent war. Few could have known of his reputation for cruelty by which he had become known in America as Bloody Ban, or of his private boast that he had butchered more men and lain with more women than anyone else in the army. Tarleton was a handsome, flamboyant character who enjoyed driving in his horse-drawn gig around the town markets and kissing the stall women, although this did not make him popular with all. He made great play of having lost two fingers during the war by holding up his right hand and declaring, "These I gave for king and country."[27] He chose the green of his cavalry uniform as his election colour, which his bands of supporters displayed by wearing sprigs of vegetation, along with the usual flags and ribbons. However, Tarleton was up against Bamber Gasgoyne, who had topped the poll at the previous election and enjoyed the patronage of both the corporation and his influential father. Also standing was the recently ennobled Lord Penryhn, who as plain Richard Pennant had represented Liverpool for thirteen years until losing the previous election. Despite previous concerns about Penryhn's lack of loyalty and patriotism in opposing the war, such issues could now be laid to rest, while some felt he had been vindicated.

Given his generous financial backing, Gascoyne again topped the poll, despite memories of tough old bull and cabbage stalks at Childwall Hall.[28] However, second place was a much closer call, with Penryhn narrowly pushing Tarleton into third place by just thirteen votes. Two days later, *Williamson's Advertiser* reported that, "As soon as the numbers were declared, Col. Tarleton came forward, and in a short speech demanded a scrutiny, which he said, out of justice to his friends who had supported him during the election, he thought himself bound to require. The same was immediately granted, and is expected to last many days. The members were then chaired and carried through the principal streets of the town, amidst the acclamations of many thousands spectators, with many elegant colours and bands of music."

Clearly unhappy at the outcome, Tarleton and his committee accused his opponents of irregularities by depriving him of votes. By inference, some

[26] Brooke, op. cit., p386-387. (See Ch 10 below).
[27] A. Hochschild,, *Bury The Chains* (2006) p184.
[28] See p83 above.

freemen had been persuaded to break pledges of support for him, which meant they had cast "bad votes". But since bribery was practiced on all sides, and freemen could vote as they pleased, Tarleton was unlikely to prove his case. Letters of accusation flowed from both sides in *Williamson's Advertiser* on 22nd April. One claimed that, "Two hand-bills have been dispersed this day, which compel the friends of Lord Penryhn, tho' reluctant, to throw upon their authors the illiberal expressions they contain. The names of many worthy Freemen who had voted for his Lordship and Mr. Gascoyne were published … and the subscribed list of bad votes which the Colonel's Committee had at the same time delivered in to his Lordship's friends fully justified such action." Intent on clearing up the dispute without delay, Penrhyn invited the freemen named "to attend in person at his Lordship's Committee Room to furnish such information as might afford proper means of procuring justice for the reflections cast upon them." With this in mind, the "Friends of Colonel Tarleton" felt themselves on unsafe ground and were ready to back down. The Tarleton camp responded, "The list supposed to be referred to was printed merely to facilitate an inquiry into the votes, and contains a bare copy of names without the least doubt being expressed as to the validity of the vote of any person named in such list." Whatever the truth of the matter, the issue soon blew over, and both Gascoyne and Penrhyn took their seats in Parliament.

The journey to and from London was, however, an arduous business, and not without risk. The quickest option for men like Gascoyne and Penrhyn was to travel by horse, although the bulk of their luggage would have to be sent by coach and was liable to loss or theft. An alternative to such men of means was a light carriage such as a gig or post chaise, but this increased the risk of interception by highwaymen. A third option was a luxury 'diligence' coach, or a 'flying machine' that could reach London in forty-eight hours or less, allowing perhaps for one or two brief overnight stops at reputable inns. But, since few could afford their own transport, or the £2 15s for the journey by 'diligence', most travellers had to settle for a cheaper alternative. A recent innovation was the mail coach that left for London three days a week from the *Cross Keys* in Dale Street. Teams of horses were changed every twenty miles or so at coaching inns along the way, allowing a brief opportunity for relief and refreshment. After travelling through the night by the dim light of lanterns, exhausted travellers took breakfast in Derby, dined in Leicester, and stayed for part of the second night at the *Angel Inn* in Northampton, but had to leave at three the next morning.[29] 1s 6d would buy a private room, but most paid from nine pence to a shilling to share. More regular, however, was a

29 A.H. Arkle, *Early Liverpool Coaching*, Historic Society of Lancashire and Cheshire, Vol. 73 (1921) p18.

coach from the *Talbot* in Water Street, which went each day except Saturday, and arrived two days later at the *Swan With Two Necks* in Lad Lane.[30] Either way, inside travellers were charged £1 11s 6d for the full distance, while those outside paid a guinea, and children on the lap went half price.

Coaches also went to Warrington, Manchester, and Wigan, although the latter could also be reached by packet boat along the unfinished Liverpool to Leeds canal at a penny per mile. The Union Stage Coach Company operated a service between Liverpool and Lancaster four days a week, starting at half past six from the *Horse and Rainbow Inn.* Travellers could expect to take breakfast at Burscough Bridge near Ormskirk, dine at Mr. Cooper's at Preston, and arrive at Mr. Reynold's *New Inn* at Lancaster early the same evening, where connections to Kendal and beyond could be made. Luggage allowances were 14lbs for inside travellers, and 7lbs for those outside, with a penny surcharge for each additional pound.[31]

Most main routes were built and maintained by turnpike trusts in return for tolls, enabling coaches to travel at reduced speed overnight, but damage by iron-rimmed wheels caused frequent breakdowns and delays. However, minor roads were usually full of ruts and potholes, becoming quagmires in wet weather and passable only on foot, or by horse for those who could afford one. Although coaches were sprung and had padded seats and glass windows, inside passengers still swayed with the constant motion and felt the winter cold, while those outside froze on hard wooden seats as they hung on for dear life. However, other than walking, the cheapest form of travel was by goods wagon, which offered neither comfort nor speed. Wagons came to Liverpool from all over the country, and, having reloaded, picked up passengers at an allotted inn or tavern before setting off on the return journey.

Although all parts of Liverpool were easily accessible on foot, eight hackney carriages were licensed to operate from outside the Exchange, charging a shilling for any part of a mile. These generally carried four people who shared the fare. Alternatively, single passengers could hire a sedan chair at six pence for up to a thousand yards, or a shilling thereafter up to a mile. Several of the finer inns also operated a superior post-chaise for the private use of their clientele, although some people of wealth owned a light carriage or a two-wheeled gig. For journeys to outlying villages such as Everton, West Derby or Garston, the hire of a coach and two horses at 12s 6d a day was often the best solution. However, most of Liverpool's vehicles were carts carrying items of cargo between ships and warehouses. Charges for the services of 'carmen', or carters, were strictly regulated according to load and distance. For example, a load carted up to

---

[30] *Gore's Directory*, 1781. The next directory did not appear until 1788.
[31] *Williamson's Advertiser*, 30th October 1783.

six hundred yards weighing no more than nineteen hundredweight cost four pence, but this increased with distance.[32] 7s 6d would hire a cart, two horses and the driver for seven hours from October to March, while nine shillings for ten hours was the standard rate for the rest of the year.[33] Both coachmen and carters faced fines for jumping queues, leaving vehicles unattended, speeding, or mounting footpaths, and notices of these offences appeared regularly in the local press. Fatal accidents were not unknown, as in the case of a man tragically killed early in 1785. Soon after the event, *Williamson's Advertiser* misleadingly reported that, "Yesterday William Hesketh Esq., Coroner of this town, and a very respectable Jury, sat on the body of John Bradshaw, killed by means of one John Bibby, a waterside carter, carelessly driving his cart." Hopefully, Bradshaw's corpse was not subjected to the weight of twelve good

Looking east along Dale Street from the top of Water Street, with the town hall on the left, showing the variety of transport around 1790 (Herman Collection B1110, LRO)

men and true, but Bibby certainly felt the full weight of the law as he was found guilty of manslaughter and committed to stand trial at the Lancaster Assizes. The magistrates also issued a warning by stating, "The offence of carters riding on their carts, and driving them furiously thro' the public streets, is so frequent that we think it our duty on this melancholy occasion to take notice that there are cases where the accident of death to an individual, thro' the misbehaviour of the carter, is no less than *Murder* and punishable by death."[34]

---

[32] There are 20 hundredweights to a ton.
[33] *Gore's Directory*, 1781.
[34] *Williamson's Advertiser*, 17th February 1785.

With the recent introduction of special mail coaches, Liverpool was receiving post on a daily basis, although the volume was small and some letters still arrived by dispatch rider. The post office was a house in John Street, which had a letterbox for outgoing letters and a hatch for the postman to collect and deliver mail. *Williamson's* and *Gore's Advertisers* both depended on postal correspondence for much of their content, particularly from London and abroad. Indeed, there was now barely a week that went by when readers would not find news of a strange mode of transport that excited observers wherever it was demonstrated. Since the first ascents by the French Montgolfier brothers in 1783, ballooning was becoming something of a craze, although many of the first flights were unmanned. This was the case in Liverpool in June 1784, when an experimental flight was witnessed by most of the townspeople. *Williamson's Advertiser* reported that "its form was in some sort that of a double pyramid, flat at the top. The bottom only was open; and from the center within the balloon were suspended two tin trays, one above the other, in which a quantity of cotton wick and spirits of wine were placed. These were no sooner set on fire than the machine began to ascend, tho' rather obliquely. It passed almost close to the battlements of St. Thomas's church steeple, and thence proceeding and ascending very gradually, affording a new, grand and pleasing sight to a vast multitude of people whom curiosity had drawn together, till it came near the Mount, when a gust of wind driving it much on one side, the flaming spirit, which was spilled, set fire to the whole, and it soon burned out and fell down in the field beyond St. James's Walk."[35]

Just over a year later, however, the Italian balloonist Vincenzo Lunardi came to Liverpool, having gained notoriety in London by making the first manned ascent in Britain in September 1784. Lunardi's balloon was 33 feet across, and was made from oiled silk woven as a giant Union Jack.[36] This was filled with hydrogen, which took several hours, as the gas was produced by dissolving small pieces of iron in sulphuric acid in an apparatus under the balloon.[37] His ascent in Liverpool the following July was to take place from the fort by the river to the north of the town. Spectators would be "accommodated at Five Shillings the first, and Half-a-Crown the second places, to see the process of filling his Balloon, and his ascension into the atmosphere." In the meantime, "the balloon with all its appendages" was to be exhibited, attended by Lunardi, "to gratify the curiosity of those ladies and gentlemen who may favour him with their company, by explaining the principles of aerostation, and the construction of his balloon. Admittance to the Pantheon, One Shilling."[38]

---

[35] *Williamson's Advertiser*, 1st July 1784.
[36] See www.fiddlersgreen.net/AC/aircraft/Balloon/info/info.htm
[37] Henry Cavendish discovered hydrogen by this method in 1766. Although he wasn't sure of what he'd found, he realised that the gas was extremely light and flammable.
[38] *The General Advertiser*, 14th July 1785.

On the morning of the 20th, while ticket holders took up their ringside seats, crowds had assembled nearby to witness a midday launch. But the occasion was dampened by heavy rain with thunder and lightning, which made inflating the balloon out of the question. By one o'clock, however, the rain had been cleared by fresh variable winds, perhaps aided by the collective will of the throng. Hoping the wind would calm, Lunardi announced his intention to ascend later that afternoon, but the crowd was now clearly getting impatient. Anxious not to disappoint, a gun was fired at two o'clock to signal the filling of his tethered balloon. By five, Lunardi decided his balloon was sufficiently inflated, and a second gun was fired to signal the start of the ascent. As *Williamson's Advertiser* later reported, he now got into the "boat" or basket, "but upon trying the rising power, the weight was found too great, he immediately threw out his two boxes of ballast, but still the balloon was deficient in levity. He therefore slung down his pistols, his speaking trumpet, and even his cork jacket. About six the last gun was fired, and he rose majestically in a perpendicular direction – for a moment an awful silence took place, but this immediately gave way to loud and repeated bursts of applause – again all was hushed, and he gracefully waved his hat, and saluted the spectators." The balloon then started heading north-west over the river towards the sea, "which occasioned much anxiety." Luckily, it was blown back, then turned north and kept going for fifty minutes before landing ten miles away at Symmonds Wood. By that time Lunardi had thrown everything else out of his basket to keep himself suspended, including his hat, coat and waistcoat.[39]

Despite the ticket sales, *Williamson's* reported that Mr. Lunardi was very much out of pocket, and on Thursday 4th August invited generous public subscriptions for a second ascent. Improvements were to have been made to both the balloon and the "apparatus used for filling it," but there were now scurrilous rumours circulating about Lunardi's integrity. The following week's paper reported, "Highly enraged at the scandalous reports propagated that it was not his intention to ascend, Mr. Lunardi went to the fort on Monday afternoon fully determined not to stir from thence till he had entirely vindicated his reputation." Early on Tuesday 9th, "while the fierce blasts of the north west wind howled dreadfully in his ears," he decided to risk another ascent. Having rigged up sails as windbreakers, Lunardi started filling his balloon at midday, by which time the winds had eased. By three o'clock it was fully inflated and he got into the basket, but "no sooner did the people see the balloon tost to and fro, than, injudiciously apprehending the danger greater than it really was, they rushed forward with the utmost violence; and, as if seized with sudden frenzy, every hand was extended to catch hold of the balloon, nettings, &c. In

---

[39] *Williamson's Advertiser*, 21st July 1785.

vain did he cry out 'Let me go, for God's sake, let me go!' they still persisted to keep him down by holding the hoop to which the boat was fastened. The balloon was burst in two places, several of the cords loosened, and the netting almost torn to pieces. At this moment he seemed giving way to despondency, and, lying down, cast up his eyes and exclaimed 'Oh, Dio!' But in a moment, as if started by a sudden recollection, he arose, drew his hanger [sword] and threatened to cut every hand that should touch the hoop. Awed by his intrepidity, they let go, and he ascended with astonishing celerity. No sounds but those of affright and horror were heard, when the beholders saw him rising in the air, with the rent netting and broken ropes streaming in the wind, and the boat leaning so much as to terrify everybody with the idea of his tumbling out; yet so perfectly composed was he as to fasten the strings and salute the company by waving his flag. In about four minutes he disappeared behind a cloud, but soon was in view again, and continued to be seen at intervals for near half an hour." Lunardi landed near Tarporley in Cheshire about twenty miles away, having been dragged in his "boat" some considerable distance before finally coming to a halt.[40]

Lunardi had first come to Britain as secretary to the Neapolitan ambassador in London. Clearly, he wished to make his name as a pioneering aeronaut, but not without making his exploits pay. Whether scripted by himself, or by his friend and sometimes co-balloonist George Biggin, the plea for donations went out in *Williamson's* on the same day as the account of his second intrepid exploit. It read, "To the Ladies of Liverpool, if generosity is more than a name, and if true courage is not become worthless in the eyes of the Fair Sex, your hearts must be alive to the full power of sensibility! Your tenderest feelings must have been excited by the dangers Mr. Lunardi went through on Tuesday last. Did a female behold him and not shed tears? Then prove that the sensations of pity have sufficient power in your hearts to awaken more noble ones; it has never been doubted that you possess generosity. Now let it publickly appear, for virtue ought never to hide her head. Act like yourselves, and sacrifice some trifling gratifications, to the sublime pleasure of rewarding merit and intrepidity." The writer revealed himself as a friend of Lunardi and appealed for generosity by concluding, "Let each lady suppose that her favoured lover speaks in this address. She will then have a double interest in doing a good action, and every pulsation of the heart will be to her a tribute of praise for listening to the advice of the ladies' most devoted humble Servant, PHILO."[41]

The public appetite for spectacle, however, was more usually satisfied by the repertory company of the Theatre Royal in Williamson's Square. As in

---

[40] *Williamson's Advertiser,* 11th August 1785.
[41] Ibid, 11th August 1785.

London and elsewhere, acting was more about scoring points with the audience than with realism. Performances were expected to be over the top, the more over-dramatic the better. Standing on a stage lit by candles in footlights and chandeliers, wearing gaudy costumes and thick greasepaint before brightly painted scenery, actors always played to the crowd. Audiences showed little discipline, treated serious plays as pantomime, and pelted actors with rotten fruit and vegetables if they were unhappy with the performance. The company's repertoire, a year or so before Lunadi's appearance, included a comic opera, *The Maid of the Mill.* Mr. Mattocks played *Lord Aimsworth,* Mr. Quick played *Sir Harry Sycamore*, *Lady Sycamore* was played by Mrs. Pitt, and *Fanny* by Mrs. Kemble.[42] But to give the audience its money's worth the company also performed the *Masque of Comus* that same night. A few weeks later, however, a far greater spectacle was planned. *Williamson's* advertised the celebration of a "Jubilee in Commemoration of Handel, in which will be introduced The Passions, an Ode to Music by Mr. Collins. The stage will be formed into an orchestra; the scene represents the principal Aisle at Westminster Abbey, and the whole performance conducted as it was at the Theatre Royal, Covent Garden, last winter." This was to be followed by "Shakespeare's admired Play called *The Winter's Tale,* or *The Royal Shepherd*, as altered by Garrick into three acts, and performed at both theatres in London, with universal applause." The company then went on to perform *The Tempest* during mid-August, followed each evening by a "*Grand Masque between Neptune and Amphitrye*." To these performances were added a short dramatic piece called *The Toy Shop* and a farce called *Barnaby Brittle*. The evenings were concluded with fireworks consisting of three "Vetrical Wheels, four Brilliant Suns, and fifteen Chinese Trees." As always, tickets for the pit cost 2s 6d, and boxes 3s 6d, but cheaper tickets could be had in the gallery at a shilling each.[43]

But many found the odd spare shilling or two unaffordable, and were unable to make ends meet. In October 1784 many of the journeymen joiners went on strike, and there were reports of several "unlawful meetings in the adjoining fields and waste lands, where they enter into combinations and conspiracies for the express purpose of compelling their employers to raise their wages, contrary to law." The strikers also stood accused of having "the audacity to repair to premises, where others their fellows where peaceably and quietly working for their employers, and have intimidated them from continuing to work, using threats and menaces to those who refused to accede to their unlawful purposes."[44] But perhaps more troubling than conspiracies to strike, however, was a recent spate of thefts of fine plate from the houses of wealthy

---

42 *Williamson's Advertiser,* 12th August 1784.
43 Ibid, 24th June 1784.
44 Ibid, 14th October 1784. Journeymen were craftsmen who had served an apprenticeship.

merchants and professional men. This was followed by a break-in at the Exchange, when two ceremonial maces and other pieces of gold and silver regalia worth several hundred pounds were stolen. Apparently, the villains made their escape through an upstairs window by means of a rope attached to the staircase, but no one could work out whether they had entered by ladder or had concealed themselves in the building earlier that day with the help of an insider.[45]

Three months after the joiners' strike, eight men pleaded guilty to the crime of "combining to raise their wages" and were ordered to pay a £10 fine or face twenty days imprisonment. However, these men got off very lightly and could count themselves lucky. At the same magistrates' session William Parr was convicted of cheating a shopkeeper of money and sentenced to seven years transportation, although he was a noted swindler. Thomas Battman was sentenced to two floggings and six months imprisonment merely for stealing raw cotton, but William Hughes got just three months for stealing a quantity of rum. Roger M'Ginnis was sentenced to a public whipping in the market place for stealing "a piece of money and wearing apparel", yet for the theft of a mere few items of clothing Mary Wearin got three months imprisonment and was whipped on her release. Justice was unpredictable, the same sentence being given to John Roberts for stealing some silver plate and other valuable articles.[46] Six months later Thomas Beyendoff got three months and a flogging for "stealing and embezzling a quantity of gold and silver," yet James Moor was given seven years transportation for cheating a man of three watches. Among the lesser items of theft were pieces of old rope oakum and flax, a handkerchief, a looking glass and some wheat, each resulting in confinement or a flogging. Joseph Timms ended up in the pillory and was publicly whipped for stealing 8s 6d, while Elizabeth Murphy was "exposed" at the Old Fish Market Stones with the label "Receiver of Stolen Goods".[47]

Meanwhile, with the renewed influx of mainly unskilled migrants to Liverpool, the pressure on the parish rates, or local taxes, continued to grow. At their Easter vestry meeting in 1786 the parish committee agreed to build four houses "for the relief and accommodation of casual sick poor, whose several disorders may happen to be such as to render them unfit objects to be took into a publick Hospital."[48] The committee decided at the same time to raise funds through public subscriptions to build a "lunatic hospital" close to the infirmary, and a new range of almshouses was built

[45] *Williamson's Advertiser,* 28th October 1784.
[46] Ibid, 3rd February 1785.
[47] Ibid, 11th August 1785.
[48] Easter Vestry meeting, 18th April 1786, Peet, op. cit., p287.

soon after in St. Mary's Lane on Mount Pleasant. However, when the committee decided to tax dock duties to help raise funds, the corporation, as dock trustees, refused to pay. The parish committee then responded by adding a rate on corporation tolls for markets and fairs. At this point the corporation retaliated by demanding arrears of rent for the workhouse site to cover the fifteen years since it had been built. Although the legal responsibility for poor relief did indeed rest with the parish, it was clear that the wealthy corporation was unwilling to pay its share of the burden, and a dispute began that would last another twenty years.

Among the many immigrants who sought new opportunities in Liverpool was James Irving, but his skills were much in demand. His father was an innkeeper in the village of Langholm about twenty miles north of the Scottish border, but Irving clearly felt his future lay elsewhere. Despite having no connections with the sea during childhood, Irving studied to become a ship's surgeon, and in April 1779, at just nineteen, he had gained his certificate.[49] This by no means put him on the same footing as a qualified surgeon doctor, but given the state of medical knowledge the distinction was perhaps meaningless. Although the skills of a 'sawbones' were much in demand on a man-of-war or privateer, a surgeon on board a merchant vessel was more likely to be applying leeches, remedies and poultices rather than the blade of a knife or saw. Irving first sailed from Liverpool early in 1782 to Tortola in the Virgin Islands, a trip he repeated on his next voyage. He then completed two slaving voyages to Africa and Jamaica, after which he married Mary Tunstall. They made their home in College Lane between Paradise and Hanover Streets, but in May 1786 Irving sailed again for Africa on board the *Jane*.[50]

As he sat in his cabin in August 1786, the pain of separation from his young wife was almost too much to bear. Even before his ship had left the Mersey three months earlier James had written, "Oh! For a volley of these endearing embraces that I have so often received, I could at this moment almost smother you with caresses. I feel as if I was dismembered or deficient of a part essential to my existence."[51] Now, as the *Jane* lay off the African coast, Irving was anxious to send his third letter since his arrival

49 S. Schwarz, *Slave Captain: The Career of James Irving in the Liverpool Slave Trade*, p11-12.
50 Ibid, p13.
51 Letter dated 19th May 1786, quoted in Schwarz, op. cit., p109. Irving must have asked the river pilot to deliver it.

at New Calabar a month earlier via the ship *Ally* that was due to sail next day. Writing to "My dearest Mary", Irving was soon admonishing his young wife for apparently not writing. "The Princess Venus from Liverpool arrived here a week ago, and I had the mortification to find that you had neglected the opportunity. I readily excused you when I heard that the Vulture sailed the same day but had called at Lisbon. She is not yet arrived, but when she does I flatter myself that what she will bring me will sufficiently compensate for my disappointment, but still my girl you should not have neglected or overlooked any opportunity." Irving reported that trade was "dull" and slaves were selling at an "exorbitant price", which would delay his leaving for the West Indies for another two months. He continued, "The above intelligence you may communicate to any person concerned or acquainted with our employers, as the captain's letter may miscarry, and the least intelligence of the ship will be very satisfactory. I'm all impatience for the arrival of the Vulture and Golden Age, as you certainly have put two or three sweet billets on board each of them. You cannot be a stranger to the comfort and pleasure they will afford to an affectionate husband, who is toiling away with the sweat on his brow in a pestiferous climate under a vertical sun."[52]

Happily for Irving, the *Ally* was itself delayed, and he was able to add a postscript telling her that he had since received two letters from her via Captain Amoss. The *Jane* finally left New Calabar early in October and arrived in Barbados forty-six days later, having lost forty-eight of its six hundred slaves.[53] Irving wrote hurriedly, "a boat hath just arrived with the letters … bless you my dear girl for your kind letter."[54] He wrote from Tobago ten days later, intimating, "I'm nearly wearied of this unnatural accursed trade and think (if no change of station takes place) when convenience suits of adopting some other mode of life." Irving noted that, being a French island, he was unlikely to be able to buy anything with his British currency, but would try to get "Brother George" the parrot he wanted, and would "bring the returns of my voyage home in my pocket." Irving ended, "I think I'll desist, as our black cattle are intolerably noisy and I'm almost melted in the midst of five or six hundred of them."[55]

---

[52] Letter dated 13th August 1786, quoted in Schwarz, op. cit., p109-110.
[53] This represents 8%. In addition, seven crew members died before reaching Liverpool, and five deserted in the West Indies.
[54] Letter dated 22nd November 1786, quoted in Schwarz, op. cit., p112. Many ships traded directly with the West Indies, and were not involved in slavery. Mail was taken by these vessels to Barbados, the most easterly Caribbean island, enabling letters to be collected or sent from there by incoming slave ships before continuing on to other islands.
[55] Letter dated 2nd December 1786, quote in Schwarz, op. cit., p112-113.

Irving's letter went by schooner to Barbados, where it joined mail frm other Caribbean Islands before being taken to Liverpool by whatever vessel was next to sail. He himself was next reunited with Mary early in 1787, and would make two further slaving voyages as a surgeon before embarking on a fateful voyage as master of his own ship. Meanwhile, merchants and abolitionists were soon to become locked in a struggle that would only be resolved twenty years later.

At about seven o'clock on Sunday morning 23rd December 1787, John Silvester Dowling, Patrick Burne, Harry Neale and a man named Hunter broke into the lodging house of Mrs. Graham on Rose Hill Street armed with pistols and knives. While one stood guard below, three of the men rushed upstairs and burst into the bedrooms of Mrs. Graham and her two lodgers, Mr. Matthews and Mr. Harrison. The three startled victims were met with violent and "horrid imprecations of death" if they resisted, and were firmly tied to their beds before the robbers set about rifling their belongings. Before long, Mrs. Graham's best silverware, plus nineteen guineas, a quantity of silver coins, a pair of pocket pistols, various letters and papers, and other sundry items were in the robbers' possession. But the most precious part of the haul were various money bills with values of ten and thirty pounds, and even larger bills of exchange for sums between one and three hundred pounds belonging to Mr. Harrison.[56] Being on the very edge of Liverpool, the four men were soon making their escape along the country lanes to the north east of the town, well ahead of any watchmen in pursuit who could be stirred that early Sunday morning.

This was an audacious crime indeed, and was one that suggested the perpetrators chose both their victims and the location with care. But any thought of disguise seemed to have escaped them, as two were to find to their cost. Details of the robbery were published next day in *Williamson's Advertiser*, and a reward of up to eighty pounds was offered for information leading to the arrest of the men. Dowling and Burne were identified early next January, as both had lodged with Ann Eaton in Frederick Street on the other side of the town. Burne had been working as a 'lumper' unloading cargo on the docks, and had last been seen with a large sailor's knife. Described as having "lusty" short curled hair and a fair complexion, he had been wearing a light drab coat

---

[56] *Williamson's Advertiser*, 24th December 1787.

mended at the elbows, a brown velvet waistcoat and white breeches. Dowling had worked as a painter, and was a short, thin man with long black hair tied in a pigtail, but was partly bald. He wore a dark brown double-breasted frock coat with yellow buttons, a brown velvet Manchester waistcoat, brown corduroy breeches, "salt and pepper" coloured worsted stockings, and "very large pair of plated buckles much worn, so as to have the appearance of lead." Both were from the Dublin area, but less was known about their accomplices, except that both were Irish, and that one had skin pitted by smallpox and a missing front tooth.

By the time these details were published in Liverpool Burne and Dowling had been arrested in Bristol, from where they intended to sail to Dublin. One was arrested in his bed, while the other ran and nearly made his escape. Unfortunately for him, however, the peace officer's dog followed in hot pursuit, attached its jaw to his leg, and "detained him till he was properly secured."[57] After their packages had been found to contain much of the stolen booty, Burne and Dowling were taken back to Liverpool for identification, and then on to Lancaster to await trial towards the end of March. The matter was an open and shut case, and the two men were sentenced to death, along with John Bradburn and Mary Chadderton for burglaries in Manchester, and Francis Hancock for merely stealing ribbons in Lancaster.[58]

Executions for crimes committed within the county were normally held in Lancaster, but on this occasion the Liverpool authorities were determined to set an example "by deterring the guilty from a perseverance in the commission of such crimes as must bring on them an ignominious punishment." A scaffold and gallows were hastily built, and were assembled on the morning of 31st March outside the Water Street gaol and draped in black. One writer described the scene of the preparations as "truly awful", adding that it would stamp a lasting impression on any that viewed it. This was to be Liverpool's first execution since 1715, and every effort was made to publicise it. By mid-morning fifteen to twenty thousand people thronged the area around St. George's dock to view the awful spectacle. Shortly after ten, the prisoners, with arms bound, were led along a passage from the gaol, attended by a clergyman, the under-sheriff, and several "proper officers." As they climbed the scaffold the crowd fell silent, and prayers were said for the doomed men. These were their last moments

---

[57] *Williamson's Advertiser*, 21st January 1788.

[58] Ibid, 31st March 1788. Others were more fortunate. James Jones was committed to seven years transportation for stealing cotton from Richard Arkwright's mill near Manchester, as was Robert Towers for stealing plate in Ulverston, while John Redford got fourteen years for stealing cotton and linen handkerchiefs from a bleaching ground in Cheetham. Meanwhile, for abusing a six-year-old girl, John Greenless was sentenced merely to stand in the pillory for an hour, and then to be imprisoned for a year. Such was eighteenth century justice.

before each was hooded and the nooses placed around their necks. Seconds later they were "launched into eternity," their bodies twisting and writhing, before finally coming to rest in death. [59]

---

[59] *Williamson's Advertiser*, 7th April 1788.

Chapter Six

In May 1787, four years after the case of Gregson v. Gilbert concerning 'cargo' jettisoned from the *Zong*, the Society for Effecting the Abolition of the Slave Trade was formed in London. Among its founding members was Granville Sharp, who had tried unsuccessfully to have the crew tried for murder. But it would be Thomas Clarkson who would prove its most active foot soldier. Clarkson had won first prize in 1785 for an essay in a Latin competition at Cambridge, where he had studied divinity. Clarkson could expect a promising career in the Church of England following his literary honour, but the subject of the competition - whether it was lawful to make slaves of others against their will - changed his life and set him on a course from which he would seldom be diverted. His research had affected him deeply, and he found himself consumed as he made his way home to London from Cambridge. As he later recorded, "I sat down disconsolate on the turf by the roadside and held my horse. Here a thought came into my mind, that if the contents of the Essay were true, it was time some person should see these calamities to their end."[1] After translating his work into English and adding to its contents, Clarkson sought a publisher in London and was introduced to James Phillips at his printing shop in Lombard Street. Clarkson agreed that Phillips should print his book, and was introduced to Granville Sharp and others who told him about their long-standing campaign against slavery. He set about investigating the trade from those with first hand experience of its horrors, and soon found an ally in Parliament when he presented William Wilberforce with his findings.[2] But this was just the start of a long quest for the facts that might persuade others of the evils of slavery, during which he was to ride over thirty thousand miles gathering information. Clarkson would work long into the night by dim candlelight writing copious notes of conversations with seafarers to use as evidence, and would often be haunted by his findings.

Years later, when Parliament had finally been persuaded to outlaw the trade, Clarkson would write an account of the struggle for abolition in which he shared his reflections on a living nightmare. He began with the tragedy played out daily on the plains of Africa. "Who is that wretched woman, whom we discover under that noble tree, wringing her hands and beating her breast, as if in the agonies of despair? Three days she has been there at intervals to look and to watch, and this is the fourth morning, and no tidings of her children yet. Beneath its spreading boughs they were accustomed to play – but alas! – the savage man-stealer interrupted their playful mirth, and has taken them

---

[1] Thomas Clarkson, *The History of the Rise, Progress and Accomplishment of the Abolition of the African Slave Trade* (1808) Vol. 1, p210.
[2] Ibid., p241-242.

forever from her sight….But let us leave the cries of this unfortunate woman, and hasten into another district. And what do we first see here? Who is he that just now started across the narrow pathway, as if afraid of a human face?

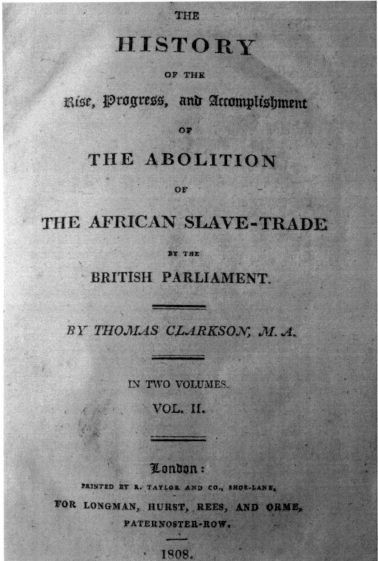

THE

HISTORY

OF THE

Rise, Progress, and Accomplishment

OF

THE ABOLITION

OF

THE AFRICAN SLAVE-TRADE

BY THE

BRITISH PARLIAMENT.

BY THOMAS CLARKSON, M.A.

IN TWO VOLUMES.

VOL. II.

London:

PRINTED BY R. TAYLOR AND CO., SHOE-LANE,

FOR LONGMAN, HURST, REES, AND ORME,

PATERNOSTER-ROW.

1808.

Title page of the second volume of Clarkson's history of the abolition movement (LRO)

What is the sudden rustling among the leaves? Why are those persons flying from our approach, and hiding themselves in yon darkest thicket? Behold, as we get into the plain, a deserted village! The rice field has been trodden down around it. An aged man, venerable by his silver beard, lies wounded and dying near the threshold of his hut. War, suddenly instigated by avarice, has just visited the dwellings which we see. The old have been butchered, because unfit for slavery, and the young have been carried off, except such as have fallen in the conflict, or have escaped among the woods behind us."

"And whither shall we go now? The night is approaching fast. Let us find some friendly hut, where sleep may make us forget for a while the sorrows of the day. Behold a hospitable native ready to receive us at his door! And now let us give ourselves to repose. But why, when our eyelids are but just closed, do we find ourselves thus suddenly awakened? What is the meaning of the noise around us, of the trampling of people's feet, of the rustling of the bow, the quiver, and the lance? Let us rise up and inquire. Behold! The inhabitants are all alarmed. A wakeful woman has shown them yon distant column of smoke and blaze. The neighbouring village is on fire. The prince, unfaithful to the sacred duty of the protection of his subjects, has surrounded them. He is now burning their habitations, and seizing, as saleable booty, the fugitives from the flames. Where shall I find words to express properly their sorrow, as arising from the reflection of being parted for ever from their friends, their relatives, and their country?" Is no justice manifest in the land, where the prince, unfaithful to his duty, seizes his innocent subjects, and sells them for slaves? Are no moral evils produced among those communities, which make war upon other communities for the sake of plunder, and without any previous provocation or offence?"

When Clarkson turned his mind's eye to the ships' owners, masters and crews, he reasoned, "The counterpart of the evil is to be seen in the conduct of those who purchase the miserable slaves in their own country, and convey them to distant lands. Do they experience no corruption of their nature, or become chargeable with no violation of right, who, when they go with their ships to this continent, know the enormities which their visits will occasion, who buy their fellow-creature man, and this, knowing the way in which he comes into his hands, and who chain, and imprison, and scourge him? Do the moral feelings of those persons escape without injury, whose hearts are hardened? And can the hearts of those be otherwise than hardened, who are familiar with the tears and groans of innocent strangers forcibly torn away from everything that is dear to them in life, who are accustomed to see them on board their vessels in a state of suffocation and in the agonies of despair, and who are themselves in the habit of the cruel use of arbitrary power?"

Finally, Clarkson considered the fate of the captives in the West Indies, where their torment continued unabated for the rest of their miserable lives. "We are to see them examined, handled, selected, separated, and sold. We are next to see them labouring, and this for the benefit of those to whom they are under no obligation, by any law either natural or divine, to obey. We are to see them, if refusing the commands of their purchasers, however weary or feeble, or indisposed, subject to corporal punishments, and if forcibly resisting them, to death. Hence the whip – the chain – the iron collar. Hence the various modes of private torture, of which so many accounts have been truly given. Nor can such horrible cruelties be discovered so as to be made punishable, while the testimony of any number of the oppressed is invalid against the oppressors. And lastly, we are to see their innocent offspring, against whose personal liberty the shadow of an argument cannot be advanced, inheriting all the miseries of their parents' lot."[3]

There were just twelve members at the first meeting of the Abolition Society at James Phillip's print shop on 22nd May 1787, including Clarkson, Sharp and Phillips himself. Their number grew rapidly, and branch committees were established in most of Britain's ports and other major towns, but its aim would be limited to banning the trade rather than slavery itself for fear of taking on

---

[3] Clarkson, op. cit., p11-19. In selecting from Clarkson's writing, I have taken the liberty of some minor rearrangement of extracts from his original text, while keeping to his original words.

too many vested interests. The Society set about collecting evidence, printing and distributing pamphlets on a nationwide scale, and soliciting the support of politicians, bishops and others of influence. It soon had widespread support, including that of first minister William Pitt, who sent representatives to Paris to invite the French government to join Britain in banning the trade. Pitt's friend and political ally, William Wilberforce, was to steer a bill through Parliament, and there seemed little to stand in its way. But this enthusiasm was not shared in Liverpool, which now conducted the lion's share of the trade, so much so that local abolitionists felt unable to set up a branch of the Society for fear of reprisals.[4]

While the rest of the Society's founding members were busy organising their campaign from London, Clarkson went off to Bristol, which was more or less equal to London in the volume of its slave trade. While gathering evidence for a parliamentary enquiry, Clarkson met Alexander Falconbridge, who had recent experience as a surgeon on several voyages to Africa, but had left the trade on grounds of conscience. Not only did Falconbridge prove to be a mine of information, but he also agreed to join Clarkson on his fact-finding mission. They arrived in together Liverpool in September 1787, and within a day or so had seen a shop display of handcuffs, shackles, thumbscrews, and a speculum oris used in force-feeding, and bought one of each. They were soon introduced to Robert Norris, an ex-slave ship captain who had become a merchant in a different line of business, and met him several times at his own house. Norris had written a book on the slave trade, and

A detail from Clarkson's book showing drawings of wrist and ankle shackles, a thumbscrew and a speculum oris (LRO)

---

4 Although slavery accounted for only around 10% of Liverpool's trade by the 1780s, figures given by Lamb, *Volume and Tonnage of the Liverpool Slave Trade, 1772-1807*, in Anstey and Hair, op cit., p93, suggest that Liverpool's share of the British slave trade was almost two-thirds in 1789, growing to 78% in 1794. Lamb's only gives figures for Liverpool, London and Bristol, but these three ports now accounted for nearly all of Britain's slave trade.

was working on another about the despotic king of Dahomey, who made no scruple of abducting his own subjects.[5] Norris had learned the local language, enabling him to find out much that would otherwise be hidden to the ordinary seaman, and he related what he knew to the visitors. He provided evidence of the mistreatment of seamen, and proposed encouraging the trade in African produce rather than its people, all of which seemed a most promising start.

Clarkson and Falconbridge took rooms in the *King's Arms* in Water Street, and were soon the focus of attention when the purpose of their visit became known. While some merchants and captains calmly tried to justify their trade to them, others were more provocative. Clarkson recalled, "The King's Arms became now daily the place for discussion on this subject. Many tried to insult me, but to no purpose. In all these discussions I found the great advantage of having brought Mr. Falconbridge with me from Bristol, for he was always at the table; and when my opponents, with a disdainful look, tried to ridicule my knowledge, by asking me if I had ever been on the coast of Africa, he used generally to reply, 'But I have. I know all your proceedings there, and his statements are true.' " [6] However, Clarkson was soon thinking about changing lodgings or dining in private, but decided against both to avoid being seen as "unmanly". He knew that by listening to their arguments he could learn how the traders would later put their case, and he tried hard not to get ruffled. He also felt that many local people supported them and showed them warmth. However, as Clarkson lamented, "I could never get any one to come forward as an evidence to serve the cause. There were, I believe, hundreds of persons in Liverpool, and in the neighbourhood of it, who had been concerned in this traffic and who had left it, all of whom could have given such testimony concerning it as would have ensured its abolition. But none of them would now speak out. Of these indeed there were some who were alive to the horrors of it, and who lamented that it should still continue. But even these were backward in supporting me. All they did was just privately to see me, to tell me that I was right, and to exhort me to persevere: but as to coming forward to be examined publicly, my object was so unpopular, and would become more so when brought into Parliament, that they would have their houses pulled down if they should then appear as public instruments in the annihilation of the trade." Clarkson also noted, "that these fears were not groundless appeared afterwards; for Dr. Binns, a respectable physician belonging to the religious society of the Quakers ... was near falling into a mischievous plot, which had been laid against him because he was one of the subscribers to the Institution

---

[5] Robert Norris, *A Short History of the African Slave Trade*, 1787; *Memoirs of the Reign of Bossa Ahadee, King of Dahomey* (1788). Dahomey lay in the region which is now modern Benin.
[6] Clarkson, op. cit., p387-388.

for the Abolition of the Slave Trade, and because he was suspected of having aided me in promoting that object."[7]

Before long, Clarkson and Falconbridge concentrated on getting information from seamen arriving off slaving vessels, many of whom seemed more willing to help. Some started visiting them at the *King's Arms*, which increased the hostilities of the trade's supporters, and the tavern owner was put under pressure to get rid of his troublesome tenants. The two men now took lodgings in Williamson's Square, where their investigations uncovered many tales of hardship and misuse. Since many seamen refused to serve in the slave trade, whether because of its cruelties or the personal risks involved, a common means of recruitment was worked between landlords, crimps and captains. Having been enticed into debt, and then incarcerated in the debtors' tower at the Water Street gaol, the seamen were bought out by crimps and sold to awaiting ships. Clarkson wrote, "How many have I seen, with tears in their eyes, put into boats and conveyed into vessels, which were lying at the Black Rock, and which were only waiting to receive them to sail away."[8] Clarkson also saw for himself the "sickly and ulcerated crews" returning from their voyages, many of who ended up in the infirmary or wandering the streets in a state of destitution.

During his investigations into the treatment of sailors on slaving voyages by brutal captains and their officers, Clarkson found strong evidence of the murder of a steward named Peter Green while off the coast of Africa. On checking the ship's muster roll, he found that another fifteen of the crew had died during the voyage. He intended reporting the case, but was told that the magistrates, "when applied to for warrants of apprehension, would contrive to give notice to the officers to escape." He was also told, "that so many in the town were already incensed against me, that I would be torn to pieces, and the house where I lodged burnt down if I were to make the attempt."[9] He added, "The temper of the many interested people of Liverpool had now become still more irritable, and their hostility more apparent than before. I received anonymous letters entreating me to leave it, or I should never leave it alive. There was certainly a time when I had reason to believe that I had a narrow escape. I was one day on the pier head with many others looking at the same little boats below at the time of a heavy gale. Several persons, probably out of curiosity, were hastened thither. I had seen all I intended to see, and was departing, when I noticed eight or nine persons making towards me. I was then only about eight or nine yards from the precipice of the pier, but going from

---

[7] Clarkson, op. cit., p388-390.
[8] Ibid., p394
[9] Ibid., p407.

it. I expected that they would have divided to let me through them; instead of which they closed upon me and bore me back. I was borne within a yard of the precipice, when I discovered my danger; and perceiving among them the murderer of Peter Green, and two others who had insulted me at the King's Arms, it instantly struck me that they had a design to throw me over the pier head; which they might have done at this time, and yet have pleaded that I had been killed by accident. There was not a moment to lose. Vigorous on account of the danger, I darted forward. One of them, against whom I pushed myself, fell down. Their ranks were broken, and I escaped, not without blows, amidst their imprecations and abuse."[10]

Clarkson and Falconbridge soon left Liverpool, taking with them only hearsay evidence, and unable to secure anyone willing to testify before an enquiry. Far more had been gained in London and Bristol, but the reliance on slavery had declined in both those ports. Liverpool's abolitionists were highly critical of Clarkson for a lack of diplomacy and tact, claiming that he was not sufficiently prepared to engage with merchants and captains. They also criticised his many contacts with ordinary seamen, believing this to have led to the level of hostility that emerged. Physician James Currie even wrote to the Abolition Society's London Committee complaining of Clarkson's behaviour, especially his reliance on evidence from the "lowest class of seamen." Currie went on to add, "Nor is this all: conceiving that every enormity might be expected from the masters of vessels who could conduct such a trade, they have listened eagerly to the accounts of their cruel usage of the seamen, and to the rumours of the dreadful barbarities of various kinds, with which the ears of the credulous have been abused. That there is no foundation for any of these reports I am, however, far from asserting…. When they assert that the slave trade is the destruction of two thousand seamen annually, and that the masters of the ships employed are, in general, men of such barbaric dispositions as to inflict unprovoked cruelties on their crews, they bring forward positions, which in my opinion, cannot be proved, and which, I doubt not, may be opposed by reference to the facts."[11] The outraged Currie acknowledged that he was well acquainted with many slave captains, believing them to be men of integrity and "fair character". In his view, their merchant employers were men of "liberal education, enlightened understandings, and very much distinguished." Dismissively, Currie believed "A sailor is seldom a nice casuist. He takes a trip to Guinea because the wages are very good; and, if he lives, rises perhaps first to be a mate, and afterwards a master. In this station, a few more voyages

---

[10] Clarkson, op. cit., p409-410. It may be that, given that this happened in daylight and in public view, this was not a serious attempt at murder rather than a warning to scare Clarkson off. Whatever the case, Clarkson was a very tall, well-built man, which would have helped him considerably.
[11] Quoted in F.E. Sanderson, *The Liverpool Abolitionists,* in Anstey and Heir, op. cit,. p209-210.

enable him to live at home, and to take shares in vessels commanded by younger adventurers. His children inherit his fortune, his commerce, and his opinions of the slave trade; in which, perhaps, they are deeply engaged before they have ever heard that a doubt is entertained of its lawfulness."[12]

Other Liverpool abolitionists shared Currie's relationship with men of social standing, and were each concerned to maintain their position within the town by avoiding the wrath of friends and neighbours. Most felt that abolition should be a gradual process to avoid damaging Liverpool's economy, and were therefore regarded by the London Committee with suspicion. However, they were committed to the abolition cause, and shared radical, non-conformist religious and political views that already distinguished them from most of their class. Several made literary contributions, most notably William Roscoe, but each was careful to do so anonymously, such was the need for covert action. Having attacked the slave trade in his poem *Mount Pleasant* some years previously, Roscoe now did so again with *The Wrongs of Africa*, which was published and distributed by the Abolition Society. In 1788 he also wrote *A General View of the African Slave Trade, Demonstrating its Injustice and Impolicy; with Hints Towards a Bill for its Abolition.* Although Roscoe condemned slavery, he argued for phased abolition and compensation for traders. He also called for the ending of the East India Company's monopoly to allow Liverpool merchants to compete, but his pamphlet still caused much local concern. Raymond Harris, formerly a Jesuit, but now working as a clerk to a slave merchant, replied with his *Scriptural Researched on the Licitness of the Slave Trade, Showing its Conformity with the Principles of Natural and Revealed Religion, Delineated in the Sacred Writings of the Word of God.* As the lengthy title suggests, Harris argued that slavery was perfectly compatible with religious teaching and even had the backing of divine authority. Roscoe replied, again anonymously, with *A Scriptural Refutation of a Pamphlet Published by the Rev. Raymond Harris,* but Harris's work received local accolades, and the Corporation awarded him a hundred pounds in recognition of his services in defending slavery. When Harris died the following year, his obituary described him as "a great scholar and a very worthy man ….He died in peace and charity with all men."[13] This was not a view shared by the Reverend John Yates, whose anti-slavery credentials were well known through his sermons at the Unitarian chapel. Nor, too, by Edward Rushton, who for a time published a newspaper, *The Liverpool Weekly Herald,* which was largely devoted to the abolition cause. But, perhaps the most useful contribution was

---

[12] Sanderson, *The Liverpool Abolitionists,* op. cit,. p210. The word 'nice' was used here to mean simple or ignorant, while a casuist is someone who applies unsound reasoning to moral issues (Oxford Dictionary of English).

[13] Cited in G. Cameron and S. Crooke, *Liverpool – Capital of the Slave Trade* (1992) p43.

that of William Rathbone, who supplied Clarkson with the muster rolls of fifty-two Liverpool slave ships showing the high rate of mortality among seamen, evidence that was soon to prove very useful at a parliamentary enquiry.

Soon after leaving Liverpool, Alexander Falconbridge wrote an account of the slave trade, which was published by the Abolition Society.[14] Early on, he described a typical scene at Bonny, a busy slaving town just east of the Niger Delta with which he was familiar. There were often around fifteen mainly English ships anchored in seven or eight fathoms of water in the River Bonny about a mile from the town. Their masters went on shore as soon as they arrived to invite the local dignitaries on board and offer dashes, or gifts of cloths, brandy and wine, while making enquiries about the state of trade. Two kings, Norfolk and Peppel, controlled the local trade. They lived in large huts in Bonny, surrounded by stores containing produce exchanged for slaves. They also received a duty on every slave sold by local traders, which was collected by their officials. Although elected, these kings were absolute in their power, and were assisted by a small group of high-ranking people who styled themselves "parliament gentlemen", an office generally held for life. These also expected gifts, and often went on board the ships to be treated. Only then was permission given for trading to begin, which was usually expected to last about three months. Slaves arrived on board most days, their numbers varying and unpredictable, their price dependent on demand.

On his last visit to Bonny Falconbridge had spoken with a local black trader about the effects of the American war on trade. He was told that the *Mosely Hill* from Liverpool was the only ship to arrive for three years, enabling Captain Ewing to buy slaves at a premium. When asked what effect this had on the local economy the trader replied, "only making us traders poorer, and obliging us to work for our maintenance." Falconbridge added that, when told that English Quakers were for abolishing slavery, the trader had said "it was a very bad thing, as they should then be reduced to the same state as they were in during the war, when, through poverty, they were obliged to dig the ground and plant yams."[15] For Falconbridge this was no bad thing. He had also been to Angola during the war, and discovered that kidnapping had stopped, which had restored "peace and confidence."

Falconbridge found out through interpreters that the majority of captives were abducted hundreds of miles inland, but care was taken to prevent Europeans from discovering how this was organised. Victims were forcibly taken to markets about two hundred miles from the coast, where several thousand might find themselves on sale at any one time. Many measured the distances they travelled

14 A. Falconbridge, *An Account of the Slave Trade on the Coast of Africa* (1788).
15 Ibid, p9.

by "the revolution of several moons", and were treated with great cruelty, some perishing along the way. They were sold to traders from the coast, who regularly came up rivers with their trading goods in convoys of twenty to thirty canoes. Each would buy from forty and two hundred slaves, about a third of whom were women, and prices depended on intelligence about the level of demand on the coast, and therefore how much the coastal traders could charge the Europeans. Once bundled into large canoes, the captives' ordeal continued on long journeys to the coast under heavy guard, and with no protection from the torrential rains that occurred almost daily. Falconbridge had himself witnessed between twelve and fifteen hundred being brought back to a coastal trading station, with each canoe carrying thirty to forty people. However, some operations were on a far smaller scale involving the kidnapping of one or two people at a time, after which the perpetrators took captives in small numbers directly to the traders on the coast.[16] The methods used often involved some form of trickery, and even the traders themselves were not immune from being taken captive.

Although told that most captives were taken in wars, Falconbridge rejected this theory due to the lack of battle scars he had observed as a surgeon. He also learned that inland of the Windward Coast, where there were apparently no slave markets, ships' crews were themselves sent up river to trade for slaves at villages along the way. It was alleged that these captives were being sold as punishment for crimes, but Falconbridge was sceptical, believing them also to have been kidnapped. This method was slow and less productive, with crews sometimes returning to their ship with less than a dozen slaves after having been away for two or three weeks.

Having reached the trading posts, the captives were cleaned and oiled with palm oil. The ships' captains would inspect them minutely when they were ready for sale, checking teeth, eyes, limbs and joints, and rejecting any with signs of infirmity or disease. Traders at New Calabar were often known to put unsold slaves to death, which occasionally happened in sight of captains to persuade them to buy any that remained. But some would have welcomed death, knowing their ordeal had only just begun. For now they were handcuffed and shackled in pairs and sent on board ship, where the men and boys were placed in their separate compartments, while women and girls shared a smaller third section. Once below deck, and locked in by a heavy iron grating, only the females and boys were released from their bindings. Yet there was very little room to move

---

[16] One small trader, Antera Duke, recorded his activities in pidgin English in a logbook, which was later discovered and transcribed. Duke belonged to the Efik ethnic group, which was a major supplier of slaves operating from Old Calabar. His name also appears in the account book of the *Dobson*, a Liverpool ship buying slaves from Old Calabar in 1769 over a period of nearly six months. During this time, Duke sold 37 slaves in small numbers spread out over 14 separate visits, but was one of about thirty traders selling to the ship. By the time he began his diary in 1785, Duke had acquired enough wealth to build a house made from materials imported from Liverpool, and he regularly entertained captains. See J. Reader, *Africa: A Biography of a Continent* (1997) p393-395.

about, especially as more arrived, since the compartments were largely taken up by the platforms built halfway between the deck and ceiling, and extending towards the centre.

Falconbridge provided an extreme example of a 235-ton ship carrying between six and seven hundred slaves, so that "the publick may be able to form some idea of the almost incredible small space into which so large a number of Negroes were crammed." Its width across the beam was just twenty-five feet, and its ninety-two-foot length was divided into four compartments. A storeroom measured fifteen feet in length, the men's room forty-five, and the boys' twenty-two, while the women and girls shared a space no greater than ten feet long. The slaves were so crowded in such a small area that "they were even obliged to lie one upon the other," and nearly half died during the Atlantic crossing. Even at the lower figure, six hundred slaves would have needed about 4,500 square feet had they been laid out shoulder to shoulder, head to foot, but there were only about 3,300 available, including the space provided on the raised platforms.[17] It may have been possible to cram six hundred people, providing they sat permanently with bended knees. However, the height between decks on most ships was little more than five feet, so that the available headroom for the majority would have been less than half that, once the thickness of the platforms is taken into account. In short, the situation must have been one of sheer hell, although few ships would have been packed as tightly as this to lose so many slaves.[18]

Most deaths were caused by the flux, or dysentery, accompanied by fevers. Given that slaves were so crammed, and had no means of hygiene, this is not surprising. Toilet facilities consisted of conical buckets measuring about two

[17] This assumes the average slave was five feet tall and eighteen inches broad, giving a minimum requirement of 7.5 square feet each. Deck space works out at about 1925 square feet (25 width by 77 length) but this does not take into account the curvature of the ship. Falconbridge gave the breadth of the platforms as 8 or 9 feet, but they were usually about five feet ten inches, just enough to accommodate all but the tallest slaves. Having broader platforms suggests space may have been maximised by cramming two rows of slaves opposite each other, each with his or her feet wedged roughly between two people facing. Using the higher figure, they would have provided about 1386 square feet (77 by 9 by 2), providing a total area of 3311 square feet for the slaves to share.

[18] It made no commercial sense to crowd a ship to such extent, given that every slave had a monetary value. The loss of half the cargo would be a very damaging financial blow to the merchants, and could even mean financial ruin. At 250 tons, the Badger's dimensions must have been similar to those given by Falconbridge. Captain Potter took 415 slaves on board who would still have been dreadfully overcrowded, but 94% survived the voyage. Klein and Engerman, *Slave Mortality on British Ships, 1791-97*, in Anstey and Hair, op. cit. p118, show that average mortality was 5.65%, but varied according to region. It was lowest on ships trading on the Gold Coast, averaging 2.75%. Further west, from the Ivory Coast to Senegal, it averaged about 3.4%, and from Congo and Angola, 3.65%. However, the highest rates were in the Bight of Biafra, including Bonny and New Calabar, where mortality averaged 10.56%. Although these figures are for a period following legislation to regulate the number of slaves ships could carry (see below), Klein and Engerman believe that this made little difference to mortality rates, since these were linked more closely with local conditions and the health of captives once they reached the coast (p122).

feet across the base and one across the top, and twenty-eight inches in depth. Since they were shackled in pairs, and bodies lay everywhere across the deck, any man with an urgent need to reach the nearest bucket was unlikely to make it in time. Quarrels frequently broke out as people stumbled and stepped on one another, and many had to give in to the indignities of relieving themselves where they lay. Infections soon spread, especially as slaves had skin from their shoulders, elbows and hips rubbed off by constant friction with bare planks as the ship pitched and rolled. In the worst cases, even the flesh was worn away down to the bones, the effects of which were almost always fatal.

Seasickness added to problem, particularly during rough weather, when it was necessary to close the ventilation ports and hatches to keep seawater out. Falconbridge explained that during his last voyage, "I was frequently a witness to the fatal effects of this exclusion of the fresh air…Some wet and blowing weather having occasioned the port-holes to be shut and the grating to be covered, fluxes and fevers among the negroes ensued. While they were in this situation, my profession requiring it, I frequently went down among them, till at length their apartments became so extremely hot as to be only sufferable for a very short time. But the excessive heat was not the only thing that rendered their situation intolerable. The deck, that is, the floor of their rooms, was so covered with the blood and mucus which had proceeded from them in consequence of the flux, that it resembled a slaughter-house. It is not in the power of the human imagination to picture to itself a situation more dreadful or disgusting. Numbers of the slaves had fainted; they were carried upon deck, where several of them died, and the rest were, with difficulty, restored. It had nearly proved fatal to me also. The climate was too warm to admit the wearing of any clothing but a shirt, and that I had pulled off before I went down; notwithstanding which, by only continuing with them for about a quarter of an hour, I was so overcome with the heat, stench, and foul air, that I had nearly fainted; and it was not without assistance that I could get upon deck. The consequence was that I soon after fell sick of the same disorder, from which I did not recover for several months."[19] Over a quarter of the slaves died during the voyage. Under such conditions the captives' tempers were not unnaturally frayed to breaking point, the threat of insurrection constantly lurked, and there were frequent exchanges of violence. Only when calmer conditions returned could the routine of taking the slaves on deck be resumed. This enabled them to get some relief as the crew did what they could to clean and scrub their compartments below.

At about eight in the morning, when the weather allowed, the slaves were taken above and confined within the deck house of lashed wooden spars and rush matting. A long chain, secured to the deck by ringbolts, was passed

---

[19] Falconbridge, op. cit., p24-25.

through the men's shackles, securing them to the woodwork. The slaves were washed down with seawater, then fed on a gruel of boiled rice, beans, corn or yams, which was mixed with a little palm oil and served up in tubs. If slaves lost their wooden spoons they were given no replacements, so disease spread as they used their hands to feed themselves. Food and water were rationed if supplies ran low, leading to further squabbles, and slaves were frequently beaten or whipped as a warning to others if they became too dominant. While on deck, they were made to dance to music to give them exercise, the cat-o'-nine tails being applied to any that were not energetic enough. At about four in the afternoon, the slaves received a second meal and were then taken down for the night.

Meanwhile, the seamen fared little better, and the percentage that died often exceeded the mortality rate of their captives. Apart from catching the 'bloody flux' that afflicted so many slaves, seamen had no immunity from tropical fevers. They were constantly exposed to the wind and the rain, and had to sleep on the main deck under tarpaulins during the middle passage. Their food was little better than that of the slaves, and if alcohol was allowed, this was usually sold to seamen at an exorbitant price, along with anything else they might need. Many were beaten or whipped by the masters or officers, and ended up deserting in Africa or the West Indies.

On arriving in the West Indies, the slaves were cleaned and oiled before going to auction, although they were often sold by 'scramble', a fixed price having been set beforehand. Describing the process, Falconbridge wrote, "On a day appointed, the negroes were landed, and placed together in a large yard belonging to the merchants to whom the ship was consigned. As soon as the hour agreed on arrived, the doors of the yard were suddenly thrown open, and in rushed a considerable number of purchasers, with all the ferocity of brutes. Some instantly seized such of the negroes as they could conveniently lay hold of with their hands. Others, being prepared with handkerchiefs tied together, encircled with these as many as they were able, while others, by means of a rope, effected the same purpose. It is scarcely possible to describe the confusion of which this mode of selling is productive. It likewise causes much animosity among the purchasers, who, not infrequently upon these occasions, fall out and quarrel with each other. The poor astonished negroes were so much terrified by these proceedings, that several of them, through fear, climbed over the walls of the court yard and ran wild about the town, but were soon hunted down and retaken." Falconbridge described another scramble on board a ship moored at Port Maria in Jamaica, when the female slaves especially, "clang to each other in agonies scarcely to be conceived, shrieking through excess of terror at the savage manner in which their brutal purchasers rushed upon them and seized them." Sick slaves were usually sold off at five or six dollars a head, and many did not survive long thereafter. But, for those that did, the ordeal was far from over, their fate being to toil from dawn to dusk, day after endless day, under the constant gaze of plantation taskmasters. But first they were branded with red-hot irons to identify ownership, and then they were 'seasoned' over several months to break their spirit. Punishments were brutal, and any who attempted insurrection was severely flogged as a warning to others.

But human suffering was far from the mind of John Tarleton, brother of Colonel Banastre ('Bloody Ban, the Butcher') when he met with William Pitt on 3rd February 1788. Since Tarleton and Backhouse was one of Britain's leading slaving partnerships, he and others believed they had much to lose if their trade was to end. While on business in London, therefore, Tarleton hoped to gain the first minister's confidence and support by presenting slavery as a virtue. He learned instead of Pitt's intention to back his friend, William Wilberforce, who was determined to bring an abolition bill before Parliament. Tarleton wrote to Mayor Thomas Earle of Liverpool, who was also a leading African merchant, and then to his brother Clayton, explaining how he had attempted to convince Pitt, "that should Mr. Wilberforce's plan for the prohibition of a farther importation of Negroes into our islands take place, or that even any unnecessary & injudicious instructions should be adopted, that the consequence would be total ruin." Tarleton continued, "I concluded by assuring him that I did not hesitate in saying that I had not the least doubt but that the African Merchants of Liverpool would prove to the satisfaction of every unprejudiced mind in the House of Commons that, so far from the African Trade being founded in blood and a series of fraud, violence and oppression on the coast of Africa, we should be able to prove the reverse of our opponents positions, that the basis of it was founded on humanity, and justice to the Natives. His whole reply to these immense considerations, particularly with respect to his situation as the Minister of a great commercial Country whose existence depended on the resources her Trade afforded both to her Marine and her finances, was that his present sentiments were for the *Abolition of the Slave Trade*, and that I had authority from him to communicate them immediately to my friends in Liverpool ... and I am sorry to add that agreeable to my letter to the Mayor yesterday that I think we shall have little chance of success, or that the African Trade will remain on its present footing, except we can prove that it is not carried on with that shocking unhumanity that is imagined by all ranks of Mankind out of doors."[20]

After consulting the Liverpool merchants, the mayor wrote to Tarleton

[20] Quoted in F.E. Sanderson, *The Liverpool Delegates and Sir William Dolben's Bill,* Historic Society of Lancashire and Cheshire, Vol. 124, 1972, p61-62.

asking him to stay on in London to head a delegation. Tarleton was shortly joined by four others. James Penny had captained the *Count Du Nord* four years earlier, and was now a wealthy slave merchant. More surprising was Robert Norris, who had now changed sides after having been considered a good catch by the abolitionists. Archibald Dalziel had worked for eight years on the coast of Dahomey, and had since unsuccessfully tried his hand in merchant ventures. Finally, John Matthews had been an agent on the Windward coast. His book, *A Voyage to the River Sierra Leone*, had recently been published to coincide with the current abolition debate. Although it was not wholly unsympathetic towards indigenous customs, appended to the text was a long letter in which he justified the slave trade and contradicted some of his previous observations. He claimed that during the American War, when the slave trade was virtually suspended, there was such a glut of slaves on the coast that many were slaughtered. He also claimed that Africa was so over-populated, its numbers doubling every thirty to forty years, that there would be even more wars and bloodshed in the region than he had described[21]

William Pitt had originally wanted to introduce a resolution in the House of Commons to condemn the slave trade, which, if successful, would lead to a bill for its abolition. However, Wilberforce argued for an official enquiry first, knowing there were some in Parliament, particularly the Lords, with strong interests in the trade. Pitt agreed to this, and a privy council committee of the House of Lords was established on 11th February to investigate the trade. But things did not go according to plan, and Liverpool's delegates were soon making an impact. The 'African interest' argued from the start that slavery and inter-tribal warfare were endemic in West Africa. They denied that kidnapping took place, or that wars were waged for the specific purpose of supplying the Europeans, but claimed that prisoners of war and criminals had long been made slaves.[22] They soon laid emphasis on the despotism and cruelty of some African rulers, and particularly on the conditions in the kingdom of Dahomey, about which Robert Norris had written. Norris claimed to have seen two piles of human skulls outside the gates of the king's palace, "like those of shot in

---

21 Sanderson, *The Liverpool Delegates*, op. cit., p64-65. Reader, op. cit., p284 & 289, suggests Africa has never been overpopulated; if anything, it has suffered from under-population.

22 There is no doubt that slavery existed within Africa, both before and after the Europeans arrived, and that Arabs were also heavily involved. It took many forms, some more benign than others, and was more prevalent in some regions than others. M. Johnson, The Atlantic Slave Trade and the Economy of West Africa, in Anstey and Hair, op. cit. p27-29, cites a study of slaves freed in America and then taken to Sierra Leone. 11% had been found guilty of crimes; 7% had been sold as a result of debts, usually incurred by others; 7% were sold by relatives or superiors; 30% had been kidnapped; and 34% taken in war. Johnson also points out that the Islamic Fulani people were perpetually at war with their neighbours, enslaving any who refused to embrace their faith, and often supplying the Europeans.

an arsenal." The heads of recently killed victims apparently lined a passage leading to his apartments, and the roof of the palace was decorated with yet more skulls. Norris added, "and when the King means to make War, it is an Expression in use to say, 'The Palace wants Thatching'."[23] At least a thousand people a year were sacrificed, and the greatest carnage was said to occur when the annual poll tax was collected. Slaves rejected by traders were put to death, and if the king felt he had enough European goods, more would be sacrificed. One Liverpool trader even claimed he had "now and then, but rarely, met with an Instance of a Slave shewing Signs of Terror on being sold. Nine out of Ten rejoice at falling into our Hands."[24]

By arguing that the European slave trade therefore saved people from barbarities, the Liverpool delegation were effective in winning over the support of many on the committee. Clarkson recalled, "Some of them began immediately to be prejudiced against us. There were others who even thought that it was unnecessary to proceed in the inquiry, for that the Trade was actually a blessing." They now doubted the assertions made by the abolitionists, and the Bishop of London questioned whether Falconbridge's account, which had been published as a pamphlet and sent to the enquiry members, was worthy of belief.[25] Various witnesses for the slavery lobby pressed their case home. John Barnes stated that during his eight years on the coast of Senegal he learned that people convicted of theft, adultery or witchcraft at fair trials were customarily sentenced by slavery. Richard Miles said he had never known the local Fante tribe to be at war or engage in kidnapping during his sixteen years on the Gold Coast.[26] Within weeks, the credibility of the abolitionists had been dashed, and John Barton of the London committee wrote to William Roscoe warning, "It is very doubtful whether anything will be obtained at all. Since the matter has been before the privy council, I understand much cold water has been thrown upon it, and some who were once friendly to our cause have advised that the business should not be brought before Parliament at all."[27]

---

23 *Report of the Lords of Committee of Council*, published 28th March 1789, Parliamentary Accounts and Papers, Vol. XXVI No. 646, Part 1, p15, and quoted in Clarkson, op. cit. p480.

24 Quoted in Sanderson, *The Liverpool Delegates*, p68. John Reader, op. cit., p394-395, notes that torture and execution were customary punishments used by the Efik people of the Calabar region. Slaves were sacrificed to placate wrathful gods, and their spirits were believed to accompany elite members of society on their journey to the afterlife. In 1786, Antera Duke (see p139, footnote 16 above) recorded the events at a wake. He noted, "About 4 am. I got up; there was a great rain, so I walked to the town palaver house and I found all the gentlemen here. So we got ready to cut heads off and at 5 o'clock in the morning we began to cut slaves' heads off, fifty heads off that day. I carried 29 cases of brandy, and 15 calabashes of chop [food] for everybody, and there was play in every yard in town." Antera Duke wrote more about human sacrifices than he did about his sales of slaves.

25 Clarkson, op. cit. p481-482.

26 Sanderson, *The Liverpool Delegates*, p67. Miles had been governor of Cape Coast castle at the time of the *Blayd's* first slaving voyage (see p.99 above).

27 Quoted in Sanderson, *Liverpool Delegates*, p68.

Gradually, however, the tide began to turn, despite the shortage of witnesses with experience in Africa willing to support the abolition case. Having seen Clarkson's record of the evidence supplied to him by Norris in Liverpool, Pitt arranged for copies to be circulated to the committee. Norris now came under increasing attack as it was shown that he had held back on vital evidence condemning the slave trade. The committee began to doubt the motives of pro-slavery witnesses and the credibility of their evidence, and their case began to buckle. Although supporting some of Norris's testimony, Archibald Dalziel agreed that his claims had been exaggerated, and that various customs had been misrepresented. William Devaynes, who had long experience as an agent in Dahomey, also differed with Norris over various points of detail. He accepted that wars and kidnapping were conducted to supply the European market, but had visited the king on a number of occasions and had seen no more than two or three heads lying in the palace. He knew of no poll tax, and disputed Norris's claim of a thousand human sacrifices during its supposed annual payment. He suggested instead that "about Sixty Men and Women, besides all Kinds of Animals, are put to death, and sent to the deceased, in order that he or she may remain quiet and not trouble the king….These consisted of Persons sacrificed on Occasion of the Ceremony of watering the Graves of the King's Ancestors; of Prisoners taken in War; or of Delinquents of Note."[28]

Although it was clear that Dahomey was a despotic kingdom, evidence given by a number of witnesses showed that it could not be considered typical of West Africa. Along the coast from Gambia to Sierra Leone there were many petty states, although each was ruled by an absolute monarch who regarded his subjects as slaves and had power over life and death. Further inland, however, the rulers had far less power, as did most along the Gold Coast, where government was generally shared with councils of elders. Here, as in most regions, pagan beliefs led to some human sacrifice. The victims were normally the personal slaves of wealthy Africans, and were sacrificed to accompany their deceased owners. This was not viewed with horror by the local inhabitants, but rather as an accepted religious ritual. A similar situation held at Bonny on the eastern side of the Niger Delta, where both humans and animals were ritually sacrificed. The monarch here was elected from the members of the royal family, and was advised by a council of elders. Three kings ruled the region of New Calabar, one as head of civil government, another over the law, and the third as religious leader. Important issues were settled between all three, together with a council of elders, although real power rested with the principal slave traders. Further south, both Congo and Angola were limited monarchies, where government was conducted through councils of princes.[29]

[28] *Report of the Lords of the Committee of Council*, op. cit., p16-17.
[29] Ibid, p10-15 & 18-21.

The slave traders' evidence soon began to rebound on them. Several admitted having rejected unhealthy slaves knowing they would be killed, and James Penny even admitted witnessing rejected slaves being thrown from a cliff at Mellimba. Thus implicated in cruelties, the slavers then found their arguments undermined by Swedish scientists Dr. Andrew Speerman and Charles Wadstrom. While exploring West Africa to study its plants and minerals on a fact-finding mission, they had also documented reliable evidence of wars, raids and kidnapping to feed the slave trade. As guest of a local king, they had even witnessed their host send out raiding parties, and then seen the return of captives, some in a wounded state. Being sponsored by King Gustavus, and having no personal involvement in slavery, their testimony made a considerable impact.[30] But perhaps most damaging of all was the use made by Clarkson of the muster rolls given to him by William Rathbone while in Liverpool. The statistics showed that of 3,170 seamen leaving Liverpool for Africa in 1786-87, twenty per cent died or were lost on the coast. Another third deserted or were discharged in the West Indies, implying widespread friction between captains and crews, leaving less than half of their original number who returned home in their original ships.[31]

Although an initial report of the Privy Council in April 1788 was highly critical of the slave trade, it merely recommended regulation. Pitt argued that further investigations were needed, but with little time left that parliamentary session, and Wilberforce unable to attend due to illness, he suggested that the proposed abolition bill should be postponed until the following year. This left a friend of Wilberforce, Sir William Dolben, to propose a temporary bill to limit the numbers of slaves a ship could carry to three for every two tons of vessel. When the Dolben Bill was introduced in the Commons near the end of May, Liverpool MPs Lord Penrhyn and Bamber Gascoyne attacked it clause by clause. But when Norris and Penny were called to testify on the conditions on board ships, both exaggerated the care taken in providing for slaves, and neither would admit of exceptions. Penny suggested, "If the Weather is sultry, and there appears the least Perspiration upon their Skins when they come upon Deck, there are two men attending with Cloths to rub them perfectly dry, and another to give them a little Cordial." He added that after eating "they are then supplied with Pipes and Tobacco …they are amused with Instruments of Music peculiar to their own Country … and when tired of Music and Dancing, they then go to Games of Chance." When Norris was asked how the slaves slept, he replied, "On clean boards…those Apartments are clean washed and fumigated with Tar, the fumes of Tar, or Frankincense, and sprinkled with Vinegar; this is done Daily. Whenever the Weather permits, the Negroes come

30 Clarkson, op. cit. p488-491.
31 Percentages derived from raw figures in Sanderson, *The Liverpool Delegates*, op. cit, p69.

out of their Rooms. This is never omitted. They sleep on those clean Boards, which in that sultry Climate are better than sleeping in Blankets or other soft Matter." Norris denied that the smell could be overpowering until he was pressed, when he finally responded, "that must depend on every Person's own Feelings."[32]

However, a very different impression was created when Dalziel was questioned about a recent voyage in 1786, when he had captained the 200- ton *Tarter*, and a third of the slaves and crew died:[33]

Q. "How many seamen did you lose?"

A. "A third of my Ship's Company – Thirteen out of Thirty-seven to the best of my Recollection."

Q. "Are not the Negroes often fed with Horse Beans, softened with Palm Oil?"

A. "No Doubt, well boiled first – and I have often eat them myself, when the Pease were expended. – Every Body knows that Beans may be eat; and as for Palm Oil, I always eat rather than rank Butter."

Q. "What Number of Slaves did you take on Board the Tarter that Voyage?"

A. "Three hundred and Sixty, and upwards, I sailed with."

Q. "How many did you lose?"

A. "About a Third – I speak from memory, not having the Account about me."

Q. "How many Slaves died before they left the Coast?"

A. "I cannot exactly say. – I had eight drowned by Accident at One Time, and Two or Three at another. I had a badly assorted Cargo; great Competition, few slaves in the Country; Provisions scarce in the Country - in short, I was detained a Twelvemonth upon the Coast at Benin, constantly exposed to all the Vicissitudes of Weather, Rain, the Smokes or Exhalations of vapour by the Sun after the Rain, which are reckoned very unwholesome. A Scarcity of Acid Fruits particularly prevailed, and once I was obliged to quit the Bar with my Ship to get a Supply of Water elsewhere, having unfortunately lost One of my Boats, and being unable to keep up my Water with the others. All these Circumstances conspiring, detained me, as I have already said, and most were the Occasion of the Scurvy getting among the Slaves, and rendering the Voyage so fatal."

Q. "How many died of Distemper before you sailed?"

A. "I do not recollect, but I believe they might exceed Twelve."

---

[32] Sanderson, *The Liverpool Delegates*, op. cit., p71.
[33] 12th June 1788, Parliamentary Accounts and Papers, Vol.XX1V, p34-35.

Pitt had anticipated the slave traders' response to Dolben's proposals, and had sent royal naval Captain Parry to Liverpool to check the dimensions of slave ships. When the Liverpool delegates said that slaving vessels were purpose built, Parry showed this to be true of only ten of the twenty-six ships he surveyed. Likewise, claims that ships under two hundred tons were not fitted with slave platforms were shown to be false, and the average height between decks was shown to be less than the five feet, four inches that was stated. When Gascoyne claimed that slave ships were not profitable unless carrying two slaves per ton, Parry found that only about a quarter of Liverpool ships had actually taken that many on board.

When John Matthews was questioned about how the number of slaves a ship could take on board was calculated, he provided the following example:[34]

Q. "Have you made a Calculation on the Ship Brooks, supposing her to contain 297 Tons?"

A. "Yes"

Q. "Have you calculated how many Men and Women, allowing each a space of Sixteen Inches Breadth, and a Length of Five Feet Six Inches, that ship would contain, in the Common Proportion of great slaves to Boys?"

A. "In the Admeasurement of the Ship Brooks, sent up by Captain Parry, of different Apartments, measured 4,178 Square Feet – On a Supposition that the Average Height of Negroes was Four Feet Eight Inches, the Breadth Fifteen Inches (which, brought into Square superficial Feet, would be Five Feet Nine Inches) that Space would contain 568 Negroes, nearly."

After such evidence, further hearings from the London delegates were refused, and Dolben's bill passed the committee stage by fifty-six to five votes. A lawyer for the abolitionists mocked the Liverpool delegates, remarking that, "One would think that ….the solid pestilence, the thick contagion, the

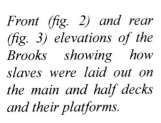
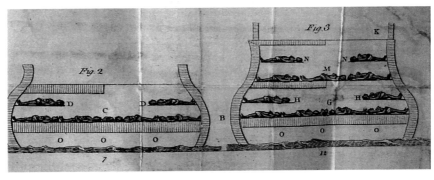

Front (fig. 2) and rear (fig. 3) elevations of the Brooks showing how slaves were laid out on the main and half decks and their platforms.

---

34 16th June 1788, Parliamentary Accounts and Papers, Vol.XXIV, p42.

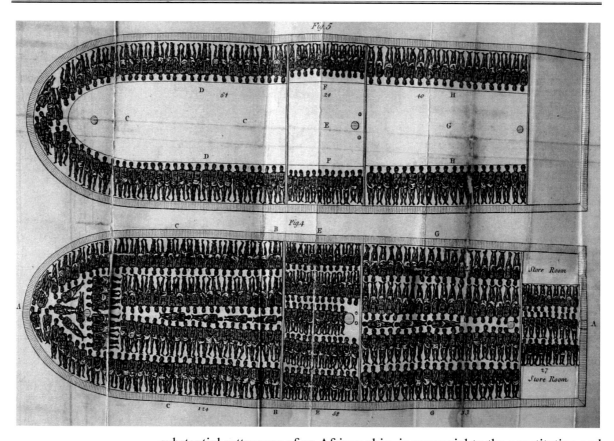

Main detail from the folded illustration in Clarkson's history of the abolition movement showing a plan view of the main slave deck on board the ship Brooks. The lower drawing (fig. 4) shows the layout of slaves on the deck floor, while the upper drawing (fig. 5) shows an extra layer of slaves laid out on the platforms built about 30-36 inches above the deck.

substantial rottenness of an African ship, is congenial to the constitution and exhilarating to the spirit of a negro.'[35] Reactions from the Liverpool merchants were bitter and furious, and instructions to the delegates to continue fighting were unambiguous. Writing to the Board of Trade, Tarleton argued that ships of about a hundred tons carried an average of five slaves for every two tons, on which a ten per cent profit was made, allowing for five per cent mortality. This amounted to about £736, which in his view was not excessive, given the financial risks. If capacity was reduced to three slaves per two tons, this would produce a net loss of about £200, and if only one per ton, the loss would be nearly six hundred. Tarleton also warned that the French would simply take over the slave trade, and British competitiveness would be lost. This made a big impression on the Lords, who began to amend the bill out of all recognition, encouraged by petitions from merchants in Liverpool, Bristol, London, and the West Indies. There were so many amendments when it was returned to the Commons that Dolben simply presented a new bill to avoid

[35] Quoted in Sanderson, *The Liverpool Delegates*, op. cit, p72.

further delay. The legislation was rushed through its final stages within a week, in spite of fresh petitions, new evidence, and further amendments proposed by the Lords. Faced with a resignation threat from William Pitt, the Lords voted to accept Dolben's bill on 11th July, and it was then passed by the Commons without further debate.

After much wrangling over numbers, the final Act allowed five slaves for every three tons up to 201 tons, and one per ton thereafter. It also imposed a fine of thirty pounds per slave over the limit. Each ship was to carry at least one surgeon, whose duties included keeping an accurate register of mortality amongst the slaves and crew. Surgeons also had to swear to the accuracy of their records before a collector of statistics at the first British port of entry after leaving Africa, the fine for non-compliance being a hundred pounds. In addition, the law would no longer regard slaves as mere goods, and merchants would not be able to claim insurance for jettisoned cargo as Gregson had tried to do for the *Zong*. Instead, bounties of a hundred pounds for the captain, and fifty for the surgeon, were to be awarded where mortality did not exceed two per cent, or half those amounts where it did not exceed three. Although the Act ended the more extreme levels of overcrowding and mortality, its impact was slight, and thousands of slaves continued to perish annually.[36]

However, rather than being the prelude it was intended to be, the Dolben Act effectively took the wind out of the abolitionists' sails. The Privy Council's report was issued to members of Parliament in April 1789, laying out the evidence in no less than 850 pages. When William Wilberforce made his first speech on the issue on 12th May, having recovered from his illness, he spoke from notes for three and a half hours. He distilled the evidence with great eloquence, but was careful to avoid blame, stating that "We ought all to plead guilty." Whether tactfully or naively, he argued that slave ship owners must surely be men of humanity, and that "if the wretchedness of any one of the many hundred negroes stowed in each ship could be brought before their view… there is no one among them whose heart would bare it."[37] He also argued that, with better conditions on plantations, slave populations could increase by natural means and therefore be sustained. His greatest criticism was reserved

---

[36] Robert Norris made five voyages as captain, his last being in 1778. During the enquiry he gave figures ranging from 1.8% to 5.5% mortality among slaves, averaging 3.7%. James Penny's average as captain before his voyage with the *Count Du Nord* was 4.9%, but that voyage raised the average mortality of his slaving voyages to 6.8%. Mortality rates differed widely. Figures in Sanderson, *The Liverpool Delegates*, p77, show that for the period 1789-1795 mortality among slaves from the River Senegal to the River Volta was 4.1%; from the Volta to Angola it was 13.1%; and from Angola it was 2.8%. These figures are broadly in line with those quoted on p140, footnote 18 above, taking into account that the two sets cover different stretches of the West African coast.

[37] Quoted in Hochschild, op. cit., p160.

for the African kings and chiefs who were all too ready to wage war. "Does the king of Barbessin want brandy? He has only to send his troops in the night time to burn and desolate a village: the captives will serve as commodities that may be bartered with the British trader."[38] As for the argument that the French would take over Britain's share of the trade, Wilberforce reasoned that people may as well go out and commit any crimes they wanted on the basis that others would do so anyway. But many MPs were not convinced, and probably very few had taken the trouble to read through the lengthy report. Supporters of the trade now played for time by arguing the need for the Commons to hold its own enquiry as a matter of proper parliamentary procedure. Knowing that many MPs felt the worst aspects of slavery had been addressed by regulating the middle passage, Wilberforce reluctantly consented, and the issue was sadly deferred.

While the struggle for abolition was underway, James Irving was beginning his fifth voyage to Africa. Built at John Barton's Liverpool shipyard in 1783, the *Princess Royal* was the largest ship owned by merchants Peter Baker and John Dawson, which was probably financed partly from the proceeds of their prize French East Indiaman, *Carnatic*, seized in October 1778.[39] Dawson was under contract to supply thousands of slaves to the Spanish West Indies, and had so far made £350,000 from the deal. He owned nineteen slaving vessels, making him possibly the world's leading slave trader.[40] At nearly six hundred tons burthen, the *Princess Royal* was frigate built, with a raised deck at the stern. This was considered necessary for the crew in case of insurrection, a particular danger given that the vessel could carry more than eight hundred slaves.[41]

With so many slaves to care for, Irving's cousin and namesake had been taken on at just fifteen or sixteen as surgeon's mate. This would have been the younger James's first voyage, and a memorable one at that. For, as he wrote to his parents in Langholm, Scotland, "We would have sailed long before this, but as the ship was going out of the dock onto the river on 23rd of last month, it being high water and no wind, the strength of the tide turned her round and ran her aground, and left her there till next tide. And she being so

---

38 Quoted in Hochschild., p161.
39 See p66 above.
40 Sanderson, *The Liverpool Delegates*, op cit. p83.
41 Schwarz, op. cit. p16.

sharp bottomed lay on one side, which so strained her that she was all bent and leaked very much, and she has been in the river ever since." Although he did not mention it, the *Princess Royal* must have been a frenzy of activity as carpenters and caulkers plugged the gaps, and the crew worked the ship's pumps around the clock. They did so successfully, for the younger James was able to report, "But now she is straight and leaks so little that there is scarce enough to wash the decks, and in the course of a month we expect there will be none....But now the wind is fair and we are able to sail the first tide. And I wrote this letter to send back with the pilot who leaves us after we are past the norwest buoy."[42]

Having avoided shipwreck, the *Princess Royal* was able to complete a commercially successful voyage in remarkably short time, returning to Liverpool from Havana in January 1789. Within months, James Irving senior had been made master of his own vessel, having impressed Captain William Sherwood of being "as careful, sober and industrious a man as ever lived." The *Anna* was a newly-built and registered schooner of just fifty tons burthen, and was able to carry eighty slaves.[43] As it sailed from the Mersey on 3rd May, Irving wrote to his wife Mary advising, "Don't fret and distress yourself without cause. Providence, if you confide in him, is able and willing to support you in every situation in life. Think on these little matters and the reflection will afford balm to your mind. Go to church now and then, or as often as you please. Take plenty of exercise in the open air; that is a practice that must be followed if you hope to be healthy." Now responsible for his own ship, Irving hoped to be rounding Orme's Head on the coast of North Wales by the early afternoon, and so added hurriedly, "As the wind is so exceeding favourable the vessel runs out very fast, so that I cannot find time to say what I have within, but do rest satisfied, my sweet girl, the next time I write shall be a very long one."[44] But, Mary had every reason to be anxious. His was an unusual responsibility for one trained as a surgeon, and as she was now two months pregnant, Mary would have to face the dangers of childbearing and birth in his absence.

But, having almost been shipwrecked close to home, Irving was soon to experience the real thing in a more hostile land. As the *Anna* sailed southward, the favourable wind had given way to more adverse conditions, and by the time the *Anna* was approaching the Canary Islands, Irving and his crew were

---

[42] Quoted in Schwarz, op. cit., p117.

[43] This was a major departure for Dawson, whose smallest ship had been 325 tons. He had probably built it because the ratio of slaves to tonnage under the Dolben Act favoured smaller vessels. Figures given by Lamb, in Anstey and Heir, op. cit., p100, show that between 1789-92, 8.6% of slaving vessels clearing from Liverpool were below 99 tons, 57% were between 100-199 tons, 23% between 200-299 tons, and 11.3% were over 300 tons.

[44] Quoted in Schwarz, op. cit. p118.

confused about their position. On the afternoon of 26th May, he set a course that he believed would take the vessel towards "Lancerota or Fortaventura" before nightfall, but by six o'clock neither could be sighted. Irving later recorded, "Thus baffled in our expectations, we were unanimously of the opinion that an easterly current….had deceived us, and that we were certainly eastward of the Canaries, however unaccountably it had happened." Irving now set a course south-west-by-west, but still no land could be seen from the masthead by sunset. Irving continued, "We had then not a doubt of our being between the Canaries and the Barbary shore, and in order to avoid any probability of danger, steered W.S.W till 11pm."[45] Despite this evasive action, the *Anna* was being carried relentlessly towards the notorious Moroccan coast by the strong eastward current, and the crew's worst fears were soon realised. Irving continued, "I had not left the deck above ten minutes, when I heard the man at the helm say the water looked comically. Much alarmed at the expression, I jumped on deck, and was met by a heavy broken sea that fell on board. We instantly endeavoured to haul the sheets aft and bring her to the wind, which blew fresh at North or N.B.W., but the breakers fell on board so heavily and followed one another so quickly, that she soon lost headway and struck in the hollow of the sea so very hard, that the rudder went away in a few seconds. She bounced with every wave so far to leeward that she lifted very little, but fell with such a shock that we expected every minute to find her part asunder or overset. In about ten minutes she filled, and the danger of over-setting being thereby increased, we cut away the main-mast and hove everything of any weight that lay upon her deck overboard in order to prevent it. She lay for some time bow to sea, which considerably prevented her going to pieces."[46] Since the schooner "lay buffeted by heavy breakers, already bilged, and full of water," the crew debated whether to abandon ship, but decided it would hold together until daylight. They managed to wade ashore through heavy surf next morning, and found the keel had been beaten off and the starboard side smashed beyond repair. Also lost was the cargo of India and Manchester cloths, hardware goods, a thousand dollars, and twenty tons of salt, all of which was washed out of the hold.

Along with Irving were ten crewmembers, including second mate Matthew Dawson, nephew of the owner. Irving's younger cousin was the ship's surgeon, and among the rest were three men listed as Portuguese blacks. What happened next was described by Irving two months later from a state of captivity. No sooner had they reached the shore when the crew were spotted, "then seized on by a party of Arabs with outstretched arms and knives ready to stab us,

---

[45] Quoted in Schwarz, op. cit., p34.
[46] Ibid, p36.

next stripped to the skin, suffering a thousand deaths daily, insulted, spit upon, exposed to the sun and night dews daily, then travelled through parched deserts, wherein was no water for 9 days, afterwards torn from one another, and your poor petitioner marched to this place half dead with fatigue, whose only hope is in God and you."[47]

The crew had initially been held near the shipwreck by their captors, but were then sold and marched to a trading town some distance away, where they were re-sold and split up. Irving was then led on an exhausting journey over the Atlas Mountains, passing a party of Frenchmen along the way who had suffered a similar fate. By 25th June Irving had reached a town called Tellin, having learned he had become the property of a Sheik and was now ransomed. After being given a reed pen and some course paper, he was told to write to the British Vice-Consul, and was threatened that if there was no response within ten days he would be put to work in the cornfields. Irving received the reply that his release could only be obtained through the intervention of the Sultan, whose influence in the region was limited as it was under the control of his estranged elder son. He was put to work as threatened, and soon received news from his crewmates that they had been "beat most unmercifully and toiled from sunrise to sunset." He was allowed frequent correspondence with the Vice-consul to encourage payment of ransom money, and wrote to Mary, suggesting that he might otherwise "have missed this shipwreck, gone to Benin, and died there."

By September 1789, Irving had fallen ill with a fever, "which rendered me delirious during the hot stage of the paroxism which seized me every day." However, during Irving's months of illness, the Sultan had been negotiating with the Vice-Consul to arrange for a doctor to treat his younger son, who was nearly blind due to a cataract. The treatment somehow led to an improvement in his sight, and to the Prince arranging for the purchase of Irving and the rest of the crew. Towards the end of December, Irving found himself taken once again over the Atlas Mountains, but this time as part of a three hundred strong caravan. Irving was carried by mule, crossing the High Atlas near its highest peak, "one of the highest mountains in the universe." Irving was reunited with the rest of his crew in Marrakech, but they were soon transferred to the care of the Vice-Consul at Mogodore. Although they now had basic accommodation and new clothes, their movements were still restricted. Many months passed while the Sultan tried to extract a deal from the British government for the loan of a frigate to take him to Mecca. Eventually, after the death of the Sultan and nearly fourteen months in captivity, they were finally released and arrived at Dartmouth towards the end of October 1790.

---

[47] Quoted in Schwarz, p119-120.

However, his letter to Mary turned out to be prophetic. Irving was soon on his way to Africa again, short of money, and having spent little more than a month with his young wife and one-year old son. He left Liverpool as captain of the *Ellen* on 2nd January 1791, arriving at the Gold Coast before moving on to Benin. By the time the *Ellen* reached Trinidad James Irving had died, along with forty-seven of his human cargo.[48]

[48] Schwarz, op. cit., p65-66.

Chapter Seven

King George's madness began with distinctly odd and most unregal behaviour. Soon there were reports of his talking to trees and running around naked, and of claiming to see Germany through his telescope. He talked utter gibberish, had violent fits, and even howled like a dog. Parliament's business came to a standstill, as politicians endlessly debated his condition and talked of succession while hoping for a recovery. Meanwhile, his doctors applied emetics and purges, and blistered his skin to rid him of poisonous humours, but none of this quackery prevented poor King George from being confined in a straightjacket.[1]

Some three months after going mad the king's sanity returned, and Britain prepared to celebrate. As the good news travelled the country there were glassworkers, metal beaters, candle makers, chandlers and brewers everywhere making ready for a festival of light. In Liverpool, architect John Foster busied himself with coordinating the local display. While Mr. Knight's workshop assembled thirteen thousand lamps, townsfolk throughout the town applied themselves with ingenuity as they improvised their own creations. By midday 26th March 1789 all was ready, and a royal salute was fired as a signal to down tools and deck the whole town. Ships, quaysides, streets and houses, churches and civic buildings everywhere were adorned with bunting, coloured lanterns and ornaments of painted glass in readiness for the evening's entertainments. Meanwhile, villagers poured in from Everton, Toxteth, Wavertree, and further afield, and at seven o'clock another twenty-one-gun salute signalled one and all to light the wicks that would illuminate the town. So accustomed were they to the darkness of night that this was truly a brilliant, spectacular occasion. By eight o'clock every lamp was glowing and the celebrations were in full swing, as the people promenaded through the streets in wonderment and awe.

Centrepiece of the occasion was the Exchange, its outlines and prominent features adorned with lamps of various colours, and its columns hung with lanterns forming spirals, stars and arches. Three painted transparencies were placed in the upper front windows, displaying a portrait of the king in the centre, flanked by figures representing *Fortitude* and *Hope*. Beneath these, across the whole width of the frontage, many dozens of lamps formed the tribute *God Save the King*. To top it all, a huge crown of crystal lamps was placed on the pediment, so that the whole effect "rivalled in splendour all we read in fairy tales and enchantments."[2] At the customs house a large transparent

---

[1] It is likely that the king suffered from porphyria, a periodic and unpredictable disease that affects the nervous system. His first brief attack was in 1765, and during the last ten years of his life the condition became so serious that the Prince of Wales ruled on his behalf as regent.

[2] *Williamson's Advertiser*, 30th March 1789.

bust of the king was lit from behind, and various tributes were hung over the entrance, including *God Save great George our King* and *Long live our noble King*. At the Theatre Royal in Williamson's Square a transparent crown and sceptre were displayed from the centre window, and the facade adorned in lights.

Indeed, throughout Liverpool, inns, taverns, civic buildings and private houses competed for attention as thousands of lamps illuminated the town. There were full-length portraits of the king and queen painted on glass and illuminated from behind, with mottos such as *Britain's Glory*, *England's Pride*, and *Long May He Live*. At John Colquitt's house the king was flanked by the Liverpool Arms and a portrait of the Roman goddess *Minerva*. Mr. Wilckens displayed an inventive picture of Death pointing a dart at George III, while *Minerva* descended to protect the king as he lay calmly reclined on a couch. Mr. Foster's window displayed *Hygeia* supporting the king to represent his health, as explained by the motto *Our King is restored*. Another displayed the *Genius of Liverpool* looking towards heaven in gratitude, as shown by the word *Rejoice*. In front of Mr. Bold's house was a six-foot statue of *Britannia*, at the foot of which was the *British Lion*. But everywhere one looked there were coloured lights, figures and emblems, each designed to inspire onlookers with awe and admiration for king and country.[3]

Three weeks later, a Restoration Ball and Supper was held at the Exchange. No expense was spared in decorating the building, and extensive temporary alterations were made to accommodate eight hundred guests. Hundreds of highly polished metal stars were suspended from the crystal chandeliers, reflecting the light of thousands of candles and lamps. Among the many transparencies was the scene of *Mercury* bringing joyful news of the king's recovery to *Neptune*, and one of the Exchange itself, while a third showed the Bidston lighthouse, complete with signals. The dancing began at nine, followed by supper at midnight, which included ornamental confectioneries made at Mr. Menzies' shop in Castle Street.[4] The decorations were kept in place for the king's birthday on 4th June, when a further ball was held and a concert given by the band of the 40th regiment, tickets seven shillings each.

Later that month a freak thunderstorm crossed the country, striking Liverpool around one in the afternoon. A heavy downpour of rain was accompanied by "exceeding large hailstones, attended by the most awful and tremendous thunder and lightning ever remembered," causing considerable damage to houses throughout the town. A chimneystack was struck by lightning and collapsed into the roof at 117 Dale Street, taking with it much of the upper brickwork to one corner of the house. Every room in Mr. Davies's house was

---

3 *Williamson's Advertiser,* 30th March 1789
4 *Ibid,* 20th April, and *Gore's General Advertiser*, 23rd April 1789.

covered in dust and soot, although the occupants luckily escaped harm. The lightning came down another stack across the street, smashing a looking glass and striking Mr. Donnelly in the temple while he and his family sat ready to dine by the fireplace. Miraculously, none was harmed, but the lightning bolt continued through a double window and split the centre frame. At Mr. Harding's house next door, the lightning entered the back of the roof and stripped the tiles, passing into the room below. There it forced the chimney board from the wall and passed through the fire grate into the parlour below, where it split an oak cupboard. Mr. and Mrs. Harding and their three children were just about to dine in the front room. As Mr. Harding stood up to cut the meat, he was struck by a separate bolt, knocking him senseless into his chair. When he came to, he discovered the rest of his family in the same dazed state. The room was filled with a sulphurous vapour, but fortunately all were restored on taking the air outside.

Meanwhile, Alexander Glover was driving a cart up Dale Street when he was struck, as was one of his two horses. Happily, the horse seemed unaffected, and Glover's injuries were limited to bruises he sustained as he was thrown from his cart. At about the same time, a gentleman was standing by the handle of the water pump at the fish stones at the bottom of James Street when he was struck through one shoulder right down to his leg. He suffered minor burns, and said that the shock was greater than that from a half gallon bottle that had been highly charged by an electrical machine. The lightning also struck a stable in Vernon Street, setting fire to the hay and timbers. Fortunately, fifteen firemen and two pump engines were on the scene within minutes and were able to prevent damage to the surrounding buildings. Sadly, however, Mr. Green's twelve-year-old daughter was killed when a bolt struck the Townside Mill and was conducted by machinery and chains into the living quarters below.[5]

It might have been remembered as a portent of things to come if the lightning had struck Paris, for while King George enjoyed the devotion of his subjects, there was growing discontent towards the French monarch and his government that would later lead to a Europe-wide conflict. When Louis XV1 gathered the Estates General at his Palace of Versailles in May 1789 none could have imagined the events that would be unleashed. The king's purpose was borne out of a growing financial crisis in France. The harvests of the previous

---

[5] *Williamson's Advertiser*, 29th June 1789.

two years had been particularly bad, forcing tens of thousands of peasants to leave the countryside and swell the ranks of the urban poor. Meanwhile, the country faced bad government, high price rises, grossly unfair taxation, and chronic debts due to its funding of the American war. But perhaps most fundamental was the exclusive power of the monarchy and nobility, since even the wealthiest members of the middle class were denied a voice. The country lacked a parliament, and much of the population still lived in serfdom under a feudal system that had faded out in Britain centuries earlier.

When Louis invited representatives to bring their grievances to Versailles he had hoped for mild reforms. But his project was doomed to failure from the start, owing to the nature of the Estates General. The First and Second Estates were made up of the nobility and clergy, while the Third consisted of everyone else from the most successful entrepreneurs to the lowliest peasants. However, there were soon disagreements as to the voting power of each, and by mid-June the Third Estate had taken the title of National Assembly and committed itself to forming a constitution. The king soon found himself powerless when he ordered the Assembly to disperse, and the more liberal members of the clergy and nobility joined the new body. But events were soon to overtake the Assembly as the Paris mob stormed the Bastille on 14th July, killing the governor and several guards, releasing the prisoners, and dismantling the building. Having destroyed this symbol of oppression, although only seven prisoners were found inside, the mob set off to the Hotel de Ville, or city hall, putting the mayor to death, while violence spread throughout the city. Calm was only restored as a new National Guard was established to protect Paris and the Assembly, under the leadership of a liberal noble, the Marquis de Lafayette.

Meanwhile, unrest spread to the countryside, as peasants stormed dozens of chateaux, burning title deeds and looting property. As the nobility began to flee the country the Assembly abolished the feudal system with all its privileges and tithes, and towards the end of August issued a *Declaration of the Rights of Man and the Citizen*. Five weeks later, thousands of Parisians marched in the pouring rain to the Palace of Versailles, where they demanded bread and insisted on bringing the king to Paris to remove him from his hated ministers. Threatened by the mob, the king gave way, arriving in the city with his wife Marie Antoinette, a hundred deputies, and several wagonloads of flour, all under the protection of the National Guard. Thousands lined the streets and cheered as Louis was taken to the former royal palace at the Tuileries. He now became a virtual prisoner, and agreed under duress to all the Assembly's decrees thus far. Having tasted power, the mob was soon to be a driving force behind the revolution.

A page from the log of the Ranger showing remarks written between 17th and 21st December 1789 by Captain John Corran (LRO 387 MD 56)

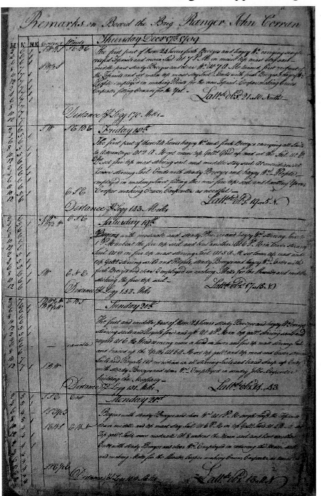

While Parisians were heading towards Versailles to fetch the king, the *Ranger* was preparing for its maiden voyage to Africa. By early January 1790 the brig was approaching the Gold Coast, having first called in at Lisbon, where several of the crew had deserted a month earlier.[6] Since then, when not working the rigging, some of the crew had been weaving rush matting for the deck enclosure, while the cooper had been making buckets. Although the *Ranger* had recently been built in Liverpool and sheathed with copper plating, the logbook recorded that the vessel had been taking in water since leaving Lisbon. This would have kept the crew busy at the pumps, but the gaps had since been plugged as there were no further references to leaks. But now the anchors were being prepared while the linesman took depth soundings, and several of the crew went off with three weeks provisions in the schooner boat *Betsey* in search of trade. On 11th January the log recorded "Soundings of 35 – 25 fathoms. Weather black and gloomy, thunder and lightning. At 6 saw the ships at Cape Lahoe. At 9 got a Canoe from the shore." The *Ranger* anchored on the 13th, but soon moved further along the coast as Captain John Corran tried to attract trade. The log noted three days later, "At 6 AM came to anchor at Afrignee in 16 Fathoms Water. At 7AM came off some of the Natives and made Trade for some Rolls of Tobacco. At 11 the Natives left us, sent 20 Rolls on Board the long Boat and sent her in Shoar. Got under way and made sail down the Coast." Six days later the *Ranger* was anchored two miles from the trading fort at Annamaboe, and the crew were busy cleaning the ship.

---

[6] LRO 387 MD 56, *Log of the Brig 'Ranger' 1789 – 1790, John Corran Master, on a voyage of to Annamaboe Africa, via Lisbon, and thence to Jamaica, trading in slaves.*

Provisions were brought from the fort over the next week or so, while preparations were made for trading in partnership with the *Gregson* from Liverpool, which was under the command of Corran's brother, William.[7] On

Logbook remarks made between 5th and 21st February off the coast of Africa (LRO 387 MD 56)

Monday 25th the log recorded, "At 10 AM the Schooner Boat came down from the Windward – Employed in taking some of the Guns from Shoar and other necessary Jobbs as useful for the Vessel – Carpenter building the Barricado." Two days later John Corran was bartering for rum on board an American vessel, while his crew were employed loading goods on board their schooner to look for trade. The first five slaves were taken on board the Ranger over the next three days, and the hold was cleaned before stowing water brought from Cape Coast in the *Gregson's* pinnace. At the end of the month a disciplinary incident was logged. "At ½ past 4PM Christian Freeze bestowed illiberal and mutinous Language to Mr. Woods the second Mate, upon which the Captn overhearing the Conversation between them desired said Freeze to desist in those proceedings to the Officers of the Vessel. Upon which orders he, the said Freeze, gave the Captn of the said Vessel abusive and ill Language. It appeared upon investigation that the said Christian Freeze and one George Hall, another seaman belonging to the said Brig, had been employed in the Hold in assisting the said Mr. Woods. But he being obliged to leave them in the hold, they, thereby taking Advantage of his Absence, embezzled part of the Cargo of Rum that lay in the hold, whereby they became intoxicated. And, for the ill conduct and drunkenness of the said Freeze and intoxication of the said George Hall, their allowance of Rum was (by the desire of the Captn) ordered not to be given to them until the Expiration of eight days as a punishment for their behaviour above expressed."

---

[7] *Lloyd's Register*, 1791. Both ships were owned by aptly named William Boats & Co.

Ten slaves were bought during the next seventeen days, while various maintenance tasks were carried out. The biggest job was careening the hull, which involved scraping off barnacles, weeds, and other debris. Where or how this was done was not recorded, except that both sides of the hull were cleaned. The ship was also painted, the men's room with two coats. Repairs were made to the rigging, and the cooper cleaned the rusty guns, while others continued the unenviable job of cleaning the hold. On 10th February the ship's "people" were served with fresh fish "in lieu of Pork and Pease," and on the next day instead of "beef and flour." But many of the crew were clearly not content with healthy dietary treats, preferring instead something a little stronger. The log recorded on the 19th, "At 2PM Daniel Chieves behaved in a mutinous manner to Mr. Woods the 2nd Mate, and all the People on Board are charged (by the confession of the Boatswain) for making away and embezzling the Cargo of Liquor on Board the Brig – and on Monday last some or one of the Officers or People broke into the hold and breached a Puncheon of Brandy which lay therein by boring a Hole with a Gimlet and thereby drawed off a Quantity of the Liquor." John Corran went to Cape Coast Castle to report the incident two days later, and "returned with the orders from the Commodore that he might put on Board of his Ship the supposed Ringleaders and Mutineers."[8] Then, next day "At 2PM the Commodore hove to abrest of Annamaboe Roads, and Captn Corran having a great suspicion against Sampson Thurston and Daniel Chieves being the two Ringleaders of the said People braking into the said Hold, and the only Persons that bestowed a great deal of mutinous language upon Mr. Woods the second Mate, therefore Captn Curran, for the safety of the Vessel and cargo, put the aforesaid Sampson Thurston and Daniel Chieves on Board the Commodore," or rather, the commodore's ship. Thurston and Chieves might well have resisted this arrest, but no details were given of any fracas that may have occurred.

Between 20th February and 4th April thirty-four slaves were taken on board, including nineteen men, eleven women, three girls and one boy. This averaged less than one a day, but others seem not to have been recorded. During this time the slaves "rooms", or compartments, were cleaned several times, and the log records "taking care of the slaves." Two women and a small anchor were traded for four puncheons of rum while various provisions were being taken on board,. The *Gregson's* pinnace and the *Ranger's* schooner were sent out on 3rd March with several weeks' provisions to trade further along the coast, but later that day "At 10PM came on a Trenado from the SE'ward, attended with heavy claps of Thunder and dismal Flashes of Lightning and rain." After the return of its schooner, the Ranger sailed west to Appalonia Fort, anchoring

---

[8] The commodore was commander of the trading fort, and was employed by the African Company.

two miles to the south-east in fourteen fathoms of water on 11th April. Corran sent forty-six slaves on board the *Gregson* and received unspecified goods in return, which were stowed on its schooner with a month's provisions for more inshore trading. Meanwhile, Corran spent the rest of April trading for gold with dealers along the coast, but the log recorded only two more slaves during a two-week period, and ended the month with "the Natives not coming to Trade." Two pages covering May are missing, but the record for early June shows further trading for gold, and exchanges of slaves and provisions between the *Ranger* and the *Gregson*. John Corran took his brig eastward again on the 7th, and the next day "met our Schooner Boat coming up to Windward and she bore away in Company with us." By 12th June the Ranger was once more at Annamaboe Fort, and sent twenty-four slaves on board the *Gregson*. Two days later, the *Princess Royal* arrived from Liverpool, the very same ship that James Irving had last served as a surgeon.

The crew now began loading large quantities of provisions, including beans and corn, eighteen canoe trips of water, and seven hundred billets of wood for cooking. On 21st June they were "Employed stowing water Casks and getting yr. Vessel ready for the slaves." Ten more canoe trips on the 23rd completed the *Ranger's* water requirements, and a dozen chests of corn were taken on board from the *Active* and the *Lovely Lass*. Meanwhile, some of the crew were "Employed in cleaning and washing betwixt Decks." Three days later the *Ranger* received 183 slaves, including one infant, from the *Gregson,* and set sail next morning for Jamaica. This was the maximum allowance under the Dolben regulations for a vessel of 110 tons.

There were several reports over the next few weeks that some of the slaves were complaining of a "Gripping in the Belly." Somewhat perversely, these alternated with comments such as "Slaves in good Health and Spirits." Meanwhile, an entry on 7th July notes, "Last night a Man Slave that slept in the Boys room endeavoured to cut his Throat with a Knife or some other Instrument, and at day light, when the Hatch was taken off to get the Tubs, the said Slave came upon Deck and jumped overboard, but was picked up with the Boat and is a fair way of recovery." The first slave burial at sea was recorded on 20th July, and nine more were to follow. Crammed in the squalid, fetid conditions below the open deck, the log made no reference to the sufferings that were felt. As they chafed against the bare timbers, sweating and puking, many must have must have embraced the very idea of death. Perhaps the ten that died were lucky, for theirs was an early release from a life of perpetual torment.

Barbados was sighted five leagues to the west early on 14th August, and by mid morning John Curran was heading ashore to collect the letters. The log added, "Burried one Man Slave of a Mortification in the Leg." The *Ranger* lay at anchor overnight in Carlisle Bay, and early next afternoon a boat came from the shore with oranges, limes and plantains. Curran rejoined the brig at half past four, having spent the night on the island. It set sail for Jamaica shortly after, reaching the island nine days later. Meanwhile, another woman had died of the flux.

The *Ranger* anchored off Kingston at midday on the 21st, taking on board plantains, cabbages and limes. Wednesday 25th began with on-shore winds and frequent showers of rain, thunder and lightning, and a few of the slaves were taken ashore and sold. At eight in the evening, "James Haseldon, Robert Pattison, & John Palmer went upon duty ashoar in the Boat and declined to return to the Brig, saying they did not approve of Mr. Woods yr. second Mate's conduct towards them, and for that reason were resolved to quit the Vessel." The next day's log notes, "People employed in overhauling and tarring the rigging – carpenter employed caulking the starboard side of the Vessel. The aforementioned People came aboard with the Lieutenant for their apparel &c." Several more slaves were sold on the 27th August, bringing the total to ten, and on the next day a "man slave" died of pleurisy. The log noted on Monday 30th, "At Meridian [noon] A Man of War's Boat came along side and enquired if any of the People were inclined to enter into his Majesty's Naval service, when John Damarain acquiesced with the Request."

The start of September saw ominous signs of severe weather approaching, and the crew "got all the spars ashoar and filled all empty casks with salt water." The entry continued, "At 11 came on a violent Gale of Wind or Hurricane attended with rain and a heavy sea. Let go the best bower Anchor and veered away long service upon both Cables. Ends with strong Gales and cloudy Wr. Several Vessels drifted ashoar in different places in the Harbour." Strong gales continued into the next day, accompanied by thunder and lightning, but the weather gradually calmed to become clear and moderate by nightfall. The Ranger escaped all but minor damage, the logbook noting merely that "The following Articles were lost in the Hurricane (viz) the rudder of both Boats, 2 bars, one Bumkin Block, one of the Arms of the Representation in the Head." However, one can only imagine the sheer terror experienced by the slaves cooped up below as they were tossed about and thrown against the timbers.

On Sunday 5th September the crew washed and oiled the slaves to prepare them for sale. Mr. Grahme, the third mate, went on shore, " but declined returning to the Vessel, the reason of such conduct is yet entirely unknown." Next morning, shackled and chained, the slaves were led off the *Ranger*. Sixty-two were "disposed of", presumably at auction, and the rest returned to the brig. Twenty-two were sold next day, and five the next, while two of the crew were taken to the hospital. Sixty-seven were sold from Thursday 9th to Saturday 11th, but only ten slaves were sold over the next four days, probably because of their poor physical condition, and on the next two days Curran was unable to sell any. On Saturday 18th "James Turner got liberty to go ashoar for three hours from Mr. Woods the second mate and never returned aboard." The logbook makes no note of taking on cargo for the return trip to Liverpool, but it does mention nine tons of ballast and a large quantity of bread. Twelve slaves remained on board by 20th September, but two were sold two days later. There the logbook finishes, and presumably the remaining slaves were virtually given away in a poor state of health to enable the *Ranger* to get underway. Whether Corran had been able to replace the missing seamen is not known, but he would have had little problem finding deserters from other vessels looking for a return passage.

In June 1790, while Louis XVI was endeavouring to stem the tide of reform, a parliamentary election was underway across the Channel. The contest in Liverpool proved more eventful than usual, although the result might otherwise have been a foregone conclusion. Bamber Gascoyne and Lord Penrhyn were confident of regaining their seats, since both had staunchly defended Liverpool's slaving interests against the abolitionists. This ensured their support from the corporation, which was anxious to see its position defended against further attacks. But, as canvassers plied the streets and alleys, it was clear that there was strong support for Colonel Banastre Tarleton, and passions were running high. With reports coming in of broken windows and cracked skulls, Mayor Thomas Smyth called a meeting of voters outside the Exchange in an effort to forestall the contest. At midday on Tuesday 16th the mayor warned of further strife and violence if the contest continued, and called for a show of support for Penrhyn and Gascoyne. The result appeared overwhelming as the hands went up, which some hoped would persuade Tarleton to bow out gracefully. But, when Penrhyn and Gascoyne spoke of *jointly* requesting the favours of freemen's votes, their attempt to forestall a contest seemed obvious. When a Tarleton supporter called for a show of hands for the Colonel, it was soon made clear the scheme had backfired.[9]

Tarleton faced an uphill struggle, since many freemen could be expected to divide their two votes between his opponents. Liverpool's printers were soon hard at work, as writers wasted no time in airing their views on handbills and posters under various pseudonyms. Among the first was *Amour Patriae*, who

---

[9] This account is based on Bass, op. cit., p284-299, and the 1790 Liverpool Poll book, containing a record of election addresses, squibs, poems, songs, and all votes cast.

claimed the support shown for Tarleton at the Exchange had been two to one. Meanwhile, *Andrew Marvel* questioned, "At a time when three candidates are on the spot, and have publickly addressed you, is it not the highest degree of arrogance and presumption for the Mayor and Bailiffs to call a meeting of the Freemen? What right have they to judge for you?" On a similar theme, *Anti-Corporate* reminded freemen of their privilege confirmed by charters and "sealed with the Blood of your Forefathers," adding that the corporation had tried "to rob you of your Blessing". Buoyed up by these and other messages, Tarleton declared, "The Experience of this Morning had plainly shewn you that the Interest of my two Opponents is one. I shall stand alone and unconnected with any Party."

Meanwhile, Penrhyn and Gascoyne supporters were far from silent. Their most powerful argument came from *Common Sense*, who weighed in by asking "Have not the Members served the Town Faithfully? Does not Colonel Tarleton himself allow that they have done so? Was not the African Trade in danger? Was not Mr. Pitt, the Minister, against it? Was not Mr. Fox, the Leader of the Opposition, against it? Was not the House of Commons against it? Who was there to stand up for it, but for LORD PENRYHN and MR. GASCOYNE? How then can any Man be so ungrateful as to give his Vote against them? The African Trade will certainly be attacked again! Suppose you elect Colonel Tarleton, and that he is ordered on foreign Service in the War that is coming on; who will there then be to support your Trade against Clamour and Ignorance? Everyone knows how slack Work was last Winter; if the African Trade is abolished you must all want Bread! You know it; These are all plain Facts; they speak for themselves. Colonel Tarleton may be a good Soldier, but he knows nothing of Trade – he is not a fit Member for the Place – every man in his Way – be not ungrateful – mind your own Interest and vote for your old Members: You have tried them, and they have stood the Trial. Do not be deluded by the senseless Noise of those who know no better, but consult your own understandings."

That Tarleton had served his country militarily was not in doubt, and many of his opponents praised his soldierly skills while wishing him well in his future military career. But others made concerted attacks on the Colonel's character, particularly his gambling and drinking, and his friendship with the unpopular, wayward Prince of Wales against the interests of the king. The effects of propaganda proved all too much, as he had to rely on persuading freemen to plump for him to deny his opponents their second votes. Faced with such expense, the next day he announced, "Gentlemen, with deep and unfeigned Regret, I am obliged to inform you that I cannot rescue you from the tyrannical Effects of a late Coalition. A Junction between Interests … must, for the present, outweigh the Liberty of the People, or Produce a Contest that would be attended with Consequences highly ruinous to a commercial Town like Liverpool." With that, Tarleton left for London, while scurrilous rumours began to spread that he had been bought off. Several of his opponents were magnanimous in bidding him farewell, as shown by *Countryside*, who ventured, "I wish our brave Townsman, the Colonel, may meet with every promotion he can deserve in the line of his profession." *Common Sense* added, "the noble colonel is a Valuable Man in the Military Line; and there he shines as much as Penrhyn and Gascoyne in the Parliament House."

June 17th, 1790.

TO ARMS !!! 'Tis now the Cause of Freedom calls upon you to assert your Rights, and independently vote in the Noble COLONEL, who is driven by the Mayor and certain great Men, with a heavy Heart, from his native Town. If you assert your Liberty, and give your Suffrages to your Townsman the Colonel, the brave Hero with Tears in his Eyes will return, with a Heart too full to speak his Gratitude.
AN INDEPENDENT FREEMAN.

A plea for support for Banastre Tarleton, and later reprinted in the 1790 Liverpool Poll Book (LRO)

Despite Tarleton's statement of withdrawal and hasty exit from Liverpool, supporters still rallied to his banner. Later that day, one calling himself *An Independent Freeman* beckoned supporters. "TO ARMS!!! 'Tis now the Cause of Freedom that calls upon you to assert your Rights and independently vote in the Noble Colonel, who is driven by the Mayor and certain Great Men, with a heavy heart, from his native Town. If you assert your Liberty, and give your Suffrages to your townsman the Colonel, the brave Hero with Tears in his Eyes will return with a Heart too full to speak his gratitude." But, despite this plea, the matter might have been laid to rest had the taps not been turned off by the apparent victors. Now that the trappings of an election contest could be dispensed with, the freemen found they were denied their usual treats and revelries. With this in mind, successful solicitor and Tarleton aide George Crump bought a cask of ale or porter and had it rolled to the top of Water Street, where the contents were distributed. Crump harangued voters not to give up the fight, and a rider was soon on his way to intercept Tarleton with a message of overwhelming support. By Saturday June 19th rumours were circulating that a poll would not take place, and a call went out from Tarleton's Brunswick Street headquarters for voters to give in their names so that a contest could be demanded. One journeyman even suggested they should march on the Exchange the following Monday morning, "and see who dare be hardy enough to refuse it."

An air of determination now pervaded the town. The canvassers were even out on Sunday 20th, and there were rumours that Lord Penrhyn was offering a coalition with Tarleton, but these were hotly denied. It was clear that sympathy and popular support for the hapless exile was growing, and on Sunday night one *Independent Burgess* issued a handbill stating, "Colonel Tarleton, in order to shew his disposition for peace, made a sacrifice for what had long been his greatest ambition, and quitted the town .....I shall this evening give my name (as 780 have already done) to vote a plumper for him." *Independent Burgess* had promised to vote for Penrhyn, but like many others felt no longer bound because of the coalition stitch up. Meanwhile, a statement was issued that "Colonel Tarleton is sent for Express, and will undoubtedly present himself to his liberal and generous Supporters the moment of his Arrival. ...The Friends of Colonel Tarleton are requested to meet in Bold Street at 8 o'clock in the morning and proceed from thence to the Hustings."

A large body was duly parading the streets early on Monday morning, headed by William Rigg of the counting house of merchants Tarleton and Backhouse. They soon joined a crowd at Tarleton's residence in Bold Street on the edge of the town, and the whole procession paraded along Church Street towards the Exchange. Riding at the head on a gelding was Ellis Leckonby Hodgson Esquire, who needed frequent administrations of smelling salts, being much the worse for alcohol. Meanwhile, Penryhn and Gascoyne supporters met at the *Golden Lion* just yards from their destination, but made their way via a circuit of the town centre preceded by a band. Among their procession was Mayor Thomas Smyth, accompanied by the council members, prominent merchants, and five leading clergymen who declared they were voting against Tarleton and sin. This sentiment angered *Anti-Corporate*, who wrote later that day, "When I see Clergymen at the Head of a Mob, with their Hats waving in the Air, vociferating 'Huzzah!' I own I poignantly feel the Self-violation of Respect due to the Cloth." But, as rumours of Tarleton's lifestyle continued to circulate, his supporters were told to shut their ears against malicious gossip. As the day's polling drew to a close, Penrhyn led with seventy-six votes, followed by Gascoyne on seventy-two. Tarleton was narrowly trailing with seventy-one, but his prospects were improved as his campaign managers cast their votes, bringing him level with the leader. He arrived back in Liverpool later that evening, and the taps began to flow. He then issued a statement that he would get straight down to business at his headquarters, but was soon plotting with his three brothers and George Crump as they began to organise a riot. That evening there was menace on the streets of Liverpool.

A page from the 1790 Poll Book showing further support for Tarleton during the recent election contest (LRO)

With rumours of their involvement circulating next morning, a denial was issued stating, "A REPORT having been industriously circulated that the Damage done Last Night by a numerous Set of Ruffians were the friends of Colonel TARLETON, the public are assured that the Perpetrators of this outrage, in general, were not FREEMEN, but a Band of Ruffians who spread the desolation around indiscriminately. The Chief Agent, however, was a FRIEND of the CORPORATION and of SLAVERY, and consequently no ADVOCATE for TARLETON, FREEDOM and LIBERTY." To cover their backs, however, a handbill was issued warning, "The Committee formed for the Conducting of Colonel Tarleton's election MOST heartily recommend to their BROTHER FREEMEN not to carry Sticks or Offensive Weapons of any kind." Meanwhile, Tarleton went early to the hustings dressed in his full green uniform. He thanked those who had voted for him in the previous election and apologised for letting them down. Striking at the core of the matter, Tarleton declared, "The point we struggle for is freedom of election," and asserted that the coalition had attempted to rob voters of their rights. After declaring himself a committed Whig, he held up his hand shorn of two fingers, and said "These gave I for King and Country." He then displayed a scar on his arm left by a sword wound, and quoted from *Henry V*, ending "And say these wounds had I on Crispin's day."

That same day, *Andrew Marvel* caused quite a stir when he alleged that he had discovered a card that had been distributed to a number of master tradesmen the previous Saturday night. It apparently read, "Lord Penryhn and Mr. Gascoyne very respectfully request the Honour of your Attendance at the Hotel on Monday at Nine o'Clock in the Morning, and THAT YOU WILL BRING WITH YOU ALL THE MEN IN YOUR EMPLOY, to proceed from thence to the Hustings." Marvel had hit upon a bombshell, and milked it for all its worth by asking, "Freemen of Liverpool, what do you think of this? Is *this* a serious and solemn call upon you to support your own rights and our glorious Constitution? Or is it the *Mandate* of an Eastern Despot, to some Bashaw of a distant Province? *Bring with you the men in your employ!* ! ! Surely it would not be the *British Freemen* who were thus to be at their Master's call! But if this tyrannical Summons was really meant for YOU, and YOU submit to such trammels – why then, YOU DESERVE TO BE GALL'D TO THE BONE." This was heady stuff, and Gascoyne now took to his bed and sent a note to his aides telling them that he was indisposed. Penryhn, on the other hand, was busy accusing Tarleton of stealing voters. Against this claim was the case cited of a man being led by force to vote for Penryhn, while protesting "Tarleton Forever! Tarleton Forever!" The man was apparently rescued, but not before a fight had broken out, one of many that day. By the end of Tuesday 22nd, there was disorder on almost every street, and events in Liverpool were gaining notoriety throughout the country. By the weekend it was being reported in London that there had been "very alarming riots which threatened even the burning down of Liverpool."

Matters were clearly getting out of hand by Wednesday 23rd. While issuing a statement of thanks for defeating the coalition, Tarleton reminded his supporters not "to commit themselves to any action contrary to the peace and harmony of the town." But that was not enough to stop the violence, and later that evening a second plea was issued stating that his committee "MOST heartily recommend to their BROTHER FREEMEN not to carry Sticks or Offensive Weapons of any kind, as the FRIENDS of FREEDOM are sufficiently protected by their cause and number from the insult of any party." Although this had some effect, the violence continued, and on Friday 25th Penrhyn issued a statement announcing that he was withdrawing from the contest as he could no longer face the disorder. However, many reasoned that the corporation had put pressure on him in the hope of saving Gascoyne, and by Sunday the Penrhyn camp was making a breathtaking attempt to salvage his position. Under the pseudonym *Justica* came the extraordinary words, "I Congratulate you on your Success in opposing a Power… It is true that you have compelled the Body-Corporate (like trembling Children) to kiss the rod that whipped them, and beg Assistance from the People, whose Judgement they derided, and whose Power they held in Contempt. You have crushed their Insolence but not extirpated their Strength… Will you hug those Serpents in your Bosom, who so lately put forth their forky Tongues to STING YOU? …I know you will say LORD PENRHYN joined your foes against you…but his heart could never be against you – it was a bad and unnatural COALITION. Colonel TARLETON was your favourite Candidate. He is now secure. Lord Penrhyn is the next in your esteem…If Lord Penrhyn is not Elected your grand Scheme cannot be accomplished."

Penrhyn's miserable effort failed, and at the final close of polling the next day he had sunk to third position with 716 votes. The result gave Tarleton a clear victory with 1269 votes, but Gascoyne had retained his seat with 888. Last, and by a long way least, was a little known candidate who had failed to make it in the public's consciousness. Poor Thomas Townley Parker barely registered on the scale, having gained a mere four votes. Celebrations were held on Thursday 1st July, when Tarleton's friends gave him dinner at the *King's Arms* in Water Street, where Thomas Clarkson and Alexander Falconbridge had lodged two years earlier. He was then chaired through the town by way of several taverns, where supporters drank the health of the man who had taken on the corporation and won. Next morning Tarleton gave a farewell speech, mounted his horse, and rode off for London to rejoin his mistress, the celebrated actress, Mary Robinson. He soon gained notoriety on the fashionable London and Brighton scenes for his drinking, gambling and womanising with the wayward Prince of Wales and the Dukes of York and Clarence. When *Williamson's Advertiser* printed messages of thanks from the candidates the following Monday, Tarleton declared that no election had been more distinguished for its harmony "from the commencement to its conclusion." But this view was not shared by Gascoyne, who summed up with a truer picture by lamenting the "anarchy and confusion which have prevailed upon the late election."[10]

The corporation was again challenged four months later, when thirty-six prominent freemen complained to Mayor John Sparling about its refusal to open up the process of filling council places. The so-called Common Council was an undemocratic body of about forty men chosen from well-established merchant families, making them a self-perpetuating oligarchy. Not only did it control the public purse, but the council also had legislative powers to make by-laws for governing the town without any reference to the freemen. Membership lasted until voluntary retirement or death; only on rare occasions did fellow members vote a colleague off the council. New members were usually chosen from merchants with an interest in the slave trade, but vacancies could be left open for years if it suited the council. Indeed, as there were now five vacancies, it seemed clear that the existing council members intended to preserve their exclusive power by keeping them unfilled.

Early in 1791 a petition was organised to call a special meeting of freemen known as the Common Hall, invoking rights under ancient charters predating those of the council. When over a thousand signatures had been collected, the mayor and his bailiffs, including Banastre Tarleton's brother Clayton, called a meeting for 17th January in the courtroom of the Exchange. Five new

---

10 *Williamson's Advertiser*, 5th July 1790.

council members were elected, and a resolution was also passed demanding that the Common Hall should be allowed to audit the corporation's accounts and records. However, the council refused to recognise the new members, and denied access to its books. Following protracted argument and obstinacy on the part of the undemocratic council, a second meeting of the Common Hall was called six months later. This claimed the right to make byelaws and regulate corporation spending, and voted to impose a penalty of forty shillings on the treasurer and town clerk if they continued to refuse an audit.[11] When the treasurer and town clerk failed to comply, and the council continued to deny the new members, the mayor and bailiffs sought legal action. The case was heard at the Lancaster Assizes late in August, when the jury supported the Common Hall's right to audit the books but not its right to elect councillors.[12] Not content with the outcome, the council applied to the Court of King's bench to challenge the verdict, since the matter had rested on various ambiguities and contradictions contained in charters issued by nearly every monarch since Elizabeth. The arguments were heard in May 1792, and the application for a new trial was granted. The case went back to Lancaster, but the same verdict was reached, and the legal process continued into the following year, when either the funds or resolve of the mayor and freemen finally gave out.[13]

While Liverpool's freemen were challenging the corporation, the parish committee was once again attempting to force it to pay taxes on its various tolls and rents, which were reckoned to be worth six thousand pounds annually. A similar attempt had failed five years earlier,[14] but the demands on the parish had grown inexorably with a huge rise in population since the end of the American war. A recent census of Liverpool's population counted nearly 56,000 people, which was a rise of more than 20,000 in just seven years.[15] This was largely due to a renewed influx of people from outside, many of who were "abandoned and dissolute characters who have no visible means or abilities to maintain themselves [and who] soon become a very great additional charge on this parish, or maintain themselves by theft or other iniquitous means, filling our streets with begging women, children, whores and thieves."[16] Managing this worsening situation was the job of Robert Oddie, who had been parish treasurer and governor of the Brownlow Hill workhouse for three years on

---

[11] *Williamson's Advertiser*, 13th and 27th June 1791.

[12] Ibid, 27th August 1791.

[13] Brook, op. cit., p224-230.

[14] See p125 above.

[15] Simmons' enumeration of October 1789 to January 1790, published in *Gore's Directory* in 1790, gave a population of 55,732. However, in his Medical Report of 1804, James Currie estimated that 4%, or 2229, should have been added to allow for mariners at sea, bringing the total to 57,961. Williams, op. cit., gives a figure of about 34,000 for 1783.

[16] T. Troughton, *A History of Liverpool*, 1810, p147, quoted in. I. C. Taylor, *Court and Cellar Dwellings: Eighteenth Century Origins of the Liverpool Slum*, Historic Society of Lancashire and Cheshire, Vol. 122 (1970), p71. Troughton was referring to the situation in the late 18th century.

an annual salary of a hundred guineas. He was also responsible for managing outdoor relief, since there were far too many paupers to accommodate within the workhouse itself. Although there were overseers and churchwardens on the ground to help him, Oddie was feeling overwhelmed by the sheer scale of his task and asked to be relieved of his post at the Easter Vestry meeting in April 1791, but agreed to continue until a replacement could be found. The meeting also accepted a motion from the recorder to investigate morals within the workhouse, "having himself been ear witness to the very great immoralities and profane swearing as he casually passed the Workhouse in going that road."[17] A select committee reported in October, "It appears that great reform is necessary...in the manner of issuing provisions, as in the quantity and kind thereof, and in keeping a regular account of the same, and of the value of the daily expenditure. No accurate list appears to have been made up of the number of persons actually in the house, which the Committee conceive ought to be done at least once every week."[18] Further details revealed that the amount of "sweet milk" drunk had greatly increased, while the consumption of cheaper buttermilk residue had declined. Oatmeal, bread, beef, ale and beer were now being issued in abundance, and the committee believed inmates were overfed. Some were also wearing shoes rather than clogs, and there was little supervision to ensure that all who were capable were working to produce clothing and other goods to help finance their upkeep.

The committee concluded that, "A general superintendence seems greatly wanting, nor does the present governor seem equal to it," but noted that he was an honest, diligent, and well disposed man who would be better employed as assistant governor. Members also noted "great reason to lament the improper plan of the house, which renders it impossible to introduce that system of regularity and decency which are so essential to the well-being of the institution. The indiscriminate accommodation of paupers of both sexes in the same dwelling is productive of many inconveniences. The sick are not disposed of in a proper and commodious manner. The infirm are inconveniently situated for the attendance of those appointed to take care of them."[19] The members then agreed a limit of two thousand pounds for alterations, rough plans were drawn up, and advertisements were later placed in the newspapers inviting tenders. The dispensary physicians were added to the committee, and Dr. James Currie soon began a campaign to fund a separate fever ward. By April 1792 Oddie had stepped aside completely to be replaced by William Haliday on a salary of £250 for himself and a clerk, while Edward Nixon was appointed as the new assistant governor.

---

[17] Peet, op. cit., p306.
[18] Ibid., p307.
[19] Ibid, p308.

The Liverpool census of 1789-90 provided a breakdown of numbers in each type of accommodation, and showed that nearly two thousand people were in charitable institutions such as the workhouse, the infirmary, the Bluecoat and seamen's hospitals, and in various almshouses. Of the general population, nearly 40,000 people lived in 6,540 'front houses' looking onto the streets. These were the more fortunate, since there were 1728 inhabited cellars shared between 6,780 people, averaging four to a cellar. Given that most cellars were less than six feet in height, and their ceilings were just above street level, living conditions were about as bad as they could get. Those along Whitechapel and Paradise Street were especially liable to flooding, as William Moss had noted in his medical report of 1784. Three years later a surveyors' report had discussed ways "to prevent the water in future incommoding the tenants of the houses of Paradise Street by flowing into the cellars on the occasion of the fall of rain."[20] But nothing was done, and *Williamson's Advertiser* noted late in 1789, "To the honour of the Trustees of that excellent Charity, our Infirmary, we have the pleasure to acquaint our readers that the vacant wards have been fitted up for the reception of the poor people who were driven out of the cellars in Whitechapel and that neighbourhood by the late very uncommon flood, which deluged their habitations."[21] The town surveyors were still declaring the situation inadequate two years later when they reported that residents were frequently "reduced to the greatest distress", and some were "not acquainted with their situation till they found the water coming into their beds."[22] Others suffered constantly from the effluent that constantly seeped through their cellar walls from privies situated nearby.

However, the number of occupied cellars continued to multiply, particularly as a feature of back-to-back developments that were being thrown up in many parts of the town. Back houses had first been built in open spaces behind houses on the main streets, either as one-storied lean-to dwellings or separate cottages. But the idea of infilling land was taken much further by property developers, many of whom, like John Yates, began re-investing profits from slavery and other shipping ventures to capitalise on an exploding population. Indeed, they viewed their tenants rather like cargo, human or otherwise, and sought to maximise every available space for the least outlay. By 1790 there were 1608 back houses inhabited by nearly eight thousand people. With just one small room measuring some thirteen feet square on each of three floors above a cellar, these tiny houses were built around narrow courtyards in groups of six, eight or ten and backed on to others behind. Each group

---

[20] Taylor, op. cit p75.
[21] *Williamson's Advertiser*, 12th October 1789.
[22] Taylor, op. cit. p75.

was arranged behind a front house overlooking the street, and was accessed through a narrow alleyway. Toilets consisted of lean-to privies with wooden seats placed over ash pits that were shared by up ten families. One such development was underway along Crosbie Street south of the Old Dock, on land originally leased from the corporation by merchant slave trader and former mayor William Crosbie. He gave his courts such names as 'King,' 'Village,' 'Oak,' 'Pine,' and 'Elm,' which was quite grotesque given their real nature. There were sixty-one houses fronting Crosbie Street in 1790, behind which were eighty-four court houses crammed in an area of about half an acre. Nearly a thousand people lived in this space, including 181 who lived in forty-two cellars.[23] Such developments continued to be built well into the next century, while the corporation, which ultimately owned the land, did nothing to regulate housing standards. Meanwhile, the exodus of the wealthy to the eastern fringes of Liverpool continued, particularly around Clayton Square and the neighbourhood of Ranelagh and Bold Streets. Fine new Georgian houses were also appearing along Rodney Street, from where investors and developers could look down upon the vista below.

Indeed, the poor of Liverpool could not help but be constantly aware of the gap between their living standards and those above them. In August 1791 a strike broke out among seamen, ship builders, carpenters, and allied tradesmen that lasted five or six weeks. The mayor and magistrates took a dim view, and issued a notice "To the Artificers, Labourers, and others who are disposed to return to their respective occupations, that they will be protected by the Civil Powers." But the decree also warned "all persons who riotously attempt to obstruct them in the execution of their lawful employment will be prosecuted according to law."[24] Following an extract from the Riot Act, the authorities gave notice that groups of twelve or more would be liable to arrest, while responsibility for any injury or death lay with the protesters. Memories of the riots of the same month sixteen years earlier clearly worried the authorities, and they sent for the military. Towards the end of the month *Williamson's Advertiser* reported, "On Friday evening arrived here from Manchester a party of Lord Pembroke's regiment of Dragoons, and we hear that two more troop are hourly expected. These, with the addition of a part of the same regiment which was before stationed here, and the assistance of near 300 gentlemen and others who have been sworn in Peace Officers, we doubt not will preserve the tranquillity of the town, which it was feared would have suffered some disturbance from the seamen, carpenters, and other mechanics who are at present off work in order to obtain an advance of wages." The paper then

---

23 Taylor, op. cit., p85.
24 *Williamson's Advertiser*, 29th August 1791.

added, "Much to the credit of Mr. Grayson's and Mr. Wright's ship building yards, all their servants attended work this morning as usual."[25] The strike was indeed dividing workers, and by early September rewards of twenty guineas were being offered for information, not only about anyone using threats or intimidation, but also for intelligence on the "several unlawful combinations" themselves. The magistrates complained of ship repairers leaving work unfinished "to the great injury and detriment of their employers, " and warned, "Such persons are to take notice that unless they return to compleat their engagements they will be prosecuted." Threats were also extended to "all seafaring men who have signed articles to proceed to sea, and who refuse to comply with the same," warning they would be apprehended and punished accordingly. But *Williamson's* was able to report that "peace and good order has been preserved throughout the week, and we doubt not that the matters will soon be settled to the satisfaction of each party."[26]

Although the strike went on into late September, the paper did not report on its outcome. However, it seems that the strike was unsuccessful, because carpenters again downed tools the following spring. On 27th May 1792, mayor Henry Blundell wrote to the Home Secretary, informing him that he had met with three representatives who told him "a great body" intended to strike unless they got an increase of four pence a day. Although the carpenters had given undertakings to be peaceful, Blundell asked Secretary Dundas to send a cavalry unit from Manchester to Warrington near Liverpool. Although there were already troops of the 30th regiment in Liverpool, Blundell thought the threat so serious that backup might be needed. His reason was that "There seems too general an appearance of discontent among all artificers and labourers, which must if possible be prevented into tumult." He added that he also had information about a wage claim from the crews of coal barges, and that " we must either comply with this demand or be guarded against the consequences." Dundas replied that it would be difficult to remove troops from Manchester as there were similar threats of civil disorder there, but he could answer the call "in a case of absolute necessity." Fortunately for the mayor, he was able to write back a few days later with news that the carpenters' claim had been agreed in part. They had decided to settle and gone back to work after only a day, although the Mersey flatmen were still on strike.[27]

The mayor could count himself lucky, since the 30th regiment was now being blighted by an outbreak of typhus. The troops were billeted throughout

---

25 *Williamson's Advertiser*, 29th August 1791.
26 Ibid, 5th September 1791.
27 Hickins, op. cit., p25-26. Coal was brought from Manchester along the Duke of Bridgewater's canal to the River Mersey at Runcorn, from where it was taken to the Duke's small private dock in Liverpool by Mersey 'flat' or river barge.

the town and mounted guard at the fort, but several infantrymen had recently been locked up in a dank, dirty cell for drunken behaviour. At the start of June two of the men showed signs of 'jail fever', but the typhus soon spread and ten soldiers were sent to the infirmary. By the middle of the month fifty-eight soldiers had been infected, the infirmary had become full, and a temporary hospital had been set up at the fort. This consisted of two low-ceilinged rooms, each about fifteen square feet, that had been cleaned and ventilated, but were soon crammed with the sick. They were attended by Dr. James Currie, who believed that fevers were best treated by dousing the patient's body with cold water, or in more serious cases involving delirium, by applying vinegar by sponge.[28] What Currie could not have known was that the disease is carried by bacteria in the faeces of lice, mites, ticks and fleas, and is most contagious in dirty, crowded conditions where these thrive. Yet, whether or not his simple treatment had any beneficial effect, only two soldiers died and the rest recovered.

Currie was a leading physician at the dispensary on Church Street, which treated more than 14,000 patient cases that year. Over three thousand of these were fevers caused largely by typhus and dysentery. This accounted for nearly six per cent of the local population, and similar numbers were affected each year. Currie and others understood that poor living conditions were chiefly to blame, but clung to the view that much depended on weather conditions. He analysed the number of fever cases seen by the dispensary each month since 1780, and came to the conclusion that the transition from winter to summer caused the greatest shock to the system, with March and April producing the highest number of cases. He also questioned the established belief that cold winters were healthier than mild ones because of their effect in killing off diseases, but showed instead that cases of fever had been fewer during recent mild winters than in colder ones. Currie's belief in the use of applying water to fever patients, which presumably helped to reduce high body temperature, was not part of general practice. Treatment of fever at the dispensary consisted of antimonial emetics to cause vomiting, followed by liberal amounts of a cordial of bark, opium and wine.

Apart from civil disturbances, poverty, overcrowding, poor sanitation, and fever, the town was beset by problems of crime. While pickpockets and cut-purses worked the more crowded areas, usually by day, footpads plied their trade, unseen and unheard, in the narrow streets at night. Cases tried by Liverpool magistrates in September 1791 mostly involved petty theft, including watches, cloth and small quantities of money, for which the guilty received sentences ranging from one to four months in the House of Correction. Some were also

---

[28] J. Currie M.D.F.R.S., *Medical Reports on the Effects of Water, Cold and Warm, as a Remedy, in Fever and other Diseases, Whether Applied to the Surface of the Body, or Used Internally* (1804) p9-12.

whipped, but Joseph Jackson was sentenced to five years transportation. Some cases were sent to the Lancaster Assizes, including three men for burglary, two for stealing a sheep, and three for horse stealing. Others included James Gregory for "ravishment", William Bateson for "want of sureties to keep the peace", and James Worsley for returning early from transportation. The most serious cases involved Joseph Wray, John Stubbs, George Taylor and Samuel Mather, all accused of murder.[29]

One burglary that was successfully foiled was attempted early in September 1791, when four men broke into Mrs. Borkhill's house in Bold Street between two and three in the morning. Luckily, as they picked the lock of the back door and entered the yard, the family was woken. The manservant, armed with a large "horse pistol", opened a window and told them to disperse or he would fire. One of the intruders presented his own pistol, so the servant fired, then ran downstairs and grabbed another pistol. By the time he got into the yard, his assailants had got away, but daylight revealed a large quantity of blood which could be traced to the new Music Hall in the same street. This was the second attempted burglary of the Borkhill house in a month, which explained why the family was so well prepared.[30]

However, the danger was not confined to the streets of Liverpool. James Burns stood accused of highway robbery, and wine merchant Joseph Hall was the victim of five footpads while returning home on horseback shortly after dark on 25th August. As he approached Low Hill on the road from Prescot, he was stopped by five men armed with bludgeons and other weapons. When they seized his horse by the bridle, it immediately sprung round and threw Joseph Hall to the ground. The ruffians held him down "with imprecations," rifled his pockets of papers, seventeen guineas in cash, and two bills worth nearly eighty-four pounds. They also took his hat, a knife and his saddle, then let him loose with threats that they would kill him if he made a sound. After their escape Hall managed to get assistance, when he borrowed a lantern and found his horse but none of his other belongings. It was soon discovered that the bills had been cashed at Macclesfield a few days later, and a hundred guinea reward was offered for information leading to the thieves' capture. This was also extended to any of the gang members themselves, with an assurance that every effort would be made to "obtain his Majesty's most gracious Pardon." Most of them managed to avoid detection, but Thomas Fleming was later arrested and executed at Lancaster in April the following year. Meanwhile, on Liverpool's outskirts, residents were asked to give information of all suspicious persons lurking in their neighbourhoods.[31] Indeed, four years earlier, residents of

---

[29] *Williamson's Advertiser*, 29th August and 5th September 1791.
[30] Ibid, 5th September 1791.
[31] Ibid, 25th August and 5th September 1791.

Toxteth Park had become so alarmed at the number of thefts and burglaries that the residents had joined the Earl of Sefton in forming a neighbourhood watch. The idea had spread to other outlying areas, and the number of watchmen employed by the parish had been increased in response.[32]

In the meantime, Thomas Clarkson continued relentlessly with his struggle against the slave trade. Following his quest for facts in Bristol, Liverpool and elsewhere, Clarkson had been to Paris to persuade the National Assembly to end slavery in the French Caribbean. He returned a disappointed man, having found little support for extending liberty to slaves, but soon resumed work seeking information for the ongoing parliamentary enquiry. By early 1791 Clarkson had added sixteen hundred miles in his search for potential witnesses, but could only find nine who were willing to give evidence and risk intimidation. He also received letters detailing the ill-treatment of seamen and abuse of slaves. He later wrote, "the effect of these accounts was in some instances to overwhelm me for a time in tears, and in others to produce a vivid indignation, which affected my whole frame." Plagued by visions of cruelty during restless nights, Clarkson added, "my mind was confined to one gloomy and heart-breaking subject for months. It had no respite, and my health began now materially to suffer."[33]

However, apart from gambling debts and female conquests, Banastre Tarleton had other concerns. As Liverpool's new Member of Parliament, and as brother to a leading slave trader, Tarleton was charged with defending their interests to the hilt. No matter that during his election campaign he had claimed to be an advocate of freedom and liberty, or that he had accused his opponents of being friends to slavery. When William Wilberforce proposed a new abolition bill in April 1791, Tarleton responded with a long speech in defence of the trade. The Commons rejected the bill by 163 votes to 88 after only two days of debate, and the church bells rung in celebration throughout Liverpool.

This led to a nationwide campaign to boycott West Indian sugar, which was supported by at least 300,000 people nationally within a year.[34] By the time Wilberforce put forward another abolition motion in April 1792, over five hundred petitions had also been organised and presented to Parliament.

---

32 Peet, op. cit., pLi.
33 Clarkson, op. cit., Vol. 2, p22-23.
34 Hochschild, op. cit., p193.

These contained nearly 400,000 signatures, including twenty thousand from Manchester, representing nearly a third of its population.[35] Meanwhile, during a year in which a record number of its ships sailed to Africa, Liverpool sent one of only four petitions supporting the trade. Although there were some in the town who were quietly opposed, the majority of Liverpool's workforce believed their livelihoods depended on building, maintaining, supplying and manning the 'Guinea' ships. Known abolitionists faced open hostility, as was acknowledged in a letter from mayor Henry Blundell to William Pitt. He warned, "I am well informed the journeymen carpenters of this town (who are a very powerful body of men) had a meeting of some of the heads of them on Sat. evening last, and were heard to say that if the abolition of the slave trade takes place, some houses in the town (which they had marked) should be pulled down. As Chief Magistrate of this great trading town, I conceive it my duty to apprise you of it, and tho I do not (I confess) apprehend much danger myself (having the 30th Regt of Foot here) yet with submission, Sir, to yourself (and His Majesty's service will admit of it) I should recommend three troops of horse to be quartered in the neighbourhood till the present ferment subsides a little."[36]

When the debate began in Parliament, Tarleton accused the abolitionists of a sham. He suggested their petitions were too similar in form and language to be genuine, and added mockingly that they had "exercised almost unexampled zeal and industry to extort names from the sick, the indigent, and the traveller…. boys have been indulged with the gladsome tidings of a holiday, provided they would sign."[37] After Tarleton had rubbished stories of the horrors of the middle passage, the debate continued long into the night, with the trade's supporters again claiming that the French would take over Britain's share, and that slavery rescued Africans from barbarity. In the early hours of 3rd April, Home Secretary Henry Dundas tabled an amendment to Wilberforce's bill that would allow for gradual abolition. Frustrated by his colleague's suggestion, William Pitt questioned, "How, Sir, is this enormous evil ever to be eradicated if every nation is thus prudentially to wait till the concurrence of all the world shall have been obtained?" With vehement passion he added, "There is no nation in Europe that has, on the one hand, plunged so deeply into this guilt as Great Britain, or that is so likely, on the other, to be looked up to as an example." [38] But, with record profits being made from slavery, Dundas won the day, and the Commons agreed to postpone abolition for four years. This would still have been a triumph had the Lords endorsed the bill, but with

---

35 Hochschild, op cit., p230-231.
36 Quoted in Hickins, op.cit., p25.
37 Quoted in Hochschild, op. cit., p231.
38 Quoted in Hochschild, p233.

even more members involved in slavery than in the Commons they rejected it outright.

Across the channel, meanwhile, events were unfolding rapidly towards another conflict that would soon engulf most of Europe for more than twenty years. When news of the fall of the Bastille reached London, Charles James Fox declared it the greatest moment in history. Many shared his belief that the French Revolution was long overdue, and that major reforms were also needed in Britain. But others were alarmed by the power of the mob, and even extending the franchise in Britain beyond its present narrow limits was regarded as a threat to the established order. Mob violence was commonplace, the most serious examples being London's Gordon Riots of 1780, and the Liverpool seamen's riots five years before that. In October 1790, Fox's erstwhile friend and Whig colleague, Edmund Burke, published his *Reflections on the Revolution in France*, in which he predicted anarchy, bloodshed, war and dictatorship, and warned of revolution spreading to English shores. This publication was soon countered by Tom Paine, who had publicly welcomed the American Revolution, and now did the same for the French in his *Rights of Man*, which sold hundreds of thousands of copies.

Yet, despite much hot air both inside Parliament and out, the revolution in France had thus far been relatively peaceful. After abolishing the privileges of church and nobility, and issuing its *Declaration of Rights*, the National Assembly had set about forming a constitution and reforming the economy and legal system. Most of its members wanted a constitutional monarchy rather than a republic, and to bring France more into line with Britain by allowing more power for the *bourgeois* middle class. But even this proved too much for Louis, who began secret negotiations with Marie Antoinette's Austrian brother, the Emperor Leopold II. Troops were promised if Louis could reach the stronghold of Montmédy near southern Belgium and raise a sizable force. With French *émigrés* forces preparing at Brussels, Coblenz and Turin, Louis was confident of success. In June 1791 he and Marie Antoinette fled Paris in disguise, but were recognised and arrested en route. When they were brought back to Paris under heavy guard the streets were lined with spectators, many no longer regarding their king with affection but rather as a traitor. A huge crowd gathered on the Champ-de-Mars on 17th July to sign a petition for the king's removal, spurred on by the speeches of their more radical elements. When the National Assembly became alarmed and called upon the National Guard to restore order, the crowd responded with a barrage of stones. At first the solders fired into the air, but then fired into the crowd as the mob continued its attacks, killing at least fifty people and injuring hundreds more.

Along with Louis' brother, the Comte d'Artois, and Frederick Wilhelm II of Prussia, Leopold was soon demanding an end to the Assembly and the restoration of the French king's right to rule. These autocratic rulers feared the spread of revolution across their borders, and threatened military intervention. However, by the end of September the Assembly had drawn up a constitution that offered parliamentary government, equality before the law, and a system based on merit rather than birthright. Louis accepted this, and even promised to defend France against any external attack. Some Assembly members now considered their work finished, and looked forward to an enlightened government under a liberal king and parliament. A new Legislative Assembly was formed in October, but was riven by factions from the start. While some members supported the monarchy, they were outnumbered by republicans, particularly the Girondins and the Jacobins.[39] In January 1792, aware of its fragile position, the new Assembly sent an ultimatum to the Austrian Emperor to recognise the new government and renounce any notion of hostility. In the meantime, it ordered that all property of French émigrés be confiscated. Leopold died while considering the situation, and his son Francis rejected the ultimatum outright. The Assembly declared war on Austria in April, drawing Prussia into the fray as its ally. As war erupted in July, the Duke of Brunswick, commander-in-chief of the combined forces of Austria and Prussia, declared his intention to restore the old order in France. He further warned Parisians of his "resolve to inflict on them the most terrible punishments if the least insult should be offered to his Most Christian Majesty, for whom the city of Paris is particularly responsible."[40]

But there were others equally concerned within France itself about the course of the revolution, since the Assembly chiefly represented middle class interests. The labouring classes had no more wish to be dominated by the *bourgeoisie* than by the aristocracy, and believed egalitarian principles should be driven further to encompass their interests. They wanted wage increases, fixed prices, and an end to food shortages and hording. Beyond these demands they wanted a more equal distribution of wealth, and an economy that favoured

---

[39] Girondists favoured decentralised government and were named after the Gironde region of S.W. France, from where their leading deputies came. Jacobins favoured strong centralised government and were so-called because their headquarters was based in the St. Jacques area of Paris.
[40] *Williamson's Advertiser,* 13th August 1792.

small farmers, shopkeepers and artisans. In short, they had become politicised by the revolution, roused by the most extreme revolutionary activists, the Jacobins. A report from Paris on 20th July suggested that, "In proportion as the danger approaches, our National Assembly seems to become riotous and unreasonable. They are even exciting discord in the army that is to defend and preserve them; and if M. de la Fayette was to appear in Paris, he would be torn limb from limb, so violent, or rather furious, are the populace become. Nothing is heard in the streets but the most horrible and sanguinary declarations, and that with so much earnestness, and in a manner so determined, that we have everything to fear the instant the Prussian and Austrian troops enter France....I inform you that it is no longer safe to declare our opinion, if we are more than two or three; and moderation – in the eyes of the mob – is a crime deserving of death, which they inflict the instant they pronounce it."[41]

A mob stormed the Tuileries on 12th August, intent on imprisoning the royal family and bringing the Assembly to its knees. The palace was under the protection of Swiss guards, who soon found themselves in a critical situation on an already excessively hot day. An observer noted, "There is no doubt that the Swiss fired first, but not until they were pressed upon in the most violent way, and their guns forcibly turned round and planted against the palace. M. de Affray gave the order to fire. The federate of Brest and Marseilles rushed forward, and in a few minutes there was a dreadful slaughter. The Swiss retreated to the palace, and kept a most fateful fire from the windows. The dead lay in heaps. The Quays were full of people, armed and unarmed, and directing their fire deliberately into this multitude, the massacre was dreadful. It did not, however, intimidate the assailants. Seven pieces were played on the Thuilleries and the Louvre. They made breaches in the old wall in a short time, but their impetuosity from the Place de Carousel was irresistible. They broke in, and in a few minutes the multitude filled the palace. Every Swiss that came in their way perished, but numbers found temporary safety in the cellars and garrets, and were with difficulty saved from the rage of the people."[42]   The mob set about its utter destruction once inside the palace, fuelled by "immense quantities" of wine discovered in the cellars. Statues, fine china and glassware were smashed in an orgy of hatred and retribution, while bonfires were made of rich furniture and tapestries, and the bodies of palace defenders were thrown on the flames. By the end of the day an estimated 2,500 people had lost their lives.

During the melee, the royal family were arrested by Jacobin members of the Legislative Assembly, partly for their protection, but also to appease the mob.

[41] *Williamson's Advertiser*, 6th August 1792.
[42] Ibid, 20th August 1792.

The Jacobins and their unruly followers now demanded the right of all adult males to elect a new body to represent their interests, and set up a revolutionary municipal government, or commune, to rival the Assembly. Anarchy now spread throughout Paris, as the mob rampaged through the streets, destroyed prisons and set up barricades, killing well over a thousand victims. Meanwhile, nearly 200,000 Austrian, Prussian and French émigrés forces were massing on France's eastern border. As their invasion began, thousands of Frenchmen were daily recruited into the National Guard to meet the threat, while around two thousand royalists went to the guillotine. By 20th September the Prussians had reached a hundred miles east of Paris, but were halted at Valmy. Two days after, the newly elected National Convention formally abolished the monarchy and declared France a republic. A month later, having reached as far as Lille, the Austrians were being driven back eastwards, and by December the French army had occupied Brussels. Confident in their successes, the revolutionaries now declared their intention to bring liberty to all of Europe by ending the powers of church and aristocracy throughout the continent. By the end of the year Louis was put on trial for conspiring with foreign forces and violating the liberties of the French people. On 21st January 1793, Louis was sent to the guillotine and executed before a huge crowd. Within a fortnight, Britain and France were at war.

High Street, from the Exchange, 1790, Herdman Collection, 1108

Chapter Eight

Passions ran high in Liverpool as the year drew to a close. A month before Christmas 1792, a thousand handbills were distributed on Liverpool's streets branding local reformers and radicals as subversive Jacobin extremists. Being the work of Mayor Clayton Tarleton this was somewhat surprising, having so recently helped his predecessor champion freemen's rights against the powerful local council.[1] But the French Revolution had taken a menacing turn and now threatened all Europe. In the meantime, Banastre Tarleton had been to Paris with his hair cropped in the new French fashion, and had even reviewed the National Guard on the Champ de Mars alongside Lafayette. But his enthusiasm had been dampened when he narrowly escaped being strung up by a Paris mob, and next day witnessed Princess Lamballe's head being paraded on a pike.[2] That September alone, around two thousand royalists were sent to the guillotine. A decree was also issued for the arrest of all English subjects on French soil, and Banastre was lucky to escape France with his life. For Clayton, the near loss of a brother was enough, but above all he was a loyal subject of the crown. Now with full council backing, his handbill questioned the loyalties of those who simply supported the Revolution's more peaceful aims. Some felt this was as an incitement to violence, and there were warnings of riots and disturbances.[3]

Days after the handbill's circulation, one of Liverpool's leading radicals published a rebuttal. William Rathbone's pamphlet '*Equality*' defended the Revolution's democratic principles, and accused the mayor of provocation. Clayton's answer was to propose a loyal address to the king that implied a threat from home-grown radicals. Outraged at this manoeuvre, moderate Whig merchants demanded a public meeting to gauge public opinion. Days later, hundreds crowded into the Exchange to hear the impassioned speeches, and a more moderate address was overwhelmingly endorsed by over a thousand signatures. But this was not the end of the matter, and Clayton was again stirring up the atmosphere. Meanwhile, his brother wrote from London advising, "A good citizen, a good Whig, and a good subject ought to look at all Measures with calmness and moderation and strive to balance the political machine." These were fine words coming from Banastre, who understood all too well how to manipulate a mob. His warnings soon proved justified, as the mayor's supporters took to the streets chanting *God Save the King*, and smashing the windows of known radicals. Serious trouble

---

[1] See p172-173 above.
[2] Bass, op. cit., p322.
[3] Tarleton Papers, LRO 920/TAR/4/44.

threatened as they reached the Exchange, where they were met by Rathbone and his supporters. A quiet man of Quaker principles, Rathbone was not normally one to lead a mob, but on this occasion he was determined to make his stand. As he attempted to pacify the new arrivals with an eloquent speech, Rathbone was shouted down, and scuffles broke out between rival groups in front of the Exchange. After being jostled and taunted, Rathbone was ushered away, and the mayor's supporters dispersed after their small victory. Having been badly shaken by this experience, Rathbone's hair turned white almost overnight.[4]

Across the country, arguments continued to rage over the merits of the Revolution, opinions being divided along lines that had little or nothing to do with social position. Radical clubs and reform societies flourished as they spread the gospel of democracy, some even calling for a British revolution. But much of their support evaporated with news of the French king's execution. In Liverpool, as elsewhere, all flags on ships and principal buildings were set at half-mast, and the townsfolk braced themselves for a war that now seemed inevitable. Diehard radicals fell silent, as memories of a previous conflict returned. Within weeks, a small delegation was invited to meet with William Pitt to discuss the protection of Liverpool's shipping, which now handled a sixth of all Britain's trade.[5] All merchant vessels were to be well armed, and Letters of Marque were issued to licence ships as privateers against French vessels. Liverpool's fighting spirit was being rekindled.

Even before the first exchange of cannon fire, however, local tragedy struck. The *Pelican* was cruising the Mersey in a moderate breeze on 20th March 1793, having recently been launched in readiness for its maiden voyage as a privateer. Besides carrying twenty guns and all its stores, about two hundred people were on board celebrating the occasion, including dignitaries, shareholders, seamen, wives and children. As the ship began to turn near Seacombe opposite Liverpool, it suddenly capsized and filled with water through its open ports. The *Pelican* sank within ten minutes, and although many were rescued by small boats or managed to swim to safety, around seventy or eighty people were drowned.[6]

But, such a loss could not be allowed to dampen the spirits of hardy seamen spoiling for a fight. The first French prize brought into Liverpool was *L'Agreable*, taken by the *Harriet* on 5th April, after which its cargo was auctioned by Messrs. Ewart and Rutson in Exchange Alley. The *Thomas* took *La Expeditif* on the 6th with a cargo valued at around £10,000, and nine days later the *Princess Elizabeth* seized *Les Bons Freres*, laden with coffee, indigo

---

[4] This account is based on Sanderson, *Politics in Liverpool,* p81-82, and Sellars, op. cit., p50-51.
[5] Tarleton Papers, LRO 920/TAR/4/54.
[6] Williams, op cit, p304-305.

and sugar. A month later, the *Prince of Wales* captured *Le Federatif* with a cargo worth £32,000, and the *Dudgeon* took two French vessels within four days valued at £20,000. So it went on, and by the middle of the year over sixty Liverpool ships were armed and crewed as privateers, while yet more were being fitted out.[7]

Meanwhile, the French were not idle. The *Swift* was seized on 26th May by a French privateer, and its cargo of thirty-three slaves and 224 elephant teeth was taken. Rather unusually, Captain Roper was allowed to keep his ship and most of his crew, although the second mate was taken as hostage for a £1,000 ransom. Others were less fortunate. After the seizure of the *Active*, captain Bower wrote to his employers, "It is with concern I inform you of our being captured on 21st ult., by the French frigate Semillante, of 44 guns and 300 men, who took me on board. She also captured, the next day, a brig privateer (the Betsey, of Guernsey), of 10 guns and 55 men. On the 27th, she fell in with an English frigate, whom she engaged two hours, had twenty men killed and forty wounded. Among the former was the captain, first lieutenant, and a petty officer, when he bore away, having five feet of water in the hold, and was chased by the English frigate, whose main-top giving way, the Frenchman (I am sorry to say it) escaped, for could the frigate have come up with her again, she would have struck immediately. She proceeded directly for Brest, where we arrived the 2nd of June, and where I have been in prison until yesterday, when I was marched for Dinant with 112 more English prisoners, and this day arrived at Morlaix on our road thither. We have been just now joined by two men belonging to the *Allanson*, Capt. Byrne, private ship of war, taken in a prize captured by that vessel." [8] About two months later, the *Olive* was attacked by a French frigate in mid-Atlantic and taken to the port of Brest. An officer from the *Olive* complained about the French captain, who he felt "behaved in a most villainous manner, sheering up alongside and pouring nine of his heavy guns right into us before he hailed, which killed one man and wounded another." With such a broadside from a man-of-war it was perhaps miraculous that more casualties were not suffered. The officer continued, "We found it impossible to get away from her, she sailed so much faster than us. They boarded and stripped us of every article but the clothes on our backs, and in that state we were landed at Brest."[9]

By now, the press gangs were back at work in Liverpool, although officially their purpose was to encourage voluntary recruitment. An argument broke out one October evening between Felix M'Ilroy, captain of the *Ann*, and a press gang from a tender lying at anchor in the Mersey. One of the gang drew a pistol

7 Williams, op. cit., p305-307.
8 Ibid, p314-315.
9 Ibid, p318.

Report in Williamson's Advertiser, 21st October 1793, concerning reaction to Felix M'Illroy's murder (LRO)

as the argument raged and shot M'Ilroy dead. The killer was arrested next morning, but that evening a large body of seamen gathered in Strand Street and wrecked a recruitment house used by the press gang. The sailors then went to New Quay, where they repeated the scene at a second rendezvous, destroying the furniture and bedding, and completely gutting its interior, so that little more than a shell was left standing. Eventually the mayor appeared and managed to persuade the men to disperse.[10] Later, after a coroner's jury had returned a verdict of murder, the killer was tried at Lancaster Assizes, but was sentenced to just one month's imprisonment.

Indeed, the law was heavily weighted in favour of press agents, since the Royal Navy largely depended on their ruthlessness in kidnapping and enslaving anyone they thought suitable to serve on board a man-of-war. Seamen were obvious candidates, and were clearly identifiable by their dress, gait, and weather-beaten features, but just about anyone was prone to kidnap. Night-time was surely the most inauspicious for any tar or landsman to be out alone, especially while venturing home along some quiet alley after several pints of ale. Once aboard the navy tender, which became a permanent floating prison on the Mersey, there was no chance of escape and little hope of return. Those on board might be held for several weeks or more, chained and shackled like their African counterparts, before being distributed among His Majesty's vessels all around the country. On the other hand, life for the pressmen could be just as risky, and any found off guard was liable to be tarred and feathered or end up in the dock. Street brawls were frequent, as small armies of sailors, riggers or carpenters would stop work at the drop of a hat once they were given the signal to rescue a mate from the press gang's clutches. However, when the navy's men were out in force, many locals preferred to take refuge in the relative safety of Cheshire across the river. Indeed, seldom

> On Friday evening an unfortunate affray took place at the bottom of Redcrofs-ftreet, between Mr. Felix M'Ilroy, mafter of the floop Ann, of Newry, and fome of the people belonging to the Ann, Tender, lying in the river; one of whom, with a piftol, fhot Captain M'Ilroy in the breaft, of which wound he immediately expired; the offending perfon got on board the Tender, but was next morning delivered to the Civil Power, to anfwer for the tranfaction.
>
> The following day a Coroners Jury was impanelled when the body being viewed, and fome witneffes examined, the meeting was poftponed to yefterday when they again affembled and after examining further evidence, they brought in their verdict—*Murder*.
>
> On Saturday evening, a large body of failors affembled and (out of revenge as is fuppofed for the death of Captain M'Ilroy,) attacked the houfe of rendezvous in Strand-ftreet, and foon after, the one on New-Quay, which they completely gutted, cutting open the beds, and throwing the feathers, bedding, and houfehold furniture, of every defcription into the ftreet; tore down the wainfcotting, mouldings, cornices and doors, which they broke to pieces and deftroyed, alfo the windows, fhutters, and every other matter, fo as to leave fcarcely any thing but the walls, floors and roof undeftroyed: our prefent, and late, worthy chief magiftrates went down to them, when they promifed to defift from any further outrage, which they accordingly did, and difperfed to their own houfes.

---

[10] *Williamson's Advertiser*, 21st October 1793.

was *Mother Redcap's* more welcoming, or its trade so busy, as when the navy's frigates made their appearance in the river. But even here tars were on their guard, ready to make their escape over Liscard moor to greater safety further inland.[11]

Whether volunteers or pressed men, many were soon serving on naval ships far and wide. Others signed up with the military as infantrymen or gunners, although Britain's land forces remained comparatively small. Around seven thousand troops were sent under the command of the Duke of York to Flanders in February 1793 to help repel a French army that was rapidly advancing into Holland. By early March they were joined by larger Austrian and Hanoverian armies, and over the next two months succeeded in driving Republican forces out of the Dutch and Austrian Netherlands. The allies were advancing towards Valenciennes in north-eastern France towards the end of May, but found their way blocked by the National Guard dug into positions along the Rhonelle river. As sixteen battalions advanced with their bridging equipment early on the 23rd, French gun batteries opened up with little effect from a distance. As General Murray reported, "They were answered and kept in awe by the Austrian and Hanoverian heavy artillery. After some time spent in cannonading, two divisions of Hussars passed the river without opposition at a ford in the village of Mershe. His Royal Highness ordered the brigade of Guards, two battalions of Austrian infantry, six squadrons of British and two of Hanoverian light cavalry, to pursue the same route, in order to take the batteries in flank and secure a passage for the rest of the troops. This movement had the desired success; the enemy retreated from all their posts, falling back upon a redoubt which they had thrown up upon the cannonading heights behind the village of Fumars." The gun batteries of both sides blazed away for several hours, but eventually the French were unable to hold their position and were forced to retreat.[12]

The coalition forces spent the next two months besieging the French at Valenciennes, eventually seizing the town at the end of July. They then attempted to capture Dunkirk to gain control of the Straight of Dover and secure a supply route from England, but met heavy resistance. After two weeks of fighting, *Williamson's Advertiser* reported, "Yesterday afternoon the French

---

[11] Williams, op. cit., p319-325.
[12] Report from Sir James Murray, Adjutant General, dated 25th May 1793, and first printed in the *London Gazette*, before appearing in *Williamson's Advertiser*, 6th June.

made a desperate attempt to raise the siege of Dunkirk. ...So vigorous was the attack made by the Garrison, assisted by and under cover of their gun-boats, that all the advanced post of the Austrians were driven in. At this moment the 14th Regiment advanced, and, opposing a firm and steady countenance to the enemy, immediately checked their career. The 37th and 53rd, with their flank companies, came to their support. The Austrians rallied, and returned to the charge, calling out *"Bons Anglaise!"* (Brave English!) and a heavy action was maintained for three hours, at the end of which the French were completely routed, and were driven back with prodigious slaughter into the town."[13] However, the siege soon ground to a halt as Austrian reinforcements were beaten back, and a report the following week did its best to avoid admitting defeat. "The late check and consequent delay of the operations before Dunkirk have excited great many alarm. In great undertakings, however, some failure must be expected, though they by no means frustrate the main design. The object now before the army is of the first importance to this country, and though great hazard and difficulties stand in the way, we trust they will finally be overcome for the interests of mankind at large, by aiding the conversion of the deluded body of Frenchmen, and punishing the lawless tyrants who govern them."[14] But, far from converting deluded Frenchmen or toppling tyrants, the siege was soon called off, and the Duke of York withdrew his much-depleted army to greater safety near Ostend. Among his commanding officers was Colonel Isaac Gascoyne from Liverpool, who would later suffer many a jibe about a wound to his heal inflicted during the retreat.

Meanwhile, widespread uprisings had broken out across large parts of the south and west of France, threatening the Republic from within, while its forces struggled to hold back the advancing armies along its eastern borders. The Girondins had dominated the National Convention until the middle of 1793 with their vision of decentralised government and the export of revolution across Europe. But late in June, with the revolution under threat, a huge Paris mob demanded their replacement, and the Jacobins seized control. Real power soon rested with the Committees of Public Safety and General Security, and a Reign of Terror was unleashed with Maximillian Robespierre at the helm. About seventeen thousand died under the guillotine during the next twelve months, and up to forty thousand were killed in summary executions as a result of the uprisings. One report noted, "At Lyon, all executions are now performed by night, and a ditch is dug under the guillotine to receive the blood of the butchered victims."[15] Describing the execution of twelve royalist sympathisers, an eyewitness wrote, "All the insults which were heaped upon

---

[13] *Williamson's Advertiser*, 16th September 1793.
[14] Ibid, 23rd September 1793.
[15] *Billinge's Liverpool Advertiser*, 6th January, 1794 (*Billinge* replaced *Williamson* from January 1794).

the sufferers did not in the least alter their behaviour; they heard the sentence of death without having any lineament of their face discomposed. When the twelve who were condemned were led out of the gaol, a part of the people called out 'Long Live the Nation, Long Live the Republic!' But from the unfortunate victims a very different shout was heard. They rose up together, and cried out in chorus, 'Long Live the King, Long Live the King!' They presented themselves to the scaffold with the most striking courage. When it came to the youngest of the women, her mother said to her, 'Go my daughter.' The people kept, for the greater part, a melancholy silence. The insults and shouts were very rare during their march, and none at all were heard about the scaffold. I have received such an impression from this event that I can think of nothing else. Many were the persons I saw shedding tears of grief and admiration. As to us, the meat at our table was untouched - nobody could eat a morsel."[16]

By early August, French royalists were fighting for control of the Mediterranean town and naval base of Toulon, and called for foreign help. A joint British and Spanish fleet arrived at the end of the month with a force of marines and took control of the town, together with its ring of forts built to defend the natural harbour. Twenty-five French warships also surrendered, and the royalists raised their flag, proclaiming Louis XVII as king. When news of this reached Liverpool in mid-September, celebrations were held throughout the town. A salute was fired from the great guns at the fort at one o'clock on the 16th, followed by a rifle salute in Castle Street from soldiers of the militia stationed in the town. While ordinary townsfolk poured into the taverns for their own celebrations, officers and gentlemen joined the mayor in the Exchange. To mark the occasion, toasts were drunk to the King, Queen, and Prince of Wales; the Duke of York and the loyal soldiers the army; the Duke of Clarence, Admiral Lord Hood, and their loyal sailors; the town of Liverpool and its Members of Parliament; the health of the wounded; the loyal Toulonese; and many, many more.[17]

But the celebrations were premature, as the defenders were soon struggling to hold the town against a growing hostile force. The two sides became locked in a struggle for control of the surrounding heights, as Republican troops kept up a constant fire from their gun batteries overlooking the town and harbour. Three weeks into September, a force of five hundred Spanish and British soldiers managed to take control of a strategic ridge overlooking the inner harbour. The British commander, General Mulgrave, reported, "The detachment embarked from Toulon on 20th, at twelve o'clock at night…we

---

[16] *Williamson's Advertiser*, 19th August 1793.
[17] Ibid, 23rd September 1793.

proceeded across the harbour, and landed at about two o'clock in the morning of 21st at Fort Balaguier, and marched immediately forward to reconnoitre the heights de la Graffe, which consisted of a ridge, divided at the top by three different knolls, covered with woods...I was determined to take the lowest and easternmost knoll, which is about 500 yards from the landing place. Having distributed the troops in the best positions the post would admit, Admiral Gravina returned with me to Toulon before noon to order the necessary supplies for the troops, and some guns for the defence of the post. At about five o'clock in the afternoon, the enemy advanced along the upper knolls of the Hauter de Graffe, to the number, we have since learnt, of about 700 men, and having driven in the piquets, began an attack under the cover of the woods, forming themselves upon a steep ascent in front of the post in three lines, so as to have the advantage of a triple fire; from which our troops were, in some degree, protected by trunks of trees which had been felled and placed to serve as a breastwork. The firing continued for an hour, when the enemy were repulsed."[18]

But this success proved short-lived, as Republican troops continued to pour in, aided by a young artillery commander by the name of Napoleon Bonaparte. Meanwhile, Captain Horatio Nelson of the *Agamemnon* had been dispatched to Naples to seek reinforcements, and returned with the promise of two thousand troops. By the end of the year, however, the defence of Toulon was cracking under the strain, as further reinforcements from Britain and Austria failed to arrive. The end came in December, as described in this account in *Williamson's Advertiser*. "For many days past, numbers of the Republican troops assembled in the woods about Toulon, besides those who were already before it. From 13th December, they made many attempts against the place, but with little success. In the evening of the 17th, a very numerous French army attacked all the advanced posts and some of the forts. The Neopolitans, who were camped on the outside of Fort Baloguie, called, *To Arms!* but they had scarce time to take them up, when they were attacked by the enemy and obliged to abandon to them their camp and the fort, and to retire under the town with some loss. The other combined troops that defended the different posts were also obliged to abandon them on account of the great superiority of the enemy."[19]

Thus overwhelmed, there was nothing for it but to abandon the town and withdraw to the fleet. While still under attack, several thousand royalists were hurriedly evacuated in small boats. During the confusion of organising so many refugees, "an insurrection of the malcontents took place, who, taking advantage of the disorder, and the flight of the Royalists, fell upon them with

---

[18] Letter dated 26th September, printed by *Williamson's Advertiser*, 28th October 1793.
[19] Letter dated 25th December, *Billinge's Advertiser*, 20th January 1794.

sabres, and every kind of weapons, and made a horrid carnage of them in order to seize their effects." As the fleet prepared to leave, orders were given to destroy the port's stores, magazines, and as many French warships as possible. By daybreak, "a most terrible fire was seen at a great distance, which consumed the arsenals, some fortifications, and even the bason of the port. It was so furious that it extended to the town; and soon two great shocks were heard, which was either the explosion of the powder magazine, or the blowing up of two large French ships, on board of which Lord Howe had placed almost the whole powder of the place, and which were stationed at the entrance of the arsenal. These shocks, so near the town, must have rent and destroyed most of the houses."[20] Ten French warships were eventually destroyed, while several more were used to evacuate the refugees, but hundreds of Royalists remained to face the wrath of the Republicans, and around eight hundred were rounded up and shot.

In Liverpool, the new parish treasurer and workhouse governor, William Haliday, was making an impact, and supervision arrangements had been greatly improved. However, the parish was now desperately short of money because of a new economic downturn since the outbreak of war. Trade had collapsed, unemployment had risen, prices were rising sharply, and the parish was now liable under a new law for the maintenance of servicemen's families. To help solve the problem, the Easter vestry meeting of 1793 supported a motion to add Liverpool owned ships to the parish rates, thus making their owners liable to pay tax. The proposer, Robert Carr, cited a recent case in the Court of King's Bench against ship owners in Pool, Dorset, in which the parish had won their claim.[21] But, as Carr and his supporters were to find, Liverpool ship owners and their corporation backers were not about to take the matter lying down. To make matters worse, Haliday had discovered that £2000 was owed to the parish due to "gross negligence in the collection of rates." When a special meeting was called in August, it was agreed to borrow the money on the understanding that it would be repaid within nine months. A new collector of taxes was to be appointed, together with several new assistants, each under very strict rules for the "discharge of their duties" and liable to huge fines of four or five hundred pounds.[22]

[20] *Billinge's Advertiser,* 20th January 1794.
[21] Peet, op. cit., p315-318.
[22] Ibid, p319.

By the next Easter meeting in 1794, Haliday had worked out that the total arrears for the five years when his predecessor had been in charge amounted to £11,376, exclusive of the disputed money owed by the corporation and ship owners. The number of workhouse inmates had risen by over two hundred, and many more needed outdoor relief. To add to the problem, the price of oatmeal, wheat and potatoes had increased sharply, none of the cotton spun in the workhouse had been sold, and there were debts due to the recent alterations in the workhouse. Haliday suggested that there ought to be a surplus of four thousand pounds on the books but for the difficulty in collecting arrears. He noted the "calamitous and universal depression in trade, and the consequent scarcity of money, are circumstances which have all combined to render these arrears so uncommonly great." Despite this, Haliday was confidant that the money would be collected, and that the parish taxes could be reduced from three shillings in the pound to two shillings and six pence, thus returning to the 1790 rate.[23] Warnings were issued in the early summer of 1794 that "the Inhabitants of this Parish, from whom taxes are owing, are desired to take Notice that, after 24th June next, legal means will be used against all, indiscriminately, who shall then be in arrear to the Parish; and that the better to enforce the Payment, the Books of Collection will then be delivered to the Committee, under whose direction the said Inhabitants will be preceded against."[24]

Haliday also presented the committee with details of the people in the workhouse and how they were employed.[25] Of over a thousand inmates, about half were described as either "lunatics", "idiots", sick, lame, infirm, very old, or very young, and were not required to work. A third were infants or children under ten, and ten per cent were over seventy. Among the workers, roughly half were employed as "cotton pickers", separating seeds and pieces of twig from the raw material. Just over a hundred were spinners of cotton, linen, or wool supplying seven weavers, and fifty-one were knitters or seamstresses. Forty-five people were embroiderers using frames known as tambours. Two smiths and eighteen boys made nails for use around the workhouse and for sale. Others worked as shoemakers, coalmen, ropers, bread makers, cooks, cleaners, servants, washerwomen, carters and swineherds. There were six nurses and servants to look after infants, and another fourteen for "lying in women," the sick and infirm, and for the venereal, fever and lunatic wards. Other specialist roles included two bookkeepers, bricklayers and plasterers, a glazier, coffin-makers, boat builders, joiners and sawyers, tailors, a barber, two schoolmasters and two schoolmistresses. Over 140 inmates had died

[23] Peet, op. cit., p327-329
[24] *Billinge's Advertiser*, 23rd June 1794.
[25] Peet, op. cit., p334.

over the previous twelve months, many of fever. As always, housekeepers, manufacturers, captains, and "others of good character" were invited to apply to the workhouse and reduce its numbers by taking on inmates as indentured servants. For many employers the workhouse was a ready source of cheap labour, since all that was required was to provide food, clothing and shelter, and the most basic of bedding.

Meanwhile, undeterred by the threat from French privateers, Captain William Young and his crew set off for the River Congo in April 1794 with a cargo of cloths from India, including "Romalls, Chelloes, Photaes, and Bejuta pants," and other "stuffs" from Manchester. His ship also carried an assortment of knives, cutlasses and guns, twenty-four barrels and over seven hundred kegs of gunpowder. There was also an assortment of dishes, plates, mugs, and calabashes, a large amount of sugar, iron bars from Sweden, and a quantity of garnets and agates. To help smooth trade, the *Enterprize* carried twenty puncheons containing over 2000 gallons of brandy, nearly sixty gallons of Spanish and Portuguese wine, and a quantity of rum. Young had specific instructions to barter for ivory and "prime young Negroes" below twenty years of age. He was also advised to include some of four feet six to four feet nine inches tall, which he could get for a "reduced Bundle" of goods, and because they would "stand the middle passage better than full grown." His employers, Leyland and Company, warned Young that "a long stay in the Zaire is always attended with great mortality among both Blacks and Europeans in the best Season." Having been cautioned against "short purchase", Young was instructed to "treat the slaves while on board with the greatest care and humanity, and require your Surgeon and Officers the most prompt execution of their Duty on all occasions." After leaving the African coast, Young was to make for Kingston, Jamaica, and contact Messrs. Taylor, Ballentine and Fairlie to arrange for the sale of the slaves.[26]

Few details remain of the voyage itself, but the *Enterprize* had an encounter with another vessel about two hundred miles west of Portugal, seized it as a prize, and then took it to Cork in southern Ireland. The *Virgini* was a Spanish-built ship that had previously been taken as a prize by the French, but it seems unlikely that it was ever returned to Spain once its cargo had been sold. The

---

[26] Account book of the *Enterprize*, Merseyside Maritime Museum, Emancipation and Abolition microfilm reel 18, DX/1732.

Enterprize sailed from Cork early in May, arriving off the coast of Angola three months later. After nine weeks of trading, the 229-ton *Enterprize* left for Jamaica with 360 slaves, taking just over five weeks to complete the middle passage, during which four slaves died. 356 slaves were sold after arriving at Kingston late in November, their individual prices ranging from £44 to £75, but averaging £62, which grossed over £22,000 for Leyland and Co. The ship set sail early in February, arriving in Liverpool on 29th March 1795 after a total voyage of fifty-one weeks.

The voyage seems to have been very profitable for Leyland and Company, although the records are not sufficiently complete to be sure just how much. However, there is no doubt that it was lucrative for William Young, as was the case for ships' masters in general on slaving voyages. His wages of £5 per month were as nothing when compared with his commission, which at nearly six per cent of the proceeds, earned him £1261 11s 10d. After three or four voyages, and having invested his money, Young could comfortably expect to set himself up as a merchant. His chief mate, William Hymers, would doubtless have been looking forward to the command of his own vessel. He earned privilege money of £62, doubling his earnings from wages of £5 per month. Surgeon William Scott earned £4 10s a month, but received the same financial privilege as Hymers, which more than doubled his wages. He also received 'head money' and a gratuity on the number of slaves delivered to Kingston, earning him nearly £46 in addition. Added to this was his bounty of £50 for helping to keep the slaves' mortality rate below two per cent, bringing his total earnings for the voyage to around £212. As for the rest of the crew, the highest paid was the carpenter on £5 10s a month. The second and third mates earned £4 10s, the boatswain £4 5s, the gunner £4, while the seamen's wages ranged from £4 down to £2 2s according to experience. Among the crew were twelve landsmen with little or no previous experience, which at one third of the total crew was a surprisingly high proportion. Most earned a mere £1 15s per month, but were probably hopeful of becoming able seamen, mates, and even captains in the fullness of time. Some no doubt dreamed of becoming merchants in their own right, but unless they were literate, numerate and fully able to navigate, there was no chance of rising beyond the level of second mate. With an average mortality rate of about one in six each voyage (although no record exists for the *Enterprize*) few could expect to live to reach even this pinnacle.

Voyages like that of the *Enterprize* were considered vital by some for Britain's economy, which helps explain the reluctance of so many politicians to support abolition. For Britain, France and Spain in particular, the West Indies were a lucrative source of wealth from cotton, tobacco and coffee, but above all, from sugar. The appetite for sugar in Europe and America was insatiable, and the British navy was virtually fuelled on the rum distilled from sugar cane. Prior to its conflict with America, Britain's imports from Jamaica alone had been around five times the value of those from its thirteen mainland colonies, while imports from tiny Grenada were worth eight times those of Canada.[27] But all this depended on labour in a climate considered unbearably hot by most Europeans, and where tropical diseases were rife. Most believed the islands were only viable on the basis of slave labour, and the native Caribbean population had long since died out.[28]

Profit was all. While most plantation owners and their families lived in opulence and ease, slaves worked from sunrise to sunset or beyond, typically fourteen hours a day or more. Harvesting was especially backbreaking and dangerous, as slaves bent low to slice through the base of the canes with heavy machetes while trying to avoid cuts from the razor sharp leaves. Meanwhile, black slave drivers used their whips liberally to prevent slacking, ever conscious of the gaze of armed white overseers. The canes were collected in bundles and taken by carts to wind-powered mills, where heavy rollers crushed them to extract the juices. Accidents were common, and there were no brakes to stop the machinery. When drowsy slaves got their fingers crushed as they fed the canes through, limbs had to be severed quickly with a machete to avoid being further consumed by the rollers. Worse still were the boiling houses, where temperatures and humidity reached satanic levels. Scalding was common, and exhausted slaves were not unknown to fall into boiling vats of sugar. Much of the processing was done at night to prevent the cane juices fermenting and turning sour soon after being cut during daylight hours. This meant that slaves had to work night shifts in addition to their field work or other tasks, leaving them with very little sleep.[29]

Conditions on West Indian plantations were generally worse than in America. Some half a million slaves were taken to the American mainland before the United States banned the slave trade in 1808, yet their population had grown to around four million when Americas slaves were emancipated in 1865. Well over two million slaves were transported to the British West Indies over a similar period, yet their numbers were only around two-thirds of a million

---

[27] Hochschild, op. cit., p55.
[28] Indigenous peoples such as the Caribs and Arawaks were mostly wiped out in the early years of colonisation by common diseases brought over from Europe, against which they had no immunity.
[29] Hochschild, op cit p63-67.

when they were finally set free in 1838. This was bad economics if nothing else, as roughly a third of all slaves died within three years of their arrival in the Caribbean. Hard labour and poor nutrition reduced fertility levels to such an extent that half the female slaves produced no offspring. But for those who did, giving birth meant condemning their children to lives of hard toil and misery. Children started work at an early age, weeding, planting, and feeding fodder to the animals, then collecting and spreading their manure, before graduating to adult work as soon as they were able.[30] However, mixed race 'mulatto' children born of rape could expect a better life. Rape was endemic, both on board slave ships and on plantations. Mulattos were generally given privileged positions on plantations, mostly as free men and women, and many ran small plantations of their own.

Little thought was given to diet to keep slaves healthy, and the best that slaves could expect was the occasional salt cod or pickled herring that was considered unfit for sale. Rickets and scurvy were common, despite a climate well suited to the growing of citrus fruits and bananas, although slaves were allowed to tend small vegetable patches on Sundays to supplement their meagre diet. They also carried out repairs to their sparse huts, mending leaky roofs with the trash that was left after the sugar canes had been crushed. Their meagre dwellings could not withstand the frequent hurricanes, and contrasted sharply, while they lasted, with the fine sturdy houses of the plantation owners. Hygiene was impossible to maintain, and many slaves who had survived the ravages of dysentery during the middle passage from Africa did so only to succumb after their arrival. Some fell victim to yellow fever, malaria or leprosy, while others caught pneumonia as they lay their exhausted bodies down in the chill night air after leaving the heat and humidity of the boiling houses.[31]

Under such conditions of hardship, attempted escapes were common but usually futile. Slaves were nearly always branded with the owner's initials using a red hot iron, a dreadful process that left them easily identifiable wherever they went. When the alarm was raised and reward notices posted, there were few places to hide. Runaways faced a severe public whipping providing they were quickly caught, and were placed in leg irons and spiked iron punishment collars to prevent further attempts at escape. Any caught after thirty days could expect death by hanging, while their oppressors were liable to a mere fine for taking their punishments too far. Rebellions were rare but not unknown, and were dealt with by the local militias. In some instances, slaves found guilty of plotting insurrection or murder were burned alive as an example.[32]

---

[30] Hochschild, op cit, p63-67.
[31] Ibid.
[32] Ibid, p61.

The jewel of the Caribbean was the French colony of St. Domingue, which was more than twice the size of Jamaica, and produced around a third of the world's sugar and over half its coffee, so rich was its fertile soil. [33] As news of France's revolution spread, its half million slaves became increasingly restless for the liberty, equality and fraternity being fought over in Europe. Meanwhile, forty thousand whites had other ideas, and the situation became a powder keg. A full-scale revolt broke out in August 1791, and under the leadership of Toussaint L'Ouverture, developed into revolution. It would end thirteen years later in the creation of a free and independent Haiti, but only after many tens of thousands had lost their lives in a bloody war marked by horrific acts of brutality committed on both sides of the conflict. Meanwhile, the uprising sent shock waves through the Caribbean islands and the colonial powers, and threatened to spread especially to neighbouring Jamaica.

There were complex divisions between various groups that further destabilised the country. Many landless white workers, or *petits blancs*, were republicans, but few sympathised with the slaves. Most of the planters were royalists who wanted independence from republican France and looked to Britain for protection. In addition, there were nearly forty thousand free blacks and mulattoes who had recently been granted full political rights by the French government to win their support. Many were men of minor property and some even owned a few slaves, which meant they had no affiliation with the rebels. However, others regarded their new rights as meaningless in a white dominated society, and threw in their lot with the Toussaint L'Ouverture's rapidly growing army. At the end of August 1793 a commissioner from the French National Convention, Leger-Felicite Sonthonax, declared an end to slavery in St. Domingue, believing this to be the only way to calm the rebellion and maintain French control over the colony. British troops from Jamaica entered the fray, landing on the south-east tip of St. Domingue in September 1793. Their aim was to exploit the divisions and take control, thus doubling the value of their Caribbean assets while preventing the spread of rebellion to nearby Jamaica. They were soon welcomed by the planters and most of the petits blancs, preferring the safeguarding of slavery under British rule to black liberation. However, the French National Convention formally declared an end to slavery throughout all its colonies on 4th February 1794. With British troops advancing, and slavery abolished, Toussaint L'Ouverture now joined with republican French forces to repel them.

By June 1794, the British had taken control of Port-au-Prince and many of St. Domingue's port towns, reinforced by some of the seven thousand

---

[33] Hochschild, p261.

troops that had arrived at Barbados in January. Meanwhile, much of this additional force was dispatched to seize control of Martinique. The island's capital, Fort Royal, was heavily protected, but came under attack on 17th March from both land and sea. Various acts of gallantry were reported in *Billinge's Liverpool Advertiser*, which now superseded *Williamson's* under its new owner. Among them was that of Lieutenant Bowen and his men, who, "with the rowing boats of the guard, boarded the *Bien Venue* French frigate, and brought off the Captain, Lieutenant, and about twenty men who were on board her, under a smart fire of grape-shot and musquetry from the ramparts and parapet of the fort." Nearby, the commander of the naval sloop *Zebra* seized the opportunity to breech the defences from the sea. It was reported that Captain Faulkner and his crew, under constant fire from grape shot, "determined to undertake the service alone, and he executed it with matchless intrepidity and conduct, running the *Zebra* close to the wall of the Fort, and leaping overboard at the head of the sloop's company, assailed and took this important post before the boats could get on shore, although they rowed with all the force and animation which characterizes English seamen in the face of an enemy." Forty ladders were then hastily constructed from "bamboo and small stretched cordage, from twenty to thirty six feet long," with which to scale the walls, and "the navy committed themselves with their usual gallantry, carrying the Fort by Escalade about twelve o'clock on the 20th inst." The fort garrison surrendered soon after, when "the Grenadiers and Light Infantry made good use of their field pieces and muskets, and…. took possession of the town by the bridge over the canal at the back of it, while a strong detachment from the Naval Battalions…in flat boats, barges, and pinnaces, approached the beach in front." The report concluded, "The rapid success of his Majesty's arms has been produced by the high courage and perseverance of his officers, soldiers and seamen in the most difficult and toilsome labours, which nothing short of the perfect unanimity and affection between them and their chiefs could have surmounted."[34]

News of this success reached Liverpool five weeks later, when the mayor gave a grand banquet to mark the occasion and honour his brother, Lieutenant Colonel Blundell, who had command the light infantry. Meanwhile, St. Lucia had also been taken at the beginning of April, and British forces had gone on to invade Guadeloupe, where they were "received with great demonstrations of joy" by French royalists. Several battalions went on to storm the forts and gun batteries protecting the capital and harbour, including Blundell's light infantry, which "forced several difficult posts of the enemy during the night." After ten days of heavy fighting, nearly six thousand Republican troops had

---

[34] *Billinge's Advertiser*, 28th April 1794.

surrendered and were allowed terms to "march out with the honors of war and lay down their arms, to be sent to France and not to serve against the British forces or their allies during the war."[35] By 22nd April Britain had added Guadeloupe and its satellite islands to its conquests.

But the conquest soon proved short-lived, when a squadron of French ships arrived to retake the island six weeks later. The Republicans stormed Fort Fleur d'Epee at midnight on 7th June, and, "after twice being repulsed, on the third attack carried the place by storm." The following morning they marched into the capital, Pointe-a-Pitre, singing songs of liberty, but they soon found themselves hemmed in by the British, both on land and at sea. *Billinge's Advertiser* reported that Blundell was soon leading his men against the attackers, and the "most dreadful revenge was taken by the British upon the Republicans, who, during their short stay, had been solely occupied in putting to death the Royalists." Meanwhile, local slaves, mockingly referred to as "democrats", had joined the attack on the British. As *Billinge's* reported, "The invasion of Guadaloupe by the French will be a very happy circumstance for that island, as all the democrats have shewn their principles, and will no doubt be shipped off, by which means the island will be purged of them."[36]

However, such optimism was misplaced, as Republican reinforcements arrived to renew the assault, aided or hindered by the hopeful slave population, while the French royalist aristocrats gave support to the British. *Billinge's Advertiser* began cautiously, "The following account is taken from a St. Kitt's paper – It appears somewhat imperfect; but as it contains many interesting particulars, we readily lay it before our readers." [37] It then reported, "Each time the Republicans attacked Fleur de Pee," [Fort Fleur d'Epee] "they made the air echo with *Vive le Republique! Vive le Nation!* – and each time they were repulsed their drums beat a peal to rally them. The aristocrats answered them by huzzas, and *Vive le Roi! Vive le George le Trois!"* But by this time the British garrison had been "so reduced to death and sickness, that it did not consist of more than 100 men, 80 of whom were in the fort, and twenty in the town to preserve order." All were forced to withdraw, as did their royalist French supporters, who reckoned to have had two hundred killed or wounded. By mid-morning the Republicans were marching into the town "with drums beating, and singing songs of liberty," while their supporters welcomed them wearing national cockades in their hats. They let the prisoners out of the gaol, and placed guards throughout the town "to prevent the Negroes from plundering, who were then busily employed at that work." Far from it being a riot, however, the slaves "observed the greatest regularity and discipline; they

---

[35] *Billinge's Advertiser*, 26th May 1794.
[36] Ibid. 28th July 1794.
[37] Ibid, 11th August 1794.

broke but one French store open to get provisions, and when they had taken what they wanted, they put a new lock on, and placed a sentinel on it."

The slaves now looked forward to their freedom, and insurrections broke out on several plantations. The report from St. Kitts continued, "The democrats at the Hays, and some other villages in that quarter, hoisted the National flag, and made some aristocratic ladies and one man prisoners." However, control of the island was still disputed, and the plantation owners were soon dealing with the rebellious slaves with sheer brutality. Reporting on these reprisals as though of little consequence, the writer explained, "General Grey sent a frigate from Basseterre to scour that coast – at the same time he wrote to the aristocratic planters to settle the fellows, which they eventually did by cutting to pieces a number of them and quelling the insurrection."

Meanwhile, having evacuated the fort, the remnants of the British garrison from Fort Fleur d'Epee and the capital managed to escape and join the main contingent under General Grey on the eastern half of the island. Grey now prepared to retake the capital, but was wary that the Republicans would set fire to the shipping in the capital's harbour. Predicting the consequences, Grey feared, "in which case the town must infallibly be destroyed, as the vessels ride close to the shore, and the wind blows directly into the harbour. In that case a beautiful town would be ruined, a number of British merchant ships and stores full of valuable goods, and upwards of 30,000 hogsheads of prize sugar, besides the prizes and English shipping, will be totally reduced to ashes."[38] But this soon proved unnecessary, as the British found themselves confronting a force swelled by slaves and mulattoes now more intent on fighting rather than looting. The fighting took a terrible toll on both sides, while soldiers sweltered in their thick woollen uniforms under the heat of the summer sun, and were periodically drenched by torrential downpours. When they had finally fought their way to the capital, the British found themselves walking into a trap. As Grey reported, "...being misled by our guides, the troops entered the town at the part where they were most exposed to the enemy's cannon and small arms, and where it was not possible to scale the walls of the fort; in consequence of which they suffered considerably from round and grape shot, together with small arms fire from the houses &c., and a retreat became unavoidable." The British pulled back from Pointe-a-Pitre to new positions overlooking the harbour, erecting batteries of 24-pounders and mortars to defend themselves and harass French ships below. However, Grey realised that his chance was lost, "The season for action being past, and the troops debilitated by the fatigue of a long campaign and the climate, so

---

[38] *Billinge's Advertiser,* 18th August 1794.

as to become unable for further contest, without shelter from the scorching heat of a vertical sun, or the heavy rains now so frequent."[39]

A letter reprinted in Billinge's Liverpool Advertiser, 26th May 1794 (LRO)

Grey's force held out for several months on the eastern half of Guadeloupe, having suffered over five hundred casualties in their attempt to retake control of the capital and the rest of the island. But far more succumbed to the ravages of yellow fever, and by early September less than five hundred men were fit for duty out of the remaining force of just over two thousand. The fever produced severe flu-like symptoms at its most benign, but more frequently led to wholesale internal bleeding and death. By December *Billinge's Advertiser* was reporting the demise of the remaining British force, "which had been obliged to capitulate, consisted of a small camp of about 400 men under the command of General Graham. The fever which has raged so violently there has subsided."[40] St Lucia was also abandoned the following year, while British troops in St. Domingue struggled against both fever and the guerrilla tactics of Toussaint's army. Meanwhile, free blacks in the north of Jamaica began a guerrilla war after several of their leaders were captured in defiance of a sixty year old treaty that had recognised their special status. The British attempt to win control of the French islands was now in tatters, having too few soldiers to spare in the region and a mortality rate of fifty per cent due to yellow fever alone.

In the meantime, swelled by military conscription, French forces in Europe had begun to roll back their enemies, and at one point the British army was close to surrender. When the British and Austrians attacked at Tourcoing in the middle of May 1794, the French

SATURDAY and SUNDAY's MAIL.

LONDON, MAY 22.

OFFICIAL accounts are received mentioning advantages gained by the Duke of York, on the 17th instant, and his discomfiture on the following day, they state that the British rejoicing in the Victory of the seventeenth, and about to march in o Tourcoin, the Austrians being posted on the left, to divert, as is imagined, the attention of the enemy, in case of a sortie; the French drew out on Sunday the 18th, at seven o'clock in the morning, the whole garrison of Lisle, with such other troops the requisition could supply, and attacked the British Detachments on every side. Thus hemmed in, the British Leader found no alternative but to surrender or cut his way, sword in hand, through the numerous hosts with which he found himself surrounded; who, tis supposed, were at least 60,000:—it was bravely resolved to cut their way through, which they, with that gallantry inseperable from British soldiers' effected: the loss (we are sorry to say) is 58 killed, 206 wounded, 568 missing, 47 horses killed, 32 wounded and 117 missing, and the Park of Light Artillery, consisting of 11 six pounders, 3 twelve do. one howitzer, 1 twelve pounder spiked and dismounted. The loss sustained would, in all probability, have been considerably less, had not a panic seized the Austrians, which made them basely desert their brave associates.—The Austrian Hussars were the first who fled; they broke through the ranks, and forced their way amidst the divisions, directing their shameful flight towards Tournay.—We flatter ourselves the Duke of Yorks next attack will be attended with that glory which every true lover of his country must delight in, against such a horde of savage ruffians.

---

[39] *Billinge's Advertiser,* 25th August 1794.
[40] Ibid, 15th December 1794.

brought in reinforcements from nearby Lille and began to attack from every side. The account of a desperate retreat was portrayed by *Billinge's Advertiser* as though the Duke of York was the last man standing against overwhelming odds. It reported, "Thus hemmed in, the British Leader found no alternative but to surrender or cut his way, sword in hand, through the numerous hosts with which he found himself surrounded; who, tis supposed, were at least 60,000." All was made clear, as the report continued in heroic terms that, "it was bravely resolved to cut their way through, which they, with that gallantry inseparable from British soldiers, effected." The report concluded, "We flatter ourselves the Duke of York's next attack will be attended with that glory which every true lover of his country must delight in, against such a horde of savage ruffians."[41]

By mid-July, Robespierre's grip on the machinery of French national politics was over. When he was arrested for tyranny, and tried by the revolutionary tribunal, one of his accusers exclaimed, "I will, with this dagger, rid the world of this tyrant, if the convention does not strike off his head with the sword of the law."[42]   Robespierre and a dozen others were sent to the guillotine at the end of the month, thus ending their Reign of Terror. Huge crowds lined the streets of Paris as the condemned were taken to the scaffold, and tens of thousands watched as the blade fell and their severed heads were held aloft.

However, the revolutionary army marched on. French forces re-took the Austrian Netherlands during the summer of 1794, and then swept into Holland to force the retreat of their opponents. The Duke of York reported in mid-September that "the actual force now advancing against me….could scarcely be less than eighty thousand men. The hazard of an action with such a great disparity of numbers could not but become a matter of the most serious consideration; and, after the most mature deliberation, I did not think myself at liberty to risk, in so unequal a contest, his Majesty's troops, or those of his allies serving with them."[43]   By the end of the year the Duke was reporting from Arnhem that French forces had reached the Rhine, and the British army was evacuated from northern Germany in March 1795. Both Prussia and Holland made peace with France soon after.

41 *Billinge's Advertiser,* 26th May 1794.
42 Ibid, 18th August 1794.
43 Ibid, 29th September 1794.

While the Republican armies were proving victorious on the field of battle, its fleet proved no match for a navy manned by men from Liverpool and ports all around Britain. In May 1794 the British fleet under Admiral Howe was searching for an expected convoy of French merchant ships and their warship escorts. Having suffered another bad harvest the previous year, France was now dependent on American grain. A fleet of French warships headed out from their base at Brest mid-way through the month to rendezvous with over a hundred merchant vessels crossing the Atlantic.[44] The Liverpool-built frigate *Phaeton* was scouting ahead of the main British fleet early on 28th May, when it sighted the warships on the horizon about three hundred miles south west of Ireland. Several British men-of-war went to investigate, and by mid-morning confirmed their presence, when "everything was done by his Majesty's fleet, per signals from the Earl Howe (preserving them in order) to get up with the enemy, who appeared to be forming in order of battle."[45] However, it soon became clear that the French hoped to avoid an engagement, and the British fleet gave chase. The lead ships caught up with the rear of their enemy by around eight o'clock that evening. As it got within range, the 74-gun *Bellerophon* fired upon the much larger *Revolutionnaire*, which then dropped back to meet the challenge with its 110 guns. After an hour and a half of broadsides, the *Bellorophon* was forced to withdraw from the action, having suffered heavy damage and her main topmast about to go overboard.[46] By this point the 74-gun *Audacious* had arrived on the scene, beginning an engagement with the *Revolutionnaire* that was later reported by its captain, William Parker. As daylight faded, "his Majesty's ship under my command arrived up with the rear ship of the enemy's line. I immediately commenced a very close action, which continued near two hours without intermission; never exceeding a distance of half a cable's length, but generally closer, and several times in the utmost difficulty to prevent falling on board, which, at his last effort to appearance, at about ten o'clock he attempted to effect. At this time his mizzen mast was gone by the board, his lower yards and main top-sail yard shot away; his fore top-sail being full (though flying out from the top-sail yard, the sheets being shot away) he fell athwart our bows, but we separated without being entangled any time. He then directed his course before the wind, and, to appearance, passed through or close astern of the ships in the rear of our line."[47] By this time the *Audacious* was itself badly damaged, having had most of its rigging shot away, and the crew worked through the night to repair what they could.

[44] Cordingly, op. cit., p68-69.
[45] Admiralty Office, 7th June 1794, reported in *Billinge's Advertiser,* 9th June.
[46] Cordingly, op. cit., p75.
[47] Reported in *Billinge's Advertiser,* 9th June 1794.

Soon after daylight next morning of the 29th, as the "greatest exertion was used by every officer and man in the ship" to bend the sails to the yards, the crew found themselves being chased by two enemy ships. As Captain Parker noted, "The ships came up with us very fast, our situation became very alarming, until we got the main topgallant sail, main topmast, and topgallant studding sail set, when it was judged we nearly preserved our distance." The *Audacious* had therefore barely managed to avoid a potentially disastrous encounter when it was soon being pursued once more. Parker continued, "However, from the foremast being in a tolerable state of security, at half past nine we were about setting a lower studding sail, when three sail that had been discovered to the eastward some time before (viz. two ships and a brig) coming pretty near to us hoisted French colours. The state of our masts did not admit of our making alteration in our course. They, observing our shattered state and two ships in chase of us, stood athwart us boldly within fire, and shot were exchanged, the one a large frigate and the other two corvettes. But, as we had so much sail out, they fell astern for a considerable time. At length, the frigate came within shot of us again, and harassed us by a constant cannonade." The French ships withdrew after an exchange of fire lasting an hour, but the *Audacious* was now badly crippled and had completely lost sight of the rest of the British fleet. Parker reported, "I considered the endeavouring to find the fleet again might put his Majesty's ship (in her defective state) too much to risque, and therefore judged it most advantageous for the service to proceed to port without loss of time to refit, which I hope might meet with their lordships approbation."[48]

Meanwhile, the *Revolutionnaire* having also made its escape for repairs, the rest of the two fleets faced each other in the early morning several miles apart. The French had the advantage of being to the windward of the British, so Admiral Howe gave the signal to tack towards it and cut through the line of ships.[49] Howe's flagship, the *Queen Charlotte*, and Rear Admiral Pasley's *Bellorophon* led the way, exposing themselves to the broadsides of several ships before they could make effective use of their own guns. As with the *Audacious*, the crew of the *Bellorophon* had spent the night repairing the damage of the previous day, but once again its sails and rigging were cut to pieces and its timbers holed and badly shattered. However, the manoeuvre isolated three French ships, which now took a heavy pounding as the rest of the British fleet followed through the French line. By the end of the day the British fleet had gained the advantage, and several French ships were so badly damaged that they were forced to try and make their way home. The French and British crews worked throughout the night mending sails, splicing ropes

---

[48] *Billinge's Advertiser,* 9th June 1794.
[49] Cordingly, op cit, p76-77.

and patching up shattered timbers, while a heavy mist descended. The fog had become so thick by morning that one ship could not identify the next. By the time it had lifted, the French fleet was about nine miles away, and no action followed that day.[50]

On the morning of 1st June, after a further night of repairs and little sleep, the decisive engagement began at around nine-thirty. The *Queen Charlotte* made for the rear of the French admiral's flagship *Montagne*, firing into and destroying the stern, and causing great loss of life as the heavy shot blasted along the length of the decks[51] As the *Bellarophon* followed, an eighteen-pound shot smashed into Rear Admiral Pasley's leg, which later had to be amputated. Meanwhile, a 36-pounder tore through the *Phaeton's* timbers, taking off a man's head and breaking the thighs of another, and injuring several more.[52] But the dead and injured lay bleeding on every ship, many having been hit by flying splinters torn from the timbers by broadsides. Before long, the scene was one of total confusion amid the dense fog of gun smoke. Everywhere was wreckage, with fallen masts, tattered sails, and rigging strewn across the decks. By early afternoon both fleets were pulverised and began to withdraw as best they could, many of the ships having no means left to manoeuvre. As Admiral Howe reported the following day, "In less than an hour after the close action commenced in the centre, the French Admiral, engaged by the Queen Charlotte, crowded off, and was followed by most of the ships of his van in condition to sail after him, leaving with us about ten or twelve of his crippled or totally dismasted ships exclusive of one sunk in the engagement. The Queen Charlotte had then lost her fore topmast, and the main topmast fell over the side very soon after." Several of the crippled ships were either towed away by French frigates or escaped under much reduced sail, but "seven remained in our possession, one of which, however, sunk before the adequate assistance could be given to her crew, but many were saved." [53]

By the end of four days of battle, 287 British seamen and marines had been killed and 811 wounded. Against these numbers, some 1,500 Frenchmen were reckoned dead, and a further 2,000 wounded, while about 3,500 were taken prisoner.[54] Meanwhile, as the two fleets limped back to their respective home ports, 117 merchant vessels completed the Atlantic crossing with their cargo of American grain. Few in Britain were aware of this detail, as they celebrated the "Glorious First of June" in towns and villages across the land. As *Billinge's Advertiser* reported on 16th June, "On Friday morning, when the news of Lord

---

[50] Coedingly, op cit., p77-78.
[51] *Billinge's Advertiser*, 16th June 1794.
[52] Cordingly, p81 & p83.
[53] Reported in *Billinge's Advertiser*, 16th June 1794.
[54] Cordingly, op. cit., p85.

Howe having defeated the French fleet arrived in Liverpool, it gave rise to the most unbounded joy. The bells of the different churches rang incessantly; flags were displayed from the ships and steeples; the ships in the different docks were gaily decorated; pendants and ensigns were hung out from the various dwellings throughout the town; and where those could not be obtained, quilts, handkerchiefs, curtains, etc. At one o'clock a royal salute was fired from the great guns of the fort. On Saturday, the flags were again displayed."

A benefit performance was held five weeks later at the Theatre Royal to raise money for the relief of the widows and orphans of local men killed during the recent naval battle. However, the threat of local press gangs using the occasion for their own purposes led "J. B." of Tarleton Street to write to their headquarters expressing his concerns, an extract from which was published in *Billinge's Advertiser*. "The only thing to be lamented on the occasion is that a set of men are precluded from attendance, whose principal characteristic is a most unbounded generosity. I mean the sailors, who dare not appear, in order to show their liberality. Being deterred by the apprehension of being impressed, this very circumstance, I should presume, will materially affect the receipts of the gallery, unless the gentlemen in power would step forward and generously guarantee the personal safety of these hardy heroes for twenty-four hours, to commence this day at noon and to continue till the noon of the following day; a circumstance this, I should presume, that would in no respect injure the general purpose of government." The reply was couched in terms of such largesse that people might have been expected to read it with gratitude for the generosity of those who would otherwise kidnap and enslave them. Signing himself as Tom Bowline, a local officer wrote, "Mr. Tim Mainstay - Being well acquainted with the disposition of the Regulating Captain, I will answer for his not suffering any man to be impressed at the time of his going to, or returning from, the Theatre this evening. Therefore, all jolly tars may subscribe their mite to the widows and orphans, and at the same time enjoy the evening's amusement, without any apprehension of being pressed. The officers, press masters, &c., will partake of the amusement without the least intention of interrupting the performers or the audience."[55] The event raised £208 18s 6d, but the press gangs resumed their work after noon next day. A subscription fund was raised soon after for the "relief of wounded soldiers and seamen in his Majesty's Service, or the wives and children of such who may fall in battle," with many of the town's merchants and businessmen donating five or ten guineas each.

James Scallon arrived back in Liverpool at the beginning of August, having made a heroic escape from captivity in France. He had been on board the *Ellen*

---

[55] Quoted in Williams, op. cit., p325.

as carpenter when it was overwhelmed by a French frigate and its crew taken captive. Scallon and six others escaped on 1st July from the notorious prison at Quimper in Britanny. Walking by night, and hiding by day, the seven men managed to reach the coast and find a small boat. They made a mast from a suitable branch found in a wood nearby, constructed a rudder from a piece of board, and made a sail from their shirts. They launched their vessel into the water with no food or water, but with a following south westerly reached Sidmouth in Devon three days later. Scallon reckoned that there were 2,700 British prisoners at Quimper, including a Lieutenant Robinson of the *Thames* frigate, whose leg had been shot off during action before his ship was taken. He had largely recovered, and was able to move on crutches, but some of the crew had been shot while attempting to escape from the prison. Scanlon also reported that British prisoners had been treated more harshly since the recent naval battle, and that a third of the fifteen hundred men on board the French admiral's flagship had been killed. Another prisoner reported being in the port of Brest when the bishop of Quimper and twenty-five others had been guillotined in the space of eleven minutes.[56]

Three fires broke out in Liverpool in January 1795, all within the space of a week. An "alarming fire" broke out in the laundry room of the workhouse on the 14th, which soon spread to the tambour room before being got under control. A fire was discovered two days later in the coffee house in Benn's Garden, "which raged with such fury, that in a little time the premises, containing a great quantity of coffee, were entirely destroyed."[57] The following day a committee sat huddled near a roaring fire in the council chamber in the Exchange. While discussing the "relief of the necessitous poor", the members became increasingly diverted by the smoke and smell coming from the fireplace. "So strongly were they impressed by this idea," that they reconvened in the vacant treasurer's office, while the room was "narrowly examined", and the chimney was swept, but no cause could be found. Little more was thought about the matter, and the members soon left for their homes and families, blissfully unaware of a smouldering timber in their beloved civic building. Whether it was caused by a spark from a coal, or a joist that had become too hot, its effect would nonetheless soon be known to all. By early that Sunday morning a fire had taken hold in the council room and spread through the

56 Williams, op. cit., p329-330.
57 *Billinge's Advertiser,* 19th January 1795.

The Exchange engulfed in flames, 1795 (Pictorial Relics, Plate 23, Herdman, LRO)

joists, floorboards, furniture and fittings, rising to the timbers supporting the roof and dome. When the alarm was eventually raised, the fire engines were unable to operate because their water tanks were frozen, and there was little that any could do but watch the flames consume the building. As hundreds stood mesmerised by the illumination, several risked life and limb saving the town charters, corporation seal, council records, and most of the title deeds. By the time the fire had burned itself out, most of the interior was gutted, and only the basement rooms and north extension had escaped destruction.[58]

At the annual Easter parish meeting that year, William Haliday reported that, although all able-bodied inmates were contributing to their upkeep, the best efforts of the rate collectors were still failing to solve the financial problems of the workhouse. Frustrated by the constant tax evasion, the meeting decided to take a firm line. The minutes noted that, "the taxes in arrear for the last or any preceding years service be immediately collected, or the payment enforced according to law; and that public notice by advertisement in Gore's and Billinge's papers be given of this order, with a view that the persons in arrear

---

[58] *Billinge's Advertiser*, 19th January 1795. Also Brooke, op. cit., p 411-412.

may not plead ignorance thereof, or that a printed copy be left at the house of each individual."[59] Meanwhile, the parish committee was still in dispute with the town council, the latter maintaining its demand for rent on the workhouse site while the former still claimed rates on corporation proceeds. However, the committee could now look forward to losing seventy-five workhouse inmates and out-poor, as the navy had been given new powers to set quotas for parishes to supply fighting men.[60]

Meanwhile, the men on board Liverpool's merchant slavers, traders, and privateers continued to risk life and limb. The *Mary Ellen* was nearing Barbados at the end of August when Captain Grierson sighted a brig in pursuit. Despite setting all sail, the *Mary Ellen's* crew were unable to shake the vessel off, which hoisted French national colours and fired its bow guns as it approached. It fired a broadside from nine guns as it came alongside, which the *Mary Ellen* returned, and the two vessels exchanged fire at close range for six hours. The brig eventually dropped astern, with her stays, topsail sheets and steering sail booms shot away. Meanwhile, the *Mary Ellen* was almost a wreck, with its hull, masts, yards, rigging and sails in a shattered condition, and its rudder destroyed. Seeing that the *Mary Ellen* was unable to steer, the brig returned for another broadside, before dropping astern and hauling away. Despite its condition, the surviving crew managed to effect repairs and reach Barbados three days later. Captain Grierson was treated as a hero on his return to Liverpool, and was married to Miss Stringfellow at St. Thomas's church in Park Lane.[61]

When the *Jamaica* was taken on its return from Gibraltar in September, six of Captain Farmer's crew deserted him by escaping in the ship's boat. Despite this, Farmer and his remaining crew managed to overpower their French captors and regain control of their ship, before putting into Portsmouth. Two months later, the *Wilding* was attacked by a French privateer of eighteen guns. The privateer blew up after two hours of fighting, and all on board perished. Captain Pemberton's wounds also proved fatal, and a memorial in his honour was later erected in St. James's church in Toxteth Park by the *Wilding's* owner, Moses Benson.[62] Yet, for the ordinary crewmen who lost their lives during these and other encounters, there were no memorials, nor even the barest mention in *Billinge's* or *Gore's* papers. The best their widows and orphaned children could hope for was charity or parish relief, as their numbers swelled the growing ranks condemned to destitution.

---

[59] Peet, op. cit., p336.
[60] Special Vestry meeting, 31st March 1795, Peet, op. cit., p335.
[61] Williams, op. cit., p334-335.
[62] Ibid, p337.

Castle Street, 1786, Pictorial Relics, Herdman, Plate 2

Chapter Nine

When Wilberforce presented Parliament with a motion for a new abolition bill early in 1796, Banastre Tarleton was quick to respond. Britain must show resolve, he argued, or face the loss of its most lucrative possessions. "The discussion of the question may have such an effect on the slaves as to turn them against their masters, and induce them to pursue the practices inculcated by Jacobin principles and the doctrine of the rights of man." Talk of abolition and the freeing of French slaves had indeed raised expectations, and there had now been serious insurrections on the British islands of Dominica, Jamaica, and Grenada. Tarleton argued that Britain's grip on its West Indian colonies depended on a constant influx of slaves, knowing that many MPs believed their loss would cripple the British economy. He then warned of the effect on Africa, claiming the slave trade "engages the attention of the petty princes and prevents mutual wars and massacres."[1]

When the debate was renewed three weeks later, Tarleton rose from his seat to warn of consequences closer to home. "Many classes of the community are deeply affected by the war, and the adoption of this measure will aggravate their distress. A variety of articles of manufacture are made merely for the carrying on of this commerce, which supports numerous bodies of mechanics. If abolished, their means of living will go along with it." Then he turned to shipping, claiming "the encouragement given the seamen by the Liverpool merchants is a great source of naval strength to this country." After reminding MPs again that the "disturbances in the West Indies renders the present period very unfit for abolition," he suggested, "The war has greatly reduced West Indian property, and the bill, if passed, will inevitably bring it to utter ruin." Tarleton concluded that the Americans and Spanish would take up Britain's share of the trade, as would Ireland, enabling it to "rise on the ruin of Liverpool."[2] Wilberforce lost the Commons vote by only four votes, thanks largely to Tarleton.

Tarleton's efforts were well received in Liverpool, and his old enemies had warmed towards him by the time of the election campaign that May. Some were now prepared to endorse him as a candidate, but remained wary of his radical Whig politics and his opposition to the war. Their natural preference was for Colonel Isaac Gascoyne, who had agreed to replace his Tory brother, Bamber, on his retiring from politics. But there the matter might have stood, the two military men being returned to Parliament unopposed, were it not for another of the Tarleton family. Unlike Banastre, John Tarleton was a loyal supporter

---

[1] Bass, op. cit., p357-358.
[2] Ibid, p358.

of William Pitt and had become a close friend, despite their differences over slavery. John had won a by-election in Seaford near Brighton the previous year, but had then been involved in a dispute over election expenses. Pitt now urged him to contest Liverpool, knowing he could count on John Tarleton's support in keeping his grip on power. As a leading merchant and employer in the town, his prospects of winning a Liverpool seat seemed strong. But his decision to stand locally was a personal blow for Banastre, since the brothers had enjoyed a close relationship and shared the same London address, despite their political differences.

John Tarleton's candidacy naturally aroused suspicions of coalition, forcing Banastre firmly to declare his independence. Any remaining doubts were soon set aside, as a battle of words was fought over Banastre's supposedly Jacobin sympathies and his stance against the war.[3] From John Tarleton's camp, *Humanus* warned of the dire calamities and distress that had afflicted France becoming the fate of England if Banastre's Whig party gained power. "Your wives, mothers, daughters would fall victim to the brutality of lawless ruffians; your property would be seized upon by triumphant robbers, and your habitations stormed – open massacre would be the order of the day, and Assassinations the order of the night." Such sentiments were echoed just as graphically by *Philotas*, who reminded voters of Banastre's "attachment to French politics – his excursion to Paris to see the beauties of the Revolution, and particularly that patriotic scene where the amiable Comtesse de Lamballe was dragged naked through the streets and torn to pieces by the independent, public-spirited Patriots of France – his various senatorial attempts to justify the conduct of the regicides respecting the war with England, and to make England appear the aggressor."

The Friends of General Tarleton (as Banastre had become) struck back with the suggestion that *Philotas* had given "such undeniable proofs of mental derangement as to induce his friends to confine him in a house of reception for lunatics." Voters were warned that their imaginations, "by indulging too great a familiarity with the horrible objects of Anarchy, Confusion and Rebellion, should unhappily triumph over their reason." *Philopolis* took a similar line, when he humbly begged the Ladies and Gentlemen of Liverpool for their generosity in forgiving *Philotas* for the contents of his handbill. He reasoned, "True, it is he [who] intruded upon your good sense with the done-way cant-word JACOBIN, which you know the Alarmists in a fatal hour brought forward as a Scarecrow to frighten you from peeping into their nefarious practices." After deriding the scant support shown for John Tarleton, Philopolis concluded, "Ye Fair Ladies! Allow me one more word. Do no bestow a single sweet kiss,

---

[3] All quotes below are from the 1796 Liverpool Poll Book and Addresses.

This page and p218 - various lampoons appearing originally as posters and handbills during electioneering, and later reprinted in the 1796 Liverpool Poll Book and Addresses (LRO)

Strayed or otherways conveyed, from the Barren Hills of Childwall, a Young Pug Dog, of the Liliputian Breed, commonly called or known by the name of *Isaac*.

THE said Dog was marked in the heel at Dunkirk races, and wears a red collar; whoever will give information to Mr. Tom. C——— where he may be found, will receive a reward of a basket of fine cabbage, and a barrel of excellent bull beef.

May, 24th.

The Report Adequate, but not Courteous.

NOT Stolen, but strayed from his Kennel in the Jacobin Society at London, a remarkable Fierce looking Animal of the Cur kind, with his Tail cut off, answers to the name of Crop, wears a black collar round his neck, and has two Claws missing on his right fore Paw. Whoever will return him to his keeper, Mrs. R———n, in C——— S———t; to any of the Gaming Houses in Covent Garden, or to any of his Grace of B———'s Grooms, shall be rewarded with a Fraternal Embrace for his trouble.

Supposed to be Stolen out of the Pocket of J. T——n, Esq. In the Neighbourhood of Brunswick-street,

A Large Packet of Papers,

CONTAINING Sir G—frey W—b—ter's draft upon him for three thousand pounds for his seat in parliament. N. B. The money is not yet paid.

Copy of a speech made in the last sessions against the Liverpool Corporation Loan Bill.

Minutes of a conversation between J. T. and his Wife, respecting the necessity of his fighting Sir G—d—rey, at which, like a true Spartan Dame, she advises him to risk his life, in support of his honor.

Copies of several private letters against common halls, and the rights of the freemen of Liverpool.

A complimentary and congratulatory epistle to Mr. W. N——n, &c.

Copy of a violent handbill, abusive of his brother. N. B. The loss of this is a great inconvenience, as he was then taking it to his Printer.

SHIP NEWS,

From new Lloyd's Lift, May, 27, 1796.

THE Britannia, Capt. Grenville, Commodore King.

The Conftitution, Capt. Loughborough.——The Hibernia, Capt. Cambden.——The Caledonian, Capt. Dundas.——The Commons, Capt. Pitt.

Are all returned from a fuccefsful cruife. Comodore King has put this laft fhip out of commiffion for a few months, on account of the difloyalty of fome of her crew, who have got their difcharge with a fevere reprimand. The loyal part received thanks of the Commodore, with orders to repair on board the moment the fhip was commiffioned.

The Cromwell, Capt. Lauderdale.——The Sans Culotte, Capt. Stanhope,——The Democrat, Capt. Derby. Are laid up as ordinary ; as is the Fraternity, Capt. Bedford.

The Revolution, Capt. Fox.
The Republican, Capt. Sheridan. } Thefe three fecond rates are condemned and ordered to be
The Bon Citizen, Capt. Erfkine. } brokeup.

The Black Joke, Capt. Wilberforce. } Are driven on fhore on the
The Abolition, Capt. Dolben, } coaft of Africa, and bulged.

The Penfion, Capt. Burke—wore out in the fervice.

LIVERPOOL SHIP NEWS,

From new Lloyd's Lift, May 28.

The Favorite frigate, Capt. Gafc—e, is out of commiffion. We hear the Captain is very fick, having caught a Welch Fever, whilft fitting out for his laft cruife.

The Childwall, a fine new frigate, is intended to be launched early in June, and the command given to Capt. I. Gafco—e. It is faid he is to accompany the fquadron under Commodore King. The Captain is now fhipping his people, and will compleat his number in a few days. He has a moft excellent fet of officers.

First page showing how freemen cast their votes, 1796 Poll Book (LRO)

a single enchanting smile to your husbands or swains, until they have given their votes."[4]

From the Gascoyne camp, *A Chip off the Old Block* urged his "honest Brother Chips" to beware of the devil in sheep's clothing. He wrote of rational liberty being the prerogative of Britons, and implored "Let us then turn a deaf ear to the enemies of our King, Church and Constitution; and don't let us leave plain wholesome roast beef of old England for the meagre, unsubstantial diet of these political French cooks." However, suggestions of Banastre being a friend to revolutionary France were answered by *Crop*, as he struck a chord with those who had suffered most as a result of the conflict. "Your present Government has dragged us into a ruinous, expensive, unnecessary and wicked war,

1796.

NOTE,——Thofe marked *g t* were for General Tarleton, thofe marked *c g* for Colonel Gafcoyne, and thofe marked *j t* for John Tarleton, Efq.

ABRAM Henry, wheelwright, Church-lane		*c g*	
Argent George, painter, Breck-ftreet			*j t*
Alcock Samuel, painter, Everton	*g t*		
Afhcroft Wm. fhipwright, Sparling-ftreet		*c g*	*j t*
Afhton David, mariner, Mafon-ftreet		*c g*	
Afpinall Wm. mariner, Shawfbrow		*c g*	
Afhton Nicholas, Efq. Much Woolton	*g t*	*c g*	.
Almond James, taylor, John-ftreet	*g t*		
Adgett George, butcher, Liverpool		*c g*	
Armftrong John, merchant, Everton	*g t*		
Afpinall James, blockmaker, Norfolk-ftreet		*c g*	
Afpinall Wm. fhipwright, Merfey-ftreet		*c g*	
Abbott Edward, letter-cafe-maker, John-ftreet,	*g t*		
Andrews Peter, roper, Manchefter			*j t*
Amery Jonathan, broker, Crofbie-ftreet	*g t*		
Aftle Robert, breadbaker, Thomas's ftreet			*j t*
Amery Thomas, mafter & mariner Kent-ftreet	*g t*		
Abram John, plaifterer, Edmund-ftreet	*g t*		
Archer Richard, cooper, Tarvin Chefhire			*j t*
Afhton Edward, blockmaker, Garden-ftreet			*j t*
Abbott James, pocket-book-maker, John-ftreet	*g t*		
Allen James, roper, Brooks's-fquare		*c g*	
Andrews John, roper, Park-lane		*c g*	
Ainfworth Thomas, boat-builder, Kitchen-ftreet	*g t*		
Agnew Jofeph, pilot, Fleet-ftreet	*g t*		
Atherton Matthew, cooper, Warrington		*c g*	*j t*.
Alben Thos. anchor fmith, Norfolk-ftreet	*g t*		
Afhburn Jon. Mo. blockmaker Circus-ftreet		*c g*	
Afpinall Richard, cooper, Atherton-ftreet	*g t*		
Ainfworth Jofeph, cooper, Gerard-ftreet	*g t*		
Aftle Wm. baker, Pall-mall		*c g*	*j t*
Afpinall Wm. tinplate-worker, Williams-ftreet	*g t*		
Amery John, ftaymaker, Warrington		*c g*	
Arthington Thomas, joiner, Harford-ftreet,		*c g*	
Arthington Jon. cordwainer, Derby-ftreet		*c g*	

which has deprived you of your husbands, your children, your trade, your supports, your comforts and necessaries in life, and almost everything dear to you; and what have they given in return for these inestimable blessings? Additional weight of taxes, plenty of poverty and distress, and in your decline of life, a very poor house to linger out the remainder of your half-starving, melancholy and miserable days in." In the meantime, there was this lyrical reminder of Banastre Tarleton's recent opposition to abolition in Parliament:

"A few months ago, Oh! Did you not hear,
The slave trade would fail, which made us to fear,
That now it's all over you need not repine,
For the General has baffled the Wilberforce design!
Oh rare Tarleton, well done, General,
We'll vote for you again and again."

---

[4] Swain – young lover or suitor (Oxford Dictionary of English).

Despite the many smears, by Monday 30th May Banastre Tarleton's position seemed safe, enabling his camp to predict, "At the Public Theatre Hustings will be performed on Wednesday evening next, The Tragedy of the Unnatural Brother Conquered." But, despite the bluff and bluster, the election proved a relatively calm affair and voting was light. By the close of the polls on 1st June, John Tarleton was trailing in third place and conceded defeat on 317 votes. Isaac Gascoyne topped the poll with 672 votes, his success seldom in doubt as the corporation's favourite, while Banastre Tarleton retained his seat in Parliament with 506.

That same year, William Moss published *The Liverpool Guide*, which he thought necessary to serve the town's many visitors. He observed, "Liverpool being the first town in the kingdom in point of size and commercial importance, the Metropolis excepted, has of late been the resort of a great number of visitors for the purpose of commerce." Moss added, "the pleasant and salubrious situation of the town, the convenience of sea bathing, its amusements, and the lively cheerful air which regularly pervades it, have of late years made it also the resort of Strangers of all descriptions for the purposes of health and amusement." Indeed, the town had become a holiday resort for wealthy families "from the interior", many hiring bathing machines on the north shore, or further along at Bootle Mills where there were two good hotels.

After helpfully referring the visitor to several other publications, including his own medical survey, Moss began his guide with a tour of the inns. The largest and most superior was *Bates' Hotel* in Lord Street, "where there are accommodations for families of the first rank, their retinues, carriages, and horses." The hotel had a coffee room where most of the London and provincial newspapers and magazines could be read. Although local subscribers paid a guinea a year for the privilege, visitors were welcome free of charge. Almost as salubrious were the *Kings Arms* and the *Talbot Inn* in Water Street, the latter being much frequented by travellers to and from Dublin, and from where coaches ran daily to London. Then came the *Crown Inn* in Redcross Street, "a commodious house" from where a coach for London set out three times a week. Both the *Star and Garter* in Paradise Street and the *Globe Tavern* in John Street offered "genteel accommodation for parties, for eating or lodging, upon the plan of a regular Tavern." Stagecoaches to Warrington and Manchester went from the *Angel Inn* in Dale Street, and also the *Golden Lion*, which was "formerly the largest and best Inn in the town."

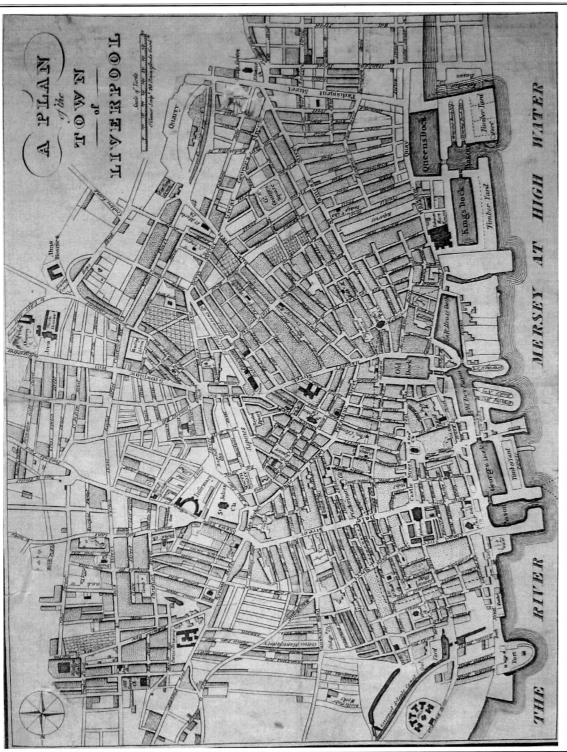

O'Connor's Plan of Liverpool, 1797 (LRO Hf 912)

Visitors could write home and expect letters to arrive two days later at most. The post office in Lord Street opened at eight and received letters until nine each evening. Mail coaches went all over the country and travelled through the night, taking under a day to reach York, and thirty-seven hours to reach London. Postage for Italy and north European destinations cost 1s 6d, but two shillings to Spain or Portugal via Lisbon. Mail was sent to North America and Jamaica on the first Wednesday each month, and twice a month to the Leeward Islands, but postage for Caribbean destinations went free of charge.

Several packet boats sailed for Dublin "for the express purpose of conveying passengers, horses, carriages, and light goods." The same were taken on open ferry boats across the Mersey to Seacombe, Woodside, Rock Ferry, New Ferry, and Eastham, along with cattle and other livestock. Good roads connected with Chester, but travellers could also take the packet boat from Eastham along the canal. Most had little other reason to make the crossing, but Moss noted that local parties did so for pleasure during the summer, and some enjoyed walking to the lighthouse on Bidston Hill. But, he warned, "ale, bread and cheese is the only fare to be met with there, except perhaps a cup of tea." However, Moss lamented the lack of price regulation, "which would prevent the daily impositions that are practiced, especially upon strangers, and which are frequently to a shameful excess." Ferry operators charged two pence for market traders and locals, but "sixpence is generally expected from the upper orders of passengers." He advised, "the smaller boats with one mast each are to be preferred to the larger with two, as they are handier, can land in shallow water, are capable of being rowed in calms or contrary winds, and are equally safe." When low water prevented boats reaching the piers, "the passengers of both sexes are carried in and out of the boats by the boatmen with great ease and safety."

Chapel Street, 1797, leading down to George's Dock (LIC 946, LRO)

Sightseers were advised to start at the Exchange and look down Castle Street, which he described as "perfectly uniform on the right hand, and nearly so on the left; all shops, containing everything useful and ornamental to indulge the taste and gratify the necessities; presents a view not to be excelled, perhaps, in the Capital." The spires of St. George's and St. Thomas's, and the ship's masts in the Old Dock, presented a view "as grand as it is novel." St. George's market offered the best vegetables in the country, and the oranges were often so plentiful "as to scent the ambient air as fully as when in their native groves." But the visitor received a note of caution, as he or she now continued on to view the ships in the Old Dock. "Pursuing the course down Pool Lane, the eye should not be turned to either side, as it would be offended by the very indecorous practice of exposing the shambles meat in the public street." On reaching the dock, the visitor should not have been surprised to see so many ships in the heart of a town with no apparent means of communication with the sea. Posts and chains had been fitted to the quays, "which became necessary to prevent strangers and others falling in in the night, from missing their way, from intoxication, &c."

Fowler's Court, off Chapel Street, 1797 (Pictorial Relics, Plate 3, Herdman, LRO)

Nearby Cleveland Square had been an "eligible residence", but had since become a market and lost both its trees and its elegance. Walking to the far end and into Pitt Street, the visitor was then directed left into York Street, passing an iron foundry owned by the Coalbrookedale Company, and into Duke Street with its engaging views. A short way up on the right in Suffolk Street was a large cotton manufactory powered by a steam engine. The upper end of Duke Street, and the land beyond, was still being developed. Great George Street showed promise as a "good street", while Rodney Street appeared "very handsome", and Moss hoped the neighbourhood would "preserve that decided superiority over other parts of the town." Sandstone for the docks and public edifices was cut from the nearby quarry, before which was the gravelled terrace of St. James' Walk offering panoramic views comparable to those at Windsor. Locals and visitors alike could admire the Cheshire hills and mountains of North Wales, the windmills and lighthouses, and the chain of flagpoles signalling new arrivals as ships approached the Mersey.

View of Liverpool from Lime Street in 1797, showing a ropery in the foreground (detail from Pictorial Relics, Plate 29, Herdman, LRO)

The walk down Parliament Street from St. James's Walk marked Liverpool's southern boundary, beyond which lay rural Toxteth, (where the riverside Herculaneum pottery would start producing fine quality porcelain soon after publication). Parliament Street led to the town's most recent dock system, comprising the King's, Queen's and two graving docks, all entered through a tidal basin protecting the dock gates from the full force of the river. (Prior to its recent opening, thousands had gathered to watch a bull being baited in the Queen's dock just before it was flooded).[5] Moss warned of the offensive smell from the processing of whale blubber at the oil works nearby, although it was far more a nuisance to those living in the neighbourhood. Alongside were several timber yards, and a tobacco warehouse built to prevent "that smuggling and pilfering so much complained of in the London river." Moss explained that "when the manufacturer wants a hogshead or more of his tobacco, he sends the duty and the tobacco is delivered accordingly."

[5] Brooke, op cit., p413.

Along nearby Wapping Quay stood several corn warehouses, along with various anchor smiths, block-makers, sail makers and a ropery, but the salt works was due to relocate up river due to pollution from coal-burning. There were also numerous lodging houses for seafarers in the locality, for as Moss noted, "fires and candles are not suffered on board the ships in the docks." The Duke of Bridgewater's small private dock received coal, pottery, and other goods brought by canals from Lancashire and Staffordshire to Runcorn, and from there down the Mersey in flatboats. Nearby, between the river and the Salthouse Dock, were the shipyards that built merchant vessels and frigates for the royal navy. The town rambler now returned to the Old Dock area, with its numerous alehouses, cheap lodgings and slop shops, and could meander round the docks over several draw bridges, eventually reaching the Parade and the ferryboat slipway by George's Dock. Apart from the larger ocean-going ships, many small trading vessels brought wares from around the coast and offered passage to travellers on their return journey, their home ports being painted on boards attached to their shroud rigging.

Moss claimed that "the docility of the carthorses of Liverpool perhaps exceeds that of any in the kingdom, or even the world." He noted that most carters directed their horses by word alone without touching the reigns "with as much precision as a regiment of soldiers." In an amusing anecdote, he recounted the story of a parrot that was frequently hung in its cage outside a house by George's Dock. The bird had acquired an extensive repertoire, "more especially that particular part which so frequently requires the horse to back his load to discharge it into the ship." One unfortunate carter had left his cart backed up to a ship, when "Pol, in a garrulous mood, unluckily happened to cry *back – back – back* – several times, so distinctly and loudly, that the well-tutored animal,

Georges Dock Quay and St. Nicholas Church, 1797 (Herdman Collection 1420, LRO)

obeying the word of command, actually backed the cart so as to precipitate it and himself into the dock." Fortunately, the horse was saved, and Moss concluded, "That two brute animals of totally different species, perfect strangers to each other, should be capable, without any assistance, of directing and executing a regular action by means of the human language, is a curiosity perhaps unparalleled in the history of the world."

Moss urged his readers to view the river traffic, which "from the variety it always affords is always entertaining, even to those who see it most frequently." A hoisted flag signalled to oncoming vessels when the dock gates were open, a lowered flag indicated their closure, and the same system operated by night using lamps. Ocean-going ships saluted the townsfolk with a blank cannonade, while friends and families gathered to welcome or see crews off as they manoeuvred their vessels along the quays with ropes and capstans. The dock masters controlled all movement of vessels, "for without such a Regulator….confusion and consequent injury would regularly ensue." With an assiduous eye on their tide tables, the masters also controlled dock water levels using sluices to enable the gates to open at high tide. Only when the levels and pressures on both sides were equal could four men on each pair of gates operate the machinery using sheer muscle power to the accompaniment of shanties.

Moss theorised that the design of ships from different nations typified their national characters. He explained, "The Dutch ships are strong and square built, misshapen and clumsy; nor, like the natives, has any attempt at the least alteration ever been made in their ornaments or equipment. They are distinguished by a considerable hollowness in the middle, and by the sudden elevation of two square ends; as also by the collosean figure of a head of Van Trump or a favourite Frow, placed, in contradiction to the custom of other nations and the order of nature, on the stern, upon the top of the rudder, with an aspect towards the crew as if for idolatrous purpose – if a Dutchman can be supposed to adore anything but wealth." Swedish ships were much the same, unlike French ships, which were "slightly built, the ornaments taudry, and the rigging and masts so light and lofty as to give the idea of a flying Mercury." In Moss's view, English ships struck a happy medium between the two, combining strength with beauty and ornament. He added, "The Guineamen here are in general the handsomest ships; being every way modelled after the Frigates, and rather more ornamented."

Having sampled the sights and sounds of the docks and the river, the visitor was guided to the market at the bottom of James Street, where flatfish, cod, herring, salmon, crabs, shrimps and prawns were plentiful according to season. As for the fish women, Moss noted wryly, "the Sisterhood will be found to enjoy as great a privilege and refinement of the tongue as at most other

Old Fish Market, James Street (Pictorial Relics, Plate 17, Herdman, 1828, LRO)

similar seminaries." Doubling back through the piazza walkway of the new Goree warehouses and passing the tower gaol, the town rambler reached the *Merchants' Coffee House* in the Old Church yard, "where the newspapers are read, and where lodgings may be had by those who prefer the situation." A little further on, between boat and shipbuilders' yards, was a small glass manufactory. Next to the river were the public baths, "which are esteemed commodious and elegant." (These consisted of two separate seawater bathing pools for ladies and gentlemen, each about thirty feet square and six deep. There were also furnished rooms heated by coal fires for relaxation, private dressing rooms, and six heated baths in private cubicles for washing).[6] Beyond these luxurious facilities stood the fort, which, "with its formidable artillery, promises an ample security against any enemy ships that may attempt an entrance into the harbour." Two hundred yards away was the terminus for the Liverpool and Leeds canal, although the Pennine section had yet to be completed. For now, the canal brought mainly Wigan coal and Lancashire textiles, while barges returned with all manner of imports, and passengers could take a packet boat as far as Wigan. The new gaol on Great Howard Street, at the north end of Liverpool, was mainly being used to hold French prisoners, who Moss thought "fortunately for themselves, have been here preserved from the famine and bloodshed that have so desolated their native country." (In reality, nothing could have been further from the truth. Over a thousand prisoners languished in conditions of overcrowding and disease, and the hearse arrived daily to bury the dead in St. John's churchyard. The inmates did their best to keep their spirits up using the seaman's ingenuity to whittle, weave and sew. Trinkets and toys, boxes and baskets, model ships and rag dolls were carved, stitched

---

[6] Brooke, op. cit., p409-410.

or woven using scraps, and put on sale at the prison entrance. Some even performed plays for the public in a small theatre within the walls, taking as much as fifty pounds in a night, but such industry could not detract from their misery).[7] Next to the prison stood a lead works, and also an iron foundry with a steam-driven mill for rolling and cutting hot metal. To return to the Exchange, the visitor was led along Old Hall Street, where the White Cross market had once been held. Although the street was

Borough Gaol, Great Howard Street (Pictorial Relics, Plate 48, Herdman, undated, LRO)

narrow and dirty, and had lost its former gentility, the area behind and around the Exchange had been made more airy by clearing away the shambles of stalls and slaughterhouses.

During the summer the visitor might be tempted to spend an evening at the Theatre Royal in Williamson Square, which had once boasted the best performers outside of London. With the growing popularity of provincial theatres, quality performers had become thinly spread, and Moss considered some no better than mere strollers. Mr. Kemble had once been hissed off the stage, and Mrs. Siddons had been forced to quit the town! But public opinion was versatile. When Mrs Siddons gained approval from London audiences, "they who had been so desirous to banish her from the theatre were now so eager to see her perform that many injuries, both of body and dress, were sustained, so great was the pressure of the crowd to get admission into the play-house." Moss regarded the present players as motley, with the exception of Mrs. Mattocks, who had played in Liverpool for thirty summer seasons with deserving estimation. However, a more refined evening might be spent at the concert hall in Bold Street to hear a recital of Bach or Handel, but performances were sadly limited to twelve a year. On the other hand, one could visit the elegant fresh water baths on Bolton Street. Ladies and gentlemen could each enjoy cold, tepid and hot plunge pools in separate facilities, the water being supplied from the well of an adjoining cotton manufactory and heated by its steam engine. Other attractions included the equestrian circus on Christian Street, an archery on Rose Hill, and a bowling green and tennis court near St. Anne's

[7] Brooke, op cit, p489-490.

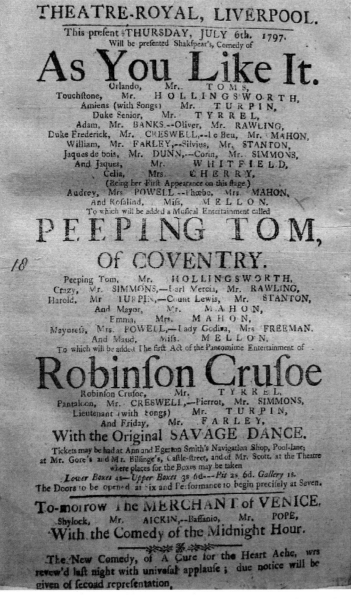

Theatre Royal Bill, 6th July 1797 (Hf 792.1, LRO)

church. But, if an alcoholic beverage was preferred, Moss advised against drinking beer from any of the forty local breweries except the Porter's. As he explained, "The indifferent quality of the Ale has lately been a means of introducing that necessary, native and wholesome beverage from many parts of the surrounding country." On the other hand, he suggested the new Porter's brewery on Scotland Road "promises to furnish as good a quality of liquor as the London Breweries."[8]

A tour of nearby villages was recommended as a pleasant ride through the countryside in a chaise. Everton village had a pleasing effect and offered good views, as did Walton along the Great North Road. Beyond West Derby village at Knowsley was the seat of the Earl of Derby, an ancient ornate mansion with extensive grounds and gardens, "well disposed both by nature and art". Childwall boasted fine views, a bath of remarkably pure spring water, a good coffee house, and Childwall Hall, home of the Gascoyne family. There was a bowling green, a pleasant villa and comfortable lodgings in Woolton, and a good dinner could be found at Mrs. Dennison's. An eminent mansion stood on Mosley Hill (paid for by the proceeds of the *Carnatic*) displaying "elegance and chastity of design", and commanding fine views. Wavertree was a pretty village with a good tavern and an inn, where locals were often joined by people from Liverpool on summer evenings. Along Smeatham (later Smithdown) Lane, the Earl of Sefton was resisting the encroachment of Liverpool towards his lands at Toxteth. As Moss noted, "Some attempts were made to improve it by building &c., but as they were entrusted to his stewards, they, of course, were frustrated."

---

[8] As far as I can tell, there is no connection with any existing brewer of the same name.

Moss also gave an account of social welfare provided by the town. Parish rates paid for the workhouse and lunatic asylum on Brownlow Hill, the almshouses on Mount Pleasant, and outdoor relief. Meanwhile, Liverpool's seafarers paid sixpence a month "for the maintenance of decayed seamen, their widows and children." Voluntary subscriptions, church collections, benefit concerts and theatre performances provided on-going finance for such institutions as the Church Street dispensary and the Liverpool Infirmary adjoining the Seamen's Hospital on Shaw's Brow (now the site of St. George's Hall). The blind asylum on Commutation Row was also charity run, its inmates being "instructed in every mechanical art they are capable of attaining", and their wares sold to help in their upkeep. Moss noted that most had lost their sight due to smallpox, but the poor still retained their prejudice against inoculation. A plan of general inoculation had been tried over two or three years, and "every persuasive means made use of to induce the lower ranks to accept it," but to little avail. The charitable Bluecoat school and hospital looked after orphaned and fatherless children, and others "whose parents are in indigent circumstances." All were taught reading and writing, the boys also receiving instruction in accounts and navigation, the girls in spinning, sewing, knitting and housewifery. Half the day was spent in the school, the rest making pins and clothing, and at fourteen they were "put out apprentices." Discipline was doubtless very harsh, child-beating being the rule rather than the exception, a practice that continued during indentured servitude.

The town also boasted an Institution for Restoring Drowned Persons, which offered a guinea reward for every successful rescue, or half a guinea for recovering the dead. Some four hundred people, half of whom were saved, had been pulled from the water over the previous twenty years using hooked poles placed at intervals along the quays. But, if proof of good works was ever needed, two charities stood out. The Ladies' Charity served to relieve poor married women, "in childbed, at their own homes; a mode that proves to have many advantages over a public hospital." Women were nursed and restored to health, while their families were fed and every basic need was met. But perhaps most worthy was the Benevolent Society, its aim being "to seek for the poor obscure objects who, from dissidence, infirmity, or as strangers, cannot obtrude themselves so as to make their wants known; and for this intention, the members alternately visit every obscure recess of poverty and distress they can discover to relieve the present urgent necessities of their suffering inmates till more effectual assistance can be procured. As Moss noted, "this society may be justly styled Benevolent."

Despite the existence of some local industries, most of Liverpool's wealth came through its docks, although it remained in the hands of the few. Trade had made wealthy men richer, while others had risen from humble origins to claim entry to the merchant ranks. But social climbing was fraught with as many obstacles as commerce itself. As Moss explained, "A man in the middle walk of life, while embracing its comforts and true elegances, will studiously avoid its ostentations for his own sake, as it invariably subjects him to the sneer of his superior, the jealousy of his equal, and the envy of his inferior." Somewhat perversely, Moss believed "the Necessitous have a peculiar advantage." In his view, the inferior orders enjoyed "a species of Charity" from employers through "indulgence, succour and protection", which cushioned them from life's hardships. He believed, "the pay of mechanics and labourers is fully adequate to the temperate subsistence of themselves and their families for the preservation of their health." Acknowledging that many families lived in cellars, he suggested, "It has an unpleasant appearance; yet that is the worst of its qualities, a cellar being found from experience a much more healthful residence than a room in a house where every room is tenanted." Some entire streets consisted of crowded multi-occupancies where people intermingled on staircases and landings, spreading their infections. For this reason, Moss was thankful that the recent intention of the council to clear the cellars had not been executed. At least cellar dwellers offered a measure of isolation from contagious diseases, even though the muck did have a tendency to flow in during heavy rainfall.

Moss was surely complacent about those less fortunate than him. As the war deprived families of men lost in action, and the numbers of destitute rose, so too did the burden on parish rates. The parish was also responsible for maintaining active servicemen's families in lieu of wages, and with the workhouse full to capacity, the system was stretched to the limit. The parish had for some time doled out poor relief to people in their homes, a practice the government finally recognised as necessary and made lawful in 1796. In the same year, a long-standing dispute as to whether the corporation should be liable to pay parish taxes on its receipts from market tolls and dock duties appeared to be resolved. When this had first been proposed ten years earlier, the corporation had retaliated by claiming back-rent for the land on which the workhouse was built[9] Furthermore, the parish still owed the corporation for a loan of £4000 to build the workhouse nearly thirty years earlier, although interest had been paid at 4½ per cent annually. To solve the dispute, the two sides agreed that the corporation would pay what it owed after deducting £1050 for a thousand year lease on the workhouse grounds. This would solve the rent issue and enable the parish to settle its loan. Meanwhile, a similar dispute had been raging with the ship owners. The parish first tried to tax ships three years earlier, but the merchants had refused to pay and the issue had lingered in the courts. The parish dropped its claim in 1796 due to legal costs, but rescinded its decision

9 See p125 above.

the following year when a rate of three pence per ton was levied, and legal proceedings resumed.

By this time Liverpool was preparing for the threat of invasion. Late in February 1797 news was received that a French force had landed at Fishguard in Wales, but had put to sea again and was expected to attack Liverpool. The mayor called a public meeting on Sunday 26th, and over a thousand men joined up as volunteers, adding to the Liverpool Yeomanry already stationed at the fort. Pilots were ordered into Liverpool Bay to warn of an enemy approach, and several merchants offered armed ships as a floating battery at the entrance to the Mersey. In addition to all this, fifty-six heavy cannon were mounted at the fort and several temporary batteries were placed along the waterfront, each with ten men to crew the guns. Meanwhile, the gunpowder at the Cheshire magazines was removed as a precaution, the barrels being stored well up river out of harm's way.

The North Fort, 1836, but much as it looked fifty years earlier (Herdman Collection 1354, LRO)

But, far from being a serious threat, the invasion turned out to be a damp squib. There were merely fourteen hundred French troops aboard two frigates, a corvette and a lugger. They made their first appearance at Ilfracombe harbour on the north Devon coast, where they scuttled a few merchant ships, but soon set sail again on learning of the North Devon volunteers marching in their direction. The tiny force then rounded St. David's Head and disembarked near Fishguard in Pembrokeshire, and after pillaging a few local farmhouses found themselves surrounded by a militia of three thousand Welshmen. Meanwhile, the four ships had sailed away leaving no means of retreat, and the farce ended in surrender without a fight. The French may have been hoping to raise a local uprising against the English, or to test out defences, but whatever the case many of the invaders were badly trained and ill-disciplined. Despite this failure, a similar attempt was made a year later in Ireland, which was prompted by an uprising of United Irishmen in both Ulster and the South. But the rebellion had effectively been crushed by the time a small French invasion force arrived at Killala Bay in County Mayo. Despite picking up some support and making halfway towards Dublin, the French were overwhelmed and forced to surrender at Ballinamuck.

In the meantime, the war of merchant shipping continued unabated. The *Tarleton* was approaching Barbados with a cargo of slaves in November 1796 when it was attacked by a large French schooner. As Captain Ratcliffe Shimmins explained, "Finding my people all healthy and well disposed, particularly my officers, and with the assistance of the best of our slaves, prepared for action. About two o'clock he got alongside of us, hoisted his French ensign, and before there was any time for hailing, gave us a broadside, which we returned warmer than he wished. The action continued without ever ceasing till five o'clock, when he sheered off and stood to the northward. The only damage we received was in our sails and rigging; not a man hurt. She was as handsome a frigate-built ship as I have seen, mounted 20 guns, nine-pounders, on her main deck, and eight guns on her quarter deck; had much the appearance of the *Princess Royal*, formerly of Liverpool."

"My people were in high spirits, and if we could have got alongside of him again we would, I am certain, have saved them the trouble of taking down their bloody flag, but our rigging and sails being a good deal cut, partly prevented us. He was much more shattered than us, and his hull pretty well moth eaten, his quarter [deck] was at one time so well cleared with our eighteen-pounders that we suppose a number of them slept under their arms. Nothing but his superior sailing saved him at last. We expended five barrels of gunpowder, and the next afternoon, about five o'clock, made the Island of Barbadoes."[10]

---

[10] Quoted in Williams, op cit., p349-350.

The crew of the *Tarleton* were lucky to have come off so lightly and to have been assisted by the slaves, but others were less fortunate. At the start of the following year, the *Thomas* was attacked on the way to Angola by a French corvette bristling with 22 guns and two to three hundred marines. The *Thomas's* crew were heavily outnumbered, but were well used to handling her sixteen heavy calibre guns. As Captain Peter M'Quie explained, the French commander "hoisted his bloody pendant for boarding, made sail, and in a short time (he sailing, comparatively speaking, two feet for my one) came off my larboard quarter, and in a very peremptory manner, ordered me to haul down my colours, otherwise he would grant me no quarter whatever. I hailed him through my Linguist that if he would come alongside I would treat upon more amicable terms, but to no effect. He then, like a man, laid his ship alongside of me, with his bowsprit entangled in my fore-shrouds, when the action became general, and for forty-seven minutes remained in this position with a determined resolution to board me on his part, and a determination on mine to resist him to the last. His bowsprit being thus entangled, I with my own hands lashed my shrouds to his main-topmast backstay, which, if the lashing had not been cut, I am convinced you would have had a good account of her. The men were all armed with tomahawks, &c. Her tops were all crowded with men, and from so well-continued and kept-up fire of small arms I am surprised the injury was not greater. The enemy threw on board hand granadoes, stinkpots (five and twenty or thirty stinkpots and hand granadoes I have now on board), marling-spikes, boarding-pikes, and even the arm of his ship's head. My first broadside, I am assured, injured her masts very materially, his foretopmast and jib boom being both shot away. In the general part of the action, my quarter guns tore him to pieces. The carnage was dreadful, sweeping every thing before them, being both well-loaded with grape, ball, and canister shot, and well conducted."[11]

The French crew got their vessel away to carry out repairs, but returned several times that evening, and again the next day, to harass the *Thomas*. Meanwhile, the *Thomas's* crew snatched whatever sleep they could by resting on their guns. The French eventually gave up when a British convoy was sighted, and the escort ship drew alongside the *Thomas* to send its surgeon on board. As for his own surgeon, M'Quie noted sorrowfully, "What must my feelings be when I inform you that my surgeon, Mr. James Beatty, was shot through the head and died instantaneously at my feet on the quarter deck, after having fired several muskets at the enemy."[12]

---

[11] Quoted in Williams, op. cit., p352.
[12] Ibid, p353.

The *Thomas* continued on to Angola, where it took on 375 slaves before setting sail for Barbados. On 2nd September 1797, just days from their destination, and while the crew were having breakfast, a couple of the female slaves noticed the armoury chest had been left unlocked. They managed to pass the weapons through the bulkheads to the captive men, who then broke through the hatches and poured on deck. The crew fought desperately with their few remaining arms but were overpowered, and many, including the captain, were killed. Twelve managed to escape in the stern boat, but only two survived by the time it reached Barbados. Meanwhile, the slaves had taken possession of the ship and forced the remaining crew to sail the *Thomas* back to Africa. Four of these escaped in the longboat, reaching the Bahamas after six days without food or water, and leaving five shipmates to crew the ship back to Africa. Six weeks after the revolt, an American brig laden with rum drew alongside. The insurgents poured on board, forcing the terrified crew to escape in their boats. After discovering and breaking open the casks of rum, the slaves got hopelessly drunk, enabling the remaining crew of the *Thomas* to recapture the brig, rescue the Americans, and set sail for Long Island. The *Thomas* was left floundering without a crew, and was later retaken by the *Thames* frigate.[13]

The crew of the slave ship *Amelia and Eleanor* had a narrow escape a year later while heading for Barbados, when it was attacked by a French privateer. Captain Alexander Speers explained, "At eleven a.m., the action commenced, and continued till half-past two p.m. Early in the action, I lost my bowsprit and foremast, close by the rigging. When he found I was disabled, he renewed the action with double vigour, and hoisted the bloody flag at his main-topgallant masthead, steered alongside within pistol shot, and hailed me, *"Strike, you____! strike!"* which I answered with a broadside, which laid him on a creen. He then stood away to the northward to plug up his shot holes, as I could see several men over the side. In about twenty minutes, he came alongside again and gave me a broadside as he passed. He then stood to the southward, and got about a mile to windward, gave me a lee gun, and hauled down his bloody flag, which I answered with three to windward. I have received a deal of damage to my hull; on my starboard bow, two ports in one; several shot between wind and water. I had not one shroud left forward but what was cut to pieces, stays, etc. I lost all headsails, and my after sails much damaged. I lost one slave, and four wounded; four of the people [crew] wounded; two are since dead of their wounds. I shall not be able to proceed from hence till January, as my hull is like a riddle."[14]

---

13 Williams, op. cit., p592-593. Brooke, op. cit., p236-237.
14 Quoted in Williams, op cit, p369.

Whatever the cargo, no ship could expect the cross the Atlantic without incident. On 1st December 1798, the *Barton* was challenged by a French privateer as it approached Barbados directly from Liverpool with passengers. Having been beaten off during their first attack, the French crew returned determined to board. As an officer explained, "...the whole of the Barton's crew being assembled on the quarter deck, and headed by their gallant commander, who was spiritedly seconded by his passengers, an attack, sword in hand, commenced, and the enemy were driven back with considerable loss, many of them being spiked from the netting and shrouds of the ship, while by a well-directed fire from the cabin guns, numbers were swept from their own deck; and a great part of her rigging being cut away, she dropped astern and gave over the contest, amidst the victorious '*Huzzas!*' of the British tars, whose bold commander, calling from his quarter deck, defied the vanquished Republicans to return to the attack. Captain Cutler's conduct on this occasion cannot be too highly spoken of, and such was the enthusiasm of all on board the ship, that his passengers bear a proportionate share of honour."[15]

Whenever possible, merchant ships travelled in convoys protected by royal naval escorts. His Majesty's ships patrolled British coastal waters, while also blockading foreign naval bases to prevent French, Spanish and Dutch warships from putting to sea. A British fleet anchored at the Nore off Sheerness to defend the Thames and Medway, while another was based at Spithead off Portsmouth, and a third at Plymouth Sound. Since Spain and Holland had sided with France, all this was essential to keep British commerce afloat and minimise the chance of invasion. But, while able seamen on merchant ships earned around £3 15s a month, those on the king's ships earned a third of this at just twenty-four shillings, and ordinary seamen and landsmen got even less. By early 1797, grievances over pay, poor food, harsh treatment, and lack of shore leave, were driving large numbers of sailors towards mutiny, bearing in mind that many had been pressed into service from all over Britain, including Liverpool. In April, sailors at Spithead presented their grievances and declared a strike, while promising to put to sea in an emergency. Their demands were accepted a week later by the Admiralty, but the men were sceptical and remained on strike until an Act of Parliament guaranteed improvements for the whole fleet. Two days before Admiral Howe personally delivered news of the settlement to the ships at Spithead, the mutiny spread to the Nore fleet. Their demands went further, and included a more equitable division of prize money, arrears of wages, and an end to brutal practices such as flogging. After tarring and feathering several officers and threatening to blockade the Thames, the government brought up warships manned by loyal sailors and set up shore batteries. The mutiny soon collapsed and thirty-six of its leaders were hanged.[16]

15 Quoted in Williams, op. cit., p369-370.
16 Cordingly, op. cit., p112-113.

In the spring of 1798, a fleet of thirteen British warships was assembling near the mouth of the Mediterranean under the command of Sir Horatio Nelson. Nelson had been blinded in one eye during action off Corsica four years earlier, and had recently had his right arm amputated after it had been shattered by a musket ball during an assault on Tenerife. This would normally have put paid to any further prospects of command, but Nelson was no ordinary leader. Before losing his arm, Nelson had won notoriety off south-west Spain, when he had helped a British fleet gain victory over a much larger Spanish force near Cape St. Vincent. He disobeyed orders by taking his ship out of the usual line of battle, drew fire from seven ships, rammed and boarded the *San Nicholas* and forced its surrender, and then seized another. Nelson became an instant hero and was knighted on his return.[17]

Such qualities made Nelson an ideal choice to lead an expedition against a French force assembling at Toulon and Marseilles, which intelligence suggested was preparing for an invasion of the kingdom of Naples and Sicily. In fact, the French intended to conquer Egypt, from where the route would be open to challenge British power in India. The idea came from Napoleon, who had been promoted to general five years earlier for his role at Toulon as artillery commander. Two years later, he had quelled a revolt against the government in Paris, using his artillery to disperse the rebels with lethal grapeshot. This had earned him command of the interior army, but he was soon put in charge of an invasion. In little more than a year, Napoleon's forces were in control of most of northern Italy and the Papal States, and several new republics were established on democratic principles. Napoleon returned home a hero and was given the task of planning an invasion of England, but realised this would be disastrous without first gaining mastery of the sea. Having come to this conclusion, Napoleon offered his Egyptian plan to the Directory of the Republic, and within two months of its approval, he was leading over thirty thousand troops and a large fleet of ships towards the eastern Mediterranean.

By the time Nelson's fleet had reached Toulon the French had put to sea. From early June to late July, Nelson searched the Mediterranean for any sign of his quarry. The French landed near Alexandria at the beginning of July, and took just three weeks to conquer northern Egypt. Nelson received news of the invasion a week after the surrender of Cairo, and the British fleet headed for the mouth of the Nile. On 1st August, thirteen French warships were discovered at anchor in Aboukir Bay, which was protected by a line of shoals, several gun batteries and a fort. But the British ships had the wind in their favour as they entered the bay late in the afternoon, and Nelson decided to concentrate

---

17 Cordingly, op. cit., p111.

an immediate attack on the front half of the French line. As a report later noted, "Sir Horatio Nelson made the signal for his fleet as they led in to get between the French line and the shore ... by the manoeuvre ...the British came upon that side on which the French were least prepared for action."[18] Half a dozen French warships now came under attack from both sides, while the 74-gun *Bellorophon* single-handedly took on the flagship *L'Orient* in the middle of the French line. This had the advantage of 120 guns on three decks, from which broadsides tore through the *Bellorophon's* timbers, severed its masts and rigging, and created carnage and wreckage on every deck. But the brave crew of the smaller ship gave as good as they got, and a fire broke out on *L'Orient* that quickly spread. The *Bellorophon* managed to drift well clear with only a spritsail, and the magazine of *L'Orient* exploded soon after, tearing the vessel apart and lighting up the night sky. By late morning on 2nd August, most of the French ships had been burnt, sunk or captured, and only four managed to escape. Over five thousand French crew were killed or reported missing, and over three thousand taken prisoner. Against these numbers, 218 British seamen were killed and 677 wounded, but despite the heavy damage to the *Bellorophon* and others, none of the British ships were sunk or beyond repair.[19] One year later, Napoleon abandoned Egypt and his eastern campaign and returned to Paris, where he engineered a coup d'etat and was proclaimed First Consul of a new government that was effectively under his full control.

On 18th November 1799 hurricane force winds hit the Mersey coast, wreaking havoc in their path. Several new but badly built houses in Liverpool were blown down, while others were damaged by falling chimneystacks or were stripped of their slates. Meanwhile, four sloops and a ferryboat were driven onto rocks opposite the town, and a fishing boat with four men on board was also destroyed. One of them was later washed ashore, leaving a widow and nine children, but the captain managed to lash himself to a wooden hatch cover and was carried back to Liverpool on the flood tide with the help a couple of oars. The *Ellis* was lying off the Black Rock at the mouth of the Mersey, when it broke from its anchors and was later stranded in Bootle Bay. Fortunately, there was no loss of life, but as the *Hope* and the *Belfast* were heading out for Ireland, both were sunk and all on board perished.[20]

---

[18] *Billinge's Advertiser*, 8th October 1798.
[19] Cordingly, op. cit., p146-154.
[20] *Billinge's Advertiser*, 18th November 1799.

But it would take more than a hurricane, or the on-going war, to dampen Liverpool's spirit. As the century drew to a close, business was booming on its quaysides and streets, and its warehouses were close to capacity. Robert Gladstone was selling new stockfish of excellent quality, while Dutton and Ferriday offered new mess beef and pork in Drury Lane. William Russell had Jamaican and Spanish hides for sale, plus prime Whitby alum for tanning and dying, and several pipes of Madeira wine. Tayleur and Park offered port, sherry and Lisbon wines in pipes and hogsheads, American tar and turpentine, white oak barrel staves, Jamaican logwood, and cotton from Georgia and New Orleans. John Palmer had carriage guns for sale, plus shot, shells, all sorts of cast iron, second hand anchors, rope, cables and junk. Others offered oak, maple, birch and ash from North America, fir timber, masts and poles from the Baltic, and mahogany from Honduras. Brimstone from Sicily, oil of vitriol, salt and potash, soap and candle tallow, lead and tin, sailcloth and rope yarn, animal skins and Florence oil – all these, and much besides, were available upon application to dealers and traders in every quarter.[21]

Typical of Liverpool's commercial life was the sale of cargoes from foreign ships taken as prizes. This was the fate of the *Ceres* on its return voyage to Bordeaux, which was taken by the *Lottery*, and its cargo auctioned "by Virtue of a Decree of the High Court of Admiralty" at Ewart and Rushton's office in Exchange Alley. Nearly seventeen hundred bags of coffee were up for grabs, along with damaged bales of cotton and casks of sugar, but most of the cargo, including pepper, nuts, tea, rice, china, skins and hides remained undamaged.[22] Several ships were also advertised for sale, all boasting copper sheathing to their hulls. The *Goodrich* was a fine Bermudan cedar-built brig lying in George's Dock, and was reckoned a "remarkably fast sailer". The 220-ton *Expedition*, with eighteen carronade guns, could carry 250 slaves under the regulations and put to sea at "very trifling expence." Brokers Mullion and Rawlinson offered the beautiful ship *Uriana*, an ideal vessel for the African trade that was "uncommonly well found in stores and sails". The *Phoebe* was pierced for 14 guns and remarkably fast, and "in most respects a complete Guineaman, having gratings and bulkheads fixed between decks, fit for the reception of slaves." Meanwhile, the brigantine *Neptune* was described as "a remarkably good vessel fit for any trade where burthen is required, sails well, shifts without ballast, carries 330 tons dead weight, stows a large cargo, having brought 180 tons Hemp and Flax."[23]

---

21 *Billinge's Advertiser*, 9th December 1799.
22 Ibid.
23 Ibid, 2nd December 1799.

Many ships took passengers in addition to freight, although departure dates were necessarily vague and dependent on uptake. In addition to the steady trickle of emigrants to North America, there were managers, agents, officials, and even the occasional plantation owner, mostly bound for the Caribbean. In December 1799, the American ships *Nancy* and *Pallas* offered good accommodation for passengers to New York, applications being made via Messrs. Rathbone, Hughes and Duncan, or directly through the captains. The *John Adams* was bound for Boston, the *Hope* for Savannah, while the *Richmond* was due to join a convoy forming at Cork on its passage to Wilmington, North Carolina. Joining the convoy were also several well-armed ships heading for Jamaica, all offering freight or passage. These included the coppered ship *Nancy* of 400 tons, mounting eighteen guns, six and eighteen pounders, "with small arms and men answerable." The 750-ton *Trelawney* carried twenty-four guns, small arms and boarding netting, while Messrs. Humble, Holland and Hurry let it be known that forty to fifty "people" were ready to defend the *London* bound for Leghorn and Naples.[24] Indeed, no matter what its business, or where its destination, no merchant vessel could afford to sail without its heavy arms, and a full complement of men willing to risk life and limb.

---

24 *Billinge's Advertiser*, 23rd December 1799.

Chapter Ten

Although mariners had every reason to fear encounters at sea, the experience could be truly terrifying for those confined below. Writing from the island of St. Vincent in February 1800, Captain Hugh Crow described an attack during the passage of the slave ship *Will* from Bonny to the Caribbean. Two brigs were spotted early on the 21st, one of which suddenly tacked towards Crow's vessel. He kept his course, but ordered the crew to prepare "to make a running fight of it." Crow continued, "At half past nine he came athwart our bows and gave us two broadsides; we returned the same, and most of our shot told. He sheered off for about one glass, and got everything ready for a boarding, and we did the same to receive him. At ten he came up again, when a most severe action took place within pistol shot and continued for nine glasses, and then sheered off leaving us in a most shattered state." All the topgallant masts were shot away, the remaining masts being "badly wounded", while most of the rigging was cut and the sails torn to shreds. In the meantime, as cannon shot slammed into the *Will*, and masts crashed onto the main deck during ten hours of heavy fighting, the slaves had been confined below in a state of utter panic. As Crow explained, "Our hull suffered very much, and one of the nine pound shot went into the men's room and wounded 12 slaves, two of which died next day, and two have their thigh bones broke. A shot likewise came in at the starboard bow gun and wounded three men, and disabled the gun."[1]

The slave ship *Dick* was heading towards Africa in October 1800 when a French corvette attacked, but the toll would have been even greater had it been carrying its intended cargo on the next leg of its voyage. As *Billinge's Advertiser* later reported, "An action commenced a few minutes past one o'clock at noon, which was most gallantly defended on both sides within pistol shot. About five o'clock, the Dick's standing and running rigging, bracings, and bowlines were cut to pieces; sails all in rags, topmasts gone, lower masts crippled, and several shots betwixt wind and water. It was about this time that an unfortunate canister shot struck poor Grahme and took away all the upper part of his skull; in this situation he was carried below. To revenge his death, which his brave crew anticipated, and for the honour of the British ensign, one of the brave tars nailed the Dick's colours to the stump of the mizzen mast, and they one and all were determined to fight the vessel as long as she could swim; and without dread or fear the chief mate and crew fought on till near eight 'o'clock, having at that time their noble captain and ten men wounded, their ammunition expended, every gun dismounted, spars and rigging shot

---

[1] *Billinge's Advertiser*, 21st April 1800.

away, 3 feet 10 inches water in the pump well, both pumps going, vessel expected to go down, and the enemy upon their quarter in the act of boarding, when Captain Grahme advised them, to prevent every man from being put to the sword, to strike their colours. He delivered up the vessel in the most courageous manner; and even had the presence of mind to desire the third mate to fling his rifle piece, pistols, sword, &c., overboard, saying no other man should ever use them: He manfully walked overboard his own vessel into the enemy's boat, refusing aid or assistance, saying to his men, '*My brave fellows, you have done your duty like Britons,*' adding (meaning his own vessel) '*Poor Dick, thou hast done thy duty likewise, but obliged to strike to superior force - I only wish thy guns had been heavier metal.*' "

"The French first lieutenant was killed; the enemy had also 27 killed and wounded, and several of her crew died after the action. She was much hurt in her masts and hull, and several holes in the side, which they were obliged to plug up with lead. On Grahme's arrival on board the La Grande Decide he was allowed a cot in the Captain's cabin, who behaved to him like a brother. The French doctor attended him night and day, his own chief mate was always with him, and his crew allowed frequently to see him. He was insensible after the first twenty-four hours, and on the 21st of October, about three o'clock in the afternoon, he departed this life, universally respected by all who knew him. He fell like a hero and a British sailor, fighting under the influence and for the honour of his country's proud ensign! God rest his soul in peace and happiness. He was launched into the deep the same evening, sewed up in his cot in as decent a manner as the situation would admit of."[2] The *Dick* was later rescued by two frigates, one of which towed it to Plymouth where the injured were taken to the naval hospital, while the other chased after the privateer.

The *Hiram* was heading directly for America that same month when it was twice overwhelmed by privateers. Captain Witney gave an account of his experiences that reads like the pages of an adventure story.[3] "I have a very unpleasant account to give you of the Hiram, which, after being twice taken and retaken, arrived here the 13th inst. after being one hundred and two days at sea. The circumstances are these. On the 13th September, being in long. 55 and lat. 30, I was overtaken by a French sloop of war brig called the Curzeuse, Captain Ratlett, from Cayenne, on a cruise of two months and then to France, who after an examination of my papers, pronounced the greater part of my property to be English. They then took out all my people, except my brother, one green hand, and a boy of 12 years of age, and put on board two officers and eight men, and ordered us for Cayenne, and after keeping us company for two days, and robbing us of a lower yard, a cask of water, a

---

[2] *Billinge's Advertiser,* 1st December 1800.

[3] *Lloyd's Register* shows the *Hiram* normally sailed between Liverpool and Pennsylvania.

ship's glass, and sundry small matters, they left us. I, on first discovering her to be French, went below, loaded my pistols, and hid them away in a crate of wares, which if I had not done I should have lost them, for no less than three different times was my trunk searched, my brother's chest and the cabin all over, and were as cautious as though they read my determination in my face. The officers would not allow the men to go off deck at any time, and they ate, drank and slept on deck themselves, never suffering but one at a time to go off deck; therefore, I found I had no other chance but to engage them openly by daylight. I directed my brother to have a couple of handspikes in readiness, and when he saw me begin, to come to my assistance. Therefore, at four o'clock in the afternoon of the fourth day after being taken, I secured my pistols in my waistband, went on deck, and found the Prize-master asleep on the weather hen-coop, his mate at the wheel, and their people on different parts of the main deck, my brother and man on the lee side of the windlass. Under the circumstances I made the attempt, by first knocking down the mate at the wheel. The prize-master jumped up so quick that I could get but a very slight stroke at him. He then drew his dirk upon me, but I closed in with him, sallied him out to the quarter rail and hove him overboard, but he caught by the main sheet, which prevented his going into the water. By this time I had the remaining eight upon me, two of whom I knocked backwards off the quarterdeck. My people got aft with handspikes, and played their parts so well that I was soon at liberty again. I then drew a pistol and shot a black fellow in the head, who was coming to me with a broad axe uplifted. The ball cut him into the skull bone and then glanced, but it stunned him and amazed all the rest, who had no suspicion of my having pistols.

By this time, the mate whom I first knocked down had recovered and got a loaded pistol out of his trunk, and apparently fired it directly in my man's face, but the ball missed him. The prize-master got on board again and stabbed my brother in the side, but not so bad as to oblige him to give out until we had got the day. In this situation we had it pell mell for about a quarter of an hour, when at last we got them a running, and followed them so close, knocking down the hindermost as we came up with them, until part made their escape below. The rest then began to cry for mercy, which we granted on their delivering up their arms, which consisted of a discharged horseman's pistol, a midshipman's dirk, a broad axe, a handsaw, and two empty junk bottles. We then marched them all aft into the cabin and brought them up one at a time, and after examining for knives, etc., we confined them down forward.

By this time it was quite dark, and my brother was obliged to give out, and lay in extreme pain for forty-eight hours, expecting every moment to be his last, but he afterwards recovered astonishingly, and was soon able to keep his watch. My man got so drunk that I could not keep him awake at night, so that there was only my little boy and I to work the ship, watch the French, and attend my brother. I kept a French lad upon deck, the only one that was not wounded, and kept him at the wheel all night. The weather was extremely fine and the Frenchmen quite peaceable, so that I met with little difficulty. Thus we kept possession of her for ten days, when we had reached within two or three days sail of Savannah, being in the long. of 75. On the 27th September, was again overtaken by a French privateer, from Guadeloupe, who, without any ceremony of examining papers (only to find out the contents of my packages) came immediately on board, broke open the hatches, and filled the deck with bales, trunks, cases, etc., and after examining for the most valuable goods, sent them on board the privateer. As her cruise was nearly at an end, having sent off their men, they hove overboard all their empty water casks and lumber of all kinds, and filled themselves as full as an egg out of us, not leaving room for their people to sleep below. They were two days at work upon us. They then took out my brother, man and boy, (leaving me on board) and all the former French crew, except four men, and put on board eleven more of their own men, and after plundering me of part of my cloaths, brass hanging compass, carpenter's tools, spare cordage, deep-sea line, and many other like stores, they left us, ordering us for Guadaloupe; and after being forty-six days longer in their hands, we were taken by his Majesty's ship Unite, and sent into Martinique."[4]

Travel on land may have been a safer prospect when undertaken by coach, but lone travellers or smaller parties were at constant risk from highwaymen. One evening, Mr. Gore, a local linen draper, and two associates from Leeds and Manchester, were returning from a visit to Prescot in their post chaise, when three armed men stopped them near the Liverpool Infirmary. One ordered the driver to stop, and fired when his command was not immediately obeyed, but fortunately the shot missed. The three ruffians then presented their pistols through the chaise windows and demanded money. One of the gentlemen handed over ten guineas, another a one-pound note, but Mr. Gore had the presence of mind to conceal his pocket book "containing property to a considerable amount" under his seat. He also dropped his watch into his boot, and presented one of the robbers with half a guinea wrapped up in a

---

[4] Quoted in Williams, op. cit., p381-383.

Coaching advertisement from Billinge's Advertiser, 20th January 1800 (LRO)

piece of paper, claiming that it was a bank note for fifty-pounds. The robbers accepted this, and ordered the chaise driver to make speed or they would blow his brains out. Despite being so close to the town, no one witnessed the robbery, and the perpetrators made their escape.[5]

Although coach passengers had less reason to fear, long-distance travel was not to be undertaken lightly. Bretherton and Co. ran coaches from the *Crown Inn* in Redcross Street every evening at seven, reaching Warrington eighteen miles away three hours later. Passengers could then sup at Mr. Key's at 10.30, before setting off through the night. After a change of horses at Mr. Gibbins' *Red Bull* at four in the morning, the coach reached Stone in Staffordshire at eight, where breakfast was served at Mr. Gothard's establishment. Coaches reached the *Saracen's Head*, Bull Street, Birmingham by three pm., where there was a three-hour stop for refreshment. Having re-grouped at six, the weary travellers reached Warwick at ten thirty, having covered a further twenty-one miles. After supping at Mr. Plant's, they continued on to Banbury in Oxfordshire, where they reached Mr. Wyatt's at three next morning to change horses, before reaching Buckingham at six-thirty for breakfast. Following a change of horses at Aylesbury at ten, the now exhausted travellers reached another *Saracen's Head* at Snow Hill in London at three in the afternoon, forty-four hours after setting off. Allowing for total breaks of about seven hours, the 218-mile journey was covered at an average speed of just under six miles per hour. As Bretherton and Co were wont to point

B. BRETHERTON AND Co.

RESPECTFULLY inform their Friends and the Public, that they have purchased Mr. STANTTON's share in the following COACHES; and that no exertion in their power shall be wanting to render travelling as expeditious and as comfortable in every respect as possible. The Coaches will set out as usual from the Crown Inn, Redcross-street, viz.

LONDON EXPEDITION—FARE—*Inside* 2l. 12s. 6d. *Outside* 1l. 11s. 6d.) sets out every evening at seven o'clock, and arrives at Mr. Key's, Warrington, distance 18 miles, at ten o'clock, (sup at half past) and arrives at Mr. Gibbin's Red Bull, 32 miles, at four o'clock in the morning —Mr. Gothard's, Stone, 17 miles, at eight o'clock, in the morning, (breakfast)—Mr. Coleman's, Colwich, 11 miles, at half past ten o'clock.—Arrives at Mr. Evett's, the Saracen's Head, Bull-street, Birmingham, 26 miles, at three o'clock, stops three hours, and sets off at six o'clock, and arrives at Mr. Plant's, Warwick, 21 miles, at ten o'clock, (sup.)—Mr. Wyatt's, Banbury, 18 miles, at three o'clock in the morning.—Mr. Osborn's Buckingham, 17¾ miles, at half past six o'clock, (breakfast.)——Mr. Walton's, Ailsbury, 16¾ miles, at ten o'clock.——Mr. Mountain's, the Saracen's Head, Snow-Hill, London, 40½ miles, at three o'clock in the afternoon.

This Coach has good Horses, is well Lighted, and has a Guard all the way the same as the Mail.

FARE.	INSIDE.	OUTSIDE
BIRMINGHAM EXPEDITION,	£1 11 6	£1 0 0
BATH DITTO,	2 12 6	1 11 6
BRISTOL DITTO,	2 12 6	1 11 6
EXETER and PLYMOUTH.		

Small Parcels not above 12lb. weight, to Birmingham 1s. and to London 2s.; large or heavy Packages to Birmingham 1½d. per lb. and to London 3d.

The Proprietors of the above Coach will not be accountable for any parcel, box, &c. above 5l. value, unless entered as such, and paid for accordingly.

N. B. The CARLISLE COACH goes from the above Inn, through PRESTON, LANCASTER, and KENDAL, carrying Passengers to all Parts of the North.

It is the desire of the Proprietors, that if any Passenger has any complaint against any of the Coachmen or Guard, that they will not fail mentioning it, as they are determined that every attention which is possible shall be paid to their passengers.

[5] *Billinge's Advertiser*, 15th March 1802.

Advertisement in Billinge's Advertiser, 23rd December, for the final production of 1799 (LRO)

out, "this Coach has good Horses, is well lighted, and has a Guard all the way the same as the Mail." Given the risk posed by highwaymen, especially at night, guards were essential, and at least one blunderbuss was always primed at the ready. Passengers paid £2 12s 6d inside or £1 11s 6d outside, the same fares applying for coaches to Bristol and Bath. Such journeys were advertised as expeditions, which surely they were, and one can only imagine the discomfort experienced, especially by those who travelled on top. Parcels up to twelve pounds in weight could be sent to London for two shillings, or half that to Birmingham, while anything in excess cost 1½d per pound to Birmingham or 3d to London.[6]

Like it or not, travel was inescapable for those in the entertainment business. For the final performance of the 18th century, the Theatre Royal offered a grand spectacle. "This evening, December 23, Mrs. Moritz, just arrived from Germany, and who has had the honour of performing before their Majesties and the Royal Family at Frogmore House, will make her third appearance and go through her astonishing feats of agility." Mr. Moritz added strength to the routine, but also promised to amaze the audience by balancing "a real egg on the top of a straw." This was to be followed by a "comic dialogue duette called the Musical Courtship," after which Master Parker, the celebrated musical phenomenon, was to perform a sonata composed by Joseph Haydn on the pianoforte. Theatregoers could expect further delights in the form of Miss Grey, who by particular desire would sing "the favourite Song called Crazy Jane." Yet there was more to come, the highlight of the evening

Liverpool, Dec. 16, 1799.

Last Night of performing before the Holidays.
New Grand Spectacle—Last Night of Harlequin Highlander.
THEATRE-ROYAL, LIVERPOOL.
THIS EVENING, DECEMBER 23,
Mrs. MORITZ, just arrived from Germany, and who has had the honour of performing before their Majesties and the Royal Family, at Frogmore-house will make her third appearance, and go through her astonishing feats of agility.
Mr. MORITZ will for this night only exhibit various new Feats of Strength and Agility, in particular he will
BALLANCE A REAL EGG ON THE TOP OF A STRAW.
A comic Dialogue Duetto, called
THE MUSICAL COURTSHIP.
Mr. JOHANNOT will sing a new comic Song, written by C. Dibden jun. called THE KING'S PICTURE; or a Guinea before a Pound Note—Tom Bowling's Answer to Abraham Newland.
MASTER PARKER,
The celebrated Musical Phænomenon, will perform a Sonata on the Piano Forte, composed by Hayden, &c. also the favorite air of the " Plough Boy," and will recite
ROLLA'S ADDRESS.
By particular desire, Miss Grey will sing the favorite Song, called
"CRAZY JANE."
After which, (never performed) a grand serio-comic Spectacle, interspersed with song and action, called
THE RENEGADOES;
Or, ALGERINE CORSAIR.
In the course of the piece will be introduced the following new Scenes, &c.—An Indian View, with the widow of an Indian Chief watching the Arms of her Husband—A war dance and Sacrifice—Between Decks of an Algerine Corsair—The Inside of the Cabin, and Deck of the Corsair—With Galley Slaves chain'd to the oar.
To conclude with (last time) an entire new Scotch Pantomime, with new scenes, music, &c. called
HARLEQUIN HIGHLANDER; Or, Sawney Bean's Cave.
Further particulars in the Bills of the Day.
The doors to be opened at six, and the performance begin exactly at seven o'clock.—Lower Boxes, 4s.—Upper Boxes, 3s. 6d.—Pit, 2s. 6d.—Gallery, 1s.
Places for the Boxes to be taken of Mrs. Adams, No. 12, Dawson Street, Williamson-square.

6 *Billinge's Advertiser*, 20th January 1800.

being "a grand serio-comic Spectacle, interspersed with song and action, called THE RENEGADOES: or ALGERINE CORSAIR," never before performed. But the players were surely confused in their sense of geography. Opening with scenes of North American Indians, including a war dance and sacrifice, the next was "Between Decks of an Algerine Corsair – the inside of the Cabin, and the deck of the Corsair – With Galley Slaves chain'd to the oar." As though this was not enough, the finale was to be "an entire new Scotch Pantomime with new scenes, music &c. called HARLEQUIN HIGHLANDER, or Sawney Bean's Cave," based on the gruesome legend of a cannibalistic mass murderer who hid out on the Galloway coast. Tickets for boxes cost four shillings or 3s 6d, while those for the pit and gallery cost 2s 6d and 1s respectively.

Given the closeness and heat of the atmosphere of a theatre - the tobacco smoke and fumes from hundreds of tallow candles lighting both stage and auditorium, the smell of grease paint and sweat, ale and liquor - together with the thunderous din of cheering, clapping and foot-stamping - the theatregoer may well have been left in need of a tonic. One might resort to a spoonful of Robberd's Nervous Volatile Essence, "by far the most invigorating and strengthening medicine in the world; particularly adapted for nervous debility," but at nearly five and a half shillings a bottle it was well beyond the budget of most.[7] Robberd's Essence treated "head-achs, derangement of thought, confusion and giddiness, depression of spirits, timidity, startings, faintings, spasms, tremours, hypochondriac and hysterical affections, weaknesses, and a whole train of endless disorders arising from an irritable state of the nervous system." Bottles were available from "respectable vendors of medicines, and from newspaper publisher and printer Thomas Billinge.[8]

For any in need of a purgative, Dr. Radcliffe's Famous Purging Elixir could be expected to provide relief. Apparently unrivalled for more than fifty years, the public could not have had recourse to a more efficacious and agreeable bitter purge, "as a purifier of the blood from all Humours contracted by excess of living, surfeits, cholic, and all obstructions in the bowels; for the cure of worms in children or adults."[9] True Daffy's Elixir offered similar promises, especially in cases of the flux. However, for those suffering with "the itch", Swinfen's Ointment promised a cure to beat all others in "eradicating this malady." Swinfen's was so "innocent" that it could even be applied to children and "breeding women" without the least danger. At one shilling and three halfpence a box, Swinfens offered good value, especially since those anxious to rid themselves of the complaint often used remedies "without considering

---

[7] Experienced able seamen or skilled craftsmen may expect to earn about one pound, or twenty shillings, a week. Most of the 'labouring classes' could expect to earn around half this, or even less.
[8] *Billinge's Advertiser,* 1st September 1800 and other editions.
[9] Ibid, 13th January 1800 and others.

the consequences that probably will arise from throwing a large quantity of noxious material into the habit."[10]

Among the many cures for venereal disease was Leake's Patent Pills, an advertisement for which appeared in the form of a letter from an apparent beneficiary who had been reduced from " a stout, healthy, rather corpulent man" to become a mere shadow of his former self. Having given up on life, he was persuaded to buy six boxes of the pills, and was soon restored to perfect health. [11] De Velno's Vegetable Syrup also offered a cure for venereal disease, along with several others. Having received a fresh supply at his house in Old Hall Street, Mr. Brewer promised that De Velno's cured "obstinate complaints of Scurvy, Scrofula, Venereal impurities, and many others arising from intemperance and indiscretion of youth." Brewer also included a letter from a satisfied customer who had taken an "immense quantity of Drugs, Mercury, and every other d_____d Quack medicine that could be thought of, without effect." However, De Velno's had cured his venereal complaint, and he now intended to take a dozen bottles with him when he next went to sea. Commonly sold for five or six guineas, Brewer informed ships' captains they could stock up with any quantity of Velno's at one guinea a bottle, the syrup being warranted to keep for any length of time in any climate. [12]

Typical of advertisements in Billinge's Advertiser for quack remedies.

ROBBERDS's NERVOUS VOLATILE ESSENCE, IS particularly recommended by the inventor, a regular professional man, now in extensive practice who has a Character to lose, and would not therefore, without indisputable proof, assert, that it is by far the most invigorating and strengthening medicine in the whole world; particularly adapted for nervous debility, whether arising from indiscretion, intemperance, sickness or hereditary, speedily relieving the ordinary symptoms, such as head-achs, derangement of thought, confusion and giddiness, depression of spirits, timidity, startings, faintings, spasms, tremours, hypochondriac, and hysteric affections, weaknesses, and the whole train of endless disorders arising from an irritable state of the nervous system, one single bottle will convince any person of its superiority, and references are given on application for a bill, to he had gratis, to persons of the first respectability, who have experienced its salutary virtues, sold by the inventor, J. Robberds, surgeon, apothecary, and man-midwife, No 379, Strand, in bottles, at 5s. 5d. each, by T Billinge, Liverpool, and by most respectable venders of medicines in the three kingdoms. Where may likewise be had his Balsamic Elixir, a medicine unequalled for the cure of Coughs, Asthmas, and Consumptions.

However, when no effective relief could be found for painful ailments, many turned to raw opium, while others preferred to take it in a solution of alcohol, a preparation known as laudanum. Members of all ranks turned to the drug, and many became addicted in their attempts to control painful symptoms. However, the makers of Genuine Lancaster Black Drop offered a superior

10 *Billinge's Advertiser*, 17th March 1800 and others.
11 Ibid 3rd February 1800 and other editions.
12 Ibid, 7th July 1800 and others.

product, which they claimed had none of the side effects that debilitated its users. They claimed, "It is well known that in many constitutions the effects of common Opium or Laudanum are extremely distressing, and that in all habits it produces some inconvenience; often creating restlessness and delirium instead of producing sleep; and its use being generally succeeded by head-achs, sickness and debility. Of these deleterious effects, the BLACK DROP is, by a chemical process, wholly deprived, while it retains in the fullest degree all the desirable powers of Opium in relieving pain, soothing irritation and securing repose." The preparation was recommended for all manner of complaints, including stomach pains, depression, anxiety, gout, inflammation of wounds, chronic rheumatism, coughs, asthma, and consumption. Small bottles cost 2s 6d, large ones 5s, and were available from several outlets including Billinge's print shop in Castle Street.[13]

However, there was one preventative treatment in the offing that was genuinely effective. In October 1802 Liverpool's dispensary physicians made a plea to "the more enlightened part of the community" to persuade others of the benefits of a recent medical breakthrough by Edward Jenner against smallpox, a disease that was estimated to kill 45,000 people in Britain alone.[14] They reported that, "The Cow-Pock inoculation has undergone, during the last four years, a very rigorous investigation," and had "completely established the fact that the true Vaccine disease effectually secures the human constitution from all future hazards of receiving the Small-Pox." Having been tested widely throughout Britain, Europe and North America, and introduced by the army and navy as standard practice, they were confident that "there can now be no doubt, that if the inoculation continues to be prosecuted with spirit and zeal, it must, at no very distant period, ANHIALATE the Small-Pox." Since the cowpox vaccine had none of the ill effects of its predecessor, the physicians hoped that church ministers, overseers and others would use their influence in overcoming objections, particularly among the poorer classes where resistance was greatest.[15]

However, demands on the charitable dispensary for all other forms of free treatment grew by the month. At the dawn of the new century, Liverpool's population stood at twice the number that had witnessed the seamen's riot during that balmy August a quarter of a century earlier. In building an unparalleled network of docks, the corporation's enterprise had ensured that the business community could thrive, even in the face of adversity. But the fruits of this

---

[13] *Billinge's Advertiser*, 22nd February 1802.

[14] Britain's population was about 10.5 million in 1801.

[15] *Billinge's Advertiser*, 1st November 1802. Bear in mind that there were no hypodermic needles, and that the vaccine had to be applied to a cut made to the arm. Smallpox was eradicated on a worldwide basis in 1979 with the last case in Ethiopia.

growth were not evenly shared, and many who had come to the town in search of prosperity languished instead in poverty and unemployment. This was a constant danger to the social order, and despite the deference of the lower ranks towards their masters the threat of riot was never far away. However, the notion of a fairer, more equitable distribution of wealth was at least a century off, and even the most philanthropic minds believed that charity was sufficient to alleviate the worst of economic distress. Charities abounded, but their many unpaid officers and subscribers understood that without them society would simply fall apart. Charity was self-interest. It ensured that the poor would ever be grateful for what they received and would look upon their benefactors with some reverence. Charity was also cheap, the odd guinea or two, now and then, making little impression on the pockets of those who earned five hundred or a thousand a year. Charity also offered publicity for those who could afford to pay the most, with the local papers regularly printing lists of names of the most generous subscribers. Charity brought with it social standing, and even though most officers were unpaid, their work brought recognition and ensured the respect of recipients and peers alike.

With the war came fluctuations in employment and inflated prices. At the close of the 18th century a new local charity was born to stave off hunger. In November 1799, mayor Pudsey Dawson and "a number of respectable inhabitants" met to discuss the opening of cheap soup shops "for the Benefit of the laborious and industrious Classes, and for the Relief of the indigent Poor." Indeed, the price of staple foods was rising inexorably. In December 1799, a bushel of wheat cost 12s 3d, but the price rose to thirteen shillings early in the new year. For the consumer, this meant that the standard two-penny "household" loaf weighed 13¼ ounces in December, but had fallen to 12½ ounces six weeks later. A four-penny loaf dropped by 1½ ounces to just over 1½ pounds in weight, with corresponding losses for six, nine, twelve and eighteen-penny loaves.[16] The latter weighed in at nearly 7½ pounds in December, but was half a pound less by late January. Similarly, sugar cost shopkeepers fifty-six shillings a hundredweight to buy in December. At six pence a pound for the bulk price, sugar retailed at about seven pence a pound, but a rise in the price of a hundredweight to sixty-one shillings in January added another farthing (or quarter penny) or so for the consumer at the grocers.[17]

By the end of 1800, mayor John Shaw and other leading citizens had come to the conclusion that a fund needed to be established to buy potatoes and other essential provisions in bulk at the cheapest possible rates, which could then be sold to the poor at knockdown prices at the town markets. But the mayor

---

[16] Two and four penny loaves were roughly equivalent to the 400 and 800 gram loaves of today.
[17] *Billinge's Advertiser*, 2nd December 1799 and 20th January 1800.

was not content simply with a little economic intervention; he intended to get tough with profiteers. Shaw issued warning in the local papers that, "there being too much reason to suppose that the different Articles of Provision, and the absolute necessities of life, are greatly inhanced in their price in this town and neighbourhood, not only from the general turn and disposition of those adventurers who seek to get money without the regard to the means, but from the conduct and behaviour of persons apparently in respectable situations in life, who nevertheless are guilty of the very serious offences of Monopolising, Forestalling, Engrossing and Regrading, particularly the valuable articles of Corn and Potatoes, which tend more immediately to the detriment and injury of the industrious and labouring poor." Shaw and his magistrates continued forcefully that it was their determined resolution "to get at a discovery of these most outrageous offenders against the wholesome laws of this realm, and that whoever shall be found offending in these particulars, however high their situation might be, he and they shall be most assuredly be prosecuted, and shall receive the punishment due to such atrocious offences, and all persons who shall give their assistance to make discoveries of any such offenders shall be handsomely Rewarded."[18]

But charity alone could not cope with the level of poverty, the nearest thing to a system of social security being poor relief, administered by the parish and paid for by local taxes. However, despite its wealth, the corporation had reneged on an agreement to pay taxes on receipts from dock duties and market tolls, and it remained at loggerheads with the parish committee. Meanwhile, some merchants still refused to pay the shipping tax, even though a rate based on profits rather than tonnage had been worked out that was acceptable to most. The majority now reluctantly paid up, although the parish committee castigated others who "…living without the boundaries of the parish, but exercising their business within them, thereby added wealth to their already vastly accumulated fortunes, and increasing the number of the poor; yet, under these circumstances, have refused to contribute, in common with the poorest housekeeper of the parish, their mite to the relief of the distressed."[19]

A further dispute had emerged over the poor condition of the streets and pavements, which were roughly surfaced with uneven slabs and cobblestones. Only Clayton Square and the lower part of Islington were properly flagged, but in 1799 some owners in Lord Street began laying flagstones outside their properties at their own expense. It was clear to all that improvements were needed, but the parish and the corporation both believed the other was responsible for carrying out and paying for the work. The corporation decided

[18] *Billinge's Advertiser*, 8th December 1800.
[19] Peet, op. cit., Vol. 1, p.lxii.

to petition Parliament for a bill making the parish responsible for the expense of widening and repaving the streets after laying proper sewers, to which the parish responded with a counter-petition against the corporation. To make matters worse, work had begun to dig trenches and lay pipes to supply water to the town. Although the corporation had been empowered to provide a pipe network under the 1786 Improvement Act, nothing had been done at the time, one excuse being that this would deprive water sellers of their living. A private company later applied to Parliament for permission to supply water from springs at Bootle a few miles away, and an Act was passed to that effect in 1799. This alarmed the corporation, which revived its old scheme and set up a rival company to provide piped water from the town's own springs, all the shares at £200 pounds each being taken up within hours.

Advertisement in Billinge's, 1st December 1800 (LRO)

BOOTLE SPRINGS.

THE COMPANY of PROPRIETORS, have the pleasure to announce to the INHABITANTS of LIVERPOOL that their Works are now in such a state, that in the course of next month those residing in the Streets where their WOOD PIPES are already laid may be supplied with WATER, and they will proceed to lay Pipes in the other streets as speedily as possible.

The mode of supply will be through Lead Pipes from the Wood ones in the same manner as is done in London, by which means they will obtain EXCELLENT WATER, FIT FOR ALL PURPOSES at an expence much less than they now pay and free from all inconveniences attending its being brought by hand.

CAPTAINS of Ships, and the *Shipping Interest* in general may reap much advantage by having an uninterrupted and ample supply of such Water as will unquestionably remain PURE AND WHOLESOME IN THE LONGEST VOYAGES.

Pipes are already laid from the Custom house along all the Docks and Basons to the North, where Ships may take in their Water at the shortest notice, and with great expedition, on terms much more reasonable than they have hitherto been accustomed to pay.

Pipes are now laying round the Docks to the South, and will be compleated with all expedition.

ALL PERSONS desirous of having a supply to their *Houses* are requested to apply to Mr. REUBEN SMITH, the COMPANYS AGENT, at their office, *Angel Inn Yard*, Dale-street, between the hours of ten o'clock in the morning and two o'clock in the afternoon.

N. B. Ships will also be immediately supplied by application to the same place.

November 24th, 1800.

The two companies now went head to head in a race to dig trenches and lay wooden pipes, which were made from elm trees bored through the centre and jointed together. Residents were encouraged to have lead branch pipes fitted to their homes and pay for their supply, but street pumps provided free water for general use. Towards the end of 1800, the Bootle Water Company was proud to announce that considerable progress had been made in laying its network, and that "all persons desirous of having a supply to their Houses" were requested to apply to the company office at Angel Inn Yard, Dale Street, between 10am and 2pm. Householders were informed that "the mode of supply will be through Lead Pipes from the Wood ones in the same manner as in London, by which means they will obtain EXCELLENT WATER, FIT FOR ALL PURPOSES, at an expence much less than they now pay and free from all inconveniences attending its being brought by hand." Pipes to the north end of the town had already been laid, and were shortly to be laid to the south.[20] But, despite the terms of the Acts to make good repairs, both companies acted recklessly in a bid to out-do each other and gain customers, and each duplicated the work of the other. This made the already poor condition of Liverpool's streets many times worse, and once again the corporation and the parish went into litigation to determine overall responsibility.

The Pulling Down of Old High Street, by Thomas Gill, 1803 (Herdman Collection, 1266 LRO)

Work began shortly after to build a new Exchange behind the old one seen in this picture, which now became known once again as the Town Hall.

A legal judgement eventually went against the parish in 1803, except in the case of the most 'ancient' streets that had existed early in the previous century. The committee now had to sort out the "dangerous and ruinous state of the pavements, which must be known to every inhabitant to have been occasioned, not by time or want of a timely repair, but by the laying down of water pipes and the injudicious and imperfect manner of replacing the pavements by one or both of the two Companies of Proprietors."[21] Although the vestry tried to arrange a meeting of the two suppliers, the Bootle Water Company refused to attend, and the confusion of roughly filled trenches that criss-crossed the town meant it was almost impossible to determine which company was responsible for what. In the end a compromise was reached by the parish appointing six

20 *Billinge's Advertiser*, 1st December 1800.
21 Easter Vestry meeting, 12th April 1803, Peet, op. cit., Vol. 2, p19.

surveyors to oversee repairs, and the corporation providing the workmen and a loan, which was to be repaid by a small additional rate. The committee concluded that the expense would "bear no proportion to the comforts that will attend the measure," and were confidant that the surveyors would police the remaining work to prevent further damage.

Meanwhile, the dispute over tolls and dock duties continued to simmer. The local magistrates judged in 1803 that taxes should be paid on revenues from market tolls, but not from the docks. The corporation remained unsatisfied and took the matter to the county assizes, which endorsed the magistrates' decision the following year, when the parish was awarded £9592 in arrears and was able to pay off its debts. However, the demands on its resources were never ending. Deaths had increased in 1800 by more than a quarter due to "the prevalence of contagious diseases, exciting considerable attention and alarm." The following year, an outbreak of dysentery was followed by epidemics of scarlet fever and typhus, when "the pressure on the Dispensary was so great as to render it impossible to keep records of the practice, or even the names of the patients; and the greater part of the private practitioners had little or no remission from anxiety and fatigue." Fifteen hundred people died in three months alone, and by the end of the year mortality had risen by nearly sixty per cent.[22] This had finally galvanised the parish to agree plans for the building of a separate House of Recovery for fever victims following years of delay, and also necessitated the purchase of land for a new pauper cemetery. The new isolation hospital was to contain four wards totalling sixty beds, or ninety in an emergency, in a separate building about forty yards from the workhouse, requiring an additional levy of nine pence on the parish rates for 1802.

For a while, however, it seemed that the burden on inhabitants in providing for the defence of the town were at an end. Britain and France had signed a peace treaty at Amiens in March 1802, which seemingly guaranteed the independence of the new Dutch, Swiss and Italian republics from French control, and settled France's border with the German states along the Rhine. On its part, Britain agreed to return many of its recent conquests to France and her allies, including St. Lucia, Martinique, and Minorca. The Treaty offered respite from the financial burden of the war and enabled a scaling down of the army, navy and local defences. But Napoleon was soon annexing Piedmont in Italy and sending troops into Switzerland, and by the end of the year the French were blockading British exports to Holland and Italy. They also began building new warships and hundreds of landing craft for an invasion of Britain, so that in May 1803 the British government again

---

[22] Currie, Medical Report, op. cit., p368-369 & 398-399.

declared war. Its belief was that security lay in control of the seas while maintaining a substantial army on British soil.[23] Two Acts were passed to raise a defence militia and additional reservists, and a new shipbuilding programme was got underway. Meanwhile, the press gangs renewed their activities with added fervour, while many men were persuaded to volunteer, lured by generous bounties.

Liverpool responded in July by setting an additional rate of six pence in the pound to raise a local militia. But for many local residents this was not enough, and the mayor agreed to hold a public meeting at the Exchange in mid-September to discuss the town's defences. The meeting called for floating batteries to be positioned at the mouth of the river and nearer the port, and for fixed batteries to be built along both coasts, "to repel and resist any attack which may be made by the enemy." It was also proposed to raise £28,000 to finance these defences, £8,000 of which had already been promised from corporation coffers. £16,000 was to come from an additional rate upon property owners and £4,000 from ship owners, and returnable subscriptions were to be invited to enable work to begin to cover the extra taxes while they were being collected. However, although Napoleon was indeed determined to invade England, the proposals for Liverpool's defence were almost certainly an over-reaction to the threat. Napoleon's plans were for an invasion along the south coast using several thousand landing craft to carry a huge army and its supplies, all of which would need constant protection from the British navy using every available warship the French could muster. A successful invasion would have to take the shortest possible route; any attempt along the west coast would be vulnerable to prolonged attack and highly unlikely. Even so, when a special Vestry meeting was held to discuss the proposals there was talk of "the alarming situation in which the town stood."[24] Opinion was divided on the issue, with several speaking in favour of finding out what plans the government had for Liverpool's defence, and the meeting ended without a resolution.

By the start of the 19th century Liverpool's rapid growth had led to gross overcrowding in some areas and a curious mix of housing in others. The

---

[23] *Billinge's Advertiser* for 7th December 1801 reported that Britain's naval forces stood at 141 ships of the line, 25 ships of 50 guns, 200 frigates and 262 sloops, with a further 24 ships under construction. These had been widely deployed, including 83 vessels in the English and Irish Channels, 74 off the south-east coast and in the North Sea, 48 in the Caribbean and assisting Atlantic convoys, 44 along the route to India, 26 off the Straights of Gibraltar, and 118 in the Mediterranean. Nearly half the army was stationed on British soil, the rest being distributed between Ireland, Egypt, the West and East Indies, Canada, Gibraltar and other islands.

[24] Peet, op. cit., vol.2, p30.

population had risen from around 58,000 in 1790 to nearly 81,000 in 1801, an increase of about forty per cent in eleven years.[25] Overall, 73% lived in front houses, 15% in back-to-backs, and 12% in cellars.[26] Few districts were exclusively inhabited either by the labouring poor or opulent middle classes, many living within a stone's throw of one another. The main areas of cellar dwellings were along the northern fringe of the town and south of the Old Dock to Parliament Street. However, even the more salubrious districts had some occupied cellars, and very few areas had none at all. But while some of these were overcrowded, nearly half had fewer than four occupants. On the other hand, a quarter of those living above them in front houses were in households of ten or more people, but north of Tithebarn Street the figure was much higher. Particularly to the north and south of the town, developers were busy filling in spaces behind houses that might otherwise have made pleasant gardens, becoming instead warrens of alleys and courtyards leading to cheap back-to-backs. Here, too, overcrowding was common, nearly ten per cent of the occupants living in households of ten or more sharing just three small rooms. In other areas, once fashionable localities such as St. Paul's and Cleveland Square had gone downmarket as merchants moved towards St. James's and Islington, but they still retained a considerable social mix.

Some idea of this can be gleaned from the 1801 census, Gore's Liverpool Directories for 1800 and 1803, and Richard Horwood's detailed plan of the town in 1803. The census shows householders' names and the number of males, females and families in each dwelling, but provides no information about ages and little about occupations. Dwellings were listed street by street either as cellars, back houses or front houses, but their numbers were not written down. However, Horwood's plan shows the numbering of roughly half the houses in Liverpool, which ran consecutively down one side of each street and continued up the other. The plan is particularly useful in gauging the relative size of properties, although it may not have been entirely accurate. Gore's Directory lists businessmen, professionals, shopkeepers, and master tradesmen and tradeswomen, but subscriptions had to be paid to be included. In addition, James Currie's medical report of 1804 provides added insight into the living conditions of the poor. Together, these sources provide a glimpse of

---

[25] Simmons' enumeration of 1790 gave a population of 55,732, but, as James Currie pointed out in his Medical Report of 1804, according to rules laid down for the first official census in 1801, an extra 4% should have been added as an estimate of the number of men at sea, giving 57,961. The 1801 census counted 77,653 inhabitants, but an extra 4% makes this 80,759. Neither census was entirely accurate.

[26] P. Laxton, *Liverpool in 1801: A Manuscript Return for the First National Census of Population*, Historic Society of Lancashire and Cheshire, Vol 130 (1981) p80. These percentages are rounded to the nearest whole number.

community life, as shown in the following examples of two neighbourhoods at opposite ends of the town.[27]

In the southern quarter, next to his brewery on the corner of St. James's Street, lived Thomas Langton in a comfortably large house at 1 Crosbie Street, while William Coxhead ran a public house next door.[28] Beyond Mr. Harrabin's cooperage, Hannah Price ran a small taproom alehouse at number 23, while cow keeper Charles Goff supplied fresh milk seven doors further down. Samuel Needham ran another public house near the bottom of the street at number 40, opposite shipbroker Isaac Lemon at 43. Thomas Hanmer kept a grocery at number 55, but also worked as a carpenter. Between the houses on the north side of Crosbie Street and Sparling Street beyond, much of the land was taken up by three roperies running side by side the full length of both streets. It was on such sites that long strands of hemp and sisal yarn were attached to revolving hooks and twisted to create the ropes that secured the masts and controlled the sails of Liverpool's ships. Residents on Sparling Street were fortunate enough to have plots behind their houses for gardens or vegetables, but behind the houses on the south side of Crosbie Street (1 to 40) most of the space that was not taken up by small industries and merchants' yards was filled with narrow three-roomed houses built back-to-back over low cellars around dingy courtyards.

One of these was Elm Court, in which James Buchanan lived with his wife, son, and two daughters. Seven people shared the next backhouse to him, and next to them lived labourer John Roberts with his wife, daughter and three sons. Across the courtyard, two families shared Richard Lloyd's house, eight people sharing three small rooms, but James Webster's family of three enjoyed the luxury of more space. Caldwell Davies and Robert Evans both lived in adjacent Pine Court with families of eight, as did mariner Nicholas Jenkinson's family of nine. George Adams and Thomas Kelly lived in Fir Court with families of nine, while ten people from two families shared Richard Andrews' crowded household in Oak Court.[29] Each house had two small bedrooms, one above the other, into which a steep, narrow staircase entered directly from below. The ground floor served as kitchen, dining and living room, where families huddled to keep warm during winter months as their food was cooked on an iron grating above an open fire.

---

[27] In all but a few cases, those whose occupations are given below are listed in Gore's Directories for both 1800 and 1803, which means they were at the same address when the census was taken in March 1801. Any exceptions are listed in the census and the 1803 directory.

[28] This area was gradually redeveloped during the nineteenth century for commercial expansion and railway development. None of the original housing remains, and Crosbie Street no longer exists.

[29] The names and layout of the courts is shown in Taylor, op. cit., figure 9, p82.

A detail from Horwood's Plan of Liverpool, 1803, showing part of the southern neighbourhood (LRO)

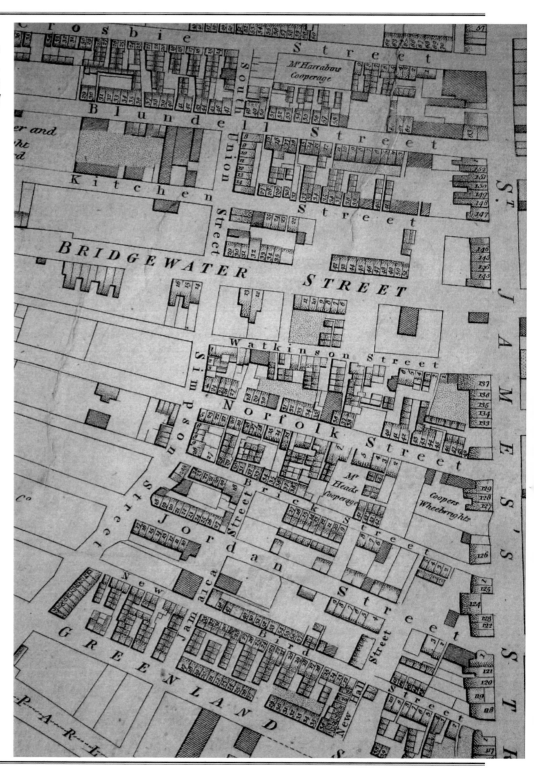

On the other side of these and similar courts was Blundell Street, where William Martin made his living as a hatter in the corner house at number 1. Four doors down at number 5, beyond Thomas Morton's anchor smithy, lived plumber and glazier John Payne, next door to cow keeper Samuel Mason. Dock surveyor William Streets lived further down at 22, next to Alice Dingwall's alehouse. Sawyer John Mason lived nearly opposite at 41, next to Captain William Ford, while mariner John Finch lived three doors up from him. Captain John Tatterson lived at 52, from where his wife Mary ran a pawn broking business, and Mary Sloan made fashionable mantua gowns for ladies at number 54, one door down from tailor James Duckworth. Corn merchants Lythgoe and Blackburne operated from a site nearby, while at the top of the street James Willcock sold groceries.

Among these local traders and professionals, mariner Richard Crosdale lived between voyages with his wife and two children, as did mariner William Carmichael with his family in the dingy cellar below. While on shore, Edward Hughes lived four doors away with his wife and five children, but John Thomas and his family of seven were crammed in the cellar below. Most of the front houses of Blundell Street had occupied cellars, while new backhouses were appearing on a piecemeal basis behind them as parcels of land were sold off to developers. These were separated from the courts behind Crosbie Street by a high brick wall, which added to the gloom and prevented a throughput of fresh air on both sides. Thomas Holland, a blacksmith at the anchor forge nearby, lived in Mason Court on the other side of the wall to Elm Court. Labourer Thomas Clark lived in nearby Wades Court, as did mariners Thomas Richards and William Maxwell, each with a wife and four children.

None of the courts had its own water supply, although pumps were soon to be provided in the main streets by the local water company. In the meantime, water for cooking and washing had to be bought by the bucketful from street carts at a farthing each. Each court had one or two stinking privies consisting of lean-tos, in which wooden seats were placed over ash pits that needed digging out on a regular basis to prevent them overflowing. Physician James Currie and his colleagues were highly critical of "the habitations of the poor in the greater part of the small and narrow courts back from the streets." He cited a report produced in 1788 advising against any further building of back-to-backs, and suggested that proprietors should be compelled to alter existing courtyards to allow a more thorough draught of air. It had also recommended that if more courts were to be built they should have wider yards and entrances, at least two "necessaries", a plentiful supply of water, and ventilation at both ends.[30] But, despite such concerns, nothing was done, the profits of greedy developers taking precedence over the more basic needs of humanity.

---

[30] Currie, op. cit., 376-377.

Blacksmith William Albin lived at 4 Watkinson Street, three away from Blundell Street. William Whitby had a small grocery shop three doors further down, and cooper Lewis Curran lived next door but one to him. Joiner Thomas Lloyd lived at number 12, and musician James Jackson at 16, while three families totalling twelve people shared Jane Lucas's household at number 18. Alice Masters lived in the cellar below her with two daughters, and William Wheeler lived two away with his family of five. Among those who lived in the courts behind Watkinson Street was millwright John Roberts, who lived at 2 Long Entry, leading off the main street. Others included mariners Andrew McDaniel and Thomas Tomlinson, both with wives and four children, and mariner Robert Garner with a family of nine. On the other side of Watkinson Street, and the jumble of backhouses and alleys between, was Norfolk Street, where Francis Alsop's family kept shop at number 3 while he worked as a wheelwright nearby. Captain Robert Marsh lived three doors away, while cow keeper and waterside carter Richard Hodson lived across the road at 36. Further down at number 19, George Wilde ran a pawnbroking business and sold slops, or cheap clothing. John Yates was a scale porter at number 22, which may well have made him envious of his merchant namesake. James Hayes lived at the bottom of the street at number 24, but he also had a shop by the Old Dock where he made navigational instruments for sale.

Jordan Street, a short distance away, was still being developed, but was home to Eleanor Holmes, a schoolmistress at number 14. Andrew Roberts was a naval officer at number 20, and Captain Robert Riddle lived three doors up from him. There was also a glass grinder, a bookkeeper and a sail maker, and John Rylance was a hairdresser at number 35. Nearby, New Bird Street was home to captains Thomas Kidney and William Needham, excise officers Michael Boyle and William Roberts, shipwright Thomas Ryding, and sail maker Daniel Wilcox, whose sail room was a short distance away on Wapping Street near the shipyards. Between them and Greenland Street, near the southern boundary of Liverpool, was perhaps the greatest concentration of courts and backhouses in the town. Union Court was home to Hugh Butler's family of nine, and Thomas Fisher's of six, while constable George Lambet's family of seven lived next to mariner Theophilus Carter's family in Cottar's Court. Yet, despite his property adjoining backhouses behind, gentleman William Ockleshaw seemed content to live at 11 Greenland Street rather than move to more salubrious surroundings. His neighbourhood was certainly well served by public alehouses. Robert Alanson, William Mason and Martha Roberts ran premises on Greenland Street, while Hugh M'Call and Mary Ann Studholme, among others, ran theirs on New Bird Street close-by.

Concerns about the level of drinking and its effects frequently exercised the authorities. There were 917 public houses in Liverpool at the end of the

18th century, although this was a reduction from the 1500 or so of a few years earlier after steps being taken to close less reputable premises.[31] The greatest problem was on Sundays when people had their day of rest, but many regarded the Sabbath differently to those who took religion seriously. An announcement in *Billinge's Advertiser* warned that, "THE MAYOR and MAGISTRATES having Information that it is a common practice among many of the lower orders of the People to resort to PUBLIC ALE-HOUSES in this Town, in the AFTERNOONS and EVENINGS of the LORD's DAY, where they sit for a considerable time, and to very late hours, DRINKING, TIPPLING and SPENDING their WAGES and EARNINGS, not only in breech of all good order and decency, but to the very great Injury and Distress of the WIVES and CHILDREN: (a distress rendered still more grievous at this time by the present HIGH PRICE of the NECESSARIES of LIFE) are determined to use their best endeavours and exertions to put an effectual stop to this most enormous Evil." Alehouse keepers were warned "not to suffer or permit any person whatever to sit DRINKING in their Houses" beyond 7pm on Sundays, and would have their licences revoked if they did. Constables had been told to be especially vigilant, and neighbours were asked to inform on licensees who contravened the rule.[32]

The authorities were also concerned about the continuing problem of detritus accumulating on streets and in courts and alleys, believing that this was linked to disease by the production of

Mayoral notice in Billinge's Advertiser, 1st December 1800 (LRO)

> BOROUGH AND TOWN OF LIVERPOOL,
> JOHN SHAW, Esq MAYOR.
>
> THE MAYOR and MAGISTRATES having Information that it is a common practice amongst many of the lower orders of the People to resort to PUBLIC ALE-HOUSES in this Town, in the AFTERNOONS and EVENINGS of the LORD's DAY, where they sit for a considerable time, and to very late hours, DRINKING, TIPPLING, and SPENDING their WAGES and EARNINGS, not only in breach of all good order and decency, but to the very great Injury and Distress of their WIVES and CHILDREN; (a distress rendered still more grievous at this time by the present HIGH PRICE of the NECESSARIES of LIFE:) are determined to use their best endeavours and exertions, to put an effectual stop to this most enormous Evil: And DO THEREFORE HEREBY STRICTLY CHARGE and COMMAND all and every the ALE-HOUSE-KEEPERS, within the Town and the Liberties thereof, not to suffer, or permit any Person whatever to sit DRINKING in their Houses beyond the Hour of SEVEN in the EVENING, on the LORD'S DAY; hereby declaring, that every ALE-HOUSE KEEPER acting contrary to this order, shall not only be forthwith deprived of his or her LICENCE, but shall be otherwise dealt with according to the Strict Letter of the Law, and the nature of their Offences as Examples to others.
>
> And with a firm resolution to detect and punish this growing evil, the MAYOR and MAGISTRATES have given the most positive directions to the CONSTABLES, to be more particularly watchful after such Offenders, and earnestly request all Persons living in the neighbourhood of any ALE-HOUSES, to give information at the TOWN CLERK's OFFICE, or to the CONSTABLES, of any breach of this Order, or to notify the same to the MAYOR and MAGISTRATES themselves.
>
> By Order, COLQUITT, Town Clerk.
>
> ---
>
> THE MAYOR and MAGISTRATES hereby give this PUBLIC NOTICE, that they are determined to put the present existing LAWS in FORCE against all HOUSEKEEPERS who do not SWEEP and CLEANSE or cause to be SWEPT and CLEANSED, the SIDE or FOOT-WALKS opposite to their respective HOUSES.
>
> By Order, COLQUITT, Town Clerk.
> Exchange, Liverpool, Nov 26, 1800.
>
> ON SALE,
> BROWN OZNABURGS, COTTON BAGGING, and BLEACH'D LINENS,

---

31 Power, op. cit., p32.
32 Billinge's Advertiser, 1st December 1800.

bad air. Residents were responsible for sweeping the areas outside their households and storing rubbish, ash and dung in their yards until scavengers were due to remove the piles in their carts. However, the system was constantly breaking down, leading the magistrates to remind townsfolk of "existing LAWS in FORCE against all HOUSHOLDERS who do not SWEEP and CLEANSE, or cause to be SWEPT and CLEANSED, the SIDE or FOOT-WALKS opposite their respective houses."[33] The sharp rise in the town's death rate at the start of the century had not only galvanised the parish into building a new fever recovery hospital, but had also led the corporation to seek advice from parish physicians about the best means of preventing the outbreak of contagious diseases. Apart from reiterating concerns about courts and cellars, James Currie and his colleagues recommended the removal of slaughterhouses, tanneries, soap works, limekilns and other manufactories from the immediate vicinity of houses, adding that smoke emissions from steam engines and other sources should be regulated. They also pointed to the need for enforcing street cleanliness and advised a review of common sewers, recommending "an improvement of their structure on the principles of a report on this particular subject addressed by them to the Mayor and Magistrates in 1788."[34]

Currie paid particular attention to the north of the town, about which he noted "repeated remonstrances … have been made for the last twenty years on the collection of standing water, including filth of every kind, which are suffered to remain in the district which extends along the termination of the streets from St. Paul's Square to Byrom Street, and to which low fevers, which in the autumnal months especially infest these streets, are principally to be imputed."[35] Although this area had fewer courts than the southern neighbourhood, the level of overcrowding in many properties was far greater. Many breadwinners were unskilled and badly paid, and the level of unemployment was almost certainly higher. Five families totalling twenty-seven people lived in Peter Jones's house on Westmoreland Street near Vauxhall Road. Seventeen people in four families lived next to him, while twenty-three lived at John Robert's house next door to that. Edward Thorpe's family of six lived in the cellar below Roberts, while James Owens' family of eight lived below customs officer John Robinson, in whose house fifteen people lived in three families. Six families totalling twenty-one people in lived in Thomas Owens' house, while there were several small backhouses with eleven or twelve people living in each.

---

[33] Billinge's Advertiser, 1st December 1800.
[34] Currie, op. cit., p372-373.
[35] Ibid, p372-373. As with the Crosbie Street area featured above, this district was redeveloped during the nineteenth century as part of the commercial centre of Liverpool.

Currie and his associates recognised that there was little hope of providing alternative accommodation for nearly ten thousand people who lived in cellars by 1801. Many were divided in two, the room next to the street gaining little light or ventilation, and the one behind practically none. Currie recommended that cellar rooms at the rear should be fitted with ventilation tubes, to which air pumps "of an easy and simple construction may be applied when necessary." He suggested, "This would in a very considerable degree facilitate the means of counteracting contagious diseases and of rendering the administration of medical assistance safe to those whose duty calls them to administer it." He added that cellars "should, in all practicable cases, have a chimney in each apartment, and open into a back yard, where there is a necessary and a supply of water; and no cellar should be inhabited, the ceiling of which is not three feet at least above the curb-stone round the door way, by which the communication with the external air may be rendered free and direct." Currie also felt that cellars should be whitewashed every year, and also when "they may have been visited by contagion."[36]

Across an open space from Westmoreland Street that had yet to be developed was a row of back-to-backs along Smithfield Street between Hargreaves' brewery and Chadwick's brick store. Jane Howell and Rosy M'Guire lived in households of ten and twelve respectively, although others were less crowded. Most of the cellars in nearby Highfield Street were occupied. John Glascons lived with his wife and two children below Charles Davies's large household, while James Hankinson lived with his wife in the next cellar. James Leat lived next to them with his wife and two sons, while Frances Perry lived with her daughter in the next cellar along. But others in the same neighbourhood lived more comfortably above ground level as professionals or small business people. Shoemaker Thomas Bell lived at 5 Highfield Street, while William Marwood lived a few doors along as a port guager in the excise service. Schoolmistress Elizabeth Norris resided at number 28, along with Alice Simpkin who operated a weighing machine, while James Smith baked bread three doors along. Captain Bryan M'Donna and customs officer William Pedley shared number 42, next to a gentleman of independent means, Nehemiah Hornby. James Hargreaves lived at 47, close to his brewery just across Pownall Square, but his neighbour, Thomas Barton, was a humble tripe seller and button mould turner.

Between Highfield and Kay Streets, where there had recently been open spaces and agricultural plots, the land was gradually being filled with back-to-backs. Kay Street itself was home to second-hand clothes dealer William Danson, gingerbread maker George Cleave, and the soap and candle

---

[36] Currie, op. cit., p375.

manufactory owned by Lund and Unsworth. Elizabeth Hollinsworth made watches at number 5, next door to gentleman Thomas Williams, while Timothy Lyon made clay pipes two doors along. Coach maker Edward Morgan lived at 51, and constable John Miller at 57, but seven families totalling 35 people lived in James Wilding's house, including a bookkeeper, a watchman, and "one in law". This must surely have been one of the larger properties looking down overcrowded Edmund Street, with one housing twenty-four people in five families. In nearby Lumber Street, John Smith made potash and Jonathon Lyon made shoes, while Thomas Harrison made his living as a gunsmith. Anthony Melling was a miller, and John Lepp a tobacconist, while Robert Naybours beat gold at number 41. Edward Jones made watchcases, but there were several others in the district who supplied the watch industry. William Joyce made springs in Old Hall Street, where there was also a hairdresser, an undertaker, and a coal merchant. In Plumbe Street, Richard Lucas engraved watchcases and Robert Simpson assembled the finished products. Jane Smith was a tea dealer in Union Street, while Hannah Bradshaw, midwife to the Ladies Charity, lived nearby at 16 Earle Street. The district also had its surgeon, brush maker, stocking weaver and "tin man", but was also well served by alehouses.

Throughout the town there were twenty-nine physicians and surgeons, seventy-seven lawyers, twenty-eight clergymen and fifty-five teachers. Liverpool also boasted seven comedians, thirty musicians and one dancing master, while working at the periphery were thirty-nine fishermen and 164 agricultural workers. In addition to nearly 500 bookkeepers, the town was also served by 412 port officials and over a hundred civic officers, including fifteen constables. The census also showed that there were 1786 prisoners of war at the Great Howard Street gaol, ten times the number of domestic prisoners held at the Old Tower and the House of Correction. Ninety-four people were in the seamen's hospital, 121 in the infirmary, and seventy-one in the lunatic asylum, while the workhouse population had risen to 1412. The Bluecoat school housed 258 children, while nine smaller schools had from two to thirty-seven pupils each.

Street cleaning scavengers, firemen, watchmen, constables and others were paid through the parish rates, which also financed the prisons and infirmary, in addition to provisions for the poor. These included the dispensary and attending the sick, the upkeep of the workhouse, and "the necessity of providing a considerable sum weekly for that of the out-poor." But, as always, many property owners were not keen to pay their local taxes. The parish committee issued a notice in *Billinge's Advertiser* in February 1802 warning that "no sufficient excuse can be urged by any inhabitant against the immediate payment of the sums charged upon him, either for the Income of his *real* or the

A detail from Horwood's Plan of Liverpool, 1803, showing part of the northern neighbourhood (LRO)

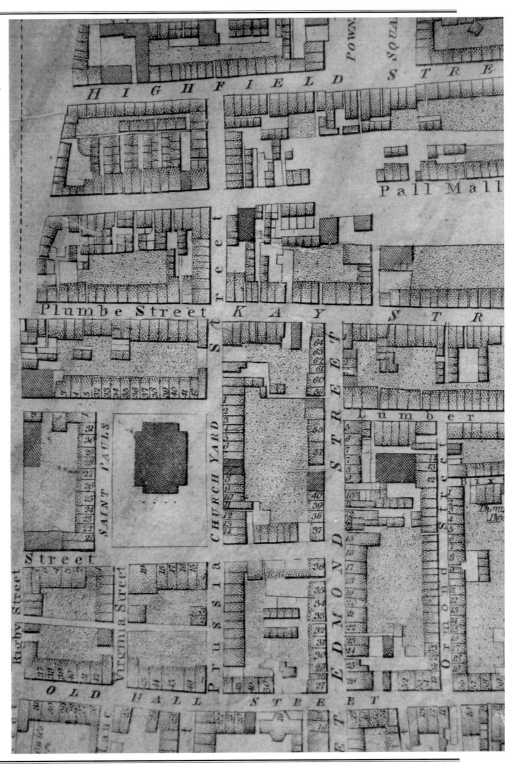

profits from his *personal* Estate." Collectors had been instructed "to be active in the discharge of their duty," and the committee added that "no inhabitants therefore may plead the want of information as an excuse for the Law being put into operation against him." As a final note, they added pointedly "That as the generous Spirit of the town of Liverpool is ever awake to the distresses of the poor by *voluntary contributions*, so it is to be hoped that on an occasion so important as the very existence of thousands of inhabitants, no other stimulus will be required to the discharge of a legal obligation than merely to make the occasion known."[37]

Liverpool's parish rates were raised by three pence to 2s 9d in the pound in 1802, although additional levies were raised for specific purposes (see above). In addition, national taxes were raised on property and the sale of a range of items from candles and newspapers to windows and private carriages, and since 1797 on income. However, the reluctance of some to pay their local rates may have had something to do with the breakdown of discipline at the workhouse since William Haliday had been relieved of the requirement to live in. While the cat was away the mouse began to play, and the system fell apart. The consumption of food and drink rose sharply, while inmates stole shoes and clothing and carried off every portable item they could. Much of the money bought 'parish wine,' which was distributed freely by the nurses and surgeons' apprentices, over three hundred gallons being consumed during six weeks in 1801 alone. Haliday had now lost his grip on the situation, and not until he was replaced was discipline restored.[38]

Elsewhere in Liverpool, the gap between the haves and have-nots inevitably fuelled petty crime. In January 1800, William Brown was sentenced before mayor Pudsey Dawson and aldermen Golightly, Naylor, Dunbar, Stanistreet and Leyland, "His Majesty's Justices of the Peace for the said Borough." He was convicted for stealing a pocket book wallet, while Peter Burns and Thomas Hall were found guilty of stealing several gold rings and a watch. All three were fined a shilling and sentenced to imprisonment in the House of Correction in Preston for a year, since Liverpool's prisons were filled to capacity. Thomas Hawkes got eighteen months "for throwing a glass bottle from the gallery at the Theatre into the pit, which struck a young Lady on the head," and then had to pay £100 for bail and sureties guaranteeing his good behaviour for another year. Thomas Landers got three months at Liverpool gaol for stealing a grey cloak, but Richard Davies got eighteen months at Preston for stealing a pair of shoes. Elizabeth Mitchell got a year at Preston for stealing two silk cloaks, and Esther Curtis six months for the theft of silk handkerchiefs, but Jane M'Coy

---

[37] *Billinge's Advertiser*, 1st February 1802. The italics are as printed in the paper.
[38] Peet, op. cit., Vol. 1, p. XLIX - L.

was recommended for mercy and was confined one month in Liverpool for stealing a pair of half boots. Servant Henry William Jones was sent to Preston "for stealing a guitar from his Master's house", while others were convicted for stealing items from various ships, including cotton, beef, lead, "trowsers" and other wearing apparel.

At the midsummer sessions that year, Philip Philips was fined a shilling and sent to Preston's House of Correction for two years for stealing coffee, a sentence reflecting the high value of that commodity. Meanwhile, George Perry got three months at Liverpool gaol for stealing tobacco from "the King's warehouse", although his sentence was reduced on a recommendation for mercy. John Lyle stole hams and articles of furniture from a house and was sentenced to seven year's transportation, while Margaret Dailey got six months at Preston for "uttering base money," or forging coins, and had to find £40 for six months bail and sureties. Jane Evans received two year's imprisonment for "a very violent Assault upon her Stepdaughter, a Child about three years old," but there were no other convictions for violence that session. Yet when violent offenders were convicted their sentences were often comparatively lenient. In October that year, William Swarsbrick was fined a shilling and sent to Preston for just six months for "an Assault upon a Peace Officer and rescuing a prisoner", while James M'Graugh got a year merely for "stealing a Watch and a Hat out of a shop." There were two separate offences of "Uttering Counterfeit Money", while James Hewitt, "an old offender", was transported for seven years for "Stealing Money out of a Counting-house." Seaman Archibald Scott received the same sentence for "Stealing Doubloons, the property of several of the ship's company."[39]

Towards the end of 1801 the issue of seamen's wages threatened a repeat of scenes that had shaken the town a generation earlier. *Billinge's Advertiser* reported, " We are very happy to be able to inform the public that the very serious and dangerous disturbances which arose on Tuesday, from the attempt made by some sailors of preventing a man's entering on board a merchant ship at the wages offered, and whom they actually threw into the Dock, from which, however, he got out alive, though very much hurt and bruised, was very speedily quelled, and we trust is now thoroughly subsided. It is to the very spirited exertions of the Mayor, who was himself attacked by one of the mob, and the very cheerful and manly assistance which he received from a number of respectable merchants and others who were present, that the mischief and riot which thus threatened the town was so happily put a stop to by taking half a dozen of the most active into custody."[40] Although they were committed for

---

[39] *Billinge's Advertiser*, 27th January, 28th July & 13th October 1800.
[40] Ibid, 2nd November 1801.

trial at Lancaster the charges appear to have been dropped, probably in the interests of public order. None of the men was actually prosecuted, and in any event the ringleader had escaped arrest and now had a bounty of fifty pounds on his head.

Early the following year, "the most dreadful storm of wind arose from the westward ever remembered by the oldest inhabitants of this town and neighbourhood, and continued with equal or increased violence until three o'clock in the afternoon." Several sloops in the river were sunk at anchor, and a number of small boats were beaten to pieces on the beach beyond the fort. The *Peggy* from Cork was driven ashore near the *Half Mile House,* where she tipped on her beam end and began filling with water before being washed back out some fifty yards from the beach. The pilot, crew and passengers lashed themselves to the masts and rigging, while a gathering on shore attempted a rescue but were foiled by the tremendous surge of the sea. All but one on board was drowned, the lucky survivor being washed ashore and plucked from a tide that ran six feet higher than the tables predicted. Meanwhile, the storm wreaked havoc in the town. Fifteen newly built houses near Vauxhall Road were levelled to the ground, hundreds more in Liverpool and the surrounding villages had their roofs entirely stripped, and many were badly damaged by collapsing chimneys. A pregnant woman was killed in her bed by falling masonry, although fortunately her husband and two children beside her escaped with minor injuries. Meanwhile, a gentleman in Ranelagh Street was lucky to escape death, having quitted his bed just minutes before the chimneys fell where he had been lying. Another in Everton had a miraculous escape and suffered only minor bruising as a chimney collapsed on top of him while he lay in bed. Fortunately, two large copingstones fell on either side of him and prevented his being crushed by the debris that followed, the weight of which broke the bed and forced it through the floor to the room below. But scarcely any property in the neighbourhood escaped damage, as leaded windows were blown in, trees were uprooted, and garden walls levelled.[41]

Later that same year the town was struck again, this time by a "calamity as singularly awful in its appearance as it was disastrous in its effects." At about ten o'clock one October evening smoke was observed coming from a storage room in the Goree Warehouse, "whose spacious and lofty front has long attracted the admiration of strangers, and which, if equalled, was not surpassed in magnitude by any similar structure in the kingdom." News soon spread throughout the town, and within minutes a large crowd had assembled nearby. At first it seemed the blaze would soon be under control, but, as firemen forced several doors and windows to gain entry, the flames were

---

[41] *Billinge's Advertiser,* 25th January 1802.

fed by a fresh supply of oxygen and were soon out of control. Within a few hours, the Goree and several warehouses nearby were completely consumed by fire, fuelled by numerous casks of brandy, wine and sugar, plus countless bales of cotton, all stacked on stout timber floors. As *Billinge's* reported, "The solemn grandeur! the majestic horror of the scene, no tongue, no pencil can describe." By the time the blaze was fully under way, much of Liverpool's population was assembled along the waterfront to gaze in awe as glowing balls of cotton floated high into the air. But "scarcely a whisper disturbed the awful stillness that prevailed," and it soon became clear that nothing could be done to quell the blaze, the fire pumps being no match for a conflagration on such a scale. Fortunately, the high tide and light breezes enabled the removal of shipping in George's Dock beyond the reach of the flames. However, for a while it seemed the fire would soon consume the housing on Water Street, but the thick walls of Mr. Dawson's warehouse and other commercial buildings arrested its progress.[42] When the fire had finely died down and the damage was surveyed, losses were estimated at nearly a third of a million pounds, leading to the collapse of the St. George's insurance company.[43] And yet, Liverpool's enterprising spirit remained undimmed.

---

[42] *Billinge's Advertiser*, 21st September 1802.
[43] Stonehouse, *The Streets of Liverpool*, p20.

Liverpool from Lime Street, 1797, Pictorial Relics, Herdman, Plate 29

Chapter Eleven

In the early morning of Sunday 26th February 1804, Lieutenant William Sparling drove in his post chaise towards rural Dingle just south of Liverpool, accompanied by his second, Captain Sam Colquitt. On reaching Toxteth Chapel, the two men alighted and walked towards the picturesque hollow known as Knot's Hole. There they waited for shipbuilder Edward Grayson, who arrived a little later accompanied by his manservant and two surgeons. Doctors Parker and McCartney had been led to believe they were on their way to an urgent case, but were soon to discover the real purpose of their mission.[1]

At stake was a matter of honour. Three months earlier Sparling had received an anonymous letter advising, "For heaven's sake, if you value your future happiness don't be so rash." That Sparling was engaged to Miss Anne Renshaw was apparently a matter of concern, the writer explaining "She is in love with your fortune, but be assured that another has a prior claim to her heart and favours, and who enjoyed them to the full – of this you may easily have proof." The letter continued, "you have friends who esteem you and who are grieved to see you throw your happiness in the power of an artful and designing girl," and concluded, "Whatever fate attends you, be assured of the sincere wishes for future happiness of an old attached friend, who thinks his name at present better suppressed."

Sparling had called off the engagement and begun an acrimonious correspondence with the Reverend Samuel Renshaw, father of the would-be bride, which soon drew Grayson into the frame. That the son of such a wealthy and respected merchant as John Sparling should act upon scurrilous accusations and impugn the Renshaw family name was all too much for Grayson. As the young lady's uncle, he was soon heard publicly to brand the Lieutenant as a scoundrel and villain, remarks that were reported back to Sparling, leaving him with little option but to lay down the gauntlet and defend his honour. Therefore, as daylight began to break upon an otherwise idyllic scene, Sparling and Grayson stood back-to-back, pistols at the ready. After taking their allotted steps, each man turned and fired, but only one shot hit its target. As the ball entered Grayson's right thigh he called out in pain, and was quickly supported by Dr. McCartney as he slumped. He was taken directly to his house in St. James Street, where the bullet was removed, but died of his wound a week later.[2]

---

[1] Grayson's firm built the *Blayds*, which had its maiden voyage in 1782 (see Ch 5 above). Sparling was son of wealthy merchant John Sparling, Mayor of Liverpool in 1790 when the Common Hall first challenged the corporation (see p172-173 above).

[2] *The Liverpool Review*, 28th June 1890, and F.H. Taylor, *Liverpool and the Athenaeum* (1965) p16-18.

An inquest was held before the mayor, and Sparling was sent for trial in Lancaster, when a jury acquitted him of murder in just twenty minutes. But the final duel in Liverpool took place at the end of the following year, when John Bolton and Major Edward Brooks faced each other in a field between Pembroke Place and Low Hill. John Bolton was a respected wealthy merchant who had raised and equipped a regiment of volunteers at his own expense, and had later used his influence to secure a senior position for Brooks with the Liverpool customs. When Brooks applied for an increase on his £700 salary, Bolton strongly disapproved and referred the matter to the West India Association, of which he was president. Brooks was enraged when the Association turned his application down, and he began making abusive comments towards his benefactor so publicly they could not be ignored. A duel was arranged to take place by the Aigburth road, but when this was leaked to the magistrates the two men were arrested and bound over to keep the peace for twelve months. They met on Castle Street the day the bond expired, when Brooks again loudly insulted Bolton in front of bystanders. They agreed to settle their differences once and for all, and the fateful meeting was arranged for that very evening of 20th December. When the duellists arrived at the field overlooking the town below, the light had so faded that they had to load their pistols by candlelight. According to custom the challenger fired first, but the major missed his target and fell dead seconds later as his opponent's shot penetrated his right eye. However, despite a verdict of wilful murder at the inquest, no prosecution was brought, public opinion being so heavily in Bolton's favour.[3]

Like many others, Bolton had come to Liverpool to seek his fortune when he was little more than a boy. He was soon off to the West Indies as an apprentice seaman, but his seafaring career was short-lived. A fellow merchant later reminisced, "The first time I ever saw you was in St. Vincent, I think in the year 1773. You had just landed from a Liverpool ship belonging to Messrs. Rawlinson and Chorley, in which ship you were an apprentice, and accordingly you were dressed in a sailor's jacket and trousers. You carried a bag of potatoes on your back, and a cheese under your arm; these, you told me, were part of your adventure. As I had always forwarded and took pleasure in encouraging young beginners, I readily eased you of your burden at the price you demanded. I recognised you soon afterwards at the store and shop of Mr. Drinkall....It seems you had been promoted from ship to this shop...On my return from England to the West Indies in 1777 I found you further promoted by the gentlemen to whom you were apprenticed, Messrs Rawlinson and Chorley. You appeared as one of their agents, retailing out one of their cargoes,

---

[3] Based on *The Liverpool Review*, 12th July 1890; James Stonehouse, *The Streets of Liverpool*, p126-128; and G.W. Matthews, *John Bolton: A Liverpool Merchant, 1756-1837*, Historical Society of Lancashire and Cheshire, Vol. 93 (1941) p102-103.

consisting of hams, bacon, herrings, cheese, beef, butter, potatoes, grits, barley, pease, checks, osnaburgs, salt, fish, tripe, frocks, trousers, jackets, etc, etc."[4] Bolton eventually made enough money to return to Liverpool in 1790, when he settled in Duke Street and set up as a merchant. However, he narrowly avoided bankruptcy three years later, when Liverpool's trade slumped with the outbreak of the war, and the bank of Messrs. Charles Caldwell & Co. had collapsed. As a major investment partner, Bolton had been lucky to get his assets out in time, having by now realised his ambitions and made a small fortune.

A fellow partner in the stricken bank, Thomas Leyland, had also been lucky to escape ruin. Ten years later, Leyland's ship *Enterprize* was fitting out for another slaving voyage to Africa. It was enterprise that drove men like Thomas Leyland in pursuit of maximum profits and blinded them to the misery they caused, even though regulations led them to caution crews against mistreating their captives. In July 1803 he instructed Captain Caesar Lawson, "Sir, Our ship Enterprize, to the command of which you are appointed, being now ready for sea, you are immediately to proceed in her, and make the best of your way to Bonny on the Coast of Africa. You will receive herewith an invoice of the Cargo on board her, which you are to barter at Bonny for prime Negroes, Ivory, and Palm Oil. By Law this vessel is allowed to carry 400 Negroes, and we request that they may all be males if possible to get them. At any rate buy as few females as in your power, because we look to a Spanish market for the disposal of your cargo, where Females are a very tedious sale. In the choice of the Negroes be very particular. Select those that are well formed and strong, and do not buy any above 24 years of age, as it may happen that you will have to go to Jamaica, where you know any exceeding that age would be liable to a Duty £10 a head. While the slaves are on board the Ship allow them every indulgence Consistent with your own Safety, and do not suffer any of your officers or Crew to abuse or insult them in any respect. Perhaps you may be able to procure some Palm Oil on reasonable terms, which is likely to bear a great price here. We therefore wish you to purchase as much as you can with any spare cargo you may have."

"We have taken out Letters of Marque against the French and Batavian [Dutch] Republics, and if you are so fortunate as to fall in with and capture any of their vessels send the same direct to this Port, under the care of an active Prize Master and a sufficient number of men out of your ship; and also put a Copy of the Commission on board her, but do not molest any neutral ship, as it would involve us in an expensive Lawsuit and subject us to heavy Damages. A considerable part of our property under your care will not be

---

[4] Letter from West India merchant, George Baillie, 1800, quoted in Matthews, op. cit., p98.

insured, and we earnestly desire you will keep a particular look out to avoid the Enemy's Cruisers, which are numerous, and you may hourly expect to be attacked by some of them. We request you will Keep strict and regular discipline on board the ship; do not suffer Drunkenness among any of your Officers or Crew, for it is sure to be attended with some misfortune, such as Insurrection, Mutiny and Fire. Allow to the ship's Company their regular portion of Provisions &c and take every care of such as may get sick. You must keep the ship very clean and see that no part of her Stores and Materials are embezzled, neglected or idly wasted. As soon as you have finished your trade and laid in a sufficient quantity of Yams, wood, water, and every other necessary for the Middle Passage, proceed with a press of sail for Barbadoes, and on your arrival there call on Messrs. Barton Higginson & Co. with whom you will find Letters from us by which you are to be govern'd in prosecuting the remainder of the voyage." The letter went on to detail the usual rates of commission, before concluding, "Any Prize that you may capture, direct the Prize Master to hoist a white flag at the fore and one at the main top Gallant Mast heads, on his approach to this Port, which will be answered by a signal at the light House. We hope you will have a happy and prosperous voyage, and remain, Sir, Your obedient Servants."[5]

After fitting out, provisioning, and buying in trading goods at a total cost of £17,000, the *Enterprize* sailed from Liverpool on 20th July. On 26th August it captured the Spanish brig *St. Augustin*, which was taken back to Liverpool by a prize crew. Two weeks later, the *Enterprize* rescued the Liverpool ship *John* with a cargo of 261 slaves, which was then able to proceed to Dominica. Lawson's ship reached Bonny on the Niger Delta late in September, where 412 Eboe slaves were taken on board over the next two months before sailing for Cuba. The *Enterprize* arrived at Havanna on 9th January, where the 393 surviving slaves were sold over a period of nearly ten weeks.[6] After the sale of the slaves, and a cargo of sugar and logwood worth over £10,000, the voyage made a profit of £24,430, of which half went to Leyland and a quarter to each of his two partners. However, the taking of the *St. Augustin* proved an expensive mistake, since Leyland had not taken out Letters of Marque against Spanish vessels. Presumably, this was because he intended to sell his slaves in Cuba and needed to remain on the best terms possible with the Spanish. Whatever the reason for seizing the vessel, this action cost Leyland & Co. just over £800 in costs and damages, and the *St. Augustin* sailed from Liverpool early in December.[7]

---

[5] Quoted in Williams, op. cit., p601-603.
[6] Presumably Lawson exceeded the legal quota knowing some slaves would die before reaching the West Indies.
[7] Leyland Papers, LRO 387 MD 43.

Soon after the *Enterprize* arrived back in Liverpool in April 1804, Napoleon Bonaparte was proclaimed Emperor of France, and his preparations for the invasion of England were almost complete.[8] The harbours at Boulogne and neighbouring ports had been enlarged to accommodate a huge invasion fleet, new forts had been built to protect them, and over 110,000 French troops had been assembled nearby. However, apart from problems of weather, which thwarted an invasion attempt in July, the vast armada needed to sail upon a single tide in the face of the Royal Navy. Napoleon had to gain mastery of the Channel to be successful, but the British were daily bombarding the ports of embarkation while blockading French warships around the coast. Napoleon's plan was to create a diversion by an attack on British possessions in the West Indies, which would lead to the Admiralty sending a large fleet to defend the islands, thereby weakening the blockade. Once a sufficient French force had been amassed in the Caribbean, it would head back across the Atlantic and into the Channel to enable the invasion to get underway. However, Britain now had nearly 400,000 men under arms, and although the south coast was the most heavily defended, there were gun batteries and militia at strategic points all around Britain, including Liverpool and the Mersey estuary.

Early in 1805, a French fleet managed to slip out of Rochefort under cover of a snowstorm, before crossing the Atlantic, recapturing Martinique, and taking several small British islands. Ten weeks later, a larger force under Admiral Villeneuve's command slipped out of Toulon, avoiding Nelson's Mediterranean fleet as it was taking on supplies in Majorca. After picking up a contingent of Spanish ships in Cadiz, Villeneuve crossed the Atlantic to rendezvous with the Rochefort squadron. On learning that two hostile fleets had put to sea, but unsure of their intentions, the Admiralty ordered an embargo on British ships from leaving their ports, and instructed press gangs to redouble their activities. As Liverpool's ships were stripped of crews to man the king's fleets, the local press reported on 13th May, "The immediate augmentation of our naval force is thought a matter of such pressing necessity, that all considerations of individual suffering must, for the present, give way. The order for an embargo at this port was announced from the Custom House on Thursday; and, during the whole week, the press gang had been indefatigable in their exertions. Persons of all

---

[8] The following account is adapted from Cordingly, op. cit., ch.12 & 13; A. Schom, *Trafalgar: Countdown to Battle, 1803-1805* (1976) p.141-151 & 180-193; and J. Terraine, *Trafalgar* (1990) p103 & 323-332.

professions, as well as seamen, have been occasionally taken; though many have been released on proper application being made. …The embargo extends to all vessels bound to foreign parts, including Ireland and the Isle of Man, with the exception of ships belonging to foreign powers, provided they have no British seamen on board. It extends, likewise, to coasting vessels of every description, except such as are laden with coals and grain."[9]

By the time Villeneuve arrived at Martinique, the Rochefort fleet had given up hope of a rendezvous and was heading home. Meanwhile, having learned that the Toulon fleet had put to sea, Nelson's ships were sailing westwards in pursuit. When Villeneuve learned of their arrival in the Caribbean early in June, and with no sign of expected French reinforcements, he headed back across the Atlantic rather than risk an engagement. On approaching the Channel in a thick mist, his force met another British fleet waiting off Cape Finisterre. Although two Spanish ships were captured, the battle was indecisive, and the rest of Villeneuve's fleet escaped southwards. It eventually took refuge at Cadiz on 14th August, but was spotted by a small British squadron under Admiral Collingwood, who immediately dispatched the news to London.

By the end of September, eighteen French and fifteen Spanish ships of the line were under a new blockade from twenty-seven of the Royal Navy. Such numerical superiority might otherwise have been regarded as an opportunity for a great victory, but Villeneuve was not optimistic. Although accused by many of being unequal to the task, he was all too aware of the shortcomings in Napoleon's plan. Experience showed that British sailors were better drilled in rapid reloading and firing with accuracy than the French and Spanish, who had had little opportunity to practice under blockade conditions. This had given the Royal Navy success in every major sea battle of the war, but Napoleon seemed ignorant of the realities. Yet when Villeneuve heard that the frustrated emperor intended to replace him, he took the fateful decision to risk putting to sea. Early on 19th October, the main British fleet having withdrawn out of sight over the horizon, the crew of a royal naval scout frigate spotted the enemy in Cadiz harbour preparing to set sail. Signals were raised, and the message they sent was passed from frigate to frigate until it reached Nelson fifty miles out from the coast. Immediate orders were given to make all sail, and over the next two days the British ships gave chase. By dawn on 21st, the sails of the French and Spanish fleets were spotted some twelve miles away under a grey sky, but the winds were now so light that it would be midday before the first shots were fired. This gave plenty of time for a hearty meal, and then to clear the decks so that gun crews would be unimpeded. Hanging tables were lashed to the ceilings, while hammocks were stowed in nets along

[9] Quoted in Williams, op. cit., p399.

the inside of the hull to help reduce splinters from incoming shot. Benches, chests, and all removables from mugs and plates to canvas bulkheads and live animals, were cleared and stowed away in the hold, while the two- and three-ton guns were unlashed from their moorings and manoeuvred into position.

Nelson toured the decks of the *Victory*, taking care to speak to as many men as time allowed, advising gun crews on their aim and to remain cool and steady under fire. Three cheers went up as he left each group, but eventually there was silence but for the creaking of timbers. Shortly before noon Nelson gave an order to signal the fleet, "England confides that every man will do his duty," but on being advised that there was no signal for the word confides he agreed to substitute "expects".[10] An officer on board later recounted, "Everything was now in order, fires extinguished, fearnought screens around the hatchways for passing powder from the magazines; shot racks drawn from under their peaceable coverings and arranged ready for their work; guns cast loose, crowbars for pointing the guns lying at hand on the deck; tompions out all ready for a game of thunder…my friend the goat sent down to the cable tier – the captain's ducks and geese left in the coops, to cackle and quake and take their chance – the doctors saws and knives and probes and bandages and tourniquets, all laid out in the cockpit; and I devoutly hoping, as tempted by curiosity I looked at them, that I might be blown away all together, rather than that he should exercise his skills on my limbs or carcass. And every man and boy was mute as he stood at his station. …all grim in lip and glistening in eye. Men shirtless, with handkerchiefs bandaged tightly round their loins and heads, stood with naked brawny arms folded on their hairy and heaving chests, looking pale and stern, but still hushed; or glancing with a hot eye through ports…I felt a difficulty in swallowing. Now, if we had gone at it at once, without this chilling prelude, why I dare say I should have known very little about that thing which we call fear. 'Stand to your guns!' at last came in a peal through the stillness from the captain's speaking trumpet; it swept fore and aft with such clear force, as though it had been spoken within a foot of the ear, and seemed to dash down into the holds and penetrate to the very keel. The instant change this produced was magical. 'Take good aim! Ready the first platoon!' Ready? Aye, every one *was* ready; stern, fixed, rigid, in soul – pliant, elastic in body. 'Captains of the guns, watch the falling of the first shot, and point accordingly.' Not a word was replied; even the everlasting 'Aye aye, sir' was refused now."[11] And so it was that the men from Liverpool stood side-by-side with sailors and marines from all over Britain in readiness for battle.

Nelson's battle plan was for the fleet to form two columns, one under his command to sail directly for the centre of the enemy line, the other under

[10] Terraine, op. cit., p141.
[11] Quoted in Terraine, p187-188

Admiral Collingwood to make towards the rear. Several ships from each column were to pass through the line, enabling the fleet to envelop the enemy from the centre to the rear and isolate them from those in the van ahead. The French and Spanish ships thus engaged would be outnumbered and out-gunned, and it would take some time for the rest to make the necessary manoeuvres to come to their aid. In addition, any attempt by the Franco-Spanish force to make a run for the safety of Cadiz thirty miles away would have been foiled. This was more or less what Villeneuve expected, having encountered Nelson and his tactics seven years earlier on the Nile. As the French admiral predicted, "The enemy will not confine himself to forming in a line of battle parallel with our own and engaging us in an artillery duel...[he] will endeavour to envelop our rear, to break through our line and to direct his ships in groups upon such of ours as he shall have cut off, so as to surround and defeat them."[12] Under other circumstances, Nelson's plan might well have been disastrous for the Royal Navy, since each oncoming vessel would be virtually defenceless against the broadsides of the enemy as it made its approach. However, not only were French and Spanish crews less experienced but their tactics were less effective. By aiming chiefly at masts, sails and rigging to disable ships, fewer British crewmen were hit, and much shot was wasted as it passed overhead. Although effective in reducing manoeuvrability, this was far less devastating than the British strategy of concentrating fire on the hulls. Although around two and a half feet in thickness, the effect of such broadsides produced terrible carnage from flying splinters at close range.

As Admiral Collingwood later explained to the admiralty office, "The action began at twelve o'clock by the leading ships of the columns breaking through the enemy's line, the Commander in Chief about the tenth ship from the Van, the second in command about the twelfth from the rear, leaving the van of the enemy unoccupied; the succeeding ships breaking through in all parts, astern of their leaders and engaging the enemy at the muzzles of their guns."[13] Collingwood's flagship, the *Royal Sovereign*, received the first broadsides as it cut through the line, passing between the bows of the *Fougueux* some distance to starboard and the stern of the *Santa Anna*. As it did so, the portside gun crews fired through the stern windows of the Spanish ship, disabling fourteen guns and causing hundreds of casualties in one long broadside. The *Royal Sovereign* now drew close alongside the *Santa Anna*, the two ships becoming locked in a deadly duel at point blank range. But Collingwood's ship was soon in desperate trouble as the *Fougueux*, *San Leandro*, *San Justo* and *Indomptable* all closed in from different angles with guns blazing. For several

---

[12] Quoted in Cordingly, op cit, p187.
[13] Letter to the admiralty office, 22nd October 1805, printed in the *London Gazette*, 6th November and reprinted by *Gore's General Advertiser*, 14th November.

minutes *Royal Sovereign* took this punishment alone, before *Belleisle* came to its aid, drawing fire and losing its mizenmast in the process. As the *Mars* and *Tonnant* followed, the *Belleisle* came under further attack from *L'Achille* and *L'Aigle*, which brought down all her masts and caused great damage to the hull.

Each successive ship faced a heavy broadside as it entered the fray, but their guns raked along the full length of the enemy's decks while passing between bow and stern. As the *Bellorophon* passed the stern of the *Monarca*, its crew fired two broadsides from its carriage guns and three from the carronades, causing great devastation and loss of life on board the stricken foe. But approaching out of the dense smoke came another, and before long the *Bellorophon* and *L'Aigle* collided and became entangled by their yards and rigging. Three ships closed in and joined *L'Aigle* to overwhelm the British vessel, and at 1pm the *Bellorophon's* main and mizzen topmasts were shattered and fell over the side, leaving rigging, sails and yards in a tangle of wreckage across the main deck and dragging in the sea. Being larger than its opponent, *L'Aigle* had the advantage, enabling marines to fire down onto the *Bellorophon's* main deck while others threw grenades through the gun ports. Captain John Cooke was killed by two musket balls while reloading his pistol, and a fire broke out near the magazine soon afterwards, but was quickly extinguished before it, or panic, could spread. But despite its desperate position, the *Bellorophon's* crew exacted the greater toll, the gunners firing relentlessly through the hull and open ports of *L'Aigle* at close range. The French ship's crew finally managed to free their stricken ship and drift away, but were soon forced to surrender to the *Defiance*.

Leading the other column, Nelson's flagship approached the centre of the line shortly after Collinwood's, but the *Victory's* speed was now reduced to one and a half knots due to the calm air. Alongside Nelson on the main deck was Captain Blackwood, who had previously suggested that it might be safer to direct the battle from his frigate, *Euryalus*. Nelson had declined, and as Blackwood took his leave, he shook hands saying, "I trust, my Lord, that on my return to the *Victory*, which will be as soon as possible, I shall find your Lordship well and in possession of twenty prizes." But Nelson had no doubt about his own fate, replying, "God bless you, Blackwood, I shall never speak to you again."[14] As Blackwood was rowed back to his vessel, he watched the slow, tortuous progress of the *Victory*. The first ranging shots fell short, but the ship was soon being subjected to a punishing barrage.

As the commander of the marines on board Villeneuve's flagship *Bucentaure* related, Nelson's column approached "in some disorder heading for our line....

---

[14] Quoted in Terraine, op cit, p148

Four of our ships, *Heros, Santisima Trinidad, Bucentaure*, and *Redoubtable*, presented him with a very brisk and solid wall of fire as he approached. All four of them were drawn up in a tight line, and it did not seem possible for him to cut through it at any place. *Victory* first wanted to pass astern of the *Santisima Trinidad*, the ship before us. We even thought she was going to board her; but just as she was about to do that, she suddenly fell off to her starboard, passing behind us. Now within musket range, she received several broadsides from our ships, including a terrible fusillade from the marines which caused her considerable damage; but it was not enough to prevent her from cutting through our line."[15] As the *Victory* crept forward, Nelson's secretary was standing next to Captain Hardy on the quarterdeck when a cannon ball took off his head. Moments later another landed between Hardy and Nelson. Hardy's foot was bruised by a flying splinter, prompting Nelson to remark, "This is too warm work, Hardy, to last long," but both men stood their ground rather than seek shelter.[16]

The mizzen topmast was brought down and the helm was smashed, which meant the ship had to be steered from the gunroom below. As double-headed shot slammed into masts and men, the *Victory* was still not in a position to return effective fire. By the time it reached the gap between the *Bucentaure* and *Redoubtable* there had been some fifty casualties on Nelson's ship and the foresail was in tatters. But as it eventually reached the *Bucentaure's* stern, its most lethal weapon was unleashed on the French crew through the cabin windows. Along with the usual 68-pound fragmenting shot, a carronade gun was also loaded with a keg containing five hundred musket balls that were fired with devastating effect. Victory's fifty portside carriage guns then opened fire with double- and triple-headed shot, causing four hundred casualties and dismounting twenty guns, and almost disabling the French vessel.

Following in *Victory's* wake was the *Temeraire*, cannonading the French *Neptune* and *Redoubtable* and drawing fire in return. Amid the sweltering heat, the dense clouds of smoke and the deafening noise, gun crews worked tirelessly reloading and re-aiming, the sweat tracing down their blackened, semi-naked bodies. At around 1.10pm, Captain Hardy brought the *Victory* alongside the *Redoubtable*, the French crews running in their carriage guns and closing the gun ports in preparation to board. The two ships closed in, and the *Victory's* gunners blasted the *Redoubtable's* hull while their opponents took up positions on the main deck and in the tops and yards above. As the vessels collided, the yards, sails, rigging and anchors became locked in a lethal embrace. Most of the French crew were now firing small arms and throwing grenades, but as the first wave prepared to storm the *Victory*, another carronade of exploding

---

[15] Quoted in Schom, op cit, p323.
[16] Quoted in Terraine, op cit, p148.

shot and musket balls blasted at them causing terrible carnage. Meanwhile, Nelson and Hardy continued to pace the quarterdeck amid the chaos and a hail of fire, the two men displaying steely courage as an example to their men. As they were about to make another turn, a musketeer shot Nelson from the *Redoubtable's* mizzen top, the ball striking his right shoulder and puncturing his lung before lodging in his spine. Within minutes, however, around forty British marines had likewise been felled, and the main deck had been virtually cleared. Nelson was taken down to the surgeon's cockpit beneath the lower gun deck, where the scene resembled a butcher's shambles, and the screams of mutilated seamen competed with the deafening explosions above. Nelson knew his spine had been hit, and he could feel the blood filling his punctured lungs. Dr. William Beatty examined him and realised that nothing could be done, so Nelson was laid against the curving timbers on the orlop deck and made as comfortable as possible away from the blood and gore. Despite his steadily worsening condition, he insisted that Hardy should keep him informed about the raging battle. On his final visit the captain informed Nelson that fifteen enemy ships had been taken, at which point the dying admiral asked his loyal friend to kiss him. Hardy obliged with a kiss on the forehead, before leaving for the last time with tears in his eyes. Nelson died an hour later. His body was later pickled in a cask of brandy to preserve it during the journey home.

Meanwhile, the two ships drifted in their deadly embrace towards the badly damaged *Temeraire*,[17] which fired at the French vessel, killing and wounding around two hundred men in several broadsides. As the *Redoubtable's* bowsprit appeared over the *Temeraire's* quarterdeck, some of the crew lashed it to their ship, but despite the pounding from both sides, the Frenchmen refused to submit and continued the fight with small arms. As several hand grenades landed in its deck, the *Redoubtable's* starboard rigging was set ablaze, the fire soon spreading to the *Temeraire's* foresail. Both crews stopped fighting to put out the fires, as did the crew of the *Victory*, where another fire had broken out. At last, the injured Captain Lucas of the *Redoubtable* struck his colours and surrendered his ship to save any further bloodshed. Of its 643 crew, 487 had been killed and 81 wounded, leaving just 75 to man and defend the ship. Against this toll the *Victory's* casualties were relatively light, with 57 killed and 102 wounded out of a crew of 821.

Soon after, however, the battle was all but over, as Collingwood explained. "About three PM, many of the enemy's ships having struck their colours, their line gave way. Admiral Gravina, with ten ships joining their frigates to leeward, stood towards Cadiz. The five headmost ships in their van tacked, and standing to the Southward to windward of the British Line, were engaged

---

[17] The Fighting *Temeraire* of later Constable fame.

and the sternmost of them taken. The others went off, leaving to His Majesty's Squadron Nineteen Ships of the Line."[18] One of them was ablaze, but the *Achille's* magazine exploded before all its crew could be rescued, and the ship blew apart.

As the last shots were being fired, Collingwood began to organise the damaged British fleet and its prizes, while the sailors searched the dark and bloodied waters for survivors amid floating wreckage. The scale of the carnage and devastation was revealed as the smoke began to clear. Many ships were totally dismasted, while hulls were smashed and streaked with blood as it flowed from the scuppers. But now that the battle was over, a new danger threatened as a storm approached. As Collingwood explained, "The Royal Sovereign, having lost her masts, except the tottering foremast, I called the Euryalus to me while the action continued, which ship lying within hail made my signal a service. Capt. Blackwood performed with great attention. After the action I shifted my flag to her that I might more easily communicate my orders to and collect the ships, and towed the Royal Sovereign out to Seaward. The whole fleet were now in a very perilous situation, many dismasted, all shattered in thirteen fathom water off the Shoals of Trafalgar, and when I made the signal to prepare to anchor, few of the ships had an anchor to let go, their cables being shot. But the same good Providence which enabled us through such a day preserved us in the night, by the wind shifting a few points and drifting the ships off the Land, except four of the captured dismasted ships which are now at anchor off Trafalgar, and I hope will ride safe until those gales are over."[19]

For some, the situation was now every bit as perilous as it had been during the battle. The heavy swell on which the ships had fought had led Nelson to warn his captains of the coming storm, but none could have guessed at its reaching hurricane force. Having no masts, sails or rigging, many ships were unable to manoeuvre and had to be towed, but securing ropes under such conditions proved exceptionally difficult, with some ships colliding and sustaining yet further damage. Many were severely holed and rapidly taking on water, and some had had their pumps knocked out during the action. Despite being totally exhausted, all the crews, friend and foe, began to work together for their mutual preservation. But for many, such efforts were in vain. After five days of storm, only four of the captured ships made it with the British fleet to Gibraltar, the rest either sinking or being wrecked on the coast. All the British ships eventually made it to port, where emergency repairs were carried out before returning to British dockyards for a more thorough overhaul. When

---

[18] Letter to Admiralty Office, dated 22nd October, printed in *Gore's General Advertiser*, 14th November 1805
[19] Ibid.

the losses were counted it was estimated that out of around 18,000 British seamen, many of them from Liverpool, 449 had been killed and 1,242 injured. The casualties among the French and Spanish were much higher, with around 2.545 wounded and 4,408 thought dead, some having drowned in the storm.

With the destruction of so many French and Spanish warships, the threat of invasion was ended. Nelson was buried at Westminster Abbey in January 1806, after his coffin was bourn through the mourning crowds on a carriage modelled on the *Victory*. With the immediate crisis now over, Britain returned to something approaching normality, although the war was far from at an end.

The country returned to the polls a year after Trafalgar, when the election in Liverpool proved no less eventful than its predecessors. Although Banastre Tarleton and Isaac Gascoyne looked set to regain their seats unopposed, the last-minute persuasion of William Roscoe to become a candidate ensured a lively affair. As a commentator noted, there were nearly three thousand voters, "…of which number five-sixths at least are working people, and generally of such thirsty constitutions that they hail the approach of an electioneering contest as the season of recreation, drunkenness and delight, and look forward to the opening of the taproom with a greater avidity of pleasure than their superiors would experience at the prospect of a jubilee, a music meeting, or a race week…The approach of a third candidate, therefore, was received by those people as a boon from heaven; and as they were insensible to the mental perfections of their hero, they were fully content to satisfy their own corporeal sensations by wallowing in the liquor which was poured down their capacious throats with lavish liberality."[20]

Roscoe was a curious choice of candidate to challenge the two generals, but several others had been approached before him and had declined to stand. Besides being an abolitionist, as an author, poet, and botanist, Roscoe preferred the quiet of his library at Allerton Hall to the bustle of Liverpool.[21] His backers were a disparate group, but what united them was their opposition

---

[20] Quoted from the Preface to the Liverpool Poll Book, 1806.

[21] Roscoe's poems include *Mount Pleasant* and *The Wrongs of Africa*, lamenting the slave trade. He wrote biographies of Lorenzo de Medici and Pope Leo X, owned a large collection of books and Italian paintings, and was a keen botanist. Roscoe not only campaigned behind the scenes for the abolition of the slave trade, but also for the emancipation of Catholics and other religious dissenters, and for parliamentary and other reforms. He bought Allerton Hall in 1799, having become a successful banker following his earlier career as a lawyer.

to the local council and their placemen. They hated Gacoyne's Tory principles, and considered Tarleton a turncoat for abandoning radical Whig ideals. Many were, like Roscoe, religious dissenters who demanded political and civil rights, including the right of all men to vote and hold public office. They included both slave traders and abolitionists, but seldom did either allow their views to bring them into conflict. Indeed, Thomas Leyland, owner of the *Enterprize*, was Roscoe's banking partner, and was one of two leading slavers to nominate him. First and foremost, Roscoe was a businessman who, like his friend James Currie, strongly defended the slave merchants' integrity. In his view, the slave trade was the whole nations' responsibility, and while it remained sanctioned by Parliament, their character could not be impugned. Perhaps what made him most acceptable to the 'African interest' was his view that abolition should be gradual and accompanied by hefty compensation. Moreover, he had long campaigned for the end of London's lucrative monopoly of the East India trade to enable Liverpool merchants to diversify.

The weakness in this argument was that over the previous ten years Liverpool's share of the British slave trade stood at roughly eighty-five per cent.[22] While merchants elsewhere *had* diversified, those in Liverpool were, like Thomas Leyland, more involved than ever. Under Napoleon's directives, France was now busy re-establishing slavery throughout its colonies. This was a double outrage to most British minds, since not only was this a retrograde step from a humanitarian view, but it strengthened the enemy's economy. Following the death of William Pitt in January 1806, his successor, Lord Grenville, had introduced a bill to outlaw British ships from supplying enemy colonies. The Foreign Slave Trade Act passed into law that May, leading Tarleton to complain that abolitionists "were now coming by a sidewind,"[23] He was right. Grenville made his views on slavery very clear, persuading the House of Lords in June 1806 finally to support a resolution to abolish the trade. The writing was on the wall, but with the breakdown of peace negotiations, and disagreements over taxation and military reforms, Grenville sought backing from an election and Parliament was dissolved.

Despite the threat to Liverpool, there was very little reference to the slave trade during the local contest. Instead, the squib writers resorted to the usual mud slinging and character bashing as though few issues were of real importance.[24] Among the lampoons was one about imaginary comedy called *John Bull's Glory*

---

[22] D. P. Lamb, *Volume and Tonnage of the Liverpool Slave Trade, 1772-1807*, p92 in Anstey and Heir, op. cit., shows the average number of ships clearing annually for Africa from Liverpool between 1793 and 1804 as 107, as against 18 from London and 5 from Bristol, giving Liverpool an 82% share. Williams, op. cit., appendix XI, cites figures showing that Liverpool's share over a similar period was 85%, reaching 86% in 1804.

[23] Quoted by Hochschild, op. cit., p303.

[24] Unless otherwise stated, all extracts below taken from Liverpool Poll Book, 1806.

at the Theatre Royal. Casting Tarleton as "General Turncoat" for abandoning his principles, and Gascoyne as "General Runaway" for retreating from Dunkirk, the writer clearly favoured Roscoe. "The public having expressed considerable dissatisfaction with the performers of last season, the Managers beg leave respectfully to say that a gentleman descended from the celebrated Roscius will undertake the part of the independent Englishman, being his first appearance on a public stage; and they flatter themselves that the abilities of this gentleman will give such satisfaction as will enable them to recommend him to tread the London Boards this ensuing winter." Another spoof offered "a valuable Collection of Books in scarce and curious Bindings." *The History of Flanders, not Moll* included an account of "the smell of gunpowder shewing its terrifying effects" on Isaac Gascoyne. *The Memoirs of a Woman of Pleasure* was a reference to Tarleton's ex-mistress, "a rare copy, but in sheets." *An Essay on the Composition of Sermons* derided Roscoe's literary achievements by purporting to show "the folly and absurdity of a man writing his own, when so many good ones may be had at so reasonable a price." Apparently a scarce book, this was "bound in black sheep, with a loose cover made of wolf's skin." Similar themes appeared in a spoof sale of horses, in which Tarleton the stallion was "not without some blemish....by a little patting may be mounted by any woman at five minute's notice." Gascoyne, the chestnut gelding, had done little useful work, and had been discharged from stud "for want of metal." The favourite was Roscoe, "that excellent horse, Willyo," who, although seeming remarkably docile, was "an astonishing leaper, and matchable with any filly in the Kingdom."

One verse writer pointed to Roscoe's humble origins, suggesting a lack of gravitas or breeding:

> *"When a boy he with scarce shoe or stocking would hop,*
> *A runner and sweeper in a stationer's shop ...*
> *Oh Liverpool, surely it never can be,*
> *That an ale-seller's son should represent Thee!"*

But perhaps the most humorous piece was this attack on establishment abuses by a Roscoe supporter in "A dialogue between a Plump Alderman and a poor Freeman."

> *ALDERMAN*
> *John, come here, you've a vote, but few brains, I divine;*
> *You'll give it in aid of a friend of mine;*
> *I'm a far better judge of what's what, than can be*
> *Imagined the case of such fellows as thee.*

FREEMAN

I acknowledge, good sir, that your dignity's great,
Your carcass well fed, shews superior state;
But from whence can you prove that the size of the skull,
Speaks the furniture good, tho' ever so full?

ALDERMAN

What a curse on the land that such blockheads as you,
Should judge for yourselves, a poor ignorant crew;
Be assured of your fate, either vote as I say,
Or from my employment you march off this day.

FREEMAN

'Tis the glory of Britain, her sons are all free! ! !
The poorest as well as such great men as thee;
Equal laws protect all, be the end what it will,
I'll give a free vote to the best of my skill.

ALDERMAN

You talk of free voting! – pray where will you find,
A man like my friend, to all interest blind;
Why he'll sport all his cash like a lord at a race,
And will never change sides – but when wanting a place.

FREEMAN

These are times when all threat'nings we ought to despise,
I feel I am free, and above all disguise;
I will tell you my choice, he well merits his fame,
He'll prove independent; and Roscoe's his name.

A BYE-STANDER - Bravo! Bravisimo!
What say you to that, Old Codger?

But behind the humorous insults of rival squib writers lay a deeper menace in the form of mob violence, fuelled by copious amounts of liquor. Trouble broke out at the start of the campaign when a mob rampaged near the Old Dock, terrifying local inhabitants and damaging several houses. Whether this was the work of Tarleton's so-called 'Butchers' gang was not clear, but Roscoe soon believed the magistrates were conniving with Tarleton by their failure to act. The 'Butchers' paraded in menacing formation near the Exchange during the first two days of voting, blocking opponents on their way to the poll. Representing Tarleton at the head of this mob was a uniformed man on horseback. Although his regimental sword remained sheathed, he brandished a menacing wooden sabre, while a man in a sheepskin stood nearby waving a large wooden cleaver. Roscoe's supporters were taunted with cries of "Church and King" and "You will beg your bread and quit your country, for you will never obtain relief from the Presbyterians." More serious for the Roscoe vote were taunts of "No African Trade! The workhouse for carpenters, coopers, riggers and sail makers, Roscoe for ever."[25] But this made his supporters more determined, and a number of skirmishes erupted as they fought their way through. Roscoe claimed, "Without the least restraint from the police of the town, many of my friends were grossly insulted, and some of them struck and wounded. Persons whose peculiar province it was to have repressed such outrages were observed actively employed in promoting them."[26] His supporters organised and brought in reinforcements on the third day of voting, and the brawling of the previous days became a serious riot. Tarleton's mob was overwhelmed and fled from the scene, enabling Roscoe to congratulate his supporters in a letter that appeared the next day in the *Liverpool Chronicle*. "At the close of the poll this day a premeditated attack was made upon you by a body of men, who…. with persons on horseback, being in possession of an axe and a sword, took advantage of your peaceable and defenceless situation, and provided with bludgeons, burst into the hustings and menaced the lives of all who opposed their fury. No sooner had you recovered from your surprise, than you repressed by your firmness and numbers their outrageous efforts." As another writer explained, "When the chair was brought to convey Mr. Roscoe from the hustings to his own house, the partisans of Gen. Tarleton resisted admission, and an affray took place between the two parties for about fifteen minutes, which terminated in broken heads and bloody noses to several of the combatants. The assailing party were, however, completely driven off from the field, and we hope will feel no inclination to try their strength in this way any more."[27] Next day, Tarleton was further humiliated with a pun-laden squib about his defeat at the battle of Cowpens in America twenty-five years earlier, "having considerable practice in America during a *slaughtering* season…. he flatters himself he is not ignorant of that branch to assist him, in which Mr. Cross has kindly lent him a lot of his butchers."

On the fourth day Roscoe still lagged behind his opponents, but the organisation of his supporters eventually brought success, bringing in many more out-voters from as far away as London and Plymouth. But more important was the size of Roscoe's purse, his wealthy backers adding generously to his own lavish funds. While Gascoyne spent three thousand, and Tarleton four, by the end of the week's polling Roscoe had laid out twelve thousand pounds on paraphernalia, out-voters' expenses, and especially the copious amounts of

---

[25] Quoted in Sellers, op. cit., p58.
[26] Quoted in Cameron and Crooke, op. cit., p59.
[27] *The Liverpool Chronicle*, 5th November 1806.

food and drink required to bribe plumpers. By the sixth day he had crept up to second place, prompting one humorous note, "The Barbers to the friends of the Generals beg leave to inform them that they can no longer afford to shave them at the usual prices. They must now charge by measure as their faces are grown much longer." Another quipped, "The Ship Banastre, of this place, and bound to St. Stephens, London, has just foundered at the mouth of the River Mersey, owing …to the unskilfulness of the pilot, but most probably to the Ship herself, not being Sea Worthy, as she has been splitting dreadfully for some days past." Cast up on the shore with the drums and green ribbons were a number of butcher's trays and cleavers.

By the close of the last day Roscoe had just tipped the poll with 1151 votes to Gascoyne's 1138, pushing Tarleton into third place with 986. As one observer put it, "It will be easily imagined that the literary fame of Mr. Roscoe would make little impression upon the minds of this description of voters. Any other person with an equal purse at his command would have had an equal influence, and it is not difficult to conceive the means usually resorted to on these occasions, but nothing can so perspicuously point out the master-key to their suffrages as a simple statement of the immense sum of money expended in ale during the continuance of the recent election."[28] Thousands turned out for his victory rally, most of them hangers-on, marching ten or twelve abreast through Castle Street and down to the Old Dock, before turning up Duke Street to Mount Pleasant and on to his party headquarters in Islington.[29] Having been plied with lavish quantities of food and drink, the revellers heard his speech, but many must have wondered whether they had cast their votes wisely. Roscoe promised to work for parliamentary reform, lower taxation and religious liberty, but went on to suggest that Liverpool should reconcile itself to the end of the slave trade. He argued that this was now inevitable, but said that he would fight for gradual abolition and compensation, while renewing his campaign to open up trade with the Far East. Weeks later, Thomas Leyland dissolved his banking partnership with Roscoe in disgust.

Having gained a majority in Parliament, Grenville kept his pledge to end the slave trade once and for all. As Clarkson was soon to note in his history of the abolition movement, "It was judged advisable by Lord Grenville that the expected motion on this subject should, contrary to the practice hitherto adopted, be agitated first in the Lords."[30] Grenville soon found he had overwhelming support, not least from the Duke of Gloucester, who described the trade as a "cruel and criminal traffic in the blood of my fellow creatures," adding that it was a foul stain on the national character and an offence against the Almighty. When the bill passed to the Commons, the foreign secretary, Lord Howick, told the House, "The merchants and planters have an undoubted right, in common with other subjects of the realm, to demand justice at our

---

[28] Liverpool Poll Book, 1806.
[29] Sanderson, *Politics in Liverpool*, p77-78.
[30] Clarkson, Vol. 2., op. cit., p569.

hands. But that which they denominate justice does not correspond with the legitimate character of that virtue, for they call upon us to violate the rights of others, and to transgress our own moral duties. That which they distinguish as justice involves in itself the greatest injury to others. It is not in fact justice which they demand, but favour – and favour to themselves at the most grievous oppression of their fellow creatures."[31] Howick pointed out that the recent Foreign Slave Trade Act had reduced slaving by more than half without harming the country's economy, and that the trade now contributed less than two per cent to Britain's exports. In his view, abolition would lead to an improvement in conditions for slaves in the West Indies, and there would be no long-term loss of produce from the colonies. When the bill went for its second reading, Gascoyne claimed that Liverpool would lose forty thousand tons of shipping and two million pounds of investments. But Parliament was opposed to compensation, and Roscoe chose not to push the issue. He argued instead that Liverpool needed just six to nine months at adjust, adding that the best compensation for Liverpool would be a share of the East India trade.[32] The Commons voted overwhelmingly in favour of the bill, which passed into law on 25th March. The Slave Trade Act prevented any ships from embarking on the trade from 1st May 1807, but allowed up to 1st March 1808 to land their last human cargoes.[33]

Grenville's government collapsed on the day the bill became law, owing to disagreements over Catholics' rights, which Roscoe had also supported. Parliament was again dissolved, and Roscoe returned to Liverpool to face the electorate. He still had some supporters, and was accompanied by a procession through the town, but a riot broke out in Castle Street when a mob of unemployed seamen attacked with sticks. A horse was stabbed in the ensuing chaos, but a shaken Roscoe managed to reach the safety of his bank, from where he announced his intention not to stand in the coming election.[34] Despite this, a group of supporters raised the funds to canvass on his behalf and nominated him as a candidate. During the poll, Roscoe was vilified for his opposition to the slave trade and his support for religious freedom. Tarleton campaigned under the slogan "The Church and Slave Trade forever," and sent two black boys through the streets with placards promising "The African Trade Restored." By 15th May, Roscoe had polled just 377 votes to Tarleton's 1461 and Gascoyne's 1277, enabling him to withdraw from the cut and thrust of politics and return to Allerton Hall.

31 Clarkson, op.cit., p571-572.

32 Sanderson, *The Liverpool Abolitionists*, in Anstey and Hair, op. cit., p224-225. The East India Company's charter was revised in 1813, ending its monopoly on trade with India, but not with China.

33 The United States legislated at about the same time, banning imports of slaves from 1st January 1808.

34 *The Liverpool Chronicle*, 6th May 1807

The last British slave ships were now heading for the African coast to reap their final legal harvest of human flesh and misery. During the last sixteen months of the trade, 185 ships from Liverpool carried between them nearly fifty thousand slaves, accounting for just about every slaving vessel in the port.[35] As the final batches were being landed in the West Indies, Thomas Clarkson was writing his history of the abolition movement and reflecting on scenes that had been played out across Africa for three centuries. No doubt he also felt a sense of victory over Liverpool's merchants, and perhaps he smiled at the memory of that day twenty years earlier when he resisted the attempt to throw him into the dock. Yet, despite fears of ruin, abolition did Liverpool no lasting harm, and by 1810 the port's revenues had increased by nearly five per cent, and the tonnage handled by ten.[36] Liverpool's merchants and local abolitionists were soon reconciled, and some ex-slavers even worked with Roscoe and others to prevent the handful of merchants who continued clandestinely to evade the Slave Trade Act. The town raised its first petition against the trade abroad in 1814, and a year later William Roscoe was presented with the freedom of the borough.[37]

The war with France finally ended in 1815 when Napoleon was beaten at Waterloo. By 1827 Liverpool was handling twice the tonnage of twenty years earlier, feeding the growing industrial towns of Lancashire and the Midlands. As the port expanded, its merchants became richer, building ever-finer houses away from the poverty and misery of the growing numbers of back-to-backs and cellars that blighted the town. As cotton poured in from American slave plantations, there was talk of white slavery in Britain's factories and mines, while slavery still provided the sugar from its West Indian colonies. Only in 1833, after renewed pressure from the abolition movement, did Parliament vote to free Britain's slaves, but it was another five years before they were finally emancipated. With his work done in Britain, Thomas Clarkson campaigned against American slavery right up to his death in 1846 at the ripe old age of eighty-six. But by that time Liverpool was at the forefront an alternative form of human traffic, having become the major port of embarkation for emigrants from all over Europe, as they set out for new lives in the United States, Canada, and Australia.

---

[35] According to Williams, op. cit., between 1st January 1806 to 1st May 1807 185 slaving vessels measuring 43,755 tons cleared the port, enabling them to carry up to 49,213 slaves according to regulations then in force. This works out as nearly 139 ships over a twelve month period, which is above the average of 101 ships for 1805-7 given by Lamb, op. cit., or the average of 122 shown in figures given by Williams, appendix X1, for 1798-1804.

[36] Williams, op. cit., p620-621., shows that Liverpool handled 662,309 tons in 1807, 734,391 tons in 1810, rising to 1,225,313 tons by 1827.

[37] Sanderson, *The Liverpool Abolitionists*, in Anstey and Hair, op. cit., p227.

Bibliography

Anstey, R., and Hair, P. E. H., (eds) *Liverpool, The African Slave Trade, and Abolition,* Historic Society of Lancashire and Cheshire, Occasional Series, Volume 2, 1976.

Arkle, A.H. *Early Liverpool Coaching,* Historic Society of Lancashire and Cheshire, Vol. 73, 1921.

Bass, R.D., *The Green Dragoon, The Lives of Banastre Tarleton and Mary Robinson,* Alvin Redman Limited, London, 1958.

Brooke, R., *Liverpool As It Was,* 1775 to 1800, Liverpool Libraries and Information Services, 2003. (First published 1853).

Brown, R. Stewart, *Liverpool Ships in the Eighteenth Century,* Liverpool University Press, 1932.

Cameron, G. and Crooke, S., *Liverpool – Capital of the Slave Trade,* Picton Press, Liverpool, 1992.

Clarkson, T., *The History of the Rise, Progress and Accomplishment of the Abolition of the African Slave Trade by the British Parliament,* Longman, Hurst, Rees and Orme, London, 1808.

Collins, R.O (Ed) *Problems in African History,* Marcus Wiener Publishing, Inc., New York and Princeton, 1993.

Currie, J., M.D.F.R.S, *Medical Reports on the Effects of Water, Cold and Warm, as a Remedy, in Fever and other Diseases, Whether Applied to the Surface of the Body, or Used Internally,* Vols. 1 and 2, Liverpool, 1804.

Cordingly, D., *Billy Ruffian: The Bellerophon and the Downfall of Napoleon,* Bloomsbury Publishing, London, 2003.

Davis, R., *The Rise of the English Shipping Industry in the Seventeenth and Eighteenth Centuries,* Macmillan, London, 1962.

Falconbridge, A., *An Account of the Slave Trade on the Coast of Africa, 1788.*

Goodwin, P. *The Construction and Fitting of the Sailing Man of War, 1650-1850,* Conway Maritime Press, London, 1987.

Hickins, H.R (Ed.) *Building the Union – Studies on the Growth of the Workers' Movement: Merseyside 1756-1967,* Toulouse Press for Liverpool Trades Council 1973

Hochschild, A., *Bury The Chains: The British Struggle to Abolish Slavery,* Pan Macmillan, London, 2006.

Ireland, B., *Naval Warfare in the Age of Sail, War at Sea 1756-1815,* Harper Collins, London, 2000.

Laxton, P., *Liverpool in 1801: A Manuscript Return for the First National Census of Population,* Historic Society of Lancashire and Cheshire, Vol. 130, 1981.

McGowan, A., *The Ship, The Century Before Steam: The Development of the Sailing Ship 1700-1820,* HMSO, London, 1980.

Matthews, G.W., *John Bolton: A Liverpool Merchant 1756-1837,* Historic Society of Lancashire and Cheshire, Vol. 93, 1941.

Marquardt, K.H., *Eighteenth Century Rigs and Rigging,* Conway Maritime Press, London, 1992.

Moss, W., *A Familiar Medical Survey Of Liverpool, Addressed To The Inhabitants At Large,* Liverpool, 1784.

Moss, W., *The Liverpool Guide,* Liverpool,1796

Muir, R., *History of Liverpool,* University Press of Liverpool, London, 1907.

Oliver, R., & Fage, J.D., *A Short History of Africa,* Penguin, Harmondworth, revised edition, 1978.

Parkinson, C. N., *The Rise of the Port of Liverpool,* Liverpool University Press, 1952.

Peet, H., *Liverpool Vestry Books,* Volumes 1 & 2, Liverpool University Press, 1912.

Plumb, J.H., *England in the Eighteenth Century,* Penguin, London, 1950.

Power, M.J. *The Growth of Liverpool,* in *Popular Politics, Riot and Labour: Essays in Liverpool History 1790-1940,* Ed. Belcham, J., Liverpool University Press, 1992.

Reader, J., *Africa: A Biography of a Continent,* Penguin, 1998, first published by Hamish Hamilton Books, 1997.

Rediker, M. *Between the Devil and the Deep Blue Sea,* Cambridge University Press, 1987.

Rose, R.B., *A Liverpool Sailors' Strike in the Eighteenth Century,* Lancashire and Cheshire Antiquarian Society, Vol. 18, 1958.

Sanderson, F. E., *The Liverpool Delegates and Sir William Dolben's Bill,* Historic Society of Lancashire and Cheshire, Vol.124, 1972.

Sanderson, F. E., *Liverpool and the Slave Trade: A Guide to Sources,* Historic Society of Lancashire and Cheshire, Vol. 125, 1973.

Sanderson, F. E., *The Structure of Politics in Liverpool,* 1780 – 1807, Historic Society of Lancashire and Cheshire, Vol. 127, 1978.

Schom, A., *Trafalgar: Countdown to Battle, 1803-1805,* Michael Joseph Publishers, 1990.

Schwarz, S (Ed.) *Slave Captain: The Career of James Irving in the Liverpool Slave Trade,* Bridge Books, Wrexham, 1995.

Sellers, I., *William Roscoe, the Roscoe Circle, and Radical Politics in Liverpool, 1787-1807,* Historic Society of Lancashire and Cheshire, Vol. 120, 1968.

Shyllon, F.O., *Black slaves in Britain,* Oxford University Press, London, 1974.

Stonehouse, J., *Recollections of Old Liverpool by a Nonagenarian,* published in Liverpool by J.F. Hughes, 1863.

Stonehouse, J., *The Streets of Liverpool,* Liverpool Libraries and Information Services, 2002 (first published 1869).

Taylor, F. H., *Liverpool and the Athenaeum,* published by Liverpool Athenaeum, 1965.

Taylor, I.C. *Court and Cellar Dwellings: Eighteenth Century Origins of the Liverpool Slum,* Historic Society of Lancashire and Cheshire, Vol. 122, 1970.

Terraine, J., *Trafalgar,* Sidgewick and Jackson Ltd., London, 1976.

Watson, S. *The Reign of George 111,* Oxford University Press, 1960

Williams, G., *History of the Liverpool Privateers and Letters of Marque, with an account of the Liverpool Slave Trade,* Frank Cass & Co, London, 1966 (first published 1897).

Wilson, C. Birbeck, *The Records of a Liverpool 'Fireside', 1775-1781,* Historic

Society of Lancashire and Cheshire, Vol.48, 1985.

Woods, E.C., *Smuggling In Wirral,* Historic Society of Lancashire and Cheshire, Vol. 79, 1927.

Woods, E.C., and Brown, P.C., *The Rise and Progress of Wallasey,* 2nd ed. Wallasey Corporation, 1960.

INDEX

About The Author

Frank Howley taught history in Liverpool for thirty years, and was head of department at a comprehensive school for most of that time. It was early in his career that the idea for this book first took root, but the demands of family life, teaching and professional development led to his initial research notes gathering dust over many years. However, in 2004, with Liverpool's year as Capital of Culture on the horizon, Frank decided to give up full-time teaching and focus on renewing his writing project. The first fruits are found within this book, but he plans to write a sequel to pick up the story of Liverpool and its worldwide connections during the nineteenth century. He lives in Wallasey, close to the site of Mother Redcap's smugglers' tavern, and now teaches part-time.